HAMLYN
JUNIOR
SCIENCE
ENCYCLOPEDIA

HAMLYN

JUNIOR SCIENCE ENCYCLOPEDIA

Editors

Valerie Pitt B.Sc., M.Phil.

John Daintith B.Sc., Ph.D.

Alan Isaacs B.Sc., Ph.D., D.I.C.

HAMLYN

LONDON · NEW YORK · SYDNEY · TORONTO

Compiled by
Laurence Urdang Associates Ltd. Aylesbury

Contributors
The publishers wish to thank
the following contributors

Writers
Edward Brace M.A.
Julia Brailsford B.Sc.
Judith Dresner
William Gould B.A.
Keith Hitchin
John Illingworth M.Sc.
Bill Lax
Elizabeth Martin M.A.
John Scott B.Sc.
Stella Walker B.Sc.

Artists and Agents
John Batchelor
Ralph Coventry
Gordon Davies
Peter Fitzjohn
Eric Jewell Associates
Ken Ody
Oxford Illustrators
Bill Stallion
Peter Thornley
Carlo Tora
Tudor Art Agency
Brian Watson
Whitecroft Designs
George Woodman

First published 1973
Tenth impression 1984
THE HAMLYN PUBLISHING GROUP LIMITED
London · New York · Sydney · Toronto
Astronaut House, Feltham, Middlesex, England
ISBN 0 600 39512 X
Printed in Czechoslovakia by P. Z. Bratislava
51133/7

Contents

The Earth and the Universe

Contents

The Zeiss planetarium projector

Above
Our galaxy, called the *Galaxy* or *Milky Way System*, seen edge on and from above. The arrows mark the position of the sun. The galaxy has a spiral shape, the *Milky Way* being one of the arms of the spiral.

The universe

Men have gazed in wonder at the heavens from the very earliest times. Before they had any understanding of what they saw they worshipped the sun, moon, and planets as gods. But as they learnt about the regular movements of the objects in the sky, they used them to measure time and to form the basis of their calendars.

On a clear night you can see a very large number of stars. Although they only appear to be tiny pinpoints of light, they are in fact very large spherical objects that give out enormous amounts of light and heat. They seem so small to us because they are millions of kilometres away. Astronomers, therefore, do not measure the distance in kilometres but in *light years*. This is the distance that light travels in a year and is equal to about 9 million million km. The nearest star to the sun, *Proxima Centauri*, is over 4 light years away. One distant star, *Deneb*, is 650 light years away.

Some stars are much bigger than others. Some are much brighter, giving out more light. They may also seem bright to us because they are fairly near us. The light emitted by stars is of different colours. A star that appears red is much cooler than a bluish-white star. The most important star to us is the sun. It emits yellow light. It seems very big to us but it is actually much smaller and less bright than some other stars.

Although stars are so far apart they fall into groups called *galaxies*. The sun is only one of countless millions of stars that make up our *Galaxy*. Part of the Galaxy can sometimes be seen as a faint band of stars stretching across the sky. This band is the *Milky Way*. The stars in the Galaxy can be divided into much smaller groups: the *constellations*. We identify them by their shape. The brighter constellations, such as *Orion*, are used to find less obvious constellations and stars. The Galaxy is enormous. To reach a neighbouring galaxy, *Andromeda*, the furthest object visible to the naked eye, it would take a spaceship travelling at the speed of light over two million years!

The Galaxy is one of thousands of millions of galaxies, all of different shapes and sizes. In space there are also large clouds of gas and dust, called *nebulae*. The galaxies, nebulae, and the empty space between them form the *universe*. We do not know how big the universe is, but we know that the galaxies are moving away from each other at very great speeds. The universe is therefore expanding like a balloon which is being blown up. Many astronomers believe that it has been expanding from the time it was formed, ten to twenty thousand million years ago. The stars and planets were formed very slowly. A star will emit light and heat for millions of years; gradually the light will lessen and the star will die. At the same time, other stars are created from gas clouds.

Right
This is the remains of a star which exploded almost 6000 years ago. It was first seen in 1054 (the light took about 5000 years to reach earth). This type of exploding star, called a *supernova*, can emit an enormous amount of light for a very long time.

Far right
The Andromeda Galaxy, one of the nearest galaxies to our own, is over two million light years away and is twice as big as our galaxy.

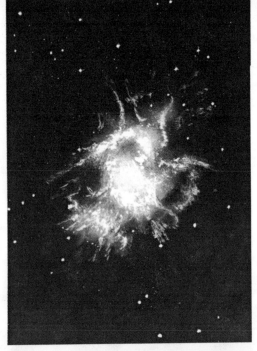

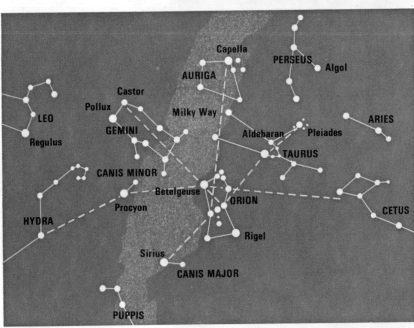

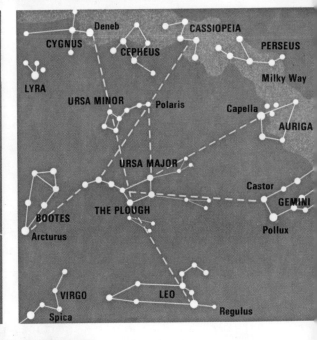

Above
The constellation *Orion* can be seen on a clear winter's night in both the N and S Hemispheres. Other stars (marked in small letters) and constellations (capital letters) can be found from the pattern of stars in Orion.

Above
The constellation *Ursa Major*, (the *Great Bear*) which can only be seen in the N Hemisphere. It contains a bright group of stars called the *Plough*.

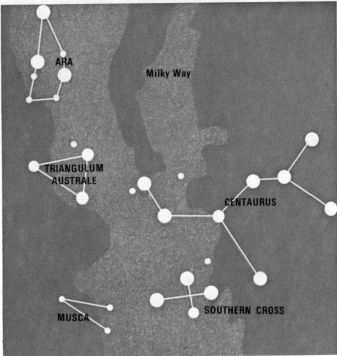

Right
The *Southern Cross*, a constellation seen only in the S Hemisphere. Its longer arm points towards the South Pole.

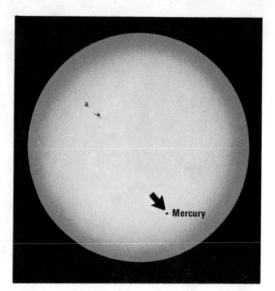

Mercury

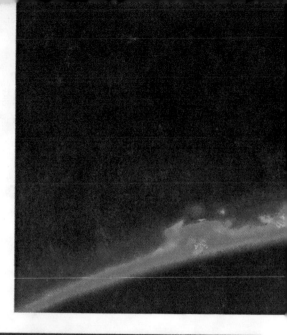

The sun

The sun is the closest star to the earth, being about 150 million kilometres away. Compared to some other stars it is rather small and insignificant. Compared to our planet it is very large. It has a diameter of about 1 392 000 kilometres. This is over 109 times the diameter of the earth. It is also 333 000 times as heavy as the earth. The sun provides heat and light needed to keep us alive.

The centre of the sun is extremely hot. It is so hot that any object normally found on earth would melt instantly. The temperature is 14 000 000°C. The temperature of the earth's surface does not usually rise above 50°C. The centre consists mainly of a gas called *hydrogen*. The high temperature of the hydrogen leads to very complicated reactions inside the sun. These are known as *fusion reactions* (see page 200). They produce the enormous amounts of heat and light which are constantly given out by the sun's surface.

The surface of the sun is called the *photosphere*. It is much cooler than the interior, but it is still extremely hot (about 6000°C). The photosphere has an irregular bubbly appearance. This is because gases are rising from inside the sun. Quite often a cloud of glowing gas erupts from the surface. This is called a *solar prominence*. Promi-

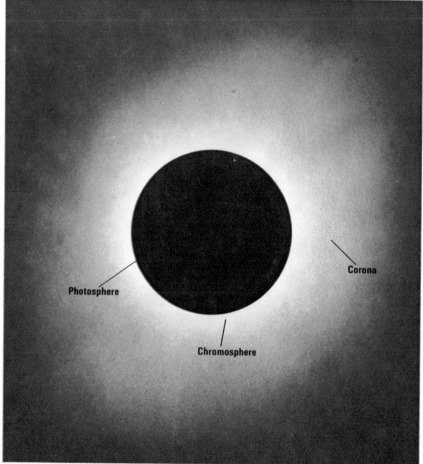

Photosphere

Chromosphere

Corona

nences are best seen during a *solar eclipse*. This occurs when the moon passes between the sun and earth, blotting out the sun's light.

The sun spins on its axis once every 25 days. Scientists measure this motion by watching the movement across the sun's face of large dark features called *sunspots*. These appear dark only because they are about 2000°C cooler than their surroundings. Sunspots are associated with very bright patches called *faculae*, and also with great

Above
A total eclipse of the sun. The moon has blotted out the sun's face and only the luminous gas surrounding it can be seen. This consists of a narrow bright inner layer called the *chromosphere* which is several thousand kilometres wide. The outer layer of gas is called the *corona*. It is extremely hot and is seen as a pearly halo reaching millions of kilometres from the sun.

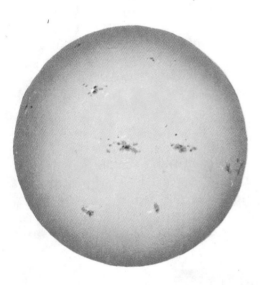

Above
The sun showing sunspots and faculae. Greater magnification of a sunspot shows the centre, called the umbra, to be darker and therefore cooler than the edge, called the *penumbra*. The temperature of the umbra is about 4200°C compared with 6000°C for the surrounding photosphere which is much brighter.

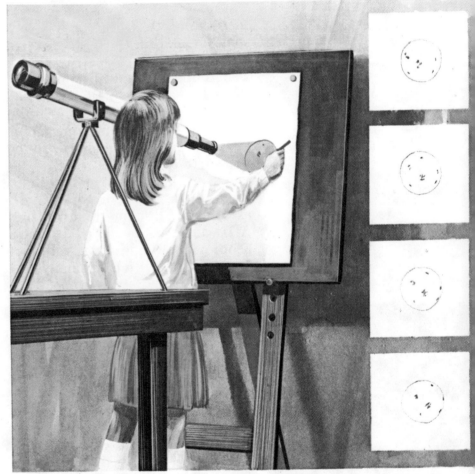

Above
An image of the sun formed by a telescope. Point the telescope in the direction of the sun. Do *not* look through the telescope but squint along the top. An image of the sun will be formed on a white card placed a few centimetres from the telescope. Move the card until the image is sharp. The visible sunspots can then be drawn in.

explosions in the sun's atmosphere, called *solar flares*. Flares only last a short time, but are very spectacular. Over a period of 11 years, the number of sunspots increases until it reaches a maximum, and then decreases again. This is called the *sunspot cycle*. When the number reaches a minimum, the cycle begins again. When sunspots reach their greatest number the solar flares also increase in brightness and in number. The flares interfere with the transmission of radio signals around the earth's surface.

Sunspots vary in size, but the very large ones often have diameters several times greater than the earth's. Some of the biggest have been seen with the naked eye. The best way to view sunspots is by producing an image of the sun on a piece of stiff white card, by using a telescope. NEVER LOOK DIRECTLY AT THE SUN THROUGH A TELESCOPE OR EVEN DARK GLASSES. The heat and light focused on your eye might cause blindness.

The solar system

The sun moves through space taking with it a large family of objects. The whole group is called the *solar system*. Its largest and most important members are the *planets*. There are nine planets known to us, of which the earth is one. They move round the sun in nearly circular paths called *orbits*. There are also smaller objects moving round the sun. These are the *asteroids* (or minor planets), *comets*, and *meteors*.

Ancient astronomers thought that the earth was flat, although some Greek thinkers, such as Aristotle (384–322 BC), realized that it was round. They also considered that the earth was the centre of the universe and that the other heavenly bodies–the sun, moon, planets, and stars–moved round the earth. This is called the *geocentric theory* of the universe. This theory was supported by the astronomer Ptolemy (2nd century AD), and was accepted by most people, including the religious leaders, for over a thousand years.

Nicolaus Copernicus (1473–1543) was the first to realize that the geocentric theory was wrong. He said that the sun, and not the earth, was the centre of the universe. His theory, the *heliocentric theory*, was bitterly opposed, mainly on religious grounds. The earth was thought to be the most important object in the sky and was therefore the centre of the universe. The astronomer Galileo was imprisoned by the Church having been forced to renounce his belief in the heliocentric theory. Copernicus was shown to be partly right by Johannes Kepler, who finally proved that the earth, and the other planets, do orbit the sun. However the motion of the stars is not connected with the sun. The sun is the centre of the solar system but it is not the centre of the universe. Almost certainly, there are many other suns, each with its own solar system.

The detailed observations of the great Danish astronomer, Tycho Brahe, helped Kepler to show that the orbits of the planets are slightly elliptical, not circular. Each planet moves in an ellipse with the sun at

Left
The solar system showing the position of the planets and asteroids. The sizes of the planets compared to the earth are approximately correct. The orbits of the four outer planets should be much bigger, Pluto being about 100 times further from the sun than Mercury.
The names of the planets are, in order of distance from the Sun, Mercury Venus, Earth, Mars, Jupiter, Saturn, Uranus, Neptune and Pluto. The orbit of Pluto comes inside that of Neptune for part of its path. The Asteroids lie between the orbits of Mars and Jupiter.

one focus. The time taken for a planet to make one complete orbit of the sun is one *year*. The length of the year is different for each planet. The planets nearer the sun have a shorter year than the ones further away. The earth's year is about 365¼ days long. So we have an ordinary year of 365 days with a leap year of 366 days once every four years to make up the ¼ day.

As a planet moves in its elliptical path, it is also rotating, or spinning like a top. A planet takes one day to make one complete rotation. The length of a day is also different for each planet. An earth day is 23 hours 56 minutes long. When a particular place on a planet faces the sun it is daytime. When it has turned away from the sun it is night. It is the rotation of the earth that causes the sun and stars to appear to move across the sky. The earth turns on an imaginary rod or *axis* passing through the North and South Poles. The axis is tilted at an angle of 23½° to the orbit of the earth. This tilt causes the four seasons, producing long warm days and short nights in summer and short cool days and long nights in winter.

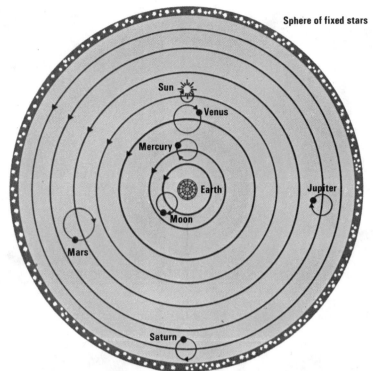

Sphere of fixed stars

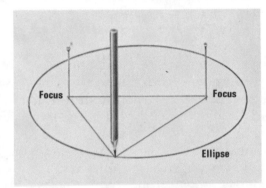

Focus   Focus

Ellipse

Above
The geocentric theory. Ptolemy assumed that the earth stood still at the centre of the universe. The sun, moon, and planets revolved around the earth in circular orbits. The stars were fixed in position on an outer sphere. The planets were thought to move in small circles centred on the circular orbit.

Left
Kepler (1571–1630) showed that the planets move in elliptical orbits round the sun. An easy way to draw an ellipse is to loop a long piece of cotton round two pins. Pull the cotton tight with a pencil and keeping it tight move the pencil round the pins. The result is an ellipse with a focus at each pinpoint.

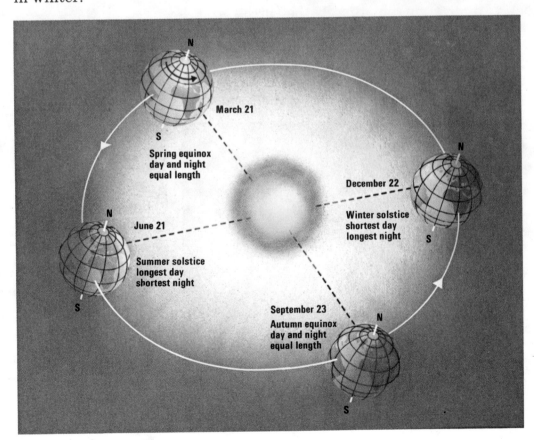

March 21

Spring equinox day and night equal length

December 22

Winter solstice shortest day longest night

June 21

Summer solstice longest day shortest night

September 23 Autumn equinox day and night equal length

Left
The earth's orbit. The tilt of the axis remains the same throughout the year. In June the North Pole faces the sun, so that it is summer in the Northern Hemisphere and winter in the Southern. In December the South Pole faces the sun, and it is summer in the Southern Hemisphere and winter in the Northern.

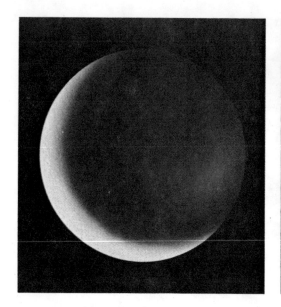

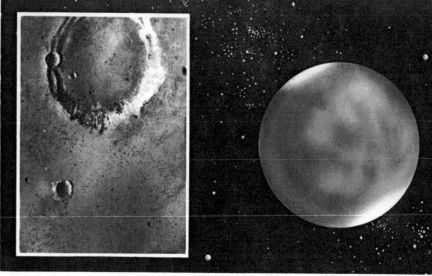

The planets

Nine planets move round (orbit) the sun, all in the same direction. The nearest planet to the sun is *Mercury* then come *Venus,* the earth, *Mars, Jupiter, Saturn, Uranus, Neptune,* and finally *Pluto.* The six inner planets were known to the Ancient Greeks. Because of their great distances, Neptune was only discovered in 1846 and Pluto in 1930. Both these planets were thought to exist before they were actually found. Astronomers now think there might be a tenth planet beyond Pluto.

The four inner planets and Pluto are approximately the same size. Jupiter, Saturn, Uranus, and Neptune, however, are much

bigger and are known as the *giant planets.* The temperature on the surface of a planet depends mainly on its distance from the sun. The giant planets and Pluto are all extremely cold. As Mercury rotates, the side facing the sun reaches a temperature of about 400°C although the dark side is very much colder. The large temperature difference is partly because of its very slow rotation (a day on Mercury lasts 59 earth days) and partly because there is no detectable *atmosphere.* A planet's atmosphere is the layer of gas surrounding it—the earth's atmosphere is the air we breathe. This layer can trap some of the sun's heat, preventing a rapid rise and fall of temperature as the planet rotates. The air on earth contains

Above
Mars and its two moons Phobos (on the left) and Deimos. Mars has no cloud covering and its atmosphere, consisting mainly of carbon dioxide, is very thin. Its reddish surface can therefore be easily seen. It is covered in craters which have been photographed by space probes. (Shown in insert.)

Above left
The crescent phase of Venus. Mercury and Venus lie within the earth's orbit and so have phases like the moon. Mercury is hard to see, but Venus is one of the brightest objects in the night sky, appearing either in the evening or early morning. It is covered in a thick layer of cloud so that the surface cannot be seen.

Below left
Halley's comet and its orbit. This spectacular comet goes round the sun every 76 years. It will next appear in 1986. As a comet comes near the sun its tail becomes visible but always faces away from the sun.

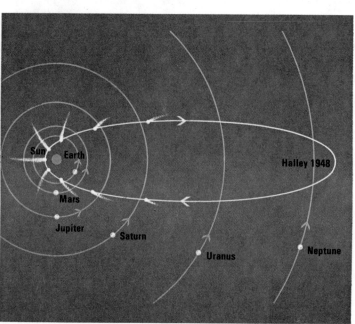

Earth (to scale)

Rings of Saturn

Jupiter

Above
Jupiter. Jupiter is not solid like the earth but seems to consist mainly of the gas *hydrogen*. The surface is not visible since the planet is covered in belts of clouds. An enormous elliptical red spot, almost the same size as the earth, can be seen in the clouds. It is not known what the spot is.

Above right
Saturn and its rings. Saturn is very similar to Jupiter, also consisting mainly of hydrogen.

Below
The meteor crater in Arizona. It is over 180 metres deep and is 1200 metres in diameter.

the gases *oxygen* (about 21%) and *nitrogen* (about 78%). Different gases surround the other planets. The different atmospheres and temperatures and also the possible lack of water on them mean that the other planets are very unlike the earth and are probably uninhabited.

Many planets have smaller objects orbiting round them. They are called *moons* or *satellites*. The Moon is the satellite of the earth. Jupiter, Saturn, and Uranus have a large number. The four largest moons of Jupiter were first seen by Galileo in 1617. The strangest feature of Saturn is its *rings*. These are thin flat belts of particles, possibly consisting of ice. They could also be fragments of a moon which has never been formed.

The *asteroids*, or *minor planets*, are also members of the solar system. They are large lumps of rock orbiting the sun mainly between Mars and Jupiter. *Ceres*, the largest one known, was discovered in 1801. Its diameter is 1000 kilometres. Some of the 2500 or more other asteroids identified are only a few hundred metres across.

Comets are objects orbiting the sun, usually in very elliptical orbits. This means they often cross the paths of the planets. As they approach the sun their tails, stretching behind them for millions of kilometres, become brightly illuminated. Small lumps of rocks, possibly the remains of comets, also move around the sun. If they enter the earth's atmosphere smaller ones, called *meteors*, burn up producing bright streaks of light (*shooting stars*). Larger ones, called *meteorites*, can reach the ground, often producing craters.

Table of the Planets

Planet	Distance from sun (millions of km)	Diameter (km)	Number of moons	Planet's year earth time	Planet's day earth time
MERCURY	58	4880	—	88 days	59 days
VENUS	108	12 100	—	225 days	243 days
EARTH	150	12 756	1	365¼ days	23 hr 56 min
MARS	228	6790	2	687 days	24 hr 37 min
JUPITER	778	142 800	16+	12 years	9 hr 50 min
SATURN	1427	120 000	15+	29½ years	10 hr 14 min
URANUS	2870	51 000	5	84 years	18 hr*
NEPTUNE	4497	49 000	2	165 years	23 hr*
PLUTO	5900	3000*	1	248 years	6 days 9 hr

Note that a day on Venus is *longer* than its year.   *Data uncertain.

The moon

The moon is our nearest neighbour in space and the first one to be visited by man. It orbits the earth at an average distance of 384 400 kilometres. Astronomically speaking, this is right on our doorstep. The moon takes about 27 days to make one orbit. It also takes 27 days to complete one rotation of its axis. This means that the same face is always turned towards us.

The moon gives out no light itself; it shines at night because of the light it reflects from the sun. Moonlight is therefore reflected sunlight. When the moon lies between the earth and the sun we

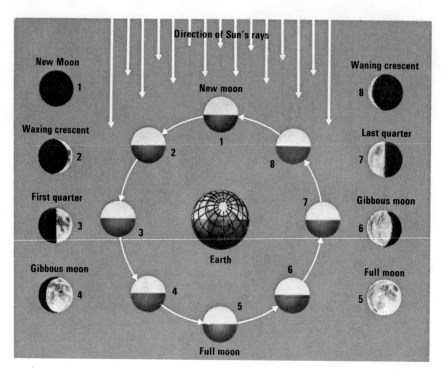

cannot see it, but as it moves in its orbit, it seems to grow and change shape as the sun illuminates more and more of it. Then it gets smaller until it disappears again. These changes of shape and size are called *phases*. The full moon is one phase. The phases repeat themselves every 29 days.

Dark markings can be seen on the moon. Galileo, who was the first man to use a telescope, thought that these dark areas were seas, because they looked very flat. Actually, they are enormous, dry plains, though we still call them seas. There is in fact no water on the moon, and no atmosphere. Man cannot live there unless he takes his own air supply. It is a most unwelcome place; by day the temperature of the surface facing the sun reaches 100°C, while at night it drops to —155°C. Day and night on the moon last about 14 earth days each.

The surface of the moon is very rocky and rugged. The seas (plains) are often surrounded by very high mountain ranges. The highest mountains on the moon reach almost 10 000 metres—higher than Mt Everest. There are wide valleys and small clefts called *rills*.

The moon is pitted with saucer-shaped features called *craters*. There are thousands of them

Above
The gibbous moon seen through a telescope. The telescope turns things upside down so that north is at the bottom, south at the top, and west on the left. Many craters and seas (dark areas) can be seen.

KEY
1 Sea of Tranquillity
2 Sea of Crises
3 Sea of Serenity
4 The Appenines
5 Aristotle
6 The Alps
7 Plato
8 Sea of Showers
9 Copernicus
10 Ptolemy
11 Sea of Clouds
12 Gassendi
13 Tycho

ranging in size from tiny holes to vast plains surrounded by mountain ranges. The largest crater, Bailey, is about 300 kilometres in diameter. Some craters are over 7000 metres deep.

The moon is much smaller than the earth. Its diameter, 3476 kilometres, is only about a quarter of the earth's and it is about 81 times lighter. Nevertheless, the moon is strong enough to pull at the seas of the earth as it orbits round it. This pull of gravity (see page 60) causes the daily *tides*.

Several rockets have been round the moon and some have landed on it. In 1959, a Russian spacecraft photographed, for the first time, the side of the moon which we never see. American astronauts first landed on the moon in 1969. Rock specimens have been brought back and scientists are examining them to find out more about the moon's age and structure. Many scientists think that the moon was formed at the same time as the earth. Because it was smaller it was captured and went into orbit around the earth, becoming its natural satellite.

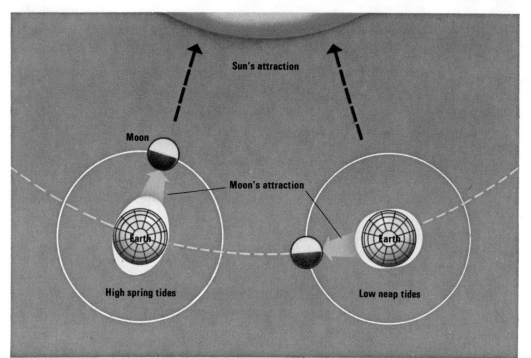

Above
A picture of the earth taken from the surface of the moon.

Left
The tides are caused by the pull of gravity of the moon on the sea. The sun has a similar but smaller effect. There are two high tides a day. The sea is furthest out six hours after these high tides. The highest tides, called *spring tides*, occur at new and full moon. The lowest high tides, *neap tides*, occur at first and last quarter.

Left
An American astronaut from *Apollo 16* standing on the moon's surface, next to the *lunar module* and the *lunar rover*. They used the lunar rover to travel over the surface and collect samples of lunar rock.

Below
A communications satellite orbits above the equator taking 24 hours to complete one orbit at a height of about 35 700 km. This is called a *stationary orbit* and means that the satellite always remains over one point of the earth's surface.

Exploring space

Man has long dreamed of journeying beyond the earth, but it is only quite recently that space travel has become reality.

In order to escape from the gravitational pull of the earth, the modern *rocket* (see page 250) has been developed. Man began to investigate space by using rockets to shoot small objects, called *artificial satellites*, into orbit round the earth. The first one, *Sputnik 1*, was launched by Russia in 1957. These complicated devices are used for various purposes: to obtain information about the sun, stars, and other things in the universe, to study weather patterns in the earth's atmosphere, or to act as communication devices.

Telstar 1, a communications satellite launched in 1962, made possible the first direct television link between Europe and America. The *Early Bird* satellites were of a better design and formed an important part of world communications.

In 1961, the first manned space flight was made by the Russian cosmonaut Yuri Gagarin. He made one orbit of the earth. John Glenn was the first American to be put into orbit round the earth.

The Russians began to study the moon using a series of space vehicles called *Lunik*. In 1959,

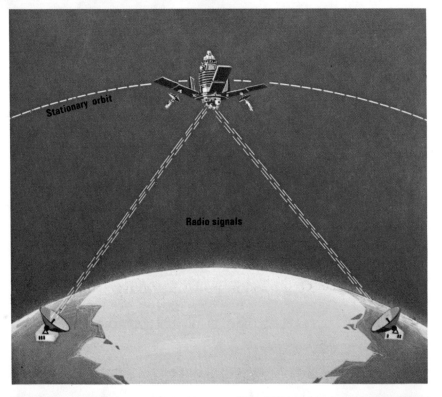

Stationary orbit

Radio signals

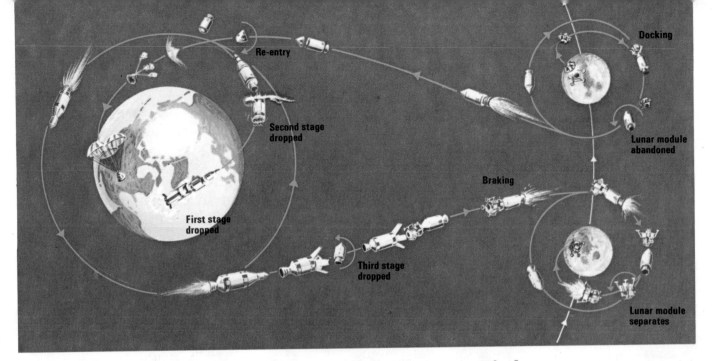

Above
The flight path of *Apollo 11* to the moon. To shoot the spaceship into earth orbit, the rocket requires three parts (*stages*). Each stage is fired in turn, for a few minutes, then dropped off and the next stage is fired. The third stage is fired for a second time to send it on its way to the moon.

Lunik 3 sent back to earth photographs of the hidden side of the moon. During the 1960's, Russia concentrated on solving the problems of orbital space flight but also continued their moon studies with the unmanned *Lunik* series.

The Americans, however, turned their efforts to becoming the first men on the moon. In their *Mercury* (one-man) and *Gemini* (two-man) orbital space flights, they studied the conditions in space and the problems, such as weightlessness, that would face man.

The unmanned *Ranger* and *Surveyor* probes were launched on a path towards the moon, in preparation for the manned *Apollo* missions. In 1969, Neil Armstrong and Edwin Aldrin of *Apollo 11* became the first men to walk on the moon.

In 1971, the Russians made a major breakthrough when they launched the *Salyut* space station. In 1972, *Skylab*, an American experimental space station was launched. This fell to earth in 1979, scattering debris across western Australia. The Russians have so far launched six Salyut space stations, and in 1980 cosmonauts set a new record by spending 180 days in orbit in *Salyut 6*.

Both America and Russia have sent out many unmanned *space probes* to the planets. The American *Mariner* probes of the late 1960s and early 1970s were sent to photograph Mars and Venus,

Mariner 10 flying on from Mars to Venus and Mercury. Further probes sent to Mars were *Vikings 1* and *2* which actually landed on the planet. In 1973 and 1974 two American *Pioneer* probes flew past Jupiter, and a later *Pioneer* landed on Venus, as did the Russian *Venera 11* and *12* probes. But the outstanding study of the planets to date is that carried out by *Voyagers 1* and *2*. These American craft flew past Jupiter and then on to have a close-up look at Saturn. *Voyager 2* will go on to Uranus and Neptune.

A recent major development in manned space flight is the American re-usable *Space Shuttle*, first launched in 1981. This is the first spacecraft which returns to earth for re-use.

Left
Alexei Leonov, a member of the crew of the Russian orbiting spacecraft *Voshkod 2*, was the first man to walk in space. His stay outside the craft lasted only 10 minutes, but it prepared the way for more prolonged EVAs (extravehicular activities).

Right
The re-usable Space Shuttle may be used in the future to carry men, food and other supplies to orbiting space stations. Additional rocket boosters separate from it about 40 km up; they can be recovered and used again too, thus reducing costs.

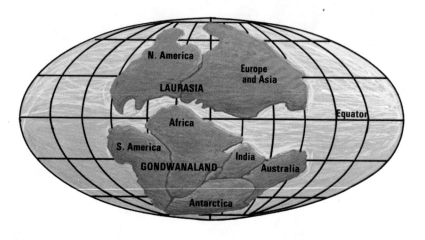

The earth

The earth was formed over four thousand million years ago and was very hot. It is believed that there was only one enormous mass of land, surrounded by ocean. About two hundred million years ago this land mass slowly broke in two. Gradually these two portions also split up forming the six continents we know today. Over millions of years the surface of the earth has changed enormously, and is still changing. Mountain ranges, rivers, deserts, and other features have appeared.

Compared with the surface, little has changed inside the earth. The distance from the surface of the earth to the centre is about 6400 km. Between the surface and the centre there are several layers made up of different substances. The outermost layer is known as the earth's *crust*; it is composed of rocks which form the continents and the bottom of the oceans. This crust is between 5 and 32 km thick, being thickest beneath mountains.

The crust itself is composed of two distinct layers. The outer layer, called the *sial*, consists of solid rocks, like granite, with a low density. Beneath the sial, in regions of higher temperature, is a layer of denser rock material called *sima* or *magma*. This is the substance from which the rocks on the surface of the earth are made.

The layer beneath the crust is called the *mantle*. It is about 2900 km thick and extends about half way to the centre of the earth. The rocks in the mantle are denser than the sial and sima of the crust, and are hotter. This material can flow and change its shape.

The very centre of the earth is called the *core*. It consists of an inner solid metallic part and an outer ring of liquid material composed mostly of *iron* and *nickel*. The core is about 3500 km thick.

An *earthquake* occurs when a series of movements or *vibrations* of the material in the crust or the

Above
A possible map of the world about 200 million years ago. The land mass, called *Laurasia*, made up of the Northern continents, has split away from *Gondwanaland*, which contains the Southern continents. They are separated by the Tethys Sea—the ancient Mediterranean Sea. The idea that parts of a single land mass split up and eventually drifted into the position of today's continents is known as the continental drift theory.

Right
A diagram showing the layers of different materials inside the earth. Rocks in the sial are composed mainly of two chemicals, *si*lica and *a*lumina (from which the sial gets its name). The sima consists of denser rocks containing mainly *si*lica and *mag*nesia. Silica, magnesia, and iron are the principal chemicals making up the mantle.

Sial

Sima

Crust
(5–32 km)

Mantle
(2900 km)

(Liquid)

Core
(3500 km)

(Solid)

Below
The materials making up the earth's crust. The boundary between crust and mantle is called the *Mohorovicic discontinuity* after the man who discovered it in 1909 while studying an earthquake.

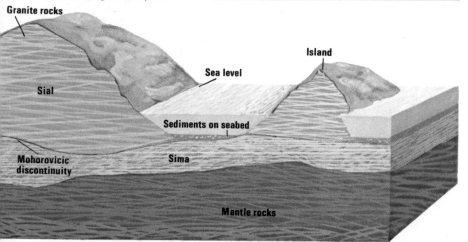

mantle causes the land on the surface to shake and move. The vibrations are called shock waves or *seismic waves*. They can be detected by delicate instruments called *seismographs*; the nature and size of the earthquake can therefore be found. Earthquakes today are much less violent than earthquakes in the past.

Volcanoes occur as a result of cracks or fractures in the surface of the earth through which liquid magma, from the lower part of the earth's crust, is forced. When it pours from a volcano this hot liquid material is called *lava*. It contains hot ashes, rock fragments, and steam. Volcanoes usually occur in the regions where most earthquakes take place, often forming mountains. Like earthquakes, they may be associated with movements of the mantle. One of the most violent volcanic eruptions was on the island of Krakatoa, near Sumatra, in 1883. This explosion produced an enormous tidal wave that affected oceans throughout the world.

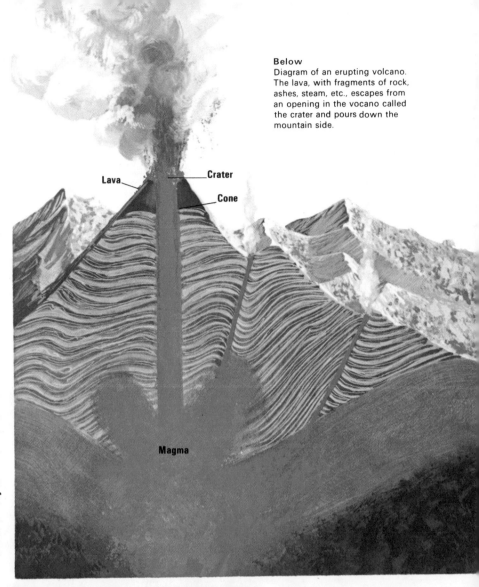

Below
Diagram of an erupting volcano. The lava, with fragments of rock, ashes, steam, etc., escapes from an opening in the vocano called the crater and pours down the mountain side.

Lava — Crater
Cone
Magma

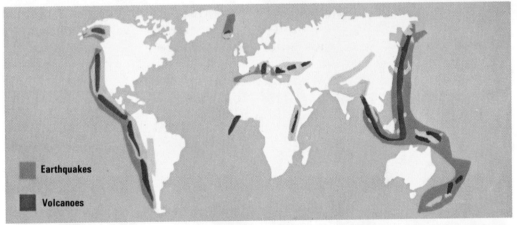

Left
Major regions of earthquakes and volcanoes. Earthquakes were once of such force and violence that they caused the formation of mountain ranges, such as the Alps, Andes, and Himalayas. Earthquakes and volcanoes occur today in regions of recently-formed mountain ranges.

Earthquakes

Volcanoes

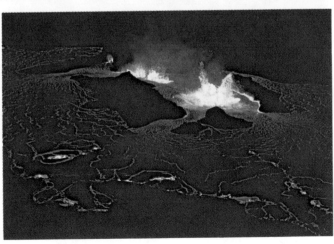

Left
A volcano in eruption. The great river of lava glows red in the dark in this night photograph.

Far left
The great column of smoke and ash rising from the new island of Surtsey, that appeared off the coast of Iceland a few years ago, as a result of submarine volcanic activity.

21

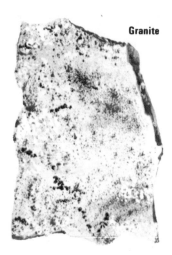

Granite

Beryl in quartz

Garnet

Rocks and minerals

The surface of the earth is cool and solid. In contrast, the material many kilometres below the surface is a very hot substance called magma. It consists of the materials that make up rocks, melted together by the very high temperature. Sometimes this magma escapes to the surface where it cools and forms *igneous rocks*. (Igneous, from the Latin word for fire, *ignis*, means produced by heat).

One of the ways in which igneous rocks are formed is when the magma shoots out through a volcano. The magma is then called *lava*. It cools and becomes solid very quickly to form several different types of rocks, such as *basalt*. Most rocks consist of particles called *crystals*. Rocks formed from lava have very small crystals. Sometimes the magma is squeezed to the surface through cracks in the earth, which gives it much longer to cool and become solid. Rocks, such as *granite*, formed in this way consist of much larger crystals.

Many other rocks are formed from igneous rocks. These other rocks can be placed in two main groups: *sedimentary rocks* and *metamorphic rocks*. Very old rocks are gradually worn away or *eroded* by the action of wind, rain, ice, rivers, and seas. The particles that are eroded from these rocks are carried away and eventually deposited, for instance at the bottom of the sea. After millions of years masses of these particles become bound together and form sedimentary

Above
Top A piece of granite. Granite is very hard and is not eroded by rain, heat, or cold. It is therefore a good building material. *Centre* A lump of quartz in which is embedded a green gemstone called *beryl*. *Bottom* Crystals of dark red garnet which are embedded in rock of a different material. Garnets make attractive jewels when cut and polished.

Right
This enormous pinnacle of sandstone occurs in Orkney, and is called the Old Man of Hoy.

Far left
The massive chalk cliffs of the Needles, Isle of Wight which continue out to sea as isolated pinnacles.

Left
These six-sided columns of basalt are part of the Giant's Causeway in Northern Ireland.

Below left
Stalactites and stalagmites. They are formed from a very slow accumulation of minerals, mainly calcite, that are contained in water continually dripping from the roof of a cave. When the water disappears the calcite remains. Sometimes a stalactite will become joined to a stalagmite to form a column of limestone.

rocks. *Sandstone* and *clay* are both sedimentary rocks. Sandstone is composed of medium-sized particles and clay consists of very small particles. Some sedimentary rocks are formed from the deposited shells and skeletons of animals that used to live in the seas and rivers millions of years ago: *limestone* and *chalk* are examples of such rocks.

Metamorphic rocks are formed by the action of great heat on igneous and sedimentary rocks. This heat often comes from an erupting volcano. *Marble* is a metamorphic rock formed from limestone; *slate* is formed from clay. Many metamorphic rocks contain large crystals of *gemstones*, such as *garnet* and *ruby*.

Most rocks consist of crystals of different chemicals called *minerals*. *Quartz* is the most common mineral and is found in most rocks. Sand on the sea shore consists of small grains of quartz that have been worn and smoothed by the action of the tides. Pebbles found on beaches are also smooth and rounded by the sea. This smoothing process by the sea takes millions of years.

The dark colour of many rocks is caused by the presence of minerals containing iron and magnesium. *Olivine* and *hornblende* are examples of such minerals. A mineral called *calcite* occurs in limestone and chalk. It consists of the same substance that can form a coating inside kettles (fur): it also forms stalactites and stalagmites in underground caves.

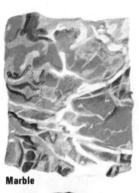

Marble

Agate

Amber

Jet

Above
A piece of marble. Marble is a beautiful rock and is used for ornamental purposes, such as statues or floors.
Specimens of agate, amber, and jet. These stones are often found as rounded pebbles on the sea shore.

Left
A limestone quarry. The limestone is removed and used for building and to manufacture chemicals. The rocks in quarries are arranged in layers called *strata*. The strata near the bottom of a quarry contain the oldest sedimentary rocks. The strata nearer the top were formed more recently and may be of a different composition.

Erosion

The scenery of the world has taken millions of years to reach its present form and is still changing. It has done so principally as a result of the erosion of wind, rain, ice, frost, seas, and rivers on the rocks which make up the surface of the earth. Erosion is the breaking down of solid rocks into smaller pieces which are then carried away. These fragments of rock may be further worn down over a very long period of time until they form minute particles and are deposited as *soil*. The type of soil depends on the type of rock from which it has been formed.

One of the most important agents of erosion is ice, especially moving ice or *glaciers*. Less than one million years ago, which is quite recent in terms of geological time, much of the northern part of the world was covered with huge sheets of ice. This period is called the *Ice Age*. When the glaciers advanced over the land they eroded and carried away much of the softer rock and soil over which they passed. This usually took place in mountainous regions. All this eroded material was deposited when the ice moved less quickly or when it finally melted on lower ground. The movement of the glaciers resulted in very rugged scenery and U-shaped valleys where erosion took place, depositing boul-

Above right: top
La Mer de Glace, a huge glacier at Chamonix in the French Alps. A glacier is a river of ice moving very slowly down a mountain, forming a U-shaped valley.
Jagged mountains, such as those in the Alps, are caused by frost shattering. When rainwater freezes in cracks in the rocks, it expands and widens the cracks.

Above right: centre
A section through a glacier showing the burden of rock fragments it carries along beneath it, called the moraine. Where two glaciers meet they form a medial moraine.

Right
The delta of a river. The delta is the place where a river joins the sea. Alluvial plains, which consist of very rich soil, occur at the deltas of many rivers.

ders, pebbles, and gravel on lower ground after the glaciers melted.

The flowing of a river creates its own scenery by erosion. When it rises in the mountains it is very swift-flowing and as it descends it erodes and carries along rock fragments of all sizes. At the same time it deepens and widens its own valley into a typical V shape. On lower ground it flows less swiftly but still carries along its load of mud, silt, sand, and pebbles. When it reaches the flat plains it slowly winds to the sea depositing its load which forms shingle beaches, sandbanks, and plains of silt and mud called *alluvium*.

Wind is a very important agent in erosion. It not only helps to wear down the rock surfaces but carries away loose dust, sand, and soil from the exposed surfaces and so leaves them ready to be acted on by other eroding forces. The action of wind is most obvious in the formation of sand dunes in deserts. Erosion of soil by the wind is another serious problem.

The sea has a very powerful erosive action. It is usually loaded with sand and pebbles which are deposited to form beaches and shingles. Waves break on the shore with such force that eventually the coastline is eroded into bays, where the rocks are soft; headlands are formed where they are harder. Wave action also causes the formation of cliffs and caves over long periods of time.

Above top
The Grand Canyon, United States. This long gorge, about 1650 metres deep and 6–29 km from rim to rim, was formed by the erosion of the Colorado River.

Above
Sand dunes. These are formed when grains of sand are picked up by the wind and deposited into crescent-shaped structures.

Left
A seashore showing caves resulting from the effects of wave erosion. The waves smash against the foot of the cliff with such force that pieces of softer rock, mud, and clay are torn away. Gradually the harder rocks making up the cliff become weaker and the continual action of the sea results in hollows or caves being formed.

Left
Erosion by the sea. Limestone cliffs in the Great Australian Bight.

■ **Warm currents**

▨ **Cold currents**

Above
Ocean currents of the world.
Currents are steady flows of water.
Movement of warm water to cool
areas and cold water to hot areas
affects the climate of nearby coastal
countries. The North Atlantic Drift,
for example, from the Gulf of
Mexico, has a warming effect on
England.

Seas and rivers

Sea water contains salt, as well as
other chemicals, whereas river
water is fresh or salt-free. The
amount of salt in the sea water
(called its *salinity*) varies in different parts of the world. The Baltic
Sea is only slightly salty because
it has a constant supply of fresh
water from the many rivers flowing
into it. The Dead Sea is very salty

because it lacks a steady supply of
fresh water and the heat in the
region causes the water to evaporate, leaving the salt behind.

Tides are rises and falls in the
sea level which occur twice a day
over most of the oceans, but in
certain areas there is only one tide
a day. Tides are controlled by the
moon (see page 17). In the open sea
the difference between high and
low tide (the *range*) may be less
than one metre, but in shallow seas
near the coast and in narrow tidal
inlets of the sea it can be over 10
metres.

Waves are caused by the action
of wind on the surface of the sea.
(You can create waves on the surface of a bowl of water by blowing
across the surface). The water
itself does not move very far in the
direction of the wind; it moves up

Above
Giant waves breaking on a reef.
The biggest waves are those which
have travelled over a large distance.

Right
Meanders in a river in its old-age
stage. The mature river has created a
wide flood plain and in its old-age
the river now meanders across it
along the easiest path. Bends which
get silted up are eventually cut off
and form oxbow lakes.

and down as the wave passes.

Tidal waves (*tsunamis*) have nothing to do with the tides. They are caused by movements in the earth's crust under or near the sea, though sometimes very strong winds can cause tidal waves. They often cause havoc as they travel very fast, sometimes up to 500 miles per hour, and they can be very high when they reach the land.

A river usually begins its course (*rises*) in hills or mountains where there is a high rainfall. As it winds its way towards the sea it gathers more and more water from smaller (tributary) streams which join the main river. The river passes through three stages along its course. They are called the youthful, mature, and old-age stages. In the youthful stage the river flows fast and is small in volume, having a V-shaped valley. In the mature stage it winds (*meanders*) across a narrow flat area called the flood plain, which in the old-age stage is very wide and the river's volume is at its maximum. Much of the silt carried along as the river's load, is deposited at this stage because its speed is reduced. *Oxbow lakes* are formed when the outer bend of a meander has become cut off from the river. Their shape is usually semi-circular.

Water is never lost from the earth and its atmosphere, though it is constantly moving in a *cycle*. It can change into a gas (*evaporate*), forming water vapour, or it can change into ice or snow.

Left
The Murchison Falls on the Nile. Waterfalls are usually formed when a band of hard rock lies across the path of a river. The force of the falling water wears away the softer rock below, undercutting the hard layer, and gradually the waterfall is worn back along the river's course, leaving a gorge.

Below
The water cycle. Water evaporates from the surface of the seas, rivers, and lakes and from vegetation on land. It rises and forms clouds in the sky where it cools and condenses back into water again. This falls as rain, snow, or sleet and eventually finds its way back into the rivers and seas, completing the cycle.

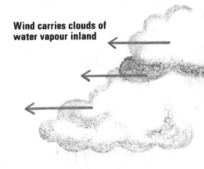

Wind carries clouds of water vapour inland

Evaporation from sea

Rainfall

ainwater seeps through round into rivers

Evaporation from rivers and land surface

Underground river

Sea

Rivers carry water back to sea

27

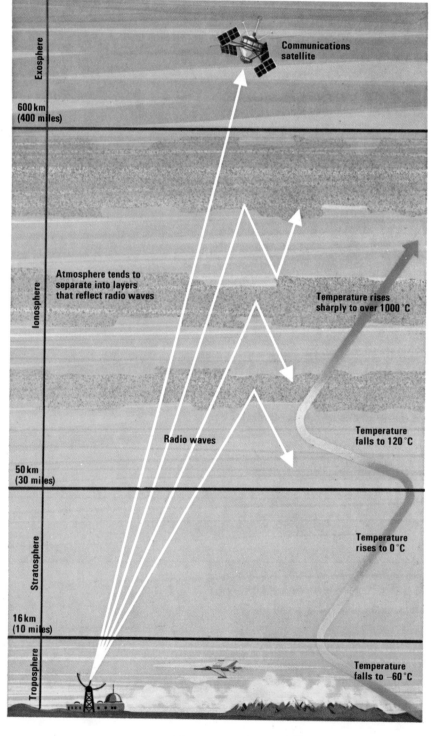

Other gases 1%

Oxygen 21%

Nitrogen 78%

Right
The proportions of gases in the atmosphere. It is easy to see that nitrogen makes up by far the greatest volume.

Below
The layers of the atmosphere. Notice how narrow the troposphere is.

Exosphere

Communications satellite

600 km
(400 miles)

Ionosphere

Atmosphere tends to separate into layers that reflect radio waves

Temperature rises sharply to over 1000 °C

Radio waves

Temperature falls to 120 °C

50 km
(30 miles)

Stratosphere

Temperature rises to 0 °C

16 km
(10 miles)

Troposphere

Temperature falls to −60 °C

The atmosphere

The atmosphere is a layer of gases surrounding the earth and extending out into space for about 800 km. It is held there by the pull of the earth's gravity. Most of it lies within 16 km of the earth's surface; above this level the amount of gas slowly decreases with height until there is very little left. This marks the beginnings of outer space.

The atmosphere performs the vital functions of protecting the earth from extremes of heat and cold and from dangerous rays from the sun. It stores and carries water and gases which are necessary for life. *Nitrogen* is the main gas by volume, followed by *oxygen* and small quantities of *argon* and *carbon dioxide*. Plants take in carbon dioxide from the air and give out oxygen (see page 48). Humans and other animals do the opposite. Oxygen allows burning to take place; without it things will not catch fire. *Water vapour*, which forms rain, is also present in the atmosphere in varying amounts. Other gases are present in very small quantities.

Dust occurs in the atmosphere in the form of tiny particles of soot (carbon), cosmic dust from the breaking up of meteorites, salt particles from evaporated seawater, and the spores of plants (by which plants reproduce). Particles of water vapour can collect around these tiny particles to form raindrops.

The air nearer the earth's surface is warmer than that higher up, because at lower levels the air is warmed more by the heat coming from the earth than by that coming directly from the sun. This lower part of the atmosphere is called the *troposphere*; it finishes at the *tropopause* where the temperature stops decreasing with height. The troposphere is where our weather is formed. Above the troposphere lie other layers, such as the *stratosphere* and *ionosphere*.

Atmospheric pressure is the force

that the weight of air above the earth exerts on the earth's surface. This also decreases with height because the higher you climb, the less air there is above you to exert pressure. At sea level the atmosphere exerts a pressure of about 1 kg per square cm (14·7 lbs per square inch or 1013·2 millibars – a a unit of pressure). To get an idea of this force, lift a weight of 1 kg (just over 2 lb) and try to imagine this weight pressing on every square cm of your body. We do not feel this weight because the liquids in our bodies exert an opposing pressure.

Pressure varies from place to place as well as at different heights. Winds, which are a flow of air, blow from areas of high pressure to areas of low pressure. High pressure tends to develop over cold areas; low pressure over hot areas.

Certain winds, which blow regularly, have names. These winds, together with sea currents, were vital to early explorers, whose ships had to depend on them for movement. They had to keep courses set by the winds and currents, otherwise they ran the risk of being becalmed.

Above
Mount Everest (8847 metres), the highest mountain in the world, was first climbed in 1953. It reaches so far through the atmosphere that the pressure is extremely low at the summit.

Far left
To prove that oxygen is necessary for burning and that it takes up about 1/5th of the air by volume, place a candle on a saucer in a washing-up bowl, add about 5 cm of water and see how the candle burns freely. Then place a jar upside down over the candle. The water rises up into the jar to take the place of the oxygen until there is no more oxygen left. The flame then goes out. You will see that the water has only risen about a fifth of the way up the jar.

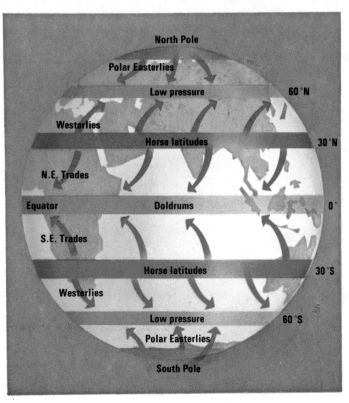

North Pole
Polar Easterlies
Low pressure — 60°N
Westerlies
Horse latitudes — 30°N
N.E. Trades
Equator — Doldrums — 0°
S.E. Trades
Horse latitudes — 30°S
Westerlies
Low pressure — 60°S
Polar Easterlies
South Pole

Left
The high and low pressure belts around the earth and the pattern of the winds. In the Northern Hemisphere winds veer to the right of their path and in the Southern Hemisphere they veer to the left, because of the spin of the earth. This is why the winds do not blow directly from high to low pressure.

Climate

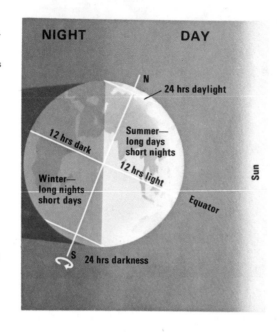

NIGHT   DAY

N
24 hrs daylight

Summer—
long days
short nights

12 hrs dark
12 hrs light

Sun

Winter—
long nights
short days

Equator

S   24 hrs darkness

Height (metres)

- 5000
- 4000
- 3000
- 2000
- 1000

Kenya
Mt Kenya, 5199 metres;
on equator

Snow

Grass

Trees

- - - - - - Snowline
· · · · · · · Treeline

New Zealand
Mt Cook, 3176 metres;
43½°S

South Georgia
(S. Atlantic)
Mt Paget, 2934 metres;
54°S

Heard Island
(S. Indian Ocean)
Big Ben, 404 metres;
54°S

Sea level   No trees   All snow

Climate is the average weather occurring in a place over a number of years. 'Greenland is a cold country' is a statement about climate. 'Isn't it rainy today' is a remark about the weather, which changes from day to day, and sometimes from hour to hour.

The climate of a place depends largely on how far north or south of the equator it is; the way in which the land and sea are arranged in the area is also very important. Mountains, ocean currents, and winds all play a part in forming climate.

The earth may be roughly divided into three areas with the same sort of climate. These areas are called *climatic zones*.

Near the North and South poles are the *polar* climatic regions. These are very cold, with snow and ice all the year round, although not much snow actually falls there. There are only two seasons: a long winter, and a short sunny summer, when there are 24 hours of daylight every day.

The *tropical* region lies each side of the equator and is hot all the

Key to Rainfall
100—200 cm
50—100 cm
25— 50 cm
0— 25 cm

year round. Parts of the tropics have fairly distinct wet and dry seasons, but in other parts there is very little change between the seasons.

The two *temperate* regions lie between the tropical and polar regions. In these areas the temperature is neither very hot nor very cold. However, some of the wettest places on earth are in these regions. There are usually four distinct seasons: spring, summer, autumn, and winter.

Other climatic zones fit in between the three main ones. The *sub-polar* regions lie between polar and temperate regions, *sub-tropical* between temperate and tropical, and *equatorial* in the middle of the tropical zone.

Another sort of climatic zone which occurs in various places on the earth is the *arid* zone. This is where there is a shortage of rainfall or snow. The most well-known arid zones are deserts, like the Sahara. Antarctica has a very low snowfall and is, therefore, an arid zone. It is sometimes called a polar desert.

The climatic zones are only a rough guide to climate. Particular places may be affected strongly by their surroundings. Places high up have colder climates than places near sea level; places near the sea have warmer winters and cooler summers than places inland.

Another way to decide what sort of climate a place has is to examine the plant and animal life in the area. If there are no trees then it is either cold or dry. In mountainous areas, tree will not grow above a particular height. This shows that the climate is colder the higher one goes.

In deserts the problem is not cold but lack of water; trees will only grow near oases or water courses. Even if there is no water in sight, a line of trees in the desert will indicate that there is water under the ground. In tropical areas the trees stay green all the year round, since there is little seasonal variation. They may bear fruit at any time of the year.

Roof allows rain and snow to run off

Temperate zone

Temperate zone

Barrel to catch rain

Wide verandah shading people and windows

Tropical zone

Hatch in case building is buried in snow

Door with high step to keep out snow

Polar zone

Polar zone

Above
The shape of houses in the different climatic zones. The temperate house has plenty of windows to let in heat and light. In the tropics, houses are raised up to allow air underneath to cool them. In polar regions, buildings have very thick walls and small windows to keep them warm. Wires hold the buildings down in strong winds.

Left
Animals can learn to live in extreme climates. A camel can travel for many days without water. It can close its nostrils to prevent sand getting into its nose. A husky can sleep in the snow when the temperature is −40°C. It has extra blood supplied to its pads (making them pink rather than black) to prevent frostbite.

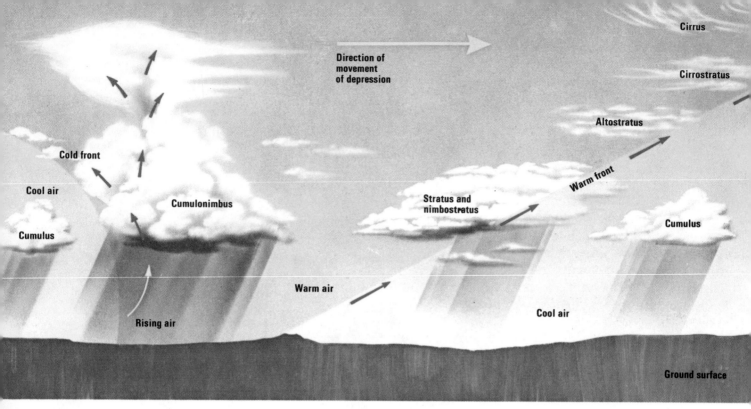

Cirrus

Cirrostratus

Altostratus

Direction of
movement
of depression

Cold front

Cool air

Cumulonimbus

Cumulus

Warm front

Stratus and
nimbostratus

Cumulus

Warm air

Cool air

Rising air

Ground surface

Weather

When we refer to weather rather than climate, we mean the particular conditions at any one time rather than the general conditions over a long period.

The weather is the result of conditions in the atmosphere and these vary for many reasons, one of them being the time of year. When we speak of weather conditions we include pressure, temperature, humidity (which is the wetness of the air), winds, clouds, rainfall, and visibility.

An important influence on tem-

perature is distance from the sea. In winter the sea has a warming effect on the land because it stores up heat from the sun in the summer and loses it much more slowly than the land. In summer it has a cooling effect because it heats up very much more slowly than the land since the surface is constantly moving. Sea winds in the summer therefore tend to feel cool.

Particles of water, condensing from water vapour in the atmosphere, can join together to form a raindrop. When the drops are heavy enough to overcome the rising air currents in a cloud, rain starts to fall.

Above
Clouds associated with the passage of a depression. Clouds are masses of condensed water vapour. The basic types of cloud are *cirrus* (thin, wispy and high in the sky), *stratus* (usually filling the sky like a complete layer on a grey day) and *cumulus* (white and puffy like cotton wool). The word *nimbus* is added to the name of the cloud if it is dark coloured, which shows that it is rain-bearing. By looking at the colour and shape of the clouds, then, we can make a good guess about our weather prospects.

Far left
Radiation fog. This type of fog occurs mainly in autumn and winter on calm nights when the sky is clear. When the ground cools quickly, by radiation, it cools the layer of air in contact with it, causing a fog of condensed moisture.

Left
An approaching tornado; a frightening sight. A tornado is a column of air which whirls around. The sudden low pressure at its centre and the gale force winds it brings can cause buildings to collapse.

Below
Snowflake crystals seen under a microscope.

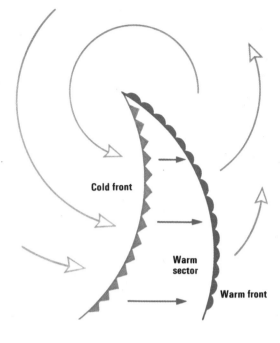

Cold front

**Warm
sector**

Warm front

There are three main types of rainfall; all are caused by the rising of moist air. *Orographic* (or *relief*) rainfall occurs when a mass of moving air is forced to rise by the presence of high ground. The air cools down as it rises, enabling the water vapour to condense. *Convectional* rainfall occurs when a mass of air is heated by the sun until it becomes lighter than the surrounding air and starts to rise (this is more common in tropical areas). Thunderstorms occur in these conditions. *Frontal* (or *cyclonic*) rainfall is caused by the movement of the warm or cold front of a *depression*, or low pressure area.

Snow falls when the atmosphere is very cold. A snow-flake consists of crystals of ice linked together. These crystals have been formed directly from water vapour that has condensed at a temperature below the freezing point of water and so missed out the liquid stage.

Hail consists of tiny balls of ice and falls from high cumulonimbus clouds when there are very strong upward air currents. Droplets of rain are carried upwards by the rising air until they freeze. More water freezes around them, and as they fall they often melt and are lifted up again until they re-freeze.

This process may be repeated several times until the hailstone is too heavy to be carried upwards again.

Fog is condensed water vapour, but unlike a cloud it rests on or near the ground. It occurs when moist air is cooled, as when in clear calm weather the earth's surface is cooled at night by radiating away its heat; air in contact with the surface is also cooled producing the most common form of fog, *radiation fog*.

Steam fog, which is not common, occurs when cold air passes over a much warmer water surface, so that the water appears to steam.

Lastly, *hill fog* occurs when a stream of moist air reaches the hills and is forced to rise; it is really low stratus cloud.

Right
Wood is an example of a solid.
Water is a liquid; it can be poured
and changes its shape. It is not so
easy to draw a picture of a gas.
The mist you see from a spray is
very small drops of water. They are
carried by the gas, which is invisible.

Matter

The stuff of which all things are made is called matter. It can be a solid such as wood or iron, a liquid such as water or oil, or a gas such as air or steam. These three forms are called *states of matter*.

If you take an ice cube and warm it gently in a saucepan it melts and becomes a liquid. As it becomes still hotter it boils to form steam, a gas.

Solids have a fixed shape and a fixed size (or volume). It takes quite a lot of energy to change the shape of a solid. Its size will not change unless it is heated or cooled.

Liquids have a fixed volume too, but have the shape of whatever container they are poured into.

Gases do not have a fixed shape or a fixed volume. They expand to fill all the space in their container; so a gas leak in one room can quickly be detected by its smell throughout a house.

There have been many ideas about the nature of matter, since ancient times. Greek philosophers thought that matter was made of vast numbers of very small particles called *atoms*. The word *atom* comes from a Greek word meaning 'unable to be divided'. In the Dark Ages the Greeks' ideas were forgotten, but they were revived by many scientific thinkers such as Boyle and Newton in the seventeenth and eighteenth centuries. Finally in 1803 an Englishman, *John Dalton*, worked out an *atomic theory*. Dalton's idea was that all matter is made up of small particles called atoms, which cannot be split up.

Different materials behave in different ways because their atoms

Right
Considerable energy is required to change the shape of a solid. If all the pieces are put together again they still occupy the same space.

Far right
One gram of solid occupies less space than the same mass of liquid. This, in turn, occupies less space than one gram of gas. The gas here occupies one thousand times as much space as the solid.

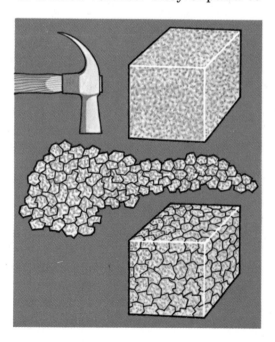

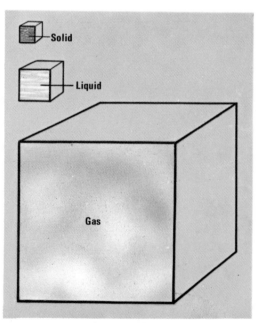

are different. For example, diamond is different from aluminium because it is made up of a different kind of atom.

The way in which the atoms are packed together decides whether a substance is a solid, a liquid, or a gas.

Atoms attract one another: if they attract strongly they are packed close together and form a solid. In a solid the atoms are fixed in position: it is this that makes it difficult for a solid to change its shape or its size.

If the atoms do not attract so strongly, they can move about and form a liquid or a gas. As a solid is heated, the particles move more and more (*vibrate*) until they break away from each other. They then form a liquid. This is called *melting*. Ice melts into water.

The particles in a liquid can move around quite freely, but cannot escape from each other completely. They are much further apart than the particles in a solid, and so take up more space.

Heating a liquid makes the particles it consists of move even faster. Eventually they are moving so quickly that they can escape from the surface of the liquid, and form a gas. This process is called *evaporation*. When the liquid gets hotter still they escape so quickly that the liquid bubbles. This is called *boiling*.

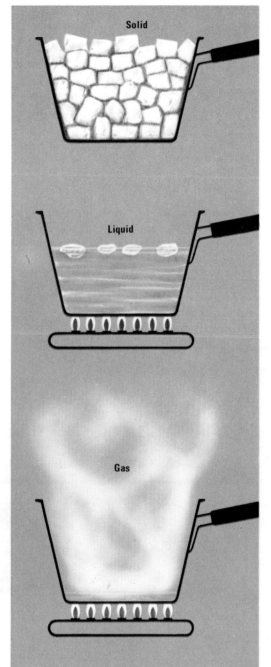

Solid

Liquid

Gas

Left
Water in its three different states; ice, the solid; water, the liquid; steam, the gas.

Above
Take a glass of still water and place a drop of milk or ink carefully on the surface. After a time the milk or ink spreads through the water because of the movement of the atoms.

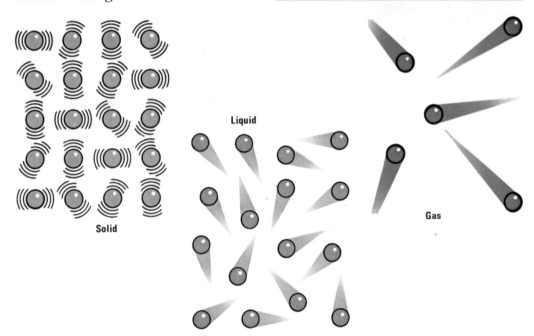

Solid

Liquid

Gas

Left
Atoms are very small. One gram of the metal copper contains nearly 10 000 000 000 000 000 000 000 atoms. In a solid they have fixed positions about which they vibrate. In a liquid they move about but are still quite close together. In a gas they are far apart, and move very quickly.

Right
The best known physical changes are the changes between solids, liquids, and gases. Water changes to steam at 100°C. When water is cooled below 0°C it changes to ice. Both these changes are reversible.

Physical and chemical changes

When ice is warmed it changes into water. This is called a *physical change*. In a physical change the material changes its appearance. It is easy to get the original material back again. If water is put in a refrigerator it *freezes* and ice is formed. We say that the change from water to ice is the reverse of the change from ice to water. The change is a *reversible change*. Another example of a physical change is the change from water to steam when a kettle boils. When the steam cools it *condenses* back to water.

A quite different kind of change takes place when a piece of paper is heated. First it goes brown and becomes brittle. Then it bursts into flames and gives out a lot of heat. It ends up as ash. When the ash is cooled it does not change

Above
The burning of a piece of paper is a chemical change. Paper and ash are quite different from one another. We say that they are different *substances*. On the other hand, water, ice, and steam are just different *states* of the same substance.

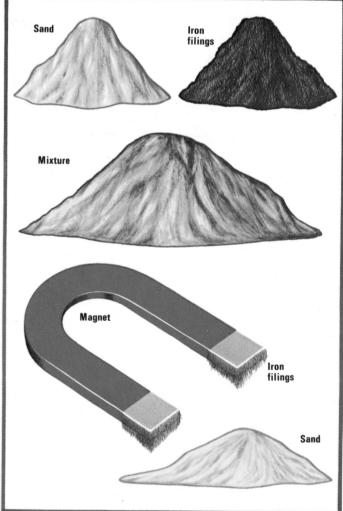

Sand

Iron filings

Mixture

Magnet

Iron filings

Sand

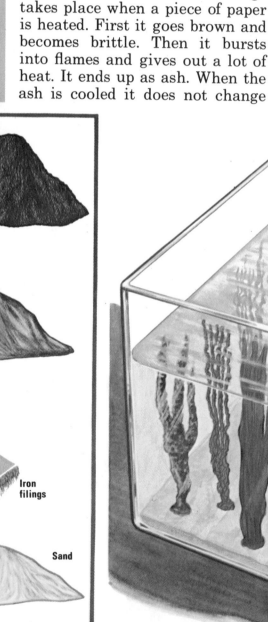

Right
A mixture of sand and iron filings can be separated with a magnet. The formation of the mixture is an entirely physical change as the sand and the iron filings do not react chemically with each other.

back into paper. A completely new substance has been made. A change of this kind is called a *chemical change*. In fact paper is changing slowly all the time. Very old paper is crumbly and yellow.

Work out whether everyday changes you see are physical changes or chemical changes. In hot weather butter becomes soft but if it gets cold it becomes hard again. The change is reversible and is an example of a physical change. On the other hand when milk is left it turns sour and there is no way of getting fresh milk from sour milk. This change is not reversible – we say it is irreversible. It is an example of a chemical change.

If iron filings are mixed with sand the mixture looks grey. However the iron filings can easily be removed by using a magnet. If you look at the mixture with a magnifying glass you can still see the grains of sand and the small pieces of iron.

No new substance has been formed. This is a physical change.

Shake some sugar and water together. The sugar *dissolves* in the water. Although the *solution* looks clear and colourless, the sugar can be obtained again by letting all the water evaporate. Crystals are left behind. This is a physical change.

If you put some shiny iron nails in water they will soon be covered with a brown coating of rust. The iron in the nails and oxygen in the water and air have formed a new substance. It would be very difficult to get the iron back from rust. Rusting is a chemical change.

Many of the changes that take place in nature are chemical. For example, inside a cow grass is turned into milk. There is no way of turning milk back into grass. The changes that occur when food is cooked are also chemical. There is no way of changing chips back into raw potatoes!

Below left
A solution of sugar in water is allowed to stand in a saucer. After a few days the water evaporates away leaving the sugar crystals. This is a physical change.

Below
In chemical changes new substances are made. One of the most striking kinds of chemical change is burning. Chemists used to think that everything contained a substance called *phlogiston* which was given off when things burn. In the sixteenth century Lavoisier proved that there was no such thing as phlogiston and that when things burn they join with oxygen in the air. This experiment shows that things cannot burn without oxygen. When the oxygen has been used up the candle goes out.

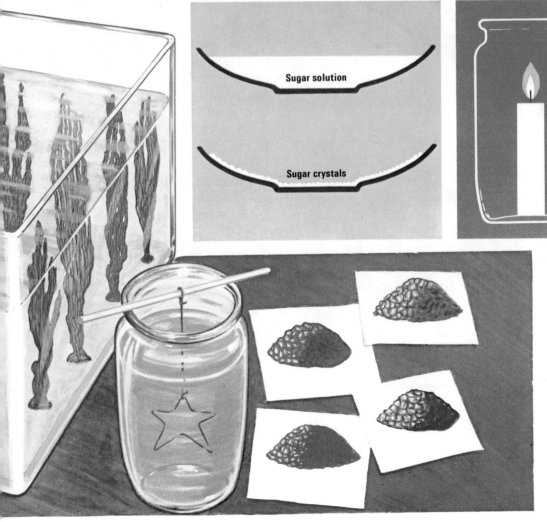

Sugar solution

Sugar crystals

Left
A chemical garden. This jungle of plant-like growths is the result of the physical and chemical changes undergone by a few crystals. To make a chemical garden, put some sand in a tank and pour in waterglass solution. Drop in a few crystals, such as iron or copper sulphate, chrome alum or potassium dichromate. They will throw up 'shoots' in a few hours. To demonstrate a purely physical change, tie a tiny crystal of alum on a thread, suspend it in a jar of alum solution and watch the crystal grow.

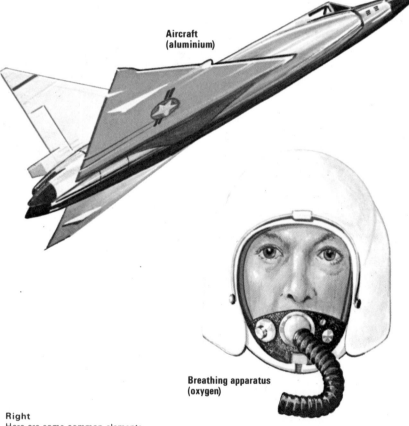

Aristotle

Mendeleev

Elements and compounds

Wood, water, air, aluminium, paper, ash, oil, milk, sugar, and grass are some examples of many millions of different known materials (substances). Over two thousand years ago a famous Greek philosopher, Aristotle, thought that all substances were made up of four *elements*. These were earth, fire, water, and air. For example he thought that wood was made up of fire and earth because it burnt to an ash.

It is only in the last two hundred years that we have discovered that the millions of different substances are made up of just over a hundred simple substances. These are also called *elements*. An element is a substance that cannot be split up into any more simple material.

Some elements are very common. One example is iron. Another is oxygen, which is a gas. It is invisible and present in the air we breathe.

You have probably seen rust on old tin cans, iron railings, and car bodies. It is a red crumbly powder quite unlike the bright hard metal iron and the invisible gas oxygen. Rust is not an element because it is made of both iron and oxygen. Chemists call it iron oxide. Iron oxide is an example of a *compound*. It is formed from the two elements iron and oxygen. The change from

Above
Aristotle was a famous Greek philosopher born in 384 B.C. He lived in Athens and wrote many books on natural science.

Above right
Dmitri Ivanovitch Mendeleev was a Russian chemist born in 1834. He constructed a table of the elements in which elements with the same properties were put into columns. One of the elements, *mendelevium,* was named in his honour.

**Thermometer
(mercury)**

**Aircraft
(aluminium)**

**Breathing apparatus
(oxygen)**

Right
Here are some common elements. Mercury is the silvery liquid you see in thermometers. It used to be called quicksilver. Aluminium is the silvery metal used in milk bottle tops. It is used for aircraft because it is a light material. Oxygen is an invisible gas. It is necessary for burning and also for breathing. Sulphur is a yellow element. When it is a powder like this it is called *flowers of sulphur.* It used to be called brimstone.

**Brimstone
(sulphur)**

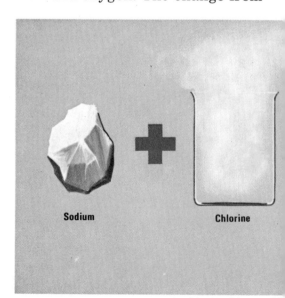

Sodium

Chlorine

iron and oxygen to rust (iron oxide) is an example of a *chemical change.* The rust is quite different from the elements from which it is made.

There are other substances besides elements and compounds. They are called *mixtures.* If powdered iron is mixed with sand the grains of sand and iron can be seen in the mixture. The iron can easily be separated from the sand. No new substance has been formed. The mixing of iron and sand is a *physical change.* Dental fillings are a mixture of the elements mercury, tin, silver, and zinc. Air is a mixture of gases, consisting mainly of nitrogen and some oxygen.

John Dalton, in 1803, explained that all elements are made up of millions and millions of small particles which are called atoms.

Iron is made up of a lot of atoms, called iron atoms. These are different from the oxygen atoms and this makes iron quite different from oxygen in its behaviour. When iron and oxygen form the compound rust the iron atoms join with oxygen atoms to give small *groups* of atoms. These groups are called *molecules.* The smallest particle in an element is an atom. The smallest particle in a compound is a molecule.

The most common compound on the earth is water. Water is made up of two elements. One is oxygen. The other is hydrogen, which is a very light invisible gas. Water molecules are made up of hydrogen

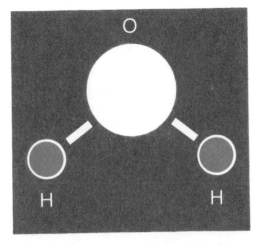

atoms and oxygen atoms. Not all compounds are as simple as water. Some have very large molecules made up of many atoms.

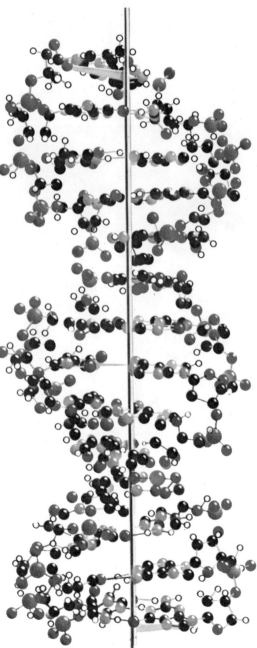

Left
Some compounds are very complicated and their molecules are very large. This is a model of the molecule of deoxyribonucleic acid (called DNA). It is found in living cells.

Sodium chloride

Far left
Sodium is a silvery-grey metallic element. Chlorine is also an element. It is a greenish-yellow poisonous gas. When the two are put together they form a compound called sodium chloride. This is better known as the salt you put on food.

Right
Acids are present in vinegar, lemon juice and rhubarb leaves. Vinegar contains acetic acid. Lemon juice contains citric acid. Rhubarb leaves contain a poisonous acid called oxalic acid.

Far right
Some animals and plants use acids and alkalis to defend themselves. Nettle leaves are covered with thin hairs that prick the skin. There is a small bulb at the bottom of each hair which is full of an acid called formic acid. This gets under the skin and causes the sting. Ant stings are also formic acid. Bee stings are acid and are relieved by putting bicarbonate of soda on them. Wasp stings are alkaline and can be treated with lemon juice or vinegar.

Right
The best known indicator is called *litmus*. It is made from lichens, a special type of plant. Litmus turns red in acids and blue in alkalis.

Right
All acids contain hydrogen. Their molecules have hydrogen atoms in them. Hydrochloric acid is a strong acid made of hydrogen and chlorine. It is also called hydrogen chloride. Caustic soda is a strong alkali. Alkalis contain oxygen atoms and hydrogen atoms and are often called hydroxides. Caustic soda is sodium hydroxide. When hydrogen chloride is mixed with sodium hydroxide they change to give sodium chloride and water. Both these new compounds are neutral. Sodium chloride is common salt. In the diagram Na is the symbol for sodium because sodium used to be called *natrium*.

Below
Many different salts exist and some of them are coloured. Here are some useful coloured salts. Chrome alum is used in dyeing and tanning leather. Copper sulphate kills fungi. Potassium dichromate is the orange substance used in the breathalyser test for drivers. Iron sulphate is used in making ink.

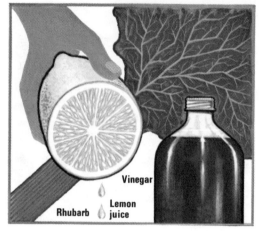

Rhubarb · Lemon juice · Vinegar

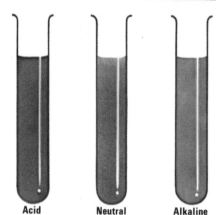

Acid · Neutral · Alkaline

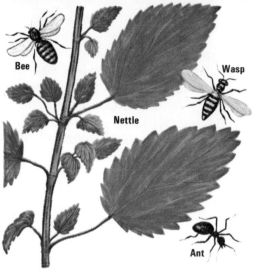

Bee · Wasp · Nettle · Ant

Acids, alkalis and salts

Although there are only 92 natural elements there are millions of chemical compounds. These behave in different ways. There are a number of very important compounds called *acids*.

One example of an acid is sulphuric acid which is used in car batteries. It is a dangerous poisonous liquid which attacks many materials and burns the skin. Acids like this are called *strong* acids. They are said to be *corrosive*.

Not all acids are so dangerous. Some familiar liquids are acids, such as vinegar and lemon juice. All acids have a sharp taste. Some plants and animals use acids as weapons. The stings of ants, bees, and nettles are acids. The gas that animals breathe out is carbon dioxide and when this dissolves in water an acid is formed. It is a very *weak* acid and is not corrosive. Soda water is water with a lot of carbon dioxide in it.

Another important kind of compound is called a *base*. If a base dissolves in water it is an *alkali*. Alkalis are often dangerous compounds and attack the skin. Wood ash contains an alkali which used to be manufactured by mixing wood ash with water so that the alkali was dissolved out and separated from the ash. The water was then boiled away in an iron pot and the alkali was left. Because of the way it was made this alkali is called *potash*. Potash is now made in a different way. Large amounts are

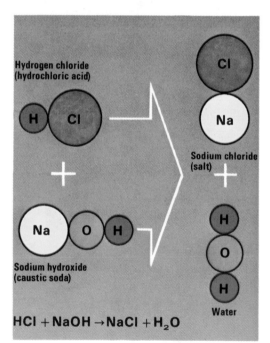

Hydrogen chloride (hydrochloric acid)

Sodium hydroxide (caustic soda)

Sodium chloride (salt)

Water

$$HCl + NaOH \rightarrow NaCl + H_2O$$

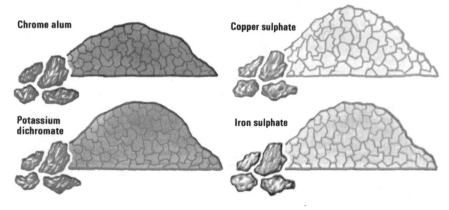

Chrome alum

Copper sulphate

Potassium dichromate

Iron sulphate

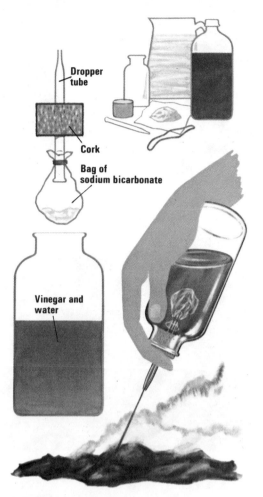

Dropper tube

Cork

Bag of sodium bicarbonate

Vinegar and water

Right
A chemical fire extinguisher contains an alkaline solution of sodium bicarbonate and sulphuric acid. When it is triggered off these two solutions come into contact and react together, and give off carbon dioxide gas. The pressure of this gas is used to drive out a strong jet of water or foam.

Left
A model fire extinguisher. To make this, push a glass tube through a cork and tie a small bag of sodium bicarbonate on the bottom end. Push the cork firmly into a bottle containing a mixture of vinegar and water.
To trigger off the extinguisher, hold the cork in with your fingers and turn the bottle upside-down. The acid solution of vinegar will leak through the paper and react with the alkaline bicarbonate, giving off carbon dioxide gas. The build-up of gas pressure in the bottle will force a jet of liquid out of the tube. Try this out-of-doors on a small piece of burning paper. Hold the cork in firmly or it may be forced out by the pressure.

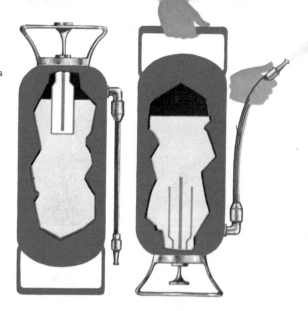

Below
Test for acid. Acids : taste sour ; turn litmus red ; react with metals ; neutralize alkaline solutions (turning them purple if they contain litmus). Only taste food acids (e.g. lemons); others are often poisonous.

Below
Tests for alkalis. Alkalis : taste brackish ; turn litmus blue ; react with fats ; neutralize acid solutions (turning them purple if they contain litmus). Many alkalis are dangerous and should not be tasted.

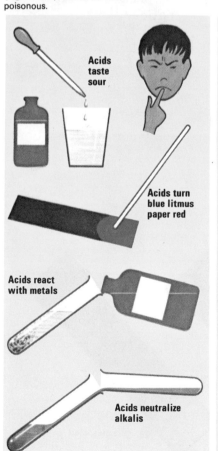

Acids taste sour

Acids turn blue litmus paper red

Acids react with metals

Acids neutralize alkalis

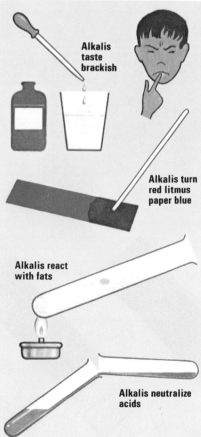

Alkalis taste brackish

Alkalis turn red litmus paper blue

Alkalis react with fats

Alkalis neutralize acids

used for making soap. Other alkalis come from lime and wasp stings. Saliva is a weak alkali.

Compounds that are not acids or alkalis are said to be *neutral*. Many flowers and fruits have a colour which depends on whether the soil contains an acid or an alkali.

Blue *hydrangeas* can produce pink flowers if planted in alkaline soil. Substances which change colour when an acid or alkali is added are called *indicators*. They can be used to test (indicate) whether a liquid is acidic or alkaline.

You can make indicators yourself. Any fruit or vegetable which has a dark colour is worth investigating. Try boiling some red cabbage in water, and strain off the coloured liquid when it is cool. If you add a drop of vinegar to this solution, it will go red, but if this is followed by a little soap (which is weakly alkaline), the solution will turn blue.

Solutions of indicators can also be made from fresh beetroot, dark red rose petals, and blackcurrants. Once you have made an indicator, test different liquids.

When an acid is mixed with an alkali a chemical change takes place and two new compounds are formed. One of them is always water. The other is a type of compound called a *salt*. The salt we eat is sodium chloride and it is often called common salt. Many other salts exist. Examples are washing soda (sodium carbonate), Epsom salts (magnesium sulphate), and limestone (calcium carbonate).

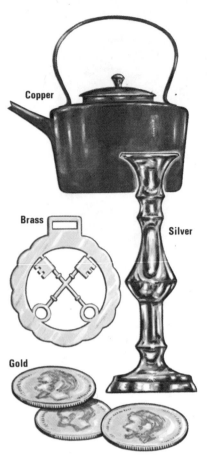

Copper

Brass

Silver

Gold

Above
Metals and alloys have a lustre.

Above right
Stand a wooden spoon and a large metal spoon at the same time, in a bowl of hot water. Then touch their handles. The metal spoon becomes hot long before the wooden one, because metal conducts heat, whilst wood is an insulator.

Right
A piece of metal hanging freely gives a musical note when it is hit. Bells are made to produce the most beautiful sound possible.

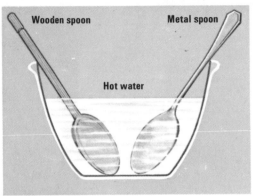

Wooden spoon   Metal spoon

Hot water

Metals

There are two kinds of elements, *metals* and *non-metals*, and each kind can be distinguished by its physical properties. Mixtures of metals are called *alloys*, and usually have some of the properties of each of their components. For example brass is an *alloy* of copper and zinc.

Probably the best test for a metal is its appearance; a polished metal has a shiny look called its *lustre*, and this applies to gold, aluminium, or even a liquid metal like mercury. Non-metallic elements can be polished, such as sulphur, or carbon

Right
Switch an electric hand-torch on, then carefully unscrew the base and see if the light has gone out. Put a large circle of paper or polythene between the base, and the batteries and the case, then screw the base up again. The bulb does not relight, because paper does not conduct electricity, but if you used a piece of aluminium kitchen foil instead, the bulb would relight as the metal allows electricity to pass through it.

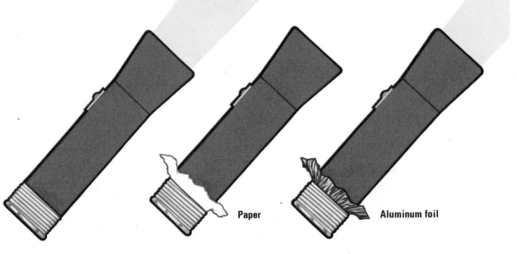

Paper   Aluminum foil

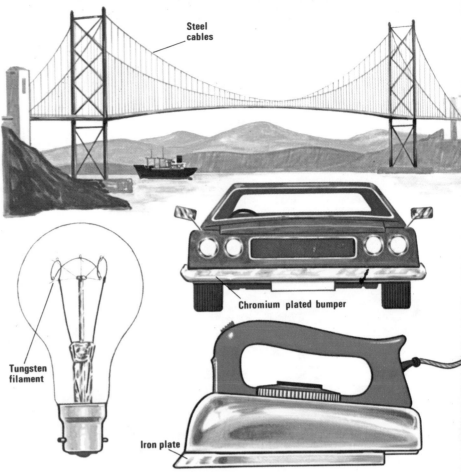

Steel cables

Chromium plated bumper

Tungsten filament

Iron plate

especially in the form of diamond, but do not have the same kind of 'sheen'. Another very simple test for a metal is that a piece which is suspended gives a ringing sound like a bell when it is hit sharply. Metals are therefore *sonorous*.

Simple experiments can be done to show that while heat and electricity can pass easily through metals, they do not do so through non-metallic materials. Because of this metals are said to be *good conductors* of heat and electricity; most non-metals are *insulators*.

The most valuable property of metals is their strength; many can be forged or hammered into any shape or made into wire, while the non-metallic elements are brittle.

The way metals are used depends on these physical properties. Lustrous metals like gold or chromium can be used for ornaments or protective plating; bells are often made of bronze, an alloy of copper and tin which is very sonorous. Two of the best conductors are aluminium and copper, so saucepans, which must heat up quickly can be made of either metal. Most electrical equipment uses metals to conduct electricity. Copper wires

carry electric currents long distances, whilst another metal, tungsten, is more suitable for the heat resistant filament in a light bulb.

The cheapest metal to produce is iron, and this is used, sometimes protected by concrete, to give strength to large structures.

Iron mixed with carbon is *steel*, which can be made in almost any shape, but is tough and springy. Steel is used for swords, car bodies, machinery, and thousands of other products. For strong light aeroplanes, alloys containing aluminium and magnesium are used.

Most non-metallic elements, or compounds, do not have these properties and in fact are often useful because of this. Saucepan handles are often made of wood or plastic, which are insulators. Porcelain or glass can be used to protect wires carrying electricity.

Many metals are expensive, but their strength and the ease with which they can be moulded is extremely valuable, so there is a constant search for new alloys which might have more interesting and useful physical properties. Scientists who study metals are called metallurgists.

Right
Making soot and making charcoal, two different types of carbon.

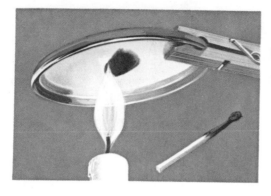

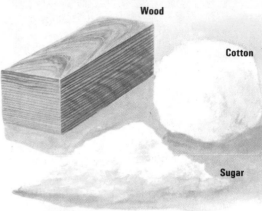

Wood

Cotton

Sugar

Far right
Wood, cotton, and sugar are *organic* chemicals. They contain carbon. Iron, brick, and salt are *inorganic* chemicals. They do not have any carbon in them. Try making lists of all the materials you can think of with carbon in them and the ones that have no carbon.

Carbon

Right
You can make a form of coal out of sugar. Heat a teaspoon of ordinary white sugar in a heat-proof dish or tin. First it will melt and then turn to brown caramel. Further heating will make it give off thick smoke which can be lit. The charred sugar turns into a pure form of coal.

If you hold a shiny tin lid in a candle flame it becomes coated with a black powder called *soot*. Soot consists of a very important *element* called *carbon*.

Soot is just one of the many forms in which carbon is found. The lead in an ordinary pencil contains a form of carbon called *graphite*. When wood is burned in the absence of air it turns into a form of carbon called *charcoal*.

Coal contains carbon; diamonds consist of it. They look and feel quite different because the atoms of carbon in them are joined together in different ways.

Atoms of carbon can link up with atoms of other elements, to form thousands of different compounds. Most of them come from living things, such as wood, sugar, and cotton, which come from plants, and candle wax and food, which come from animals. Because nearly all carbon compounds are closely connected with living organisms, they are called *organic compounds*.

Substances that do not contain carbon, such as oxygen, glass and

Graphite

Diamond

Right
Graphite and diamond are both forms of carbon. They are different because of the arrangement of the carbon atoms. Graphite has layers of atoms; this makes it soft and slippery and it does not let light through. Diamond has a quite different arrangement which makes it very hard and transparent to light.

Right
Representations of molecules of methane, which is found in North Sea gas, and butane, which is used in lighter fuel and in camping stoves. The large black balls are carbon atoms and the small white ones are hydrogen atoms.

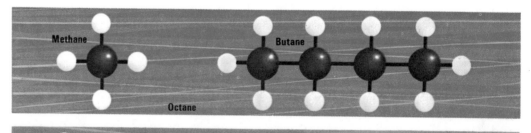

Methane

Butane

Octane

Right
A representation of a molecule of octane, which is present in petrol. In this molecule as well as in the butane and methane molecules you will see that each hydrogen atom joins to one other atom and each carbon atom is joined to four others. It is very easy to make models of molecules like these using plasticine and matchsticks.

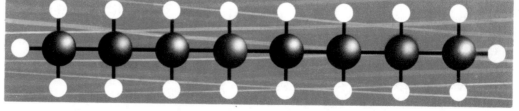

Iron

Brick

Salt

brick, are called *inorganic com-pounds*.

Some carbon compounds, such as wood and cotton, are made up of large complicated molecules. The simplest organic compounds are made of combinations of carbon and hydrogen. Such compounds are called *hydrocarbons*.

If one atom of carbon joins with four atoms of hydrogen they form a molecule of the gas called *methane*. This gas is used for cooking and heating.

Another hydrocarbon is *butane*, the liquid used as lighter fuel. A molecule of butane contains four carbon atoms and ten hydrogen atoms. One of the most important fuels is *petrol*, a mixture of hydro-carbons. It contains *octane* with eight carbon atoms and eighteen hydrogen atoms.

All these hydrocarbons have the atoms joined together in long chains. Some carbon compounds contain atoms that are linked together in rings.

By processes in which carbon compounds are heated under pres-sure, many important materials can be made, such as plastics and artificial fibres.

Fuel gas

Petrol

Paraffin

Heating oil

Lubricating oil

Wax

Asphalt

Crude oil

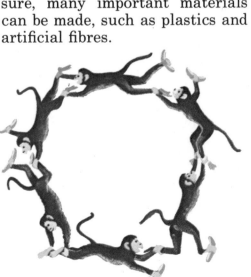

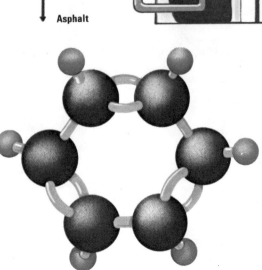

Fuels

The main fuels are coal, oil, and natural gas. All three were, most probably, formed from the remains of living matter. Until the middle of the twentieth century coal was by far the most widely used fuel but oil and natural gas are now used more and more.

Most of the world's coal began forming in the *Carboniferous period* of the geological time scale, from 345 to 280 million years ago. The remains of swamp forests were subjected to great pressure under the weight of sands and other material which was laid down on top of them. The dead vegetation turned into coal and the layers (or *seams*) of coal are divided by other rocks. There are various forms of coal. These range from brown coal – *lignite* – at the younger end of the scale to hard *anthracite* at the older end.

Oil was formed under great heat and pressure, and is found in certain types of rock formation. Great depressions or sunken parts of the earth's crust (*geosynclines*), where sedimentary rocks occur, often contain oil. It is held in rocks that are full of tiny holes (called *pores*) and therefore act as sponges. These rocks are trapped between non-porous impervious

Below
A coal mine showing the ventilation shaft on the left and the lift shaft on the right. There are three coal seam running across the drawing. The lowest one was formed earliest and the highest one latest.

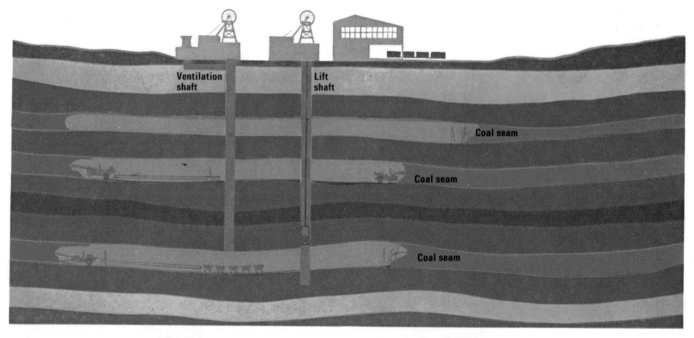

Ventilation shaft

Lift shaft

Coal seam

Coal seam

Coal seam

Left
Drilling the coal face in a mine. The more modern the colliery, the more elaborate is the machinery used.

layers which neither hold any liquid nor let it pass through them.

In its natural or *crude* form, oil is useless. In an oil refinery, however, it is divided into its various components and most of these can be used. The process is basically that of heating the crude oil; because the components change into gases (or *evaporate*) at different temperatures, they can be separated from each other. This takes place in a tall tower called a *fractionating column*.

Petrol for motor vehicles is an important product obtained from crude oil. There are many others, ranging from tar and lubricating oils at the heavy end to aircraft fuel and paraffin at the lighter end.

Natural gas also occurs underground, usually lying above a layer of oil-bearing rock. Since large amounts of it were discovered in the North Sea, natural gas has been replacing the type made from coal in the gas-works of most towns in England. In the United States it has been used for a long time.

Coal, oil, and natural gas are all used as fuels for producing heat both in the home and in industry. Some years ago, electricity generating stations in Britain used only coal as the fuel for their steam turbines; many are now using oil instead. Electricity can now be produced using another type of fuel – *uranium*, a *radioactive* element. This is used in nuclear power stations (see page 198).

A new industry has grown up in recent years as a by-product of oil refining. This is the *petrochemical industry*. The chemical industry has always been closely associated with the coal mining industry and gas works in the past, because coal is an important source of chemicals; modern petrochemical plants are on a much larger scale. The fuels are the source of chemicals for a wide range of products which we use every day. These include plastics, artificial fibres (nylon, etc.), paint, fertilizers, explosives, and many others.

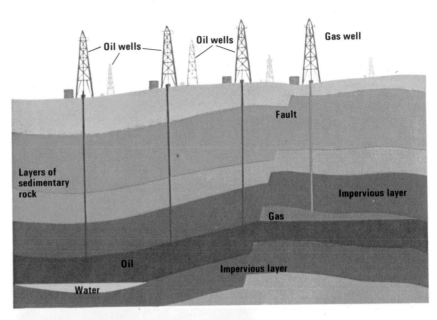

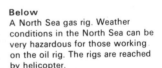

Above
A typical rock formation containing oil and natural gas. When a well is sunk, the oil can spout out under pressure or sometimes it is pumped out.

Left
A fractionating column in a refinery. The lighter fractions of the crude oil rise to the top, and the heaviest fractions remain at the bottom.

Below
A North Sea gas rig. Weather conditions in the North Sea can be very hazardous for those working on the oil rig. The rigs are reached by helicopter.

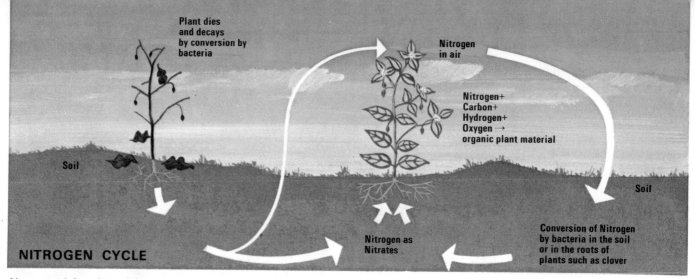

NITROGEN CYCLE

Plant dies and decays by conversion by bacteria

Soil

Nitrogen in air

Nitrogen+ Carbon+ Hydrogen+ Oxygen → organic plant material

Soil

Nitrogen as Nitrates

Conversion of Nitrogen by bacteria in the soil or in the roots of plants such as clover

Above: top left and top right
The nitrogen and carbon cycles. Plants cannot take in free nitrogen from the air. They have to obtain it from nitrates (a combination of nitrogen and oxygen) in the soil. They can, however, obtain their carbon from carbon dioxide in the air by photosynthesis. This carbon and nitrogen, together with oxygen and hydrogen (obtained from water), is used to produce organic plant material.

Below: bottom right
The alteration of a food chain. Foxes normally feed on rabbits. They have been known to make poultry one of their main foods when rabbits became very scarce.

Below
A typical rotation of crops. Certain plants, such as clover, have lumps in their roots containing bacteria which remove nitrogen from the air. When plants die, this nitrogen is released as nitrates and enriches the soil. Farmers therefore plant clover in a particular field once every few years to enrich the soil for other plants.

Ecology

Ecology is the study of living things in their natural surroundings. Plants and animals depend on one another and on the earth, air, and water in which they live for food and therefore life. All plants and animals are made up mainly of the chemicals *carbon*, *nitrogen*, *hydrogen*, and *oxygen*. These four chemicals are combined together in the organism to form complicated organic molecules called *proteins*, *fats*, and *carbohydrates*.

All living things are continually growing or, when adult, are replacing their dead cells with new ones. Therefore they are constantly needing supplies of the four basic chemicals. Oxygen comes from the air or from seas and rivers (in which it is dissolved). Hydrogen is obtained from water which is made up of atoms of hydrogen and oxygen. Carbon and nitrogen come from the air, seas, rivers, or soil. The use of these four elements by plants and animals involves two complex *cycles* which show the dependence of living things on each other and on their surroundings.

The carbon and nitrogen cycles involve the circulation of atoms of carbon and nitrogen from their surroundings (called the *environment*), through the plants and animals, and back into the environment.

In this way the composition of the environment remains the same.

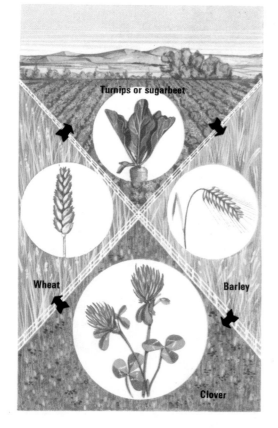

Turnips or sugarbeet

Wheat

Barley

Clover

Plankton

Eaten by small fry

Eaten by herrings

Eaten by gulls

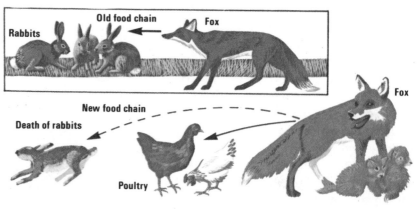

Old food chain

Rabbits

Fox

New food chain

Death of rabbits

Poultry

Fox

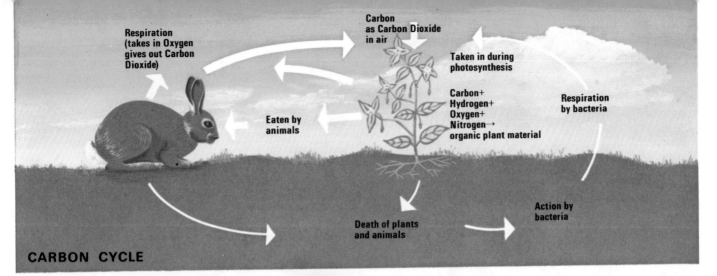

CARBON CYCLE

Carbon
as Carbon Dioxide
in air

Respiration
(takes in Oxygen
gives out Carbon
Dioxide)

Taken in during
photosynthesis

Carbon+
Hydrogen+
Oxygen+
Nitrogen→
organic plant material

Respiration
by bacteria

Eaten by
animals

Death of plants
and animals

Action by
bacteria

Right
Pyramid of Numbers. This is another way of representing a food chain. Smaller animals are often eaten by larger ones. In any one food chain, therefore, a lot of small animals eventually provide food for one large one.

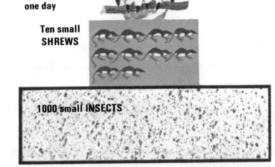

One large OWL

Eaten in
one day

Ten small
SHREWS

1000 small INSECTS

Below bottom
The poisoning of an animal low down in the food chain can result in animals higher up in the same chain being poisoned.

Below left
A food chain in the sea. Each of the animals represents a link in the chain.

Below
A food chain in a wood.

Leaves

Eaten by
Owls

Eaten by
greenfly

Eaten by
shrews

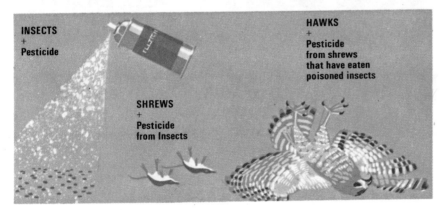

INSECTS
+
Pesticide

SHREWS
+
Pesticide
from Insects

HAWKS
+
Pesticide
from shrews
that have eaten
poisoned insects

Farmers make use of one stage in the nitrogen cycle in *crop rotation*.

The dependence of one small animal upon another is seen even more clearly in *food chains*. In nature, animals usually eat only certain kinds of food, generally certain plants or other animals. The animals are themselves eaten by larger animals which may in turn be eaten by larger animals still. This is known as a food chain: each living thing forming food for another is a link in the chain.

One animal is dependent on many others for its food, although it may not actually feed directly on them; an owl depends on insects because these form the food of shrews. If any link in the chain is removed, for instance, by killing an insect pest, the populations of the other links in the chain would be affected. This sort of interference can also cause alterations in the food chain: if an animal is unable to find one of its main foods, it will have to start eating another.

Direct action on an animal low down in a food chain can affect animals higher up in the same chain. This can be seen in the use of poisons, called *pesticides*. These poisons are used by farmers and fruit growers to kill insect pests that destroy their crops.

When shrews or other small animals eat the poisoned insects they too will become poisoned so that the hawks which feed on the shrews may also be poisoned although they have not eaten the pesticide themselves.

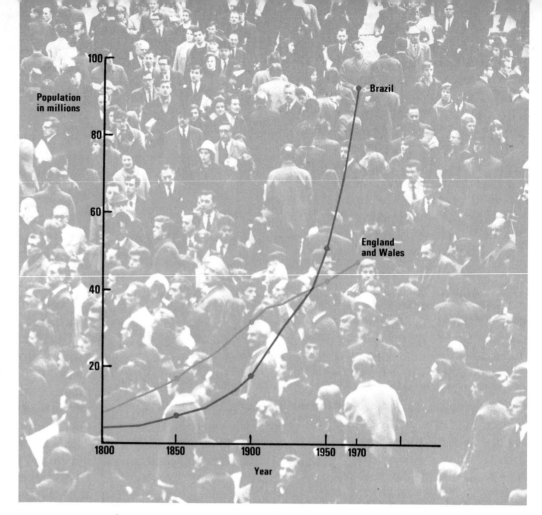

Population in millions

100

80

60

40

20

Brazil

England and Wales

1800   1850   1900   1950 1970

Year

Right
The population of the undeveloped countries has increased enormously in the last 50 years. This is largely due to the benefits of modern medicine. Brazil is a typical example; in 1800 the population was half that of England and Wales, in 1970 it was nearly double. In the developed countries the greatest increase was during the nineteenth century. Now it has tailed off and the rate of increase is much smaller. This is shown on the graph by the green line, which shows how the population of England and Wales has increased over the last 170 years.

Pollution

The population of the world today is much greater than it used to be. It has been increasing very rapidly over recent years, partly due to medical discoveries which enable people to be cured of their fatal illnesses and therefore to live longer. This means that there is also an increase in the farming, factories, fisheries, and machinery that are necessary to provide for the increased population.

Although these processes pro- vide more food for people they also produce greater quantities of waste products. These are some- times difficult to dispose of and may be harmful to people, animals, or plants. In the more highly developed countries of the world (such as in America and Europe) there is more industry and there- fore more waste products than in less well-developed countries such as India and Africa. When the waste products pile up they pollute (spoil) the countryside, rivers, seas, and air. Fortunately many coun- tries realize the dangers of pollu-

Left
Aircraft cause pollution of the atmosphere and noise. It is worse with jet engines which sometimes produce a very unpleasant black smoke. The smoke consists of incompletely burnt particles of carbon.

tion and take steps to reduce it.

Pollution of the atmosphere is one of the most serious problems. The main waste products that pollute the air are gases, such as sulphur dioxide and carbon monoxide. Smoke can also cause pollution – it consists of small particles of solid material, such as tar and carbon, suspended in the air. These are bad for health and cause plants and crops to grow less well.

The sources of these products are mainly traffic, especially exhaust fumes from cars and lorries, and factories and power stations. Lead from the exhaust fumes of cars can also cause dangerous pollution of the air we breathe.

Pollution of seas and rivers is another important problem as man needs pure water for drinking. Fish and other animals living in rivers and seas are also harmed by this type of pollution. Substances which cause pollution of rivers are detergents (washing powders), poisonous waste products of factories (effluent), pesticides (chemicals used to kill insects) and weed killers. Sewage (human waste products) is also a possible source of pollution of rivers.

One of the most serious causes of pollution of the seas is oil. The oil comes from large ships called tankers and when it escapes into the sea it causes seabirds to die and becomes spread on beaches, spoiling them for holiday-makers. Various laws have been made to reduce certain types of pollution.

Pollution of the countryside causes many plants to die. This is mostly due to the use of pesticides and weed killers which farmers and gardeners use to kill crop pests. Scientists are still trying to find less harmful ways of destroying these pests.

A rather different type of nuisance is noise pollution. In many of our larger towns and cities there is a great deal of noise. It comes from aircraft (especially near an airport), road traffic, and machinery such as pneumatic drills, as well as from radios and record-players. All this noise is very unpleasant and may actually be harmful to people.

Left
The beaches of the Mediterranean are becoming increasingly polluted. Debris from ships, sewage outlets, and factory effluents are all contributing to make the beaches unpleasant for humans and dangerous to some forms of wild life. If the pollution continues at the present rate the sea may cease to support all forms of life.

Below
Factories often discharge their waste products into rivers. If these wastes include dangerous chemicals, even in tiny quantities, the river fish can be killed.

Right
One of the most unpleasant sources of noise is the aircraft jet engine. A modern jet engine has enormous power, and this invariably means considerable noise. Various devices are used to stifle this sound, without losing too much power. The illustration shows corrugated nozzle suppressors on a Rolls-Royce powered Boeing 707.

Some Common Elements

Name	Symbol	Discovered	Properties, uses, etc.
Aluminium	Al	1827	silvery-white metal; used in light alloys for aircraft, etc.
Bromine	Br	1827	reddish-brown nonmetallic liquid
Calcium	Ca	1808	silvery metal; compounds present in bones and teeth
Carbon	C	prehistoric	solid nonmetal; occurs as diamond, graphite, and charcoal; present in living matter
Chlorine	Cl	1774	greenish-yellow gas; used as disinfectant
Copper	Cu	prehistoric	reddish-brown metal; good conductor; used in wires, cables, etc.
Gold	Au	prehistoric	yellow metal; used in jewellery
Hydrogen	H	1766	colourless gas; most common element in universe
Iodine	I	1811	black solid nonmetal
Iron	Fe	prehistoric	silvery-white metal; basis of steel
Lead	Pb	prehistoric	bluish-white metal; very heavy; used in pipes
Mercury	Hg	prehistoric	silvery liquid metal; used in thermometers
Nitrogen	N	1772	colourless gas; makes up $\frac{4}{5}$ of the air; present in living matter
Oxygen	O	1774	colourless gas; present in air; most common element on earth
Silicon	Si	1824	nonmetallic solid; present in many rocks; used in transistors
Sodium	Na	1807	silvery metal; present in salt
Sulphur	S	prehistoric	pale-yellow nonmetallic solid
Tin	Sn	prehistoric	silvery metal; used in tin cans
Uranium	U	1841	silvery-white metal; radioactive; used in nuclear fuels and weapons
Zinc	Zn	prehistoric	bluish-white metal; mixed with copper to make brass

Some simple chemical compounds

Compound	Chemical name	Formula	
water		H_2O	colourless liquid
carbon dioxide		CO_2	colourless gas
salt	sodium chloride	$NaCl$	white powder
vinegar	acetic acid	CH_3COOH	colourless liquid when pure
washing soda	sodium carbonate	Na_2CO_3	large white or colourless crystals
bicarbonate of soda	sodium hydrogen carbonate	$NaHCO_3$	white powder

Brightest Stars, seen from earth

Name	Constellation	Distance (light years)
SIRIUS (Dog Star)	Canis Major	8·8
CANOPUS	Carina	97·8
α-CENTAURI	Centaurus	4·2
ARCTURUS	Boötes	35·9
VEGA	Lyra	26·1
CAPELLA	Auriga	45·6

(1 light year = 5·9 million million miles)

Measurement, Movement and Energy

Contents

Cubit rod

One cubit

1 metre
= 100 centimetres

Metre rule

Length

Above
The ancient unit called a cubit is based on the distance between the point of a man's elbow and the tip of his middle finger. From recorded measurements of the pyramids we know that the Egyptians took the cubit as about 53 centimetres. The yard, approximately equal to two cubits, is supposed to be based on the distance between King Alfred's nose and the end of his fingers.

Above right
A metre contains 100 centimetres and each centimetre contains ten millimetres. Atomic scientists use even smaller metric units. One thousandth of a millimetre is called a micrometre (or a micron) and one thousandth of a micrometre is called a nanometre. One thousandth of a nanometre is called a picometre; this is one millionth of a millionth of a metre.

When we talk about a length we must always be comparing one measurement with another. If you say you are taller than someone else you mean that the distance from the soles of your feet to the top of your head is greater than that distance on the other person. If you wanted to find out if you were taller than a pen friend in another town it would not be possible to compare your heights by standing side-by-side. Instead you would both use a scale of some kind to compare your heights – a ruler or a tape measure. In this case, instead of comparing your heights directly you have each compared your own height with a standard length – a foot or metre. It would be impossible to use this method if the standard of length in one place was different from the standard in the other. So it is most important to make sure that the standard length is the same everywhere.

The Imperial or British system of measurement of length is based on the *yard* but in 1975 it will be changed to the *metre*.

There is a legendary tale that the yard was originally defined in terms of the distance from the tip of King Alfred's nose to the tip of his fingers when his arm was stretched out.

The first accurate standard yard was made in 1878. It consisted of a bronze bar exactly one yard long kept by the government. This was called a *primary* standard and it was thought of as being a true yard: from it, lengths a yard long could be measured on to other rods. These rods, kept in laboratories throughout the country, were called *secondary* standards. However, in 1960 the British standard yard was found to be contracting by a tiny amount (about one millionth of an inch each year) and it was decided to abandon this type of standard of length. In 1963 the yard was defined in terms of the metre, 1 yard being equal to 0·9144 metre. The metre is the

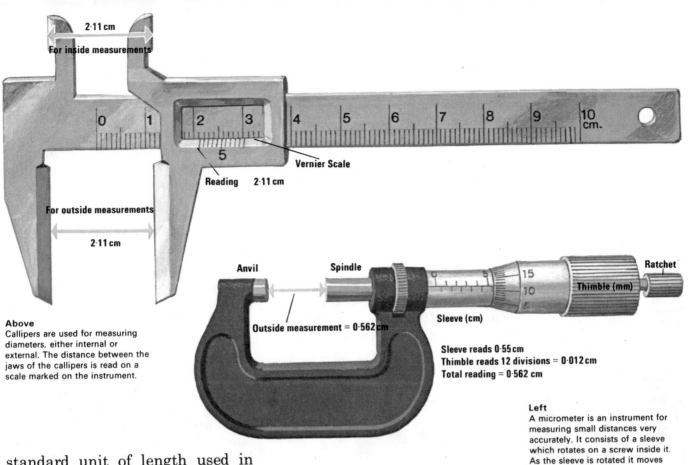

2·11 cm

For inside measurements

For outside measurements

2·11 cm

Reading   2·11 cm

Vernier Scale

Anvil   Spindle   Ratchet

Thimble (mm)

Outside measurement = 0·562 cm

Sleeve (cm)

Sleeve reads 0·55 cm
Thimble reads 12 divisions = 0·012 cm
Total reading = 0·562 cm

Above
Callipers are used for measuring
diameters, either internal or
external. The distance between the
jaws of the callipers is read on a
scale marked on the instrument.

Left
A micrometer is an instrument for
measuring small distances very
accurately. It consists of a sleeve
which rotates on a screw inside it.
As the sleeve is rotated it moves
forward until the tip of the
micrometer just touches the object
being measured. The width of the
object is then given on the scale.

Left
Distances on the ground are
measured using either a tape or a
chain. Surveyors and builders use
them to set out the foundations of
buildings. A surveyors chain
consists of 100 steel links and is
100 feet long. These are now being
replaced by metric chains.

standard unit of length used in
European countries. It was originally defined, in 1791, as one ten-
millionth of the length of the
meridian through Dunkirk in
France.

In 1927 the metre was redefined
as the length of a platinum-iridium
bar kept in Paris. But this bar was
also found to vary in length by
tiny amounts and in 1960 a new
type of definition was internation-
ally agreed. This is based on the
wavelength of the light emitted by
atoms. This length never varies;
the same atom under the same
conditions always emits light of
identical wavelength. The atom
chosen is an isotope of the gas
krypton and the metre is now
defined as 1 650 763·73 wavelengths
emitted by this atom under certain
conditions.

Astronomers sometimes use
another method of measuring
lengths when discussing the distance of stars. This is the *light-year*.
It is the distance travelled by light
in one year. As light travels at a
velocity of 300 million metres per
second and as there are about 31·5
million seconds in a year, one
light year is 9460 million million
metres or about 6 million million
miles. This is an enormous distance.

Time

In ancient times, before clocks were invented, men knew that the seasons came and went at regular intervals. The sun also rose and set regularly creating night and day. Far back in prehistory, man realized that time could be measured using these regular events. The length of time between the appearance of two summers was called a *year*. The time between one sunrise and the next was called a *day*. Another way of measuring time was by noting the occurrence of a new moon. This happens at regular intervals of about 30 days. So when someone said 'many moons have passed' he meant that the moon had waxed and waned many times. The word *month* is derived from the word *moon*.

We now know that all the regular events can be explained by astronomy. A day is the time taken for the earth to spin round on its own axis. Whilst the earth is spinning on its own axis it is also travelling around the sun. A year is the time that it takes for the earth to make one complete circuit of the sun. It actually takes us $365\frac{1}{4}$ days to travel completely round the sun so every fourth year we have a leap year of 366 days. The extra day occurs on the 29th February. This avoids the calendar getting out of step with the movements of the earth and sun. A month is created by the moon revolving around the earth, and this accounts for its regular appearances.

A day is divided into 24 equal divisions of an hour. Each hour is divided into 60 minutes and each minute into 60 seconds.

One of the first devices used to measure time was a sundial. As the earth spins round on its axis a shadow cast by the sun gradually moves round. This movement was mapped out and used for telling the time. Other methods of measuring time depend on processes that occur at regular rates. A simple example is the burning down of a candle. If you have two similar candles you can make a candle clock. Measure the time it takes for the first candle to burn down a measured distance. It may take say 3 hours to burn 3 cm. You now know that 1 cm is burned in one hour. Mark your second candle with 1 cm marks. If you now light your second candle you will be able to tell how much time has passed by seeing how many marks have disappeared. Another regular process used to measure time is the passing of sand through a small hole. An egg timer works on this principle. A larger version of the egg timer is called an hour glass.

Below
As the earth travels round the sun it creates night and day, but when one half of the earth is in darkness the other half is in sunlight.

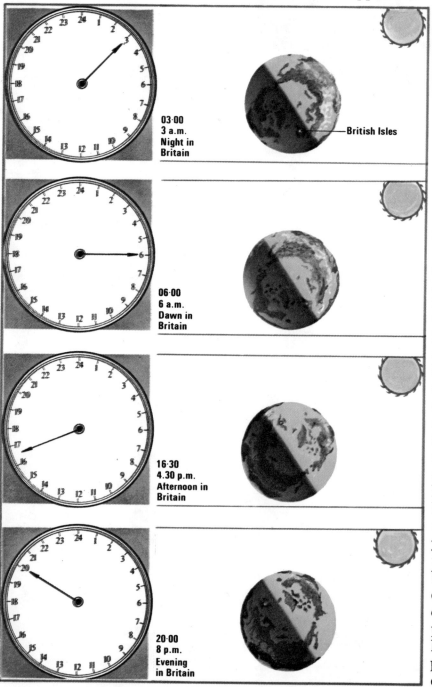

British Isles

03·00
3 a.m.
Night in Britain

06·00
6 a.m.
Dawn in Britain

16·30
4.30 p.m.
Afternoon in Britain

20·00
8 p.m.
Evening in Britain

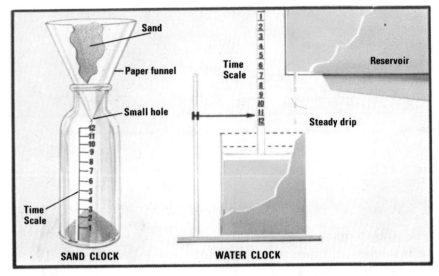

Sand

Paper funnel

Small hole

Time
Scale

12
11
10
9
8
7
6
5
4
3
2
1

SAND CLOCK

Time
Scale

1
2
3
4
5
6
7
8
9
10
11
12

Reservoir

Steady drip

WATER CLOCK

The next regular process used to measure time was the swing of a pendulum. This is a weight at the end of a stick or string. A pendulum will always take the same time to swing from one side to the other, no matter how far it travels. To obtain different periods of swing you need pendulums of different lengths.

The most modern clocks that scientists use to measure time accurately are based on the vibrations of atoms. These vibrations are very accurate and atomic clocks are correct to one second in 3000 years.

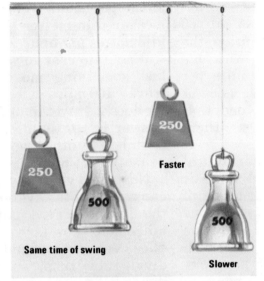

250

500

Same time of swing

250

Faster

500

Slower

Above left
Devices for measuring time depend on processes that occur at a constant rate. The hour glass depends on sand falling through a small hole. The water clock depends on water dripping from one level to another and raising a float.

Above
The first known sundials were Egyptian and through the ages many beautiful sundials have been made. This is an early eighteenth century sundial in the Science Museum in London.

Left
You can prove for yourself that the time of swing of a pendulum does not depend on how far it travels. Tie a weight to the end of a string and hang it from a hook on the wall. Make it swing gently and time five swings. Now time another five much bigger swings and you will find that the time is the same. Try changing the weight, you will find this does not alter the time of swing. It is the length that controls the time. Shorten the string and the time is reduced, lengthen it and it increases.

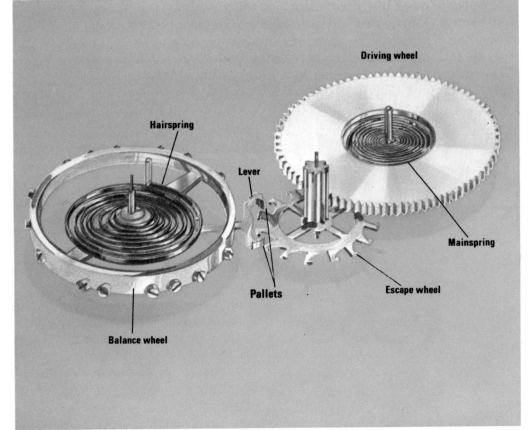

Driving wheel

Hairspring

Lever

Mainspring

Pallets

Escape wheel

Balance wheel

Left
In watches and small clocks the pendulum is replaced by a hairspring which makes a balance wheel rotate backwards and forwards. The balance wheel is kept in motion by the impulse it receives from the mainspring through the escape wheel. This device was invented two hundred years ago and is still widely used in watches.

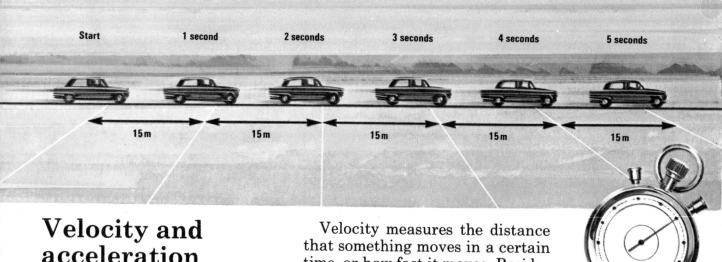

Start | 1 second | 2 seconds | 3 seconds | 4 seconds | 5 seconds

15 m | 15 m | 15 m | 15 m | 15 m

Velocity and acceleration

Imagine two towns that are 60 miles apart. Two cars drive the distance between these towns. One goes all the way at 60 miles per hour (mph) and the other goes at 30 mph. Obviously the one that travels faster will get there more quickly.

When we say that a car moves at 60 mph we mean that it takes it one hour to travel a distance of 60 miles. Therefore it gets from one town to the other in one hour. The second car only travels at 30 mph so that in one hour it has gone thirty miles. It takes two hours to go the sixty miles. We say that the speed or *velocity* of the first car is greater than that of the second car. In one hour the first car travels 60 miles whereas the second car only travels 30 miles.

Velocity measures the distance that something moves in a certain time, or how fast it moves. Besides miles per hour velocity is also measured in metres per second or kilometres per hour.

It is quite easy to work out how fast something moves. If a car travels 100 miles in four hours how far does it travel in one hour? The answer is 100 divided by four, or 25 miles. In other words the car's velocity is 25 mph.

Next time you travel by car you can work out the average speed for the journey. Find out from the mileometer how far you have travelled. Velocity is equal to distance divided by time, so divide this distance by the length of time you have been travelling. A motorway journey of 110 miles may take two hours. The average speed is 55 mph. For a town journey you may only go 20 miles in 1 hour so your velocity is 20 mph.

Snail

Man

Horse

Cheetah

Start   **1 second**   **2 seconds**   **3 seconds**

Above
This car starts off and after one second it has covered 3 metres. After two seconds it has covered another 6 metres, making 9 metres altogether. After three seconds it has gone another 12 metres, making 21 metres altogether. You can see from the diagram that as time goes by the car is moving faster and faster. This is acceleration.

Far right
The speed at which vehicles travel also varies considerably. Most ordinary cars can reach a speed of between 70 and 100 mph. The highest speed reached by a car, powered by a jet engine, is 613·995 mph. This was achieved in 1965 by the *Spirit of America—Sonic 1*. In 1970 a rocket-engined car, the *Blue Flame*, reached 631·368 mph.

Right
The fastest boat was *Bluebird* driven at 328 mph by Donald Campbell in 1967. It reached this speed on the run in which it crashed—killing its driver.

Look at the speedometer during these journeys. Sometimes it may read 60 mph, sometimes 30 mph and sometimes it may even read 0 mph when you are stuck in a traffic jam. This is because the speed of the car is changing all the time. The speedometer shows how fast the car is moving at any point. The speed of a car over a whole journey is the *average speed*.

When a car is standing still it does not have any velocity at all. As it starts to move it goes faster and faster. This is called *acceleration*. If a car goes from 0 miles per hour to 50 miles per hour it has accelerated. A racing car can move from 0 miles per hour to 50 mph very quickly. An old car may take much longer to reach this speed. The racing car has more acceleration. Acceleration is the rate at which something changes its speed. The opposite of acceleration is called *deceleration* – the rate of slowing down.

Spirit of America—Sonic I

Bluebird

Gravity

Newton

Above
Sir Isaac Newton was one of the greatest scientists who ever lived. He was born in 1642 in Woolsthorpe in Lincolnshire and went to Cambridge University where he studied science and mathematics. Besides his explanation of gravity he discovered that sunlight is a mixture of the colours of the rainbow and he also built a telescope through which he saw the moons of Jupiter. He died in 1727.

If you lift a brick and let go of it, it falls to the floor. What causes this to happen? Bricks do not move sideways without being pushed or pulled and they do not move upwards unless they are thrown or something is pulling them. This means that if anything moves downwards there must be some force pushing it or pulling it towards the ground. You can feel this force if you hold anything in your hand or try to lift anything off the floor. It is called *weight*.

The first person to discover why things have a weight and why they fall to the ground was Sir Isaac Newton. It is said that one day he was sitting in his mother's orchard when he saw an apple fall from a tree. This started him thinking why such a thing should happen. His explanation was that the earth and the apple pull each other together. The earth attracts the apple and the apple attracts the

earth. The earth is very large and is not affected by the pull of the apple. The apple, being much smaller, is pulled down towards the earth. This force attracting things through space is called *gravity*. It is this force that holds everything on the earth's surface and causes them to have a weight.

Isaac Newton also realized that the force of gravity gets smaller as things get further away from the earth. A person in an aeroplane would not weigh as much as he would weigh on the ground because the pull of gravity on him would be weaker. We do not usually notice this change in weight because it is so small.

Astronauts in a rocket notice that the pull of gravity begins to be weaker as they go up into space. Astronauts that are a long way out in space float around the cabin of their spacecraft, but this is due largely to the effects of centrifugal force (see page 64).

As a spacecraft goes further from the earth towards the moon it begins to be affected by the gravity of the moon. The gravity on the surface of the moon is less than the gravity on the earth. A man who weighs 90 kilograms on earth would be 15 kilograms on the moon. He would be able to throw things much further and jump much higher because the force pulling him down would be smaller.

The weight of things also depends on how big they are and

Right
A field of zero gravity (0g) can be created for a few seconds by flying an aircraft in a particular path called a ballistic trajectory. When the aeroplane is flying on this path, the centrifugal force (see page 64) balances the pull of gravity, with the result that any objects inside the plane become weightless. Part of an astronaut's training to deal with weightlessness involves such flights. While he is weightless, a man can fly, or swim about inside the cabin.

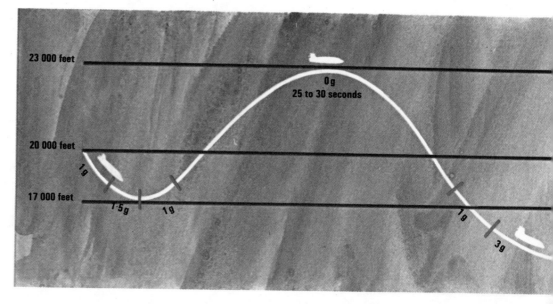

Kilometres   Kilograms

20 000	6
15 000	8
10 000	14
5 000	31
4 000	36
3 000	46
2 000	57
1 000	75
0	100

on what they are made of. What weighs more, a kilogram of lead or one of feathers? Many people without thinking say a kilogram of lead weighs more. Of course this is a trick question because they both weigh the same, but people think of feathers as being lighter than lead. If you hold a cricket ball in one hand and an apple in the other the cricket ball weighs more although they are almost the same size. This is because the stuff (or *matter*) of which cricket balls are made is more tightly packed than the matter of which apples are made. Physicists say that the cricket ball has a greater *density* than the apple. Lead has a greater *density* than feathers.

The total amount of matter in anything is called the *mass*. The cricket ball has more mass than the apple although they look the same size. The feathers and the lead have equal mass although the size of the pile of feathers would be much greater than the size of the piece of lead.

Left
A cricket ball weighs more than an apple because it has more *matter* in it. This means it has a higher *mass* than the apple. In space the cricket ball would have no weight at all because there would be no gravity to pull it. In spite of this it would still have the same mass. This is the difference between weight and mass. Weight is a force which varies from place to place. Mass is the amount of matter and it does not vary.

Far left
As we go further from the surface of the earth the effect of gravity becomes weaker and things weigh less.

Below
A spring balance measures the weight of an object, that is, the pull of gravity on it. The extension of the spring is proportional to the load hanging on it. A beam balance compares the masses of two objects. The pull of gravity is the same on both sides of the balance.
The force of gravity on the moon is only about one-sixth of the force on earth. If you were to weigh an object on the moon, this could not be detected on a beam balance. But on a spring balance the object would register only one-sixth of its weight on earth.

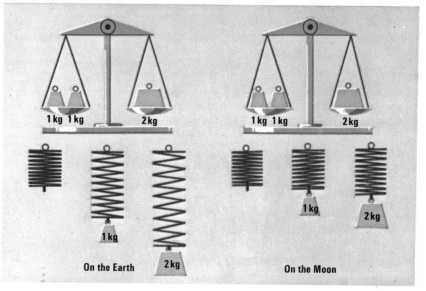

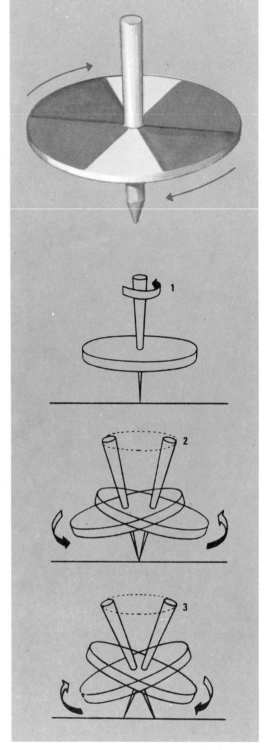

Rotation

If you spin a coin on a table it will have two kinds of motion. First of all it will move across the table, and secondly it will spin round and round on its own axis. These two motions are quite separate. In the same way, when a golf ball is flying through the air it is both spinning and changing its position.

Spinning objects have special properties. The most important of these is that they tend to resist any change in the direction of the spin. A simple experiment with the front wheel of a bicycle will illustrate this. Lift the wheel off the ground and spin it round. Now move the handlebars from side to side and you can feel a force that tries to stop you. This is the inertia of the wheel resisting a change in the direction of the axis of the spin. In the case of the bicycle wheel the axis is the wheel axle. This inertia, or resistance to change, gives the wheel a rigidity in space called gyroscopic inertia.

A *gyroscope* is a small heavy wheel mounted so that it can move about any axis; this is called a *universal mounting*. The wheel will always tend to keep spinning in the direction in space in which it started spinning.

The principle of the gyroscope is used in the *gyro-compass*. In this device, which is used in ships and aircraft, a wheel is kept spinning electrically with a compass mounted over it. The spinning wheel of

Above
Block a bicycle up so that it will not fall over sideways. Spin the wheel and try to change the direction of the axis of spin. You will feel the inertia of the wheel trying to stop you.

Above right
You can make a small top by tracing round a coin on a piece of thick paper. Cut out the circular shape. Make a small hole in the centre and push through it a used match that has had one end sharpened. By giving the top a quick flick it should spin quite easily on a table or smooth floor. Try drawing different patterns on it and see how they look when the top is spinning.

Right
When a top is spinning fast, the stick rotates vertically. As it slows down it tips over and the stick moves in the shape of a cone. As it comes to a stop and the edge touches the ground, it will roll around in the opposite direction

Below
Some ships use gyro-stabilizers. The heavy gyroscope mounted in the hull of the ship works by damping out the rolling motion of the ship.

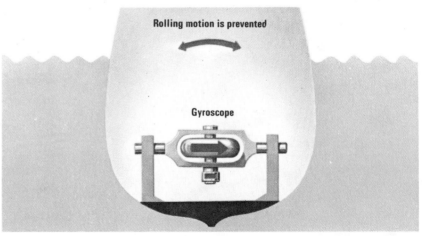

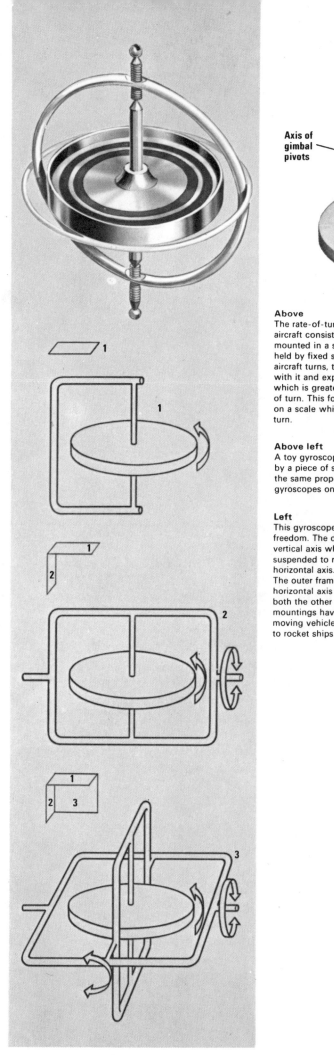

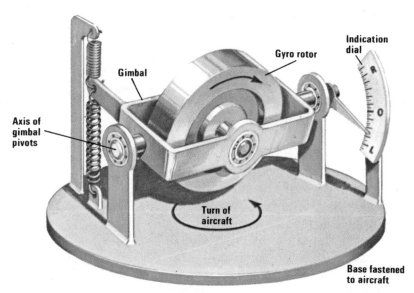

Axis of gimbal pivots

Gimbal

Gyro rotor

Indication dial

Turn of aircraft

Base fastened to aircraft

Above

The rate-of-turn indicator in an aircraft consists of a gyroscope mounted in a single gimbal which is held by fixed springs. When the aircraft turns, the gyroscope turns with it and experiences a force which is greater the greater the rate of turn. This force can be indicated on a scale which shows the rate of turn.

Above left

A toy gyroscope is started spinning by a piece of string. It has exactly the same properties as the gyroscopes on large ships.

Left

This gyroscope has three degrees of freedom. The disc rotates about a vertical axis which is itself suspended to rotate about a horizontal axis.
The outer frame rotates about a horizontal axis at right angles to both the other axes. Gyroscopic mountings have many uses in moving vehicles, from sailing ships to rocket ships.

the gyroscope, because of its inertia, is unaffected by the motion of the ship and will therefore always point to true north.

A similar device is the *gyro-pilot*. This is an instrument for steering a ship automatically. The mechanism is set to the course of the ship. Any change of course is detected by the gyro-pilot because it stays pointing in its original direction. The gyro-pilot sends a message to the motor controlling the rudder. The rudder then brings the ship back on course again.

This property of spinning objects is called spin stabilization. A frisbee spins rapidly while it is moving through the air. It is the spin that keeps it stable in the air. If it did not spin, it would not stay horizontal and so would not travel far.

You may have seen circus performers spinning plates on the tips of long sticks. The plates remain balanced because they are stabilized horizontally by their spin. The plates do not want to change the direction of the axis of their spin. Once they start slowing down, the spin stabilization gets much less and they soon fall off the stick. The skill of the juggler is to keep the stick moving so that it keeps the plate spinning. A top when spinning stays balanced for the same reason. It is stabilized by its spin.

The earth is also spinning round on its axis and this keeps the axis pointing in one direction in space, just as the spinning of a gyroscope keeps the compass pointing in its original direction.

Centrifugal force

If you swing a bucket of water over your head fast enough the water will not come out. When a body is spun round in a circle there is a force acting on it directly outwards from the centre of the circle. This is because the body wants to continue to move in a straight line. The force depends on the speed with which it is going round, the greater the speed of rotation the greater the force. So for a bucket of water which is being swung round quite quickly there is a force pushing the water into the bucket. If, when the bucket is above your head, this force is greater than the weight of the water, the water will not fall out.

This force acting outwards from the centre is called a *centrifugal force*. This centrifugal force is equal, but opposite in direction, to the *centripetal force*. This is the force acting towards the centre of the circle, that keeps the bucket moving in a circle. If there was no centripetal force the bucket would fly off in a straight line.

You can feel the pull in your arm, and this is what provides the centripetal force. The centrifugal force acts outwards from the centre while the centripetal force acts towards the centre.

If you swing the bucket more slowly you will find out what happens to these forces. The slower the swing the smaller the force. So now there is less force pushing the water into the bucket—less centrifugal force. If this force is less than the weight of the water, then the water will begin to fall out. At the same time, the centripetal force, the pull in your arm, gets less.

It is the centrifugal force that balances the force of gravity in the solar system. The earth and the sun are both very large masses and there is therefore a large force of gravity between them (see page 60). Since they do not crash into each other there must be another force pulling them apart. This is

the centrifugal force caused by the earth travelling in its orbit round the sun. So there are two forces opposing each other in the solar system. One is the force of gravity, which acts as the centripetal force. The other, which opposes the centripetal force, is the centrifugal force caused by the motion of the planets round the sun. The planets do not have air resistance to slow them down, so they will keep going.

In the same way the moon and the artificial satellites orbit the earth. The gravitational attraction between the earth and the moon or the satellites is balanced by their centrifugal forces.

You can feel centrifugal forces pushing you outwards when a car takes a bend quickly, and on roundabouts in fair grounds. On roundabouts the force is so strong, because the circle is so small, that you have to hold tight to stay on. The same effect occurs on the 'Wall of Death'. As you spin round you are pushed outwards against the wall. Because you spin very rapidly the force is great enough to stop you falling.

Above
Swing a bucket with some water in it over your head. If the centrifugal force is greater than the weight of the water then the water will stay in the bucket. When trying this experiment use a plastic bucket and do not put too much water in it to begin with, otherwise you may get very wet.

Right
Hang a cotton reel by a piece of string. Tie it on firmly. As you spin the cotton reel faster and faster it will rise higher and higher until it flies round in a horizontal circle. This is because the centripetal force is gradually overcoming the weight of the cotton reel.

Right
The spin drier depends on centrifugal force. As the clothes are rotated the clothes themselves and all the moisture they contain are thrown outwards by the centrifugal forces. The clothes cannot move outwards beyond the wire cage, but the water flies out because there is nothing to stop it.

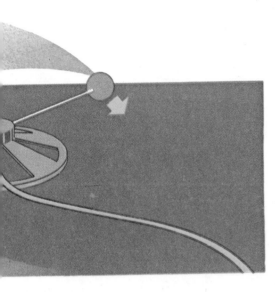

Left and far left
A rotary garden spray and a catherine wheel: two familiar sights which are examples of centrifugal force causing a fine spray of matter to fly outwards, forming a disc.

Right
The speed of both the moon and the artificial satellite depends on their distance from earth. This is because the force of gravity depends on the distance from the earth and the centrifugal force depends on the speed of the orbiting body. The body must travel just fast enough for the centrifugal force (tending to shoot it off into space) to balance exactly the gravitational attraction (tending to draw it back to earth).

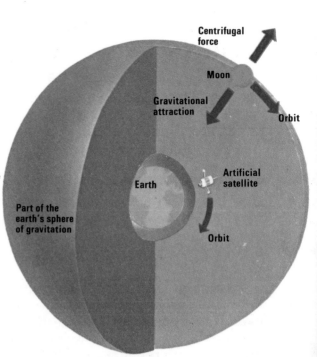

Centrifugal force

Moon

Gravitational attraction

Orbit

Earth

Artificial satellite

Orbit

Part of the earth's sphere of gravitation

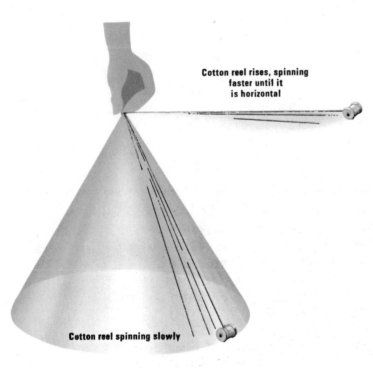

Cotton reel rises, spinning faster until it is horizontal

Cotton reel spinning slowly

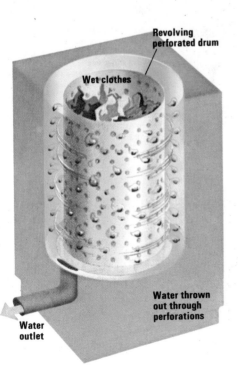

Revolving perforated drum

Wet clothes

Water thrown out through perforations

Water outlet

Right
To escape from the earth's gravity, a space ship has to go into orbit round the earth, and accelerate until the centrifugal force due to its circular motion is greater than the force of gravity which is drawing it towards the earth. The speed which has to be reached is called the escape velocity.
The force of gravity on the moon is much lower, so the escape velocity from the moon is also lower.

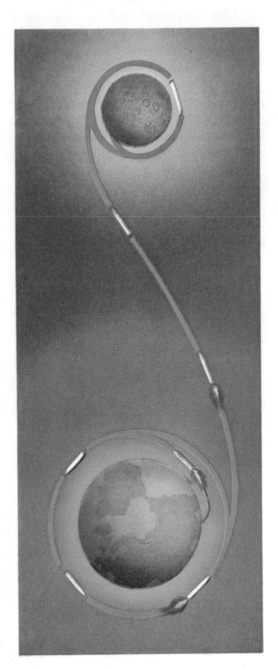

Density

Pick up a brick in one hand and a block of wood of about the same size in the other. The brick will feel heavier. It has more weight than the wood. The earth is pulling the brick with a larger force. It does this because the brick has more *mass* than the block of wood. In other words the total amount of matter in the brick is greater than in the wood.

We can see and feel that different materials have different masses even if they are the same size. The mass of a cube of gold would be nearly twenty times the mass of an ice cube of the same size.

The lightness or heaviness of a substance for a given volume is called *density*, and this depends on how tightly the molecules in the materials are packed.

We say that brick has greater density than wood. The stony particles of brick are heavy and are packed more tightly than the fibres of wood. Imagine a lift. When the lift is empty, except for the lift man, its density is low. As it begins to fill with people its density increases until it is full. It is then that its density is greatest. Its size has remained the same throughout but its mass has increased.

Density is the mass of a certain volume of material. If a cube is 1 centimetre by 1 centimetre by 1 centimetre it has a volume of 1 cubic centimetre (1cc). 1cc of water weighs 1 gram. Its density is thus 1 gram for every cc. This is written 1gm per cc. 1cc of lead weighs 11·3 grams so its density is 11·3gm per cc. Air is made up of molecules which are not very tightly packed and so its density is very low, about 0·0012 gm per cc.

Imagine a piece of material to be made up of little cubes of the same size. If you know how many of these cubes there are and the weight of just one of them, you can work out the weight of the piece. The number of small 1 centimetre cubes is the total volume of the piece.

Equal weights of different material may have different volumes.

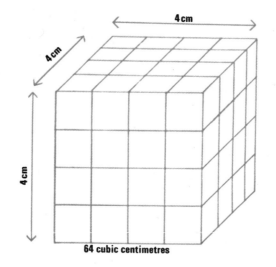

Left
People sometimes weigh their suitcases on a spring balance. At first the density of the case is low because the space is not very tightly packed. As more clothes are put in they are packed more tightly until the density is greatest when the case is full. The mass is then greatest, although the volume is the same. The heavier the case is, the more the scale pointer moves.

Using a pair of kitchen scales, put an iron pound weight on one side. Measure a pound of sugar on the other. You can see that a pound of sugar has a much larger volume than a pound of iron. This is because sugar has a much lower density than iron. Try measuring pounds of other materials and seeing how their volumes vary. The smaller the volume for a given weight, the greater the density.

Materials less dense than water can float. Icebergs which have a density less than that of water can float in it. Steel ships have an overall density of less than 1 gm per cc because their insides contain so much air. They can therefore float in water. But a piece of solid steel does not float. People are about the same density as water so they can float or swim without sinking.

The density of a material is very important. We would not want to use a very dense material to make an aeroplane because it would make the plane too heavy. So an alloy, or mixture of metals is used. It consists mainly of aluminium because it is not very dense. Other metals in the mixture give it strength. Model aeroplanes are made of balsa wood which also has a very low density. Lead is used as the sinker on the end of a fishing line because it is very dense.

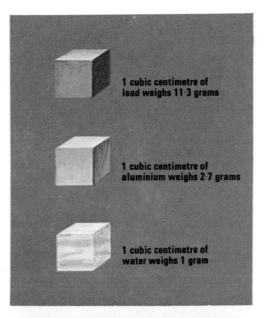

1 cubic centimetre of lead weighs 11·3 grams

1 cubic centimetre of aluminium weighs 2·7 grams

1 cubic centimetre of water weighs 1 gram

Left
Weigh some objects that look the same size. You can see that the same volume of different materials can have different weights because they have different densities.

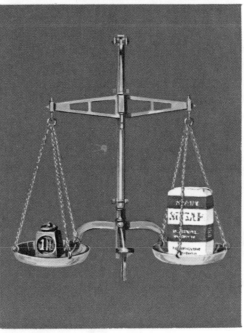

Left
Find objects of different sizes that have the same weight. Materials of different densities have different volumes for the same weights. A pound of feathers or foam rubber would have a very large volume.

Wood

Cork

Lead

Glass

Stone

Left
Some materials sink in water because their densities are greater than the density of water. Others will float. This shows that they are less dense than water.

Hard boiled egg spins   **Raw egg wobbles**

Right

Here is a trick involving the principle of inertia which enables you to tell the difference between a raw egg and a hard boiled egg, without cracking them. Spin each egg in water. The hard boiled one will stay spinning longer, the raw one will wobble and fall over. To double-check spin them again, then catch them suddenly, to stop them, and immediately let them go again. The hard boiled egg will stay still but the raw one will begin to spin round again on its own. The reason for this difference in behaviour is because the contents of the egg have a greater inertia when they are liquid. They resist spinning in the first place, but once they are in motion they keep on moving for a time, even after the shell has been brought to a stop.

Right

Liquids show the effects of inertia dramatically. Pull sharply on a still cup of water. Some of the water will splash out or be left behind because its inertia tries to keep it in the same place. Slide a cup of water along steadily towards a barrier. When it hits the barrier, the cup will stop but the water will keep on moving in the forward direction and will splash out.

Force and inertia

We know that objects that are not moving do not start moving by themselves. For example a football will not move unless it is kicked. Things that are at rest seem to want to stay there.

If you balance a postcard on your fingertip with a coin on it, you can flick the postcard away but the coin stays on your finger. You may have seen a similar trick with a tableful of plates. Some people can pull away the tablecloth so that the plates stay on the table. The plates do not want to move. Perhaps you had better not try this particular trick; it takes a lot of practice.

There are other examples of things wanting to stay in place. Look at people standing in a bus. When the bus starts they tend to fall backwards because they are not moving and their bodies want to stay like that. If the bus stops with a jerk everyone falls forward. There is nothing to stop them so they keep on moving. If someone runs into you you can feel how their body does not want to stop moving.

Generally, things do not want to move if they are at rest. Nor do they want to stop once they are moving. This tendency of something to stay at rest or stay moving is called *inertia*. An empty tea trolley has very little inertia. It is easy to get it moving and it is easy to stop it once it has started. If you load the trolley with heavy things its inertia would be much greater. It would be more difficult to start and stop it because it would have more *mass*.

Left

Balance a card with a coin on it on top of a glass. Ask someone to put the coin in the glass without touching either. The trick is to flick the card away quickly so that the coin drops into the glass. If you flick the card the coin does not move with it. This is because its inertia tries to keep it in the same place.

Right

Balance a card with a coin on it, on the tip of your finger. Flick the card away, leaving the coin sitting on your finger. Because of its inertia, the coin tends not to move.

To start and stop things you need to pull or push them. These pulls and pushes are known as *forces*. If you hold two magnets close to each other you can sometimes feel them pull and sometimes push against you. These are examples of forces.

A force is needed to start a body moving and to slow down a moving body. In other words the force overcomes the inertia of the body.

Sir Isaac Newton gave an explanation of force, motion, and inertia. He said that an object will stay at rest unless it is acted on by a force. He also said that if an object is moving at a constant speed it will continue to do this unless it is acted on by a force.

A bullet fired from a gun gradually slows down and falls to the ground. This happens because of a force due to the resistance of the air. In outer space, where there is no air, the bullet would simply continue moving. This is why a space ship, when it is outside the earth's atmosphere, can move through space without fuel. Its rockets are only necessary to slow it down, speed it up, and change its direction. Thus we see that force causes something to change its velocity (accelerate or decelerate). Newton also suggested that the bigger the force the more the acceleration (or deceleration) produced.

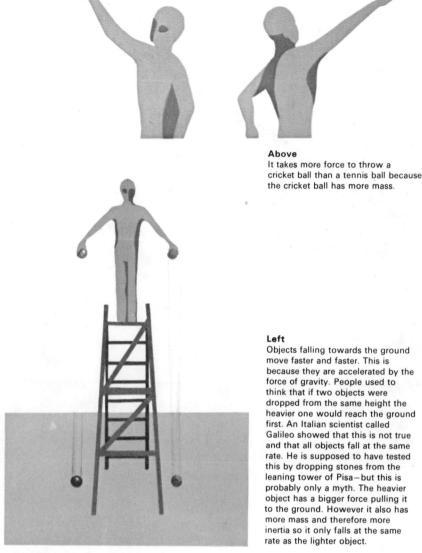

Above
It takes more force to throw a cricket ball than a tennis ball because the cricket ball has more mass.

Left
Objects falling towards the ground move faster and faster. This is because they are accelerated by the force of gravity. People used to think that if two objects were dropped from the same height the heavier one would reach the ground first. An Italian scientist called Galileo showed that this is not true and that all objects fall at the same rate. He is supposed to have tested this by dropping stones from the leaning tower of Pisa—but this is probably only a myth. The heavier object has a bigger force pulling it to the ground. However it also has more mass and therefore more inertia so it only falls at the same rate as the lighter object.

Right
Not all objects fall at the same rate. A coin will reach the ground faster than a small piece of paper. This is because the air holds the paper up. If you put the paper on the coin they both reach the ground at the same time.

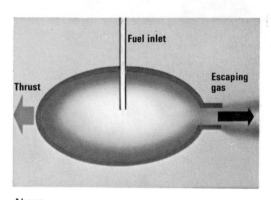

Above
Newton discovered another important fact about forces. If you push hard on a wall, you are exerting a force on it. The wall is also pushing on you with an equal force in the opposite direction. This is called a *reaction*. Newton's third law states that whenever there is a force on an object there is always an equal and opposite reaction. This is how rockets work. Hot gas is forced out of the back of the rocket. The equal force on the rocket (the reaction) pushes it forward.

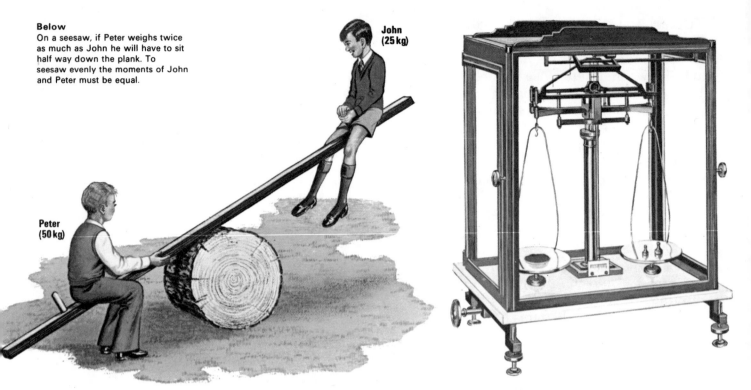

Below
On a seesaw, if Peter weighs twice as much as John he will have to sit half way down the plank. To seesaw evenly the moments of John and Peter must be equal.

John (25 kg)

Peter (50 kg)

Moments and levers

If you place a 30 cm ruler on a table with a pencil under it you will find that it only balances when the pencil is underneath the 15 cm mark. If you now place one coin on the 0 mark and another on the 30 cm mark the ruler will still balance. You will also find that one coin on the 7·5 cm mark is balanced by one on the 22·5 cm mark. The ruler is balanced by equal weights or forces at equal distances from the centre.

But what if you try to balance one coin at the 0 mark with coins at the 22·5 cm mark? You will find that for it to balance you will need two coins at this 22·5 cm point. If the distance from the centre is halved the weight or force must be doubled.

These coins are trying to turn or rotate the ruler. This tendency of a force or weight to rotate a body to which it is applied is called a *moment*. From the ruler experiment you can see that the moment depends not only on the size of the force, but also on the distance that it is from the point of balance. This point is called the *fulcrum*.

Above
Chemists use balances such as these to measure weights of substances very accurately. They place weights to the value that they want on the left hand side, and measure out the chemical on the right hand side until the scales are balanced. They then have the same weight on the right hand side as on the left.

Left
Push a hot nail through the middle of a slow-burning candle. Balance it between two glasses. Light both ends and watch it see-saw up and down. As each end of the candle drips it lightens that end, which moves up to the position of equilibrium. At the next drip from the other end, that moves up, and so on. If you make riders for your see-saw, use tinfoil, not paper, as this could catch fire.

The moment of a force is equal to the force multiplied by its distance from the fulcrum. When the ruler is balanced the moments, or turning effects, of the two forces must be equal in order to cancel each other out. In the last case we had one coin 15 cm from the centre. This gives a moment of $1 \times 15 = 15$ units. The other side had two coins 7·5 cm from the centre, giving a moment of $2 \times 7·5$ which also equals 15 units. That is why the ruler balanced. Try different weights and distances to see what happens.

This effect is used in a simple balance, like an old pair of kitchen

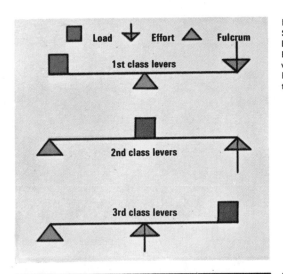

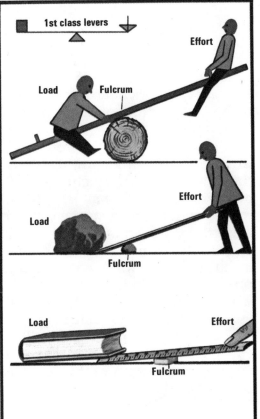

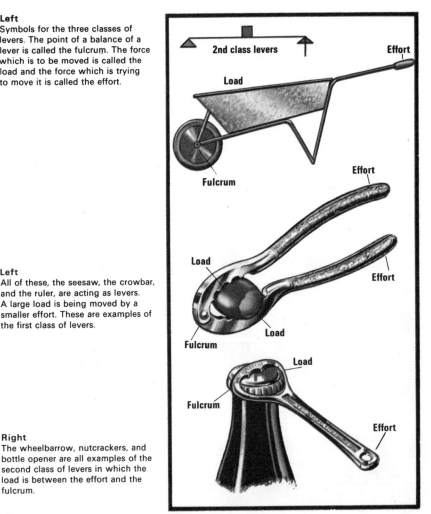

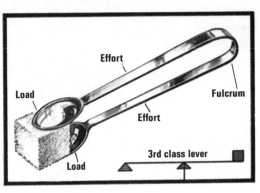

Load **Effort** **Fulcrum**

1st class levers

2nd class levers

3rd class levers

Left
Symbols for the three classes of levers. The point of a balance of a lever is called the fulcrum. The force which is to be moved is called the load and the force which is trying to move it is called the effort.

Left
All of these, the seesaw, the crowbar, and the ruler, are acting as levers. A large load is being moved by a smaller effort. These are examples of the first class of levers.

Right
The wheelbarrow, nutcrackers, and bottle opener are all examples of the second class of levers in which the load is between the effort and the fulcrum.

Right
An example of the third class of levers is the sugar tong. The effort is between the fulcrum and the load.

scales, in which weights are put on a pan on one side to balance the food to be weighed on the other side. When the correct weight is put in the pan the moments on both sides of the balance are equal, as the distances from the centre, or fulcrum, are the same.

When the force acting as load is equalled by the force acting as effort the system is said to be in equilibrium.

A lever is another application of moments. You can often prise a rock out of the ground by using a crowbar. This is because you apply the force at the end of the crowbar which is a greater distance from the fulcrum than the rock. You can therefore produce a greater moment than you could by trying to roll the rock out of the ground.

There are three classes of levers. One is like the crowbar, in which the fulcrum is between the load and the effort. The second class is where the fulcrum is at one end, the effort at the other, and the load is in between the two. An example of this is a wheelbarrow. In the third class, the fulcrum is at one end, the load at the other, and the effort in between. Sugar tongs are an example of this class.

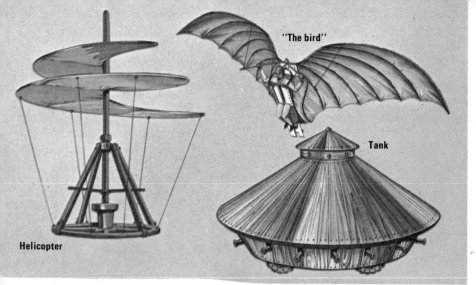

"The bird"

Tank

Helicopter

Leonardo da Vinci

Above
Leonardo da Vinci who lived in Italy from 1452 to 1519 was a musician, painter, and sculptor as well as being an engineer. He attempted to design several complicated machines including an aeroplane.

Below
The knife and the claw hammer both show how loads are overcome by using levers. They are simple machines.

Machines

Machines do not need to be complicated. A machine is simply a device that overcomes resistance at one place by enabling a force to be applied somewhere else. A knife is a very simple example of a machine. When you push on the knife this produces a cutting force in the blade. Another example is a claw hammer, which is used to pull out nails. Both of these simple machines are also levers.

Another type of machine is a pulley. A simple pulley is useful because it enables a heavy load to be lifted up by pulling downwards. It can make use of the natural downward pull of gravity on the weight of our bodies. It is much easier to remove the engine from a car using a pulley than by trying to lift it out.

If a large load can be raised using a small effort, there is clearly an advantage to be gained. This *mechanical advantage*, as it is called, is equal to the load divided by the effort. So the greater the load that can be raised for a given effort the greater is the mechanical advantage.

However we cannot get something for nothing. Pulleys allow us to lift a large weight by using a small force but we have to move the rope much further downwards than the weight moves upwards. Thus the effort we apply moves much further than the load. In fact the *work* we do raising a weight with a pulley is not less than the work we would do lifting the weight directly. Work, in physics, is defined as the force applied to anything, multiplied by the distance through which it makes a thing move. To raise a car engine weighing 100 kilograms a distance of 2 metres might require an effort of 50 kilograms applied to a pulley rope. This effort would have to move 4 metres. We say that the work done *by* the effort is the same as the work done *on* the load.

In practice the figures would not work out quite like this because they imply that the machine is 100 per cent efficient (that is, all the work put in as effort can be used to raise the load). In fact, some work is lost in friction. The efficiency of a machine is the work actually applied to the load divided by the work put in as effort. It is usually multiplied by 100 so that it can be expressed as a percentage. The efficiency is never greater than 100 per cent and in practice is always much less.

Another machine in which the effort moves a larger distance than the load is the screw. Again, large forces are produced by smaller ones. For every turn of the screwdriver the screw moves only a small distance into the wood, overcoming very large friction forces as it does so. Imagine how difficult it would be to insert a screw into wood without a screwdriver. The same principle is also used in the car jack. In this device a large turn on the handle lifts the car a very small distance.

Gears are also machines and they can operate in two ways. Not only can they make large forces from small ones but they can also make small forces from large ones.

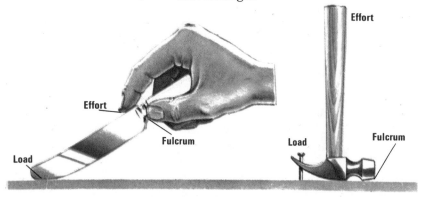

Effort

Fulcrum

Load

Effort

Load

Fulcrum

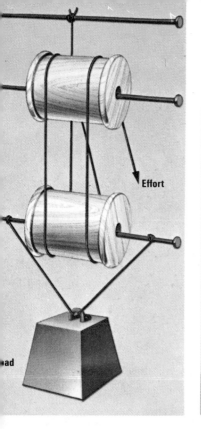

Above
Try making this more complicated pulley system yourself. Use cotton reels, thread and knitting needles.

Above right
Even a simple pulley is useful because it enables the whole weight of the body to be used as effort. This simple pulley is being used to remove an engine from a car.

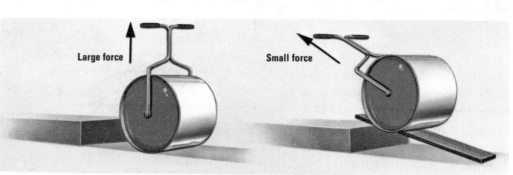

Large force

Small force

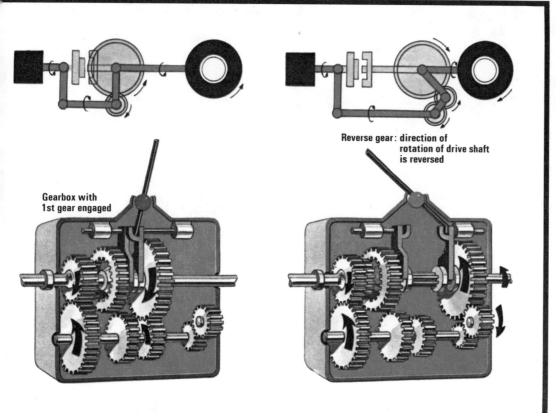

Reverse gear: direction of rotation of drive shaft is reversed

Gearbox with 1st gear engaged

Above
There are two simple ways of lifting a garden roller up a step one foot high. One way is simply to pick it up. This would certainly be difficult and might be dangerous. A better way would be to roll it up a strong plank. The inclined plane of the plank is a machine because it enables the resistance of a force (the weight of the roller) to be overcome by a smaller force (the force needed to pull it up the plank). The force required is smaller than the force needed for lifting because the roller has to travel a greater distance.

Left
Gears are used to transfer forces from the engine to the wheels. They also change the size of the forces depending on the load (for example, climbing a hill). When the car is starting or climbing a hill the engine has to turn quickly although the wheels are only turning slowly.

Springs and elasticity

If asked to think of an elastic material you would probably think of rubber. An elastic band can easily be stretched and snaps back into shape again. In the same way if you squeeze a piece of rubber to make it smaller it goes back to its original size when you let go. This is the idea of elasticity. Scientists think of a substance as being elastic if it easily recovers its shape and size after this is changed. Rubber is elastic but so also are steel and glass. Putty and plasticine are not elastic because they do not go back to their original shape. They are said to be *inelastic*. Copper and aluminium are less elastic than steel and glass but more elastic than putty and plasticine.

To change the size of anything a force has to be applied to it. The more force applied the more the thing changes its size or shape. In the case of the elastic band the force is stretching the band and making it longer. Squeezing a piece of rubber makes it smaller. This is called *compression*. If you take a wooden ruler you can bend it by a small amount. Bending is a mixture of stretching and compressing. The top face of the ruler is stretched and the bottom face is compressed. The elastic properties of materials were investigated in the seventeenth century by an English scientist, Robert Hooke (1635–1703) who was one of the greatest scientists of the seventeenth century. Besides investigating elasticity he worked on light and astronomy. He is noted for designing and making many scientific instruments, such as a microscope and a reflecting telescope. He invented the balance spring for regulating the workings of watches.

One way of finding out how elastic things are is by bouncing them. If you drop a marble onto a hard floor it bounces to quite a height. The faster it hits the floor the higher it will bounce. If you

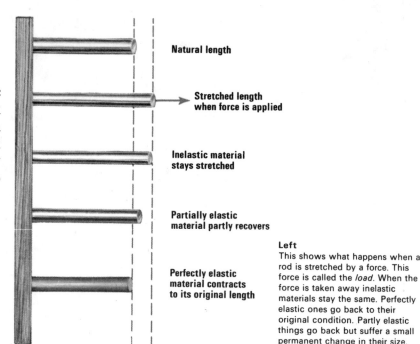

Natural length

Stretched length when force is applied

Inelastic material stays stretched

Partially elastic material partly recovers

Perfectly elastic material contracts to its original length

Left
This shows what happens when a rod is stretched by a force. This force is called the *load*. When the force is taken away inelastic materials stay the same. Perfectly elastic ones go back to their original condition. Partly elastic things go back but suffer a small permanent change in their size.

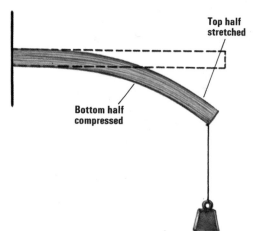

Top half stretched

Bottom half compressed

Left
When a weight is hung on a beam it bends. The top half of the beam is being stretched. The bottom half is being compressed.

Below
Coil springs are used in the spring balance for measuring weight. The spring stretches by an amount that depends on the weight. For example a weight of 10 grams stretches it twice as much as a weight of 5 grams. The weight is shown by a pointer moving over a scale.

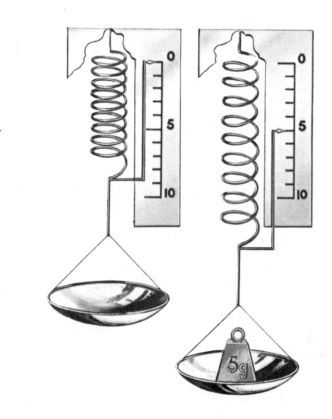

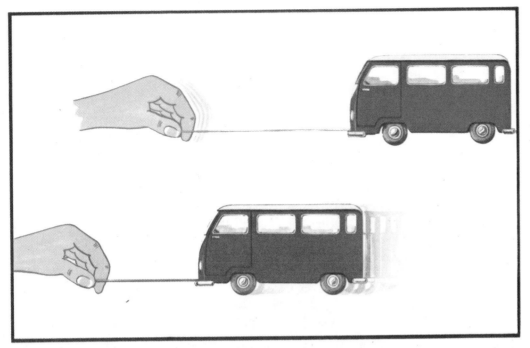

Left
Pull a toy car along on a piece of elastic. To make it begin to move you will have to stretch the elastic which gives it potential energy. As the car moves along it will accelerate as the elastic contracts back to its original length. The energy has been transferred to the car as kinetic energy.

make a ball of plasticine of the same size as the marble you will find that it does not bounce at all. It is simply flattened. As the marble hits the floor the force of the impact also squashes it slightly out of shape. Because it is elastic it regains its original shape and bounces. Notice that it does not bounce to the same height as it was dropped from. Some of its energy has been lost in the bounce.

Elastic materials are used in many ways. When a piece of wood is bent it easily springs back to its original shape. This effect is used in the bow and arrow. It is also used in springboards in swimming pools. Steel springs have many uses. They are found in mattresses, chairs, clocks, watches, and the suspension of railway engines and some cars. The suspension of a car improves the journey by absorbing shocks and bumps. This is helped by air-filled tyres. If air is compressed into a small space it is very springy. When a car goes over a bump the tyres are distorted but they quickly go back to their original shape.

Left
Here are just three of the many ways that springs are used. Mattresses use coil springs which are compressed when someone lies on the bed. Leaf springs are used on the suspension of some cars. They are made of several strips of steel joined together and work by bending. The spring in a clock is a flat coil which is wound tightly. It then unwinds to drive the mechanism.

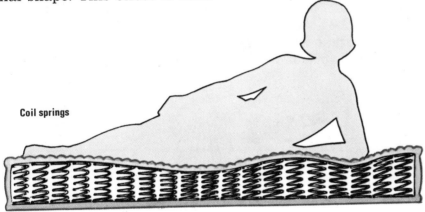

Coil springs

Mainspring

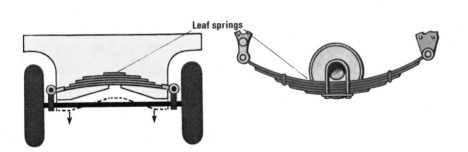

Leaf springs

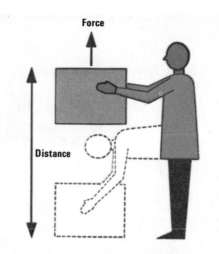

Force

Distance

Below and right
If you lift a box you exert a force on it to overcome the force of gravity. You also move this force through a certain distance. In other words you do work on the book. If you push the box along the ground you also exert a force on it to overcome the friction between the ground and the box.

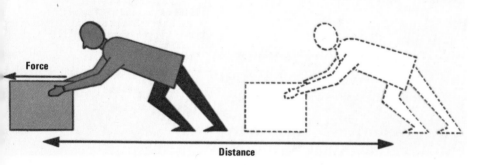

Force

Distance

Work and energy

A man carrying sacks of potatoes up some stairs is doing work. The amount of work that he does depends not only on the weight of the sacks but also on the height to which they are carried. One man carrying a sack to a height of 12 metres is doing twice as much work as a man who carries a similar sack up 6 metres. Also a man who carries a 20 kilogram sack up 6 metres has done twice as much work as a man who only carries a 10 kilogram sack up to the same height. So work involves both force and distance. The work done equals the force used multiplied by the distance for which the force is used. According to this idea work is only done when a force moves.

Strictly speaking if you hold a heavy book above your head no work is done on the book because it has not moved. However some work is done by the contraction and expansion of your muscles. If you lift a weight onto a shelf you have to do work to put it there. However this work is not wasted. The weight has more *energy* than it had when it was on the floor. This stored energy is called *potential energy*. If now the weight falls from the shelf it loses this potential energy. Because it falls faster and faster it gains a new kind of energy called *kinetic energy*. Kinetic energy is the energy due to the motion of a body.

If the weight drops onto some sand or soft soil it makes a hollow where it falls. The kinetic energy has been used up in doing work to move the soil. The energy of a body is its ability to do work. Energy is never lost but is converted from one form to another.

What happens if a falling weight hits a hard floor? Where does its energy go? Some of the kinetic energy is used in making a noise

Right
If you take a weight on one end of a piece of string and tie the other end to a fixed point you have a pendulum. If you pull the weight to one side you are doing work because you are lifting it against the force of gravity. You have increased the potential energy of the weight. Now let it go. As it moves it first increases its speed until it reaches the bottom of the swing. It is then moving fastest and all its potential energy has changed to kinetic energy. As it goes up the other side it slows down again and its kinetic energy turns back to potential energy. This picture shows a number of photographs taken of a pendulum so that you can see how it moves during one swing.

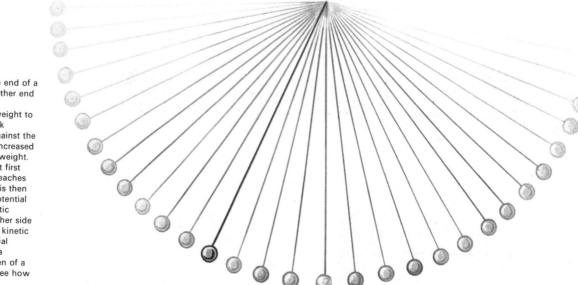

and some of it may be used to knock the weight out of shape. The remainder is turned into another form of energy, which we call *heat*. The weight gets slightly hotter. You can demonstrate how kinetic energy is turned into heat by hitting a small piece of metal with a hammer a number of times. The metal quickly becomes quite hot.

Of course hitting things is not the best way to make them hot. Burning things is a much better way of producing heat. When coal burns heat is given out. We say that the coal is a source of energy. The energy is stored in the coal and when the coal burns it forms new chemicals. These have less energy–the extra energy appears as heat. The heat from coal can be used to make steam which drives a steam engine. In turn the steam engine can be used to do work. The coal has acted as a fuel.

You also use up a fuel when you do work such as lifting a weight or pushing something. The fuel is the food you eat. Chemical changes in the food provide the energy. The energy stored in things like food, coal, petrol, and gas is called chemical energy.

There are other forms of energy. For example when things burn they give out light as well as heat. Part of the energy is converted into light energy. In an electric fire heat and some light are produced from electrical energy.

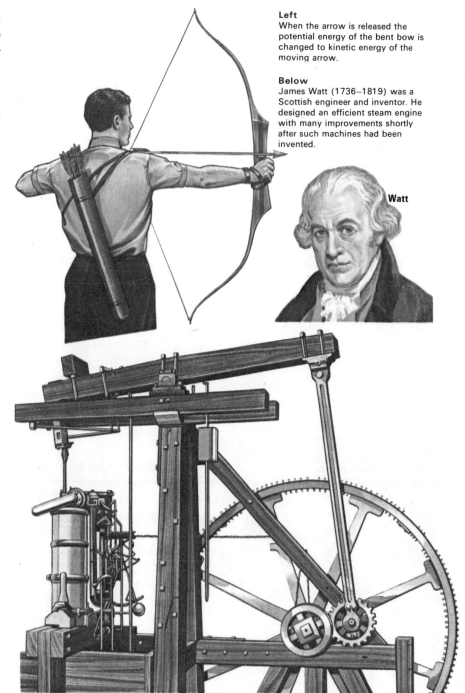

Left
When the arrow is released the potential energy of the bent bow is changed to kinetic energy of the moving arrow.

Below
James Watt (1736–1819) was a Scottish engineer and inventor. He designed an efficient steam engine with many improvements shortly after such machines had been invented.

Watt

Above
A steam engine is used to obtain useful work from the energy stored in coal. This one was made in 1788 by James Watt. It is in the Science Museum in London.

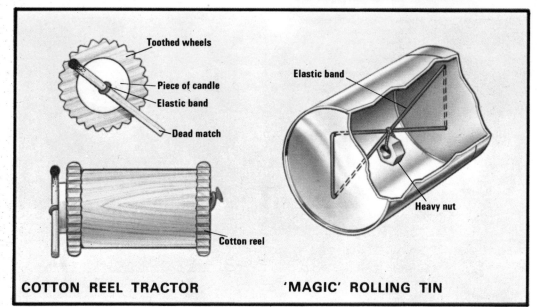

Toothed wheels
Piece of candle
Elastic band
Dead match
Cotton reel

Elastic band
Heavy nut

COTTON REEL TRACTOR

'MAGIC' ROLLING TIN

Left
Two toys that use the energy stored in a twisted elastic band. Wind the cotton reel tractor up by turning the match 'key'. It will drive itself along the floor gripping with the toothed tread. Make up a 'magic rolling tin' as in the picture. When you roll it along the floor the heavy nut will cause the elastic to twist up. When you let go it will roll backwards, apparently of its own accord, but it is really the hidden elastic unwinding.

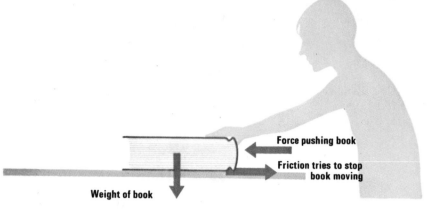

Force pushing book

Friction tries to stop
book moving

Weight of book

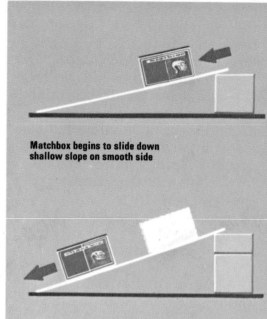

Matchbox begins to slide down
shallow slope on smooth side

Far right
You can do experiments on friction by using a piece of wood or stiff cardboard to make a slope. Put a matchbox on the wood and tilt it slowly until the box begins to slide. Does it make any difference if the matchbox is put on its edge? If the edge is rough you will find that you have to tilt the slope further. You can experiment with different surfaces to find how much friction they have.

Above
Put a book on the table and try pushing it along. Friction tries to stop it moving. Now pile some more books on top of the first one and try again. It is more difficult to push the pile of books because they are heavier. There is more force pushing the book against the table. This makes the friction greater.

Friction

Rub your finger on a smooth polished surface. Now do the same on a piece of rough stone or brick. Do you feel any difference? You will notice that in the second case there appears to be some force trying to stop your finger moving. This force is called *friction*. Friction is a force that tends to stop movement between any two surfaces which are moving over each other.

For some surfaces the friction is greater than for others. It is easy to slide on a highly polished floor or down a helter-skelter but it is difficult to slide on a rough surface. This is because friction is greater between two rough surfaces than between two smooth ones.

There are some ways in which friction is very useful. For example the brakes on a bicycle work by friction. Rubber blocks are clamped against the rim of the wheel and this stops it moving. Another use is in walking. If there were no friction between the soles of our shoes and the ground we would slip as soon as we tried to walk.

If you rub your hands together for a few seconds you will notice that they begin to get warm. Friction causes heat. Sometimes

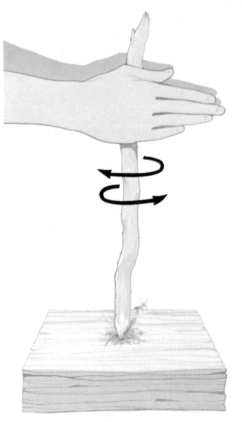

Left
Friction always causes heat. This is an old method of making fire. The pointed stick is twisted very quickly in a piece of wood and becomes hot. This sets the dry grass alight.

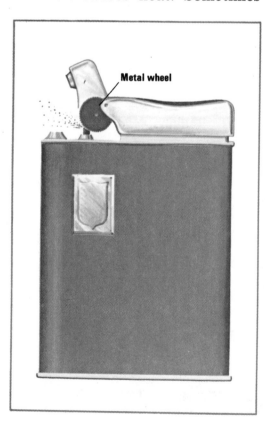

Metal wheel

Right
This is a more modern method of making fire, but it still uses friction. When the lighter is pressed the metal wheel turns and rubs against the flint. The flint is a small piece of a special metal called *cerium*. Very small pieces of flint are thrown off. The friction causes so much heat that these pieces are white hot. These are the sparks which set the gas alight.

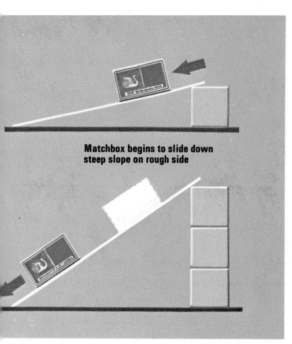

Matchbox begins to slide down steep slope on rough side

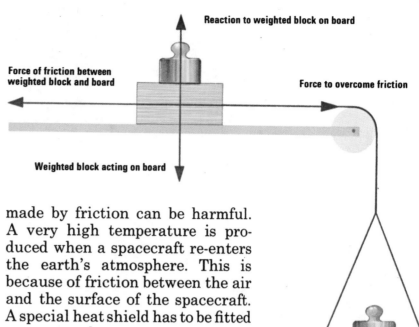

Reaction to weighted block on board

Force of friction between weighted block and board

Force to overcome friction

Weighted block acting on board

this is useful. People used to start fires by rubbing dry sticks of wood together until the friction gave enough heat to produce a flame. If you are cold you rub your hands together to make them warm. Again forces of friction are producing heat. Nowadays we often make a flame by striking a match. By rubbing or striking the match on a rough surface enough heat is made to set fire to the chemicals on the end of the match.

Sometimes however the heat made by friction can be harmful. A very high temperature is produced when a spacecraft re-enters the earth's atmosphere. This is because of friction between the air and the surface of the spacecraft. A special heat shield has to be fitted to protect the astronauts.

When a motor car engine is running there are many moving metal surfaces. Much heat would be produced between these surfaces if no oil were used in the engine. Lubricants form a film between the metal surfaces so that the metal surfaces do not rub together. This stops the engine getting too hot.

Another way of overcoming the problem of friction is to use rollers. It is always easier to roll something along than to slide it. Large objects can be moved by pushing them along on rollers.

Above
This is a laboratory experiment to measure the force of friction between two surfaces; in this case between the board and the block. The coefficient of friction, as it is called, equals the total weight of the pan and its load, divided by the total weight of the block and its load. You can study how this varies: a) for different weights on the block; b) for different surfaces, by using a variety of blocks.

Thin film of oil

Piston

Metal casing

Left
Oil reduces friction because it forms a very thin film which keeps the two surfaces apart.

Right
Ball-bearings reduce friction. To test this, take two cans with lip edges and try rotating one on top of the other. Take some small marbles or ball-bearings and place them round inside the edge. Now try rotating the cans again and see how much easier it is.

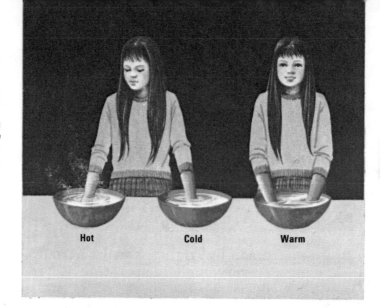

Hot   Cold   Warm

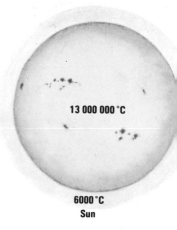

13 000 000 °C

6000 °C
Sun

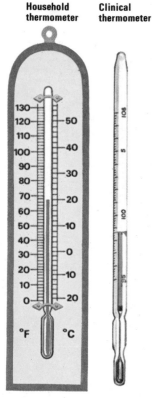

Household thermometer   Clinical thermometer

Above
Here are some examples of thermometers. The red liquid in the first one is alcohol. A red dye is added to make it visible. The clinical thermometer contains mercury. When it is put in your mouth the mercury expands and goes up the tube. When it is removed the mercury contracts but the thread breaks at the point where the tube narrows. This leaves some mercury in the stem showing the original temperature. You must shake the thermometer to get all the mercury back in the bulb again.

Right
Here we can compare the two scales of temperature.

Temperature and heat

On a cold day the temperature is low and on a hot day the temperature is high. What do we mean by temperature? The temperature of a thing is a measure of its hotness or coldness. Ice has a lower temperature than boiling water. The temperature of the sun is very high.

We can measure temperature by many methods. One way would be to simply touch things with our hands and judge how hot they are. This method is not accurate enough for scientists because the skin is not sensitive enough to notice very small changes in temperature. For accurate measurements we use *thermometers*. Ordinary thermometers are based on the fact that liquids expand when they get hotter. If we can see how much a liquid has expanded then we can find its rise in temperature.

There are many different types of thermometers. The common ones are filled with either alcohol or mercury. Alcohol is better than mercury in very cold countries because it has a lower freezing point. It can be used in conditions where mercury would freeze. Mercury thermometers are often used in laboratories because alcohol has a low boiling point and cannot be used for measuring high temperatures. If an alcohol thermometer were put into hot water the alcohol would boil and the thermometer would burst.

A special type of thermometer is used to take your temperature when you go to see the doctor. It is called a clinical thermometer. It is made so that the highest temperature it reached still shows after it has been removed from your mouth.

To get a standard scale of markings or *graduations* on a thermometer two fixed points must first be found. These points are temperatures which are easily obtained. The upper fixed point is the temperature of steam from boiling water. The lower fixed point is the temperature of melting ice. In the *centigrade scale* (°C) the difference between these two points is divided

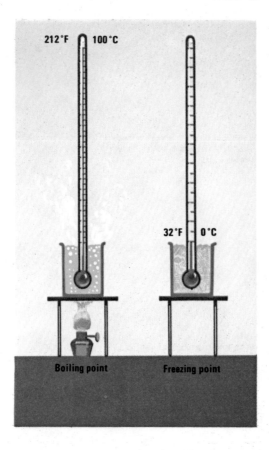

212°F   100°C

32°F   0°C

Boiling point   Freezing point

100°C

37°C
(98·4°F)

Man

0°C

Ice

Steam

Kelvin

into 100 parts or degrees. The temperature of melting ice is 0°C and the temperature of steam from boiling water is 100°C. This scale is also called the *Celsius scale*, after a Swedish scientist.

On the *Fahrenheit scale* the ice point is 32°F and the upper fixed point is 212°F. This scale came about because the two fixed points that the inventor, Fahrenheit, used were the temperature of the body, which he said was 96°F, and the temperature of a mixture of ice and salt which was 0°F. Today, most people, including scientists, use the centigrade scale. The Fahrenheit scale is much less important.

There is a difference between *heat* and *temperature*. Imagine a red-hot sewing needle and a kettle full of boiling water. The needle may be many times hotter than the water. Its temperature is much higher. However there is less *heat* in the needle than in the kettle full of water. You could prove this by dropping a red-hot needle into a kettle of cold water. It would hardly raise the temperature at all and certainly not make the kettle boil.

The amount of heat in a body does not only depend on its temperature. It also depends on how much matter it contains.

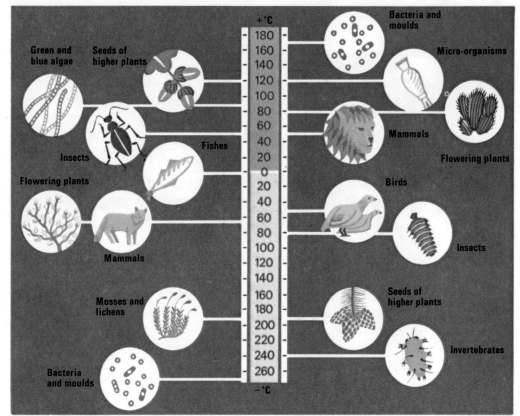

Right
When a moving marble hits a stationary one the two marbles move together. However they are slower than the original one because the total momentum is shared between them.

Right
In Newton's cradle, when the ball at one end strikes the line of stationary balls, its energy is transmitted along the line and the ball at the other end flies up. With highly polished steel balls on fine supporting threads, very little energy is lost and the movement continues for a long time without anyone touching the cradle.

Below right
The energy in this powerful laser beam is sufficient to bore a hole through a thick aluminium plate. LASER stands for *Light Amplification by Stimulated Emission of Radiation.*

Below
In an electric toaster the electric current passes through special wires. These get hot just like the element in an electric fire. Electrical energy is being converted into heat energy.

Conservation of energy

Imagine a car moving along the road. If the driver has to stop quickly he applies the brakes. In doing this he is applying a force to the wheels to stop them going round. If the car is moving at 70 mph it takes more force to stop it than if it moves at only 30 mph. Now think of a lorry moving at 70 mph. It takes more force to stop a lorry than to stop a car moving at the same speed. This is because the lorry is heavier than the car. We say that the car and the lorry have *momentum*.

Momentum depends not only on the speed of a thing but also on its mass. A lorry travelling at 70 mph has more momentum than a car travelling at 70 mph. A car travelling at 70 mph has more momentum than if it travels at 30 mph. The momentum of anything is its mass multiplied by its velocity.

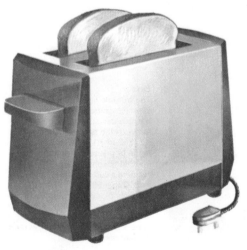

Scientists have found out that when things collide their total momentum is unchanged. This is called the *law of conservation of momentum*. If, when you are sliding on ice you catch hold of someone as you are going past them, you will both move together but the combined speed is less than the original speed. This is because your original momentum has to be shared between two people.

The law of conservation of momentum is one of the important principles in physics. There is a similar law concerning energy. It says that energy is neither created nor destroyed but is simply changed from one form to another. It is called the *law of conservation of energy*. You have already seen some examples of energy changes on page 76. It is easy to think of others.

For example, coal is burned in a power station and gives heat. This is used to produce steam for driving a turbine. The turbine turns a generator and gives electricity. In an electric fire the electrical energy is converted into heat. In this way the chemical energy in the coal has been used to provide heat energy in the electric fire. In a process like this all the chemical energy in the coal cannot be used in electric fires and electric motors. Some of the energy is lost along the way. For example, in the turbine and generator, friction in the moving parts causes heat. Also, some of the electrical energy is used in warming the wires and

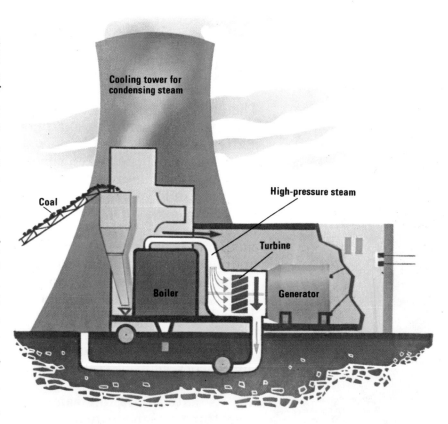

Cooling tower for condensing steam

Coal

High-pressure steam

Turbine

Boiler

Generator

cables carrying the electric current. This energy is not used for any useful purpose. However the important thing is that no energy is really lost overall. It is just converted to other forms.

In prehistoric times heat and light energy from the sun was used by growing trees and plants. These eventually changed to fuels such as coal, oil, and natural gas. When we burn these fuels the energy we get is the energy that reached the earth from the sun many years ago. This is stored in the fuel as chemical energy.

Over the last thirty years man has discovered and developed a new source of energy called nuclear energy (see page 198).

Above
A thermoelectric power station uses thermal energy from coal or oil. The fuel is used to heat the steam that drives the turbines for the turbo-generator. In a hydroelectric power station the turbines are driven by a constant flow of water using the potential energy of the water behind a dam or in a waterfall.

Below
There is a difference between power and energy. It would take a long time for the man to lift all these sacks onto the back of the lorry. The fork-lift truck does the job very quickly. Both would use the same amount of energy in doing the job but the machine is more powerful and does it quicker. Power is the amount of work that can be done in a given time.

Atoms and molecules

The ancient Greeks used to argue amongst themselves about how matter was made up. They wondered what happened when a metal bar was cut into shorter and shorter lengths. Could you go on doing this for ever, or was a point reached beyond which it could get no smaller? They had no means of finding out which theory was true.

The problem was not properly solved until the English scientist John Dalton, at the beginning of the nineteenth century, produced his theory of atoms. According to this theory matter could not be sub-divided for ever, without changing its nature. Dalton said that everything was made up of indivisible tiny particles, called *atoms*. He imagined these atoms to be like tiny billiard balls, which joined together in groups to form arrangements called *molecules*.

His theory was greatly helped by the observations of the botanist Robert Brown. Brown noticed that pollen particles in water seemed to move about haphazardly. It was later realized that the water molecules, which are far too small to see, were continually striking the particles giving them their random motion.

Imagine a very large balloon in the middle of a crowd of invisible people. The balloon would appear to move about in a very jerky manner as people bumped into it. This is what happens to the pollen grains when they are on the surface of water.

The atomic theory explains many properties of solids, liquids, and gases. In a solid, each atom and molecule has a fixed position. It cannot change places with its neighbour, it can only vibrate slightly. The atoms or molecules in solids have a regular structure called a *crystal* so that solids cannot easily change their shape.

Right
The alchemists of classical times mingled their study of chemistry with religion and philosophy. Alchemy was also linked with astrology. This table of symbols shows how each metal was linked with a planet.

Right
John Dalton (1766–1844) was the founder of modern atomic theory. He made some very careful experiments to prove the truth of his theory. He also studied gases and the weather, and discovered that people could be colour-blind.

Far right
A table of elements showing their symbols and atomic weights, drawn up by John Dalton in 1808–10.

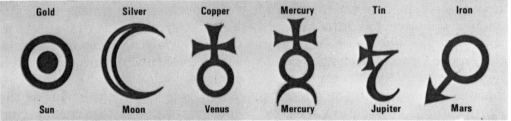

Dalton

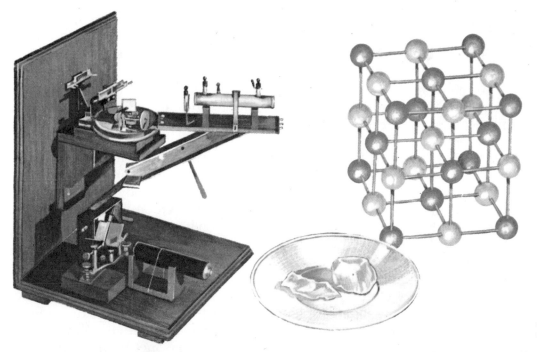

The molecules in liquids are not so firmly fixed in position. They still vibrate, but they can also move around. Liquids can therefore change their shape and flow from one place to another.

In gases the atoms or molecules are very much further apart and they move about with great speed. Since they can move about they completely fill their container.

Each molecule in solids, liquids, and gases has *kinetic energy* as a result of its motions and vibrations. This energy increases with temperature. As a solid is heated the molecules vibrate much more and the temperature of the substance rises. Because they are vibrating so much, the molecules tend to break away from their positions. This is what happens when a solid melts. As heating continues more molecules break free until all of the solid has melted. The temperature, which has not risen during melting, starts to rise again. The movement of the molecules becomes still greater until some of them break free of the surface of the liquid and evaporate off into the atmosphere. *Boiling* has now started. The temperature stays the same until all the liquid has boiled off as gas.

These processes happen in reverse when a gas cools. The temperature stays the same as it con*denses* and as it *freezes*.

Boiling

Condensing

Pure water   Salt solution

Above
As the molecules of a liquid are heated they move about more and more. Some of them escape from the surface of the liquid. This is called evaporation. When molecules from the body of the liquid form bubbles and escape this is called boiling. A gas condenses when its molecules touch a cold surface. The molecules give up some of their heat to the surface and they have less energy to move about as freely as before. This is what happens when you see steam condensing back into water on a bathroom mirror.

Left
Aristotle doubted that matter was composed of atoms because he did not believe there could be spaces between the atoms. But a simple experiment would have shown him that he was mistaken. Take a measuring cylinder and fill it with water to any marked level. Now add salt and you will see that as long as the salt dissolves there is no increase in volume. The salt atoms are fitting in between the water molecules.

Conduction and insulation

If you coat a knife blade with butter and hold the knife tip near a flame the butter will quickly melt. It melts at the tip first and then begins to melt further and further from that end. This is because the heat of the flame passes down the length of the blade. The passage of heat through a solid substance, like the knife, is called *conduction*.

It is the movement of the atoms and molecules within the solid that causes this passage of heat. When the molecules near the flame are heated they vibrate (move back and forth) more rapidly; because they vibrate faster their energy increases. They jostle the molecules next to them and these too move more rapidly. Eventually all the molecules in the solid are made to vibrate faster and therefore increase their energy. This energy is heat and as it passes down the blade the temperature of each part of the knife increases.

Some solids are better conductors of heat than others. Metals such as copper, aluminium, and silver are good conductors. Non-metals, including glass, wood, rubber, and plastic do not conduct well. These bad conductors are called *insulators*.

Materials, such as copper, that are good conductors of heat are usually also good conductors of electricity. Good heat insulators are often good electrical insulators too.

When the knife was held in the flame, the handle did not get hot because most knife handles and also saucepan handles are made of insulating substances. Saucepans however are metal or enamel so that heat can easily pass from the cooker into the pan.

Most liquids are bad conductors. Milk can be kept cool in summer by putting the bottle into a bucket full of cold water. Gases are also very bad heat conductors. Woollen clothing stops heat being lost from the body because the air trapped between the strands of wool is a bad conductor. The layer of air

Below
This experiment shows the way in which heat is slowly passing down the metal blade.

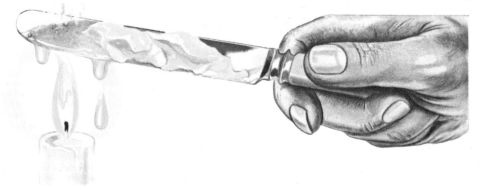

Left
In many cases we do not want heat to travel and then we use insulators. Here are a few common examples. Wooden spoons are used in cooking because a metal one would soon get hot. Insulation in the roof of a house is used to keep in the heat. Pipes are lagged with cloth to stop them freezing in winter.

Right
A vacuum does not conduct at all. This is because there are no molecules there to carry the heat. A vacuum flask is used for keeping things hot or cold. A glass bottle inside the flask has double walls. All the air is removed from this gap to stop conduction of heat. The walls are also silvered to stop heat loss by radiation.

between two jumpers say, or the pockets of air in the holes of a string vest will make the conductivity even less. This insulation keeps out cold air and prevents heat being lost from the wearer's body.

Good conductors are used when heat has to flow easily. Insulators are used to make the flow of heat as small as possible.

A car radiator is made of metal. The water inside it is used to cool the engine, and therefore gets hot. The metal is used to conduct away this heat. A rubber hot-water bottle filled with boiling water will keep warm for a long time. The small amount of heat which passes through the bottle is used to heat the bed. The bed stays warm because hot air is trapped between the blankets. Another case of insulation is the lagging on pipes, hot water tanks, or boilers. It reduces the loss of heat from a hot water system. It also prevents the water in pipes from freezing during a cold winter. (Ice occupies more room than the same amount of water, and can cause pipes to burst).

Left
Double glazing is used to keep houses warm. A double layer of glass is used and air is trapped between the panes. Since air is a bad conductor it reduces the loss of heat from the house and saves money spent on fuel bills.

Below
The string vest and the cellular blanket both work using the principle that air is a bad conductor. A cellular blanket is placed between two other blankets on the bed and traps a layer of air. It keeps the bed warm because it stops heat being lost.

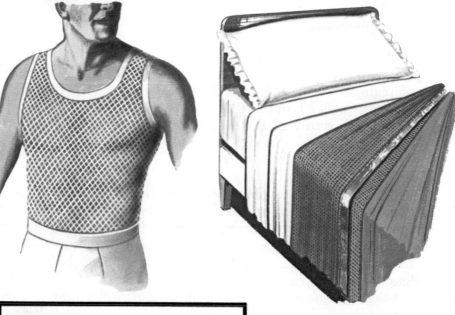

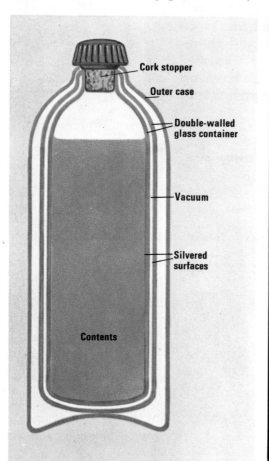

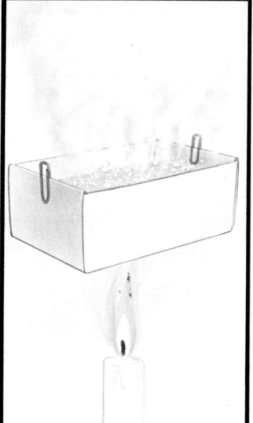

Left
Many people will not believe you if you tell them you can boil water in a paper dish, but you can. The reason is that the water conducts the heat away from the paper and prevents it from burning. If you try this experiment, make sure that your dish is quite strong and will not collapse when you put water in it. Be careful not to let the dish boil dry because then it will catch alight.

Convection

If you watch a saucepan of water as it is being heated you can see the surface is broken by ripples of water. This is caused by hot water rising and its place at the bottom being taken by colder water from the top. This process is called *convection*. It is the transferring of heat by movement of the material itself. This is unlike *conduction* in which movement of heat takes place without any movement of the material.

Convection occurs in gases as well as liquids. Carefully heat a metal rod (not so hot that it burns your fingers) and hold it in the air. Put your other hand a little above it and you can feel the warm air rising from the hot rod. If you put your hand below it you will not feel any warmth.

Convection takes place because gases and liquids expand when they are heated. This expansion makes them less dense than the surrounding material. Since they are less dense they rise and their place is taken by the denser colder fluid from above. These movements of material are called convection currents. These currents can be quite strong. Place a small paper windmill above an electric light and watch it spin around. This is

how a flickering flame effect is made in some electric fires.

This explanation of convection makes it clear why a glass of water cannot be cooled by standing it on a block of ice. The water at the bottom would become colder and colder. It would also become more and more dense and would therefore stay at the bottom. The warmer water at the top would have no chance of cooling because it would always stay at the top.

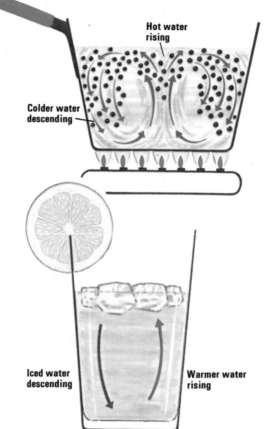

Hot water rising

Colder water descending

Iced water descending

Warmer water rising

Left
When a liquid is heated convection currents are set up in it. The warmer water rises to the top and the cooler water sinks to replace it until that too is heated and rises. The ripples show the movement of the water. A similar effect takes place when cooling a glass of water with ice. Ice cools the water which falls to the bottom of the glass and its place at the top is taken by warmer water from the bottom.

Below left
Electric convection heaters from rooms are of two types. In the natural convection heater the cold air enters at the bottom, is heated by passing over an element, and emerges at the top as warm air. The natural convection current is relied on to keep the air circulating. In the fan heater, which can be much smaller, a fan sucks in cold air from the back and blows it over the heating elements.

Below
Ventilation in a coal mine. The fire heats the air which expands, becomes less dense, and rises out of the shaft. Fresh air comes in the other shaft to ventilate the mine.

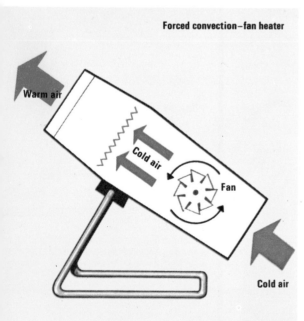

Forced convection–fan heater

Warm air

Cold air

Fan

Cold air

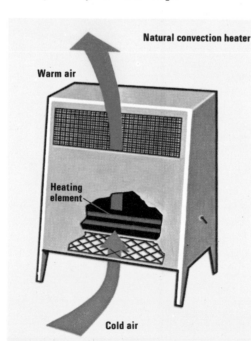

Natural convection heater

Warm air

Heating element

Cold air

Fresh air drawn in

In the early days of coal mining the mines were ventilated by convection currents. Two shafts were sunk and a fire lit at the bottom of one of them. As the heated air rose out of this shaft fresh air was drawn into the other one, thus ventilating the mine.

Convection heaters work on the principle that hot air rises. Cold air from near the floor is taken in, heated, and by convection it rises to come out of the top of the heater. In this way, a stream of warm air constantly emerges from the heater. Fan heaters and hairdriers transfer heat by convection. Air is heated by an electric element and blown out by a fan. Heat is still being transferred by the movement of air so convection is taking place. When a fan is used, it is called *forced convection.*

Convection currents take place in the atmosphere. The land is heated to a higher temperature than the sea during the day. Air over the land becomes warmer, rises, and its place is taken by cooler air from the sea. So there is usually a breeze towards the land during the day. At night the land cools down more quickly than the sea so the sea is warmer than the land. A convection current takes place the other way. The air over the sea is heated, rises and cool air from the land takes its place.

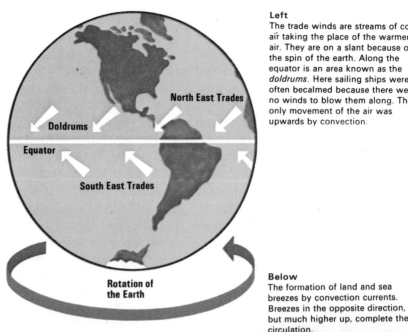

North East Trades

Doldrums

Equator

South East Trades

Rotation of the Earth

Below
The formation of land and sea breezes by convection currents. Breezes in the opposite direction, but much higher up, complete the circulation.

Sea breeze

DAY

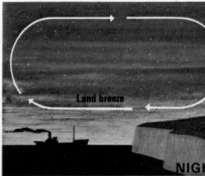

Land breeze

NIGH

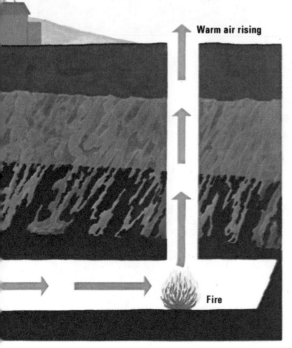

Warm air rising

Fire

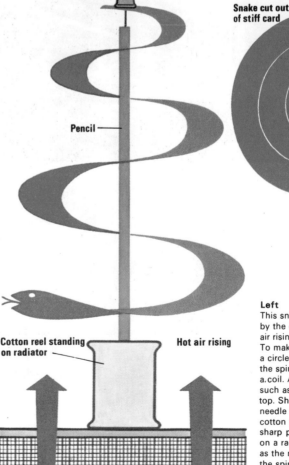

Thimble

Pencil

Cotton reel standing on radiator

Hot air rising

Snake cut out of stiff card

Left
This snake windmill is driven round by the convection currents of hot air rising from a radiator.
To make a snake, draw a spiral on a circle of card as above. Cut along the spiral and pull it out a little, into a coil. Attach the tail to a hard cap, such as a thimble or a small bottle top. Sharpen a pencil, or stick a needle in it. Hold it upright in a cotton reel. Balance the tail on the sharp point and place the windmill on a radiator. Watch it spin round as the rising air currents flow along the spirals.

Radiation

If you stand in the sunshine on a fine day you will feel warm. But if the sun is suddenly hidden by a cloud you no longer feel its warmth. This must mean that the sun has been warming you without heating the air. Heat is being transmitted without involving the material between you and the sun. Also, as there is no air beyond the earth's atmosphere the sun's heat must be able to pass through a vacuum (a space which has no particles in it). This process of transferring heat is called *radia-tion*. It is the way that energy travels across empty space.

This is also how heat is passed from the radiant type of electric fire. If you stand in front of an electric fire you will feel warm. If you move to one side, you will feel cooler. So once again the heat is being passed without using the air. It appears that heat is radiating from the fire in straight lines, just like light comes from a torch. If you put your hand in front of a torch you can block the light. In exactly the same way someone standing between you and an electric fire blocks the heat and stops it from reaching you.

Radiant heat and light are very similar—they are both *electromagnetic waves*.

Radiation is not only emitted by extremely hot things, such as the sun and electric fires. It can also be emitted by cooler objects. If too much heat is allowed to radiate from a teapot then the tea gets cold too quickly. Putting a tea cosy over it reduces the radiation loss.

Some surfaces are better radiators of heat than others. Try this experiment with an old baked bean tin. Scrape off the label and paint one half black. Leave the other side shiny. Fill the can with hot water and hold your cheek or the back of your hand first near the black side and then near the shiny side. You will find that your hand is warmer when held opposite the black side. This is because a black surface is always a good radiator of heat. A polished surface is a bad radiator. Now repeat the experiment with another can whose sides are painted white and brown. Generally, a darker surface radiates more heat than a lighter one.

From these experiments you will understand why a silver teapot with highly polished sides will not lose much heat by radiation, whereas a brown or black teapot will lose much more.

As well as radiating heat, surfaces can also reflect and absorb it. Heat, just like light, when it falls on a surface, is partly reflected and partly absorbed. Good radiating surfaces are also good absorbers of radiation. Bad radiating surfaces tend to reflect it instead of absorbing it. People who live in hot countries do not want their clothes to absorb heat. They therefore wear white clothes and hats which reflect the heat. Spacecraft have highly polished surfaces to reflect away the radiated heat from the sun. The sun radiates both heat and light to the earth. The main difference is that you can see the light rays which are radiated from objects but you cannot see the heat rays. You can only feel them as they warm you up.

Below
In hot countries people keep cool by wearing light-coloured clothes and living in white painted houses. This reduces the amount of heat absorbed.

Left
Because the firemen wear suits with highly polished surfaces, the heat from the fire is reflected and not absorbed. This enables the firemen to keep relatively cool and to approach the fire.

Right
A thermometer consists of a glass tube with a bulb at the bottom. There is mercury or alcohol inside the tube and bulb. As the liquid is heated it expands, that is its volume gets bigger and it needs more space. The only way it can do this is by rising up the tube. We use a thermometer to measure temperatures. The scale is marked off at various temperatures. The level of liquid shows the temperature.

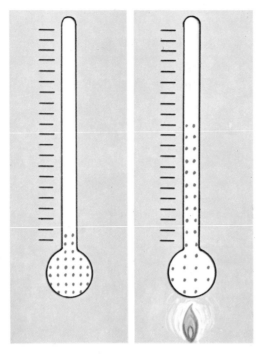

Expansion

Below
This shows the temperature of the water layers in an ice-covered pond. Because water has its maximum density at 4°C, water at this temperature sinks to the bottom. This water can now only lose heat by conduction. Since water is a poor conductor it does not lose much in this way. Therefore in deeper water there should always be some water below the ice in which fish can live.

Far right
Water expands when it freezes. If you freeze a closed glass jar of water the glass will crack under the pressure of the expanding ice. This is why pipes and radiators have to be protected from cold.

If hot water is poured into a thick glass tumbler, the glass often cracks. This is due to the inside of the glass expanding more rapidly than the cooler outside. The resulting stress cracks the glass.

When substances are heated they expand because their atoms or molecules move about more rapidly. This makes them bump into their neighbours more frequently and push each other further apart. We cannot see the atoms and molecules doing this because they are too small. We see only the effects—the volume of the substance increases. Different substances expand by different amounts, even when their temperatures are raised by the same amount. The amount a substance expands when its temperature is raised one degree is called its *coefficient of expansion*. Pyrex glass, for example, has a very low coefficient of expansion so Pyrex vessels do not crack easily from heat.

You can see many examples of expansion in everyday life. On hot days, telegraph wires sag because they have expanded. In winter they contract, that is, they become smaller (shorter), and you can see that they sag less. If they were put up on a hot day and stretched tight between their supports, the wire might break when it contracted on a cold winter's day.

Bridges with long steel girders have one end placed on rollers to allow for expansion. If both ends were firmly connected the bridge would buckle in hot weather.

Railway lines would also buckle in hot weather if the expansion was not allowed for. This is done either, in the older method, by using fishplates, or more recently by using overlapping joints.

Sometimes expansion can be useful. If a glass stopper is stuck in a bottle neck you can use expansion

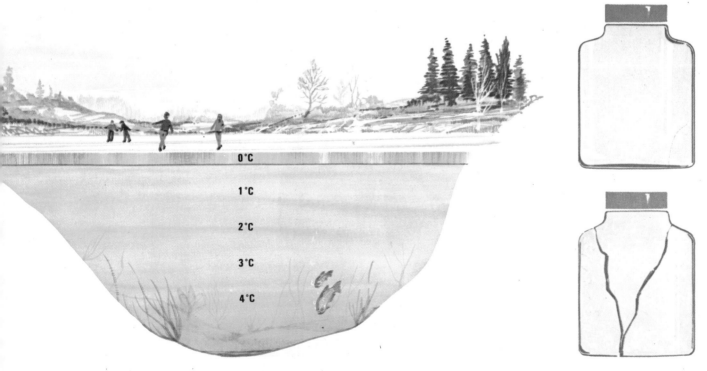

to get it out. Wrap a cloth which has been dipped in hot water around the neck of the bottle. The neck will expand but the stopper will stay the same size. The stopper should now be loose.

Liquids also expand when heated. You can see this by gently breathing on a thermometer. The mercury in the bulb is heated. Its atoms push themselves further apart and the liquid expands. In expanding it rises further up the tube.

Water has an unusual expansion. If you take some melting ice and heat it gently, it contracts or gets smaller until its temperature reaches 4°C. It then starts to expand again. This means that it takes up the least space and has its greatest density at 4°C.

Gases have a greater expansion than solids or liquids. Take a polythene bag with some air in it and firmly close one end. Dip the bag into a bowl of hot water and you will soon see it increase in size. This is because the air has expanded. Motor car engines are also driven by the expansion of gases. The gas expands when the fuel explodes and pushes a piston down in a cylinder. The piston rotates the crankshaft which, through the clutch, gearbox, and differential, moves the wheels, which drive the car along.

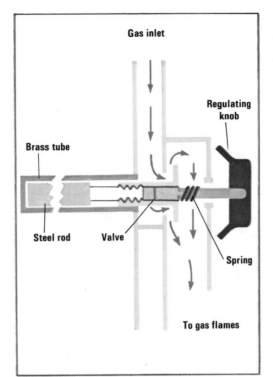

Gas inlet

Brass tube

Steel rod

Valve

Regulating knob

Spring

To gas flames

Left
Gas-oven thermostat. The diagram shows a thermostat (Regulo) for a gas oven. This is what you would see if you sliced it in half. The outside brass tube expands as the oven gets hot and pulls the steel rod with it. This closes the valve and the gas flow is cut off. When the oven cools, the brass case contracts pushing the steel rod back and opening the valve.

Above
As the bridge expands in hot weather and contracts in cold weather, the moveable end rolls backwards and forwards on the rollers. If both ends were fixed the bridge would buckle in hot weather.

Left
A petrol engine in a car depends on the expansion of gas when the fuel is exploded. When the plug fires, the petrol and air mixture explodes and the gases expand, pushing the piston down.

Water and ice at 0°C

Salt solution and ice at −10°C to −20°C

Low temperatures

It is fairly easy to produce high temperatures. Making things colder is more difficult. One way of producing low temperatures is by evaporating liquids. You can demonstrate this by wetting your hand and waving it around. Your hand will feel cold. This is because the water is turning into a vapour. When water boils heat has to be supplied to change it to vapour. In the same way heat has to be supplied to make the water evaporate from your hand. This heat is taken from your hand and it feels colder. The faster the liquid evaporates the more heat is taken away. Try the same experiment with methylated spirits or after-shave lotion which both evaporate more quickly than water. This evaporation effect is one way of producing low temperatures.

In refrigerators the working liquid is either a liquid with a very low boiling point or a gas that can easily be changed into a liquid under pressure. It is called the *refrigerant*. Some examples are ammonia, ethyl chloride, and Freon. The refrigerant is first compressed to a high pressure in one part of the refrigerator. At

this high pressure the refrigerant is a liquid. This is because its molecules are pushed close together. The compressed liquid is passed through a valve into a region of low pressure. At this low pressure the liquid boils thereby changing back into a gas. This fast evaporation takes heat from the inside of the refrigerator just as the water evaporating took heat from your hand. The refrigerant is then compressed again to turn it back to a liquid and used again.

Many domestic refrigerators work on this principle as it is an economic method of preserving food and making ice.

A slightly different method is used in producing very low temperatures. It depends on the fact that if a gas is expanded quickly it is cooled. When you pump up a bicycle tyre you are compressing the air. You have probably noticed that the pump gets hot when you do this. Now think of the opposite effect. A gas at high pressure is suddenly changed to low pressure. When this happens the gas gets slightly colder. The process is similar to the one that occurs in the refrigerator but instead of a liquid changing to a gas it is a gas at high pressure changing to one at

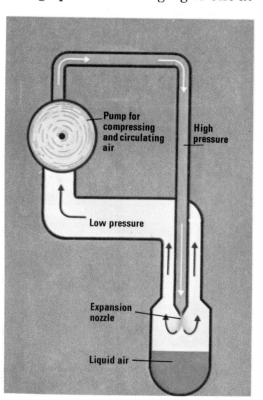

Pump for compressing and circulating air

High pressure

Low pressure

Expansion nozzle

Liquid air

low pressure. The slight fall in temperature when this occurs is called the Joule-Kelvin effect after its discoverers James Prescott Joule and Lord Kelvin. Using this effect, it is possible to cool gas so much that it becomes a liquid. Oxygen changes from a gas to a liquid at $-183°C$ and nitrogen gas changes to liquid at $-195.8°C$.

These are very low temperatures, but even lower temperatures can be produced. Liquid hydrogen has a temperature of $-259.14°C$ and liquid helium is at $-268.9°C$. It requires a great deal of energy to maintain these low temperatures.

The temperature of anything depends on how fast the atoms or molecules are moving about. If they are moving very quickly the temperature is high. If they are moving slowly the temperature is low. This means that there will be a lowest temperature below which one cannot go. At this temperature the atoms and molecules are not moving at all. It is called *absolute zero* and corresponds to a temperature of $-273.15°C$. Scientists have produced temperatures that are only a millionth of a degree above absolute zero, but they have never reached it.

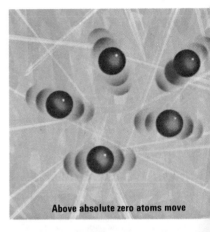

Above absolute zero atoms move

At absolute zero atoms are still

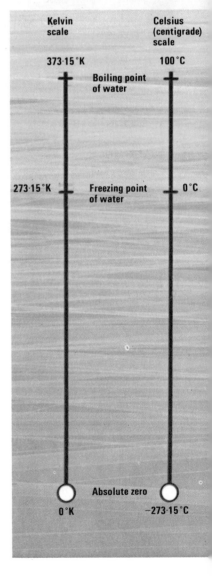

Kelvin scale | Celsius (centigrade) scale

373.15 °K — 100 °C Boiling point of water

273.15 °K — Freezing point of water — 0 °C

Absolute zero

0 °K — −273.15 °C

COMPRESSION REFRIGERATOR

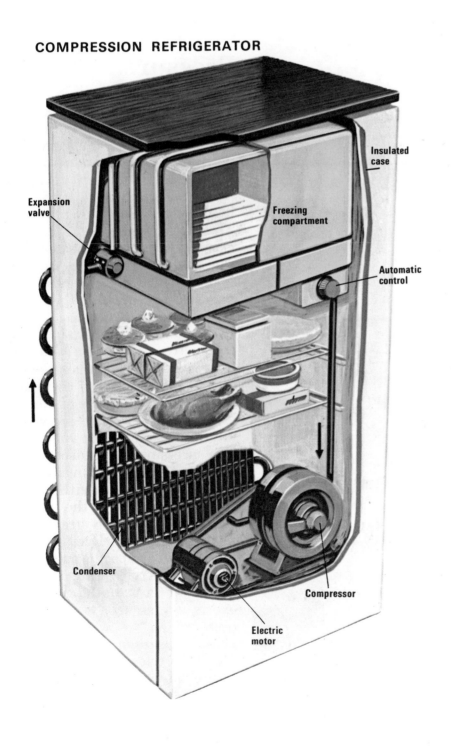

Insulated case

Expansion valve

Freezing compartment

Automatic control

Condenser

Compressor

Electric motor

Right
Gases also exert a pressure. A gas has many millions of small molecules all moving about. The pressure of the gas is caused by molecules bouncing off the walls of the container. There are so many of them that they exert a steady pressure. If twice as much gas were put into the same volume there would be twice as many molecules and the pressure would double.

Right
Gases also exert a pressure. A gas has many millions of small molecules all moving about. The pressure of the gas is caused by molecules bouncing off the walls of the container. There are so many of them that they exert a steady pressure. If twice as much gas were put into the same volume there would be twice as many molecules and the pressure would double.

Far right
Here is an experiment to show that the atmosphere exerts a pressure. Push a bottle under water so that it fills up. Then withdraw it from the water, keeping the neck of the bottle under the surface. It is the atmospheric pressure on the surface of the water that holds the water in the bottle.

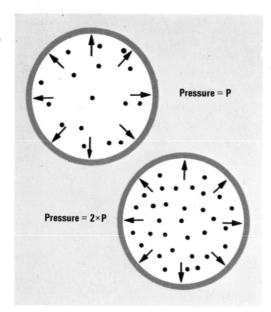

Pressure = P

Pressure = 2×P

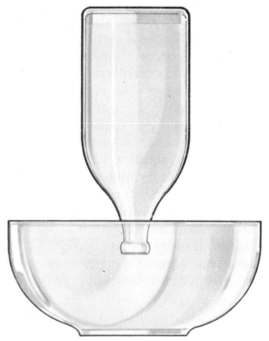

Above
If you hang two objects close together, on long threads and blow between them, you might expect them to blow apart. In fact they swing closer together because by blowing between them, you reduce the air pressure on the insides. The higher, normal air pressure on the outsides forces them to swing towards each other.

Right
This experiment shows that the pressure of a liquid increases with depth. Small holes are pierced in the can and it is filled with water. The jet of water from the bottom hole is strongest and shoots out straightest because the water at the bottom is under the greatest pressure.

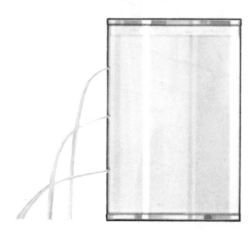

Right
A Cartesian diver. Hold a small tube or bottle upside down in a jar of water. Tip it to let a little air escape until it contains enough water to make it just float under the water. Cover the top of the jar with your hand and press down. The diver will sink. Press less hard and it will rise. By varying the pressure on the water you are changing the relative buoyancy of the diver. You may find it easier to tie a sheet of rubber over the top of the jar, to press on.

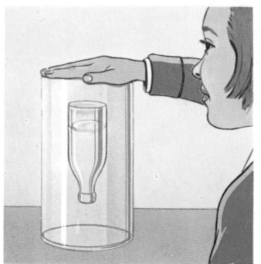

Pressure

The term pressure has an exact meaning in physics. Scientists think of pressure as a force acting down on a certain area.

Your feet sink into loose sand when you stand on it. If you lie on it you do not go down very far. This is because although in each case the force acting on the sand is the same weight, the weight of your body, in the first case it acts on a small area, but in the second a larger area is involved.

In the same way a sharp knife cuts better than a blunt one. This is because there is much less area on the cutting edge if the blade is sharp. The pressure is higher.

A pressure exists on every side of anything that is put in a liquid. The pressure is caused by the weight of liquid pressing against it. Pressure increases with depth so that the pressure at the bottom of the ocean is much greater than near the surface. Deep-sea divers have to wear special suits to prevent their bodies being crushed.

The air in the atmosphere also exerts a pressure. It is the same pressure as we would get from about 9 metres of water.

Nature tries to make pressures equal everywhere. A bicycle pump

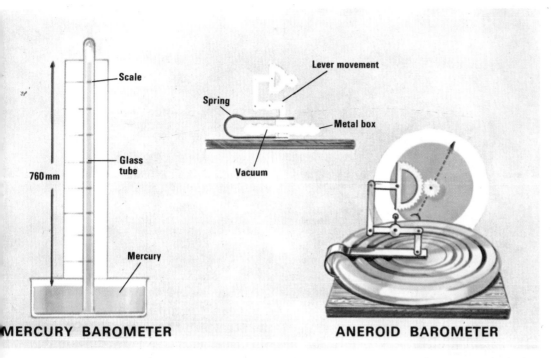

MERCURY BAROMETER

ANEROID BAROMETER

Left
Barometers measure atmospheric pressure and are used for weather forecasts. A *mercury barometer* is very simple. It just measures how much mercury the atmosphere can hold up. As the pressure changes the height of the mercury changes. An *aneroid barometer* is more complicated. A sealed metal box with thin walls is used. It has no air inside it and the sides are held apart by a spring. As the pressure outside increases or decreases the sides of the box go closer together or further apart. The movement of the top of the box moves the levers which move a pointer over a scale.

LIFT PUMP

forces air into tyres. Compressing the pump makes the pressure of the air inside the pump greater than the pressure of the air in the tyre, so air moves into the tyre.

A bicycle pump works by increasing the pressure but you suck up liquids through a drinking straw by reducing the pressure. When you suck a straw you first of all take air out of the straw. To make the pressure the same as it was before, the atmosphere pushes liquid from the glass up the straw into your mouth. You can keep drinking by keeping the pressure in your mouth lower than atmospheric pressure; in other words, you suck on the straw. A vacuum cleaner works on the same princi-

ple. The pressure in the cleaner is made lower, by the fan, than the pressure outside. So air rushes in, taking with it the dirt on the floor.

As you climb above sea level the pressure of the atmosphere decreases. This is because at great heights there are fewer air molecules around. People who climb very high mountains such as Everest have to take their own oxygen with them. There is not enough air for them, and so they breathe from oxygen cylinders. The cabins of aircraft which fly very high also have to take their air supply with them. If they did not, then the cabin would not stay at atmospheric pressure. The cabin is said to be pressurized.

Above
You can make a lift pump like the one above out of a wide tube with two stoppers, two narrow tubes and some pieces of rubber for the flaps. Dip the bottom tube into a reservoir of water and pump the top piston stopper up and down. The pump will fill up with water which gushes out of the top tube, all because of air pressure.
On a down-stroke, the air in the tube is compressed. Air presses the bottom valve flap closed and rushes out of the top valve flap. On an up-stroke, air pressure keeps the top valve flap closed so a vacuum is created under the piston. Air pressure on the surface of the reservoir makes water rush up the tube into the pump to fill this vacuum. When the pump is full, the water is forced out of the top tube.

Left
If a fixed amount of gas is compressed by a piston the molecules are pushed closer together and their pressure increases. The bicycle pump is used for compressing air into a tyre. The rubber cup forces the air into the tyre where it is kept in by a valve.

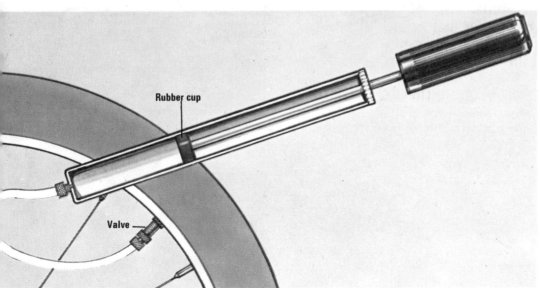

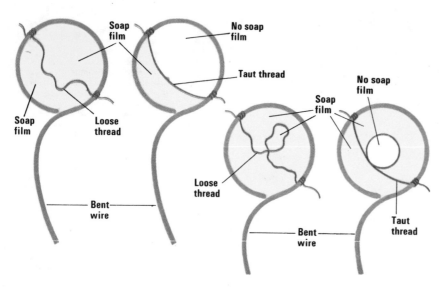

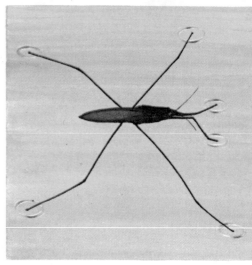

Surface tension

If you put a clean dry needle on a piece of blotting paper which is floating on a glass of water, the paper eventually sinks to the bottom but the needle stays on the surface of the water. If you fill a glass as full as you can with water, you will see that the surface of the water bulges over the glass at the top. These experiments show that the surface of water has a skin, rather like that of a blown-up balloon. The skin is made up of the layer of molecules on top of the water. They are being pulled into the centre of the liquid by the other molecules. The surface therefore shrinks and this makes it strained. This strain is known as *surface tension*. But it is important to understand that there is no real skin there, like there is on top of hot milk. It is only the top layer of molecules behaving like a skin. Nevertheless, some light insects can actually walk on water, on top of this skin.

You can see that a liquid surface is strained by doing the following experiment. Dip a wire ring, which has a piece of slack thread tied across it, into soapy water. If you break the soap film on one side of the thread, the thread is pulled by the film. This is because the remaining soap film is under strain and is trying to make itself as small as possible. Now do the experiment with a loop in the thread and break

the film inside the loop. You will find that it is pulled into a circle by the strain in the surface. The soap film that is left is again trying to shrink.

Soap and detergents lower the surface tension of water. In this way they increase the cleaning power of water by allowing it to come into greater contact with dirt and grease on the surfaces to be washed.

You can show that soap lowers the surface tension of water by making a small boat and putting a piece of soap at the back. When it is put into clean water, the boat will move about for a while. This is because the soap lowers the surface tension behind the boat and so the boat is pulled forward by the larger surface tension in front. It will only stop moving when the surface ten-

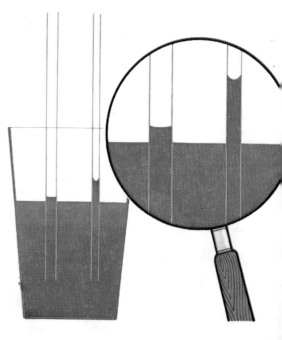

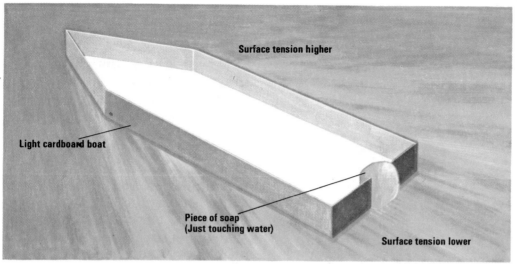

Surface tension higher

Light cardboard boat

Piece of soap
(Just touching water)

Surface tension lower

Left
Make a small boat out of a piece of
thick cardboard or a piece of wood.
Attach a lump of soap or camphor
to a little cleft at the back of the
boat and the boat will move forward
when placed in water. This is
because the surface tension behind
the boat will be lowered by the
soap, whereas it will be unchanged
at the front.

sion of the whole surface is the
same.

Soap bubbles also show surface
tension effects. Blow a bubble at
the end of a tube. The strain on the
surface makes the surface as small
as possible. So when you stop
blowing and allow the air to escape
the bubble shrinks.

Another effect of surface tension
occurs when sugar cubes or blotting paper soak up water from a
saucer. This effect is known as
capillarity. It happens because the
surface tension pulls the surface
of a liquid up into narrow tubes.
Since sugar cubes and blotting
paper are not solid, but are filled
with tiny cracks, water rises in
them. By the same means water is
pulled up into trees and plants,
which have fine internal capillary
tubes running through them.

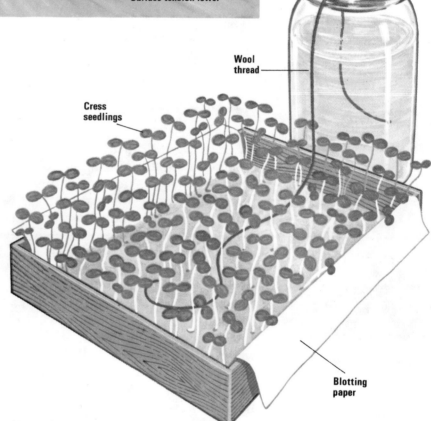

Wool
thread

Cress
seedlings

Blotting
paper

Above
Surface tension causes capillarity.
The water in the glass rises up the
thread of wool and soaks the
blotting paper. The water in the
blotting paper rises up the cress
seedlings and makes them grow.

Left
Two tricks involving surface tension.
Arrange some matches like spokes,
on a bowl of water. Dip a piece of
soap in the centre. The matches will
move outwards. Dip a piece of
blotting paper in the centre and they
will be drawn inwards again. The
soap causes a thin soap film to
spread across the surface which
reduces the surface tension. While
the surface tension is greater round
the edges of the soap film, the
matches are pulled outwards. The
blotting paper draws water up into
it by capillarity. The pull on the
water increases the surface tension
at the centre and pulls the matches
inwards.

Archimedes

Above
Archimedes was a Greek scientist and mathematician who lived in the third century B.C. He made many famous inventions and experimented with the lever. It is said that he thought of the idea of finding the volume of an object by putting it in water as he was getting into a bath filled to the brim. The volume of his body was equal to the volume of water that spilled over the top. His excitement was so great that he ran home naked from the baths shouting *Eureka* (I have found it).

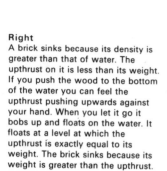

Flotation

If you throw a stone and a cork into a pond, the stone sinks and the cork floats. It is also possible to float one liquid on another. Oil floats on water. This is why oil slicks from tankers float ashore and pollute beaches. It is also difficult to put out a petrol fire with water, because the petrol floats on the top of the water and keeps burning.

If you gently lower a piece of wood into water you will find that it will appear to become lighter and lighter until finally it appears to have no weight at all. This does not mean that it has lost its weight. It means that it is now being supported by the water instead of your hand. This support from the water is called an *upthrust*, because the water is pushing up against the bottom of the wood. Eventually the upthrust supports the wood so that it can float.

There is also an upthrust against things that do not float. Lower a brick into water and it will also seem to become less heavy. But for an ordinary brick the upthrust is never great enough to enable it to float.

Archimedes, the ancient Greek scientist, was the first to study upthrusts. He came to the conclusion that the upthrust was equal to the weight of fluid displaced. This is known as *Archimedes Principle*. It means that if an object pushes aside (displaces) one kilogram of water then there will be an upthrust equal to one kilogram acting on the object.

Imagine two objects, both of identical size and shape, but made of different substances: for example, a brick and a block of wood the same size. When they are put into water so that they are both totally covered they both displace the same weight of water. This means that the upthrust on each of them is the same. In the case of the wood the upthrust is greater than its weight so it rises to the surface and floats. The brick sinks because the upthrust on it is smaller than its weight.

The property of a substance that determines whether or not it will float in water is called its *density*. Density is the weight of the substance divided by its volume. If its weight is greater than the weight of an equal volume of water it will sink. If its weight is less than the

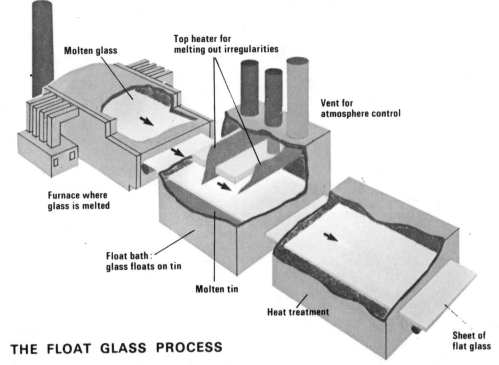

Molten glass

Top heater for melting out irregularities

Vent for atmosphere control

Furnace where glass is melted

Float bath: glass floats on tin

Molten tin

Heat treatment

Sheet of flat glass

Left
The float glass process. This is a modern method of making perfectly flat sheets of glass by floating the molten glass on a bath of liquid metal, which in this case is tin. The liquid provides a perfectly flat surface for the glass to cool on.

Below
This experiment illustrates the law of flotation. It shows that a floating body displaces a weight of water equal to its own weight. To do this, read the water level in a measuring cylinder (graduated in c.c.s). Float a weighted test tube in it. Read off the new water level. The difference in the two levels gives the volume, and hence the weight of water displaced, because one c.c. of water weighs one gram.
Take out the weighted test tube, dry it and weigh it. Its weight should be the same as the weight of water displaced.
Try it again with different weights in the test tube.

THE FLOAT GLASS PROCESS

weight of an equal volume of water it will float. The brick has a greater density than water and sinks because its weight is greater than the weight of an equal volume of water. On the other hand, the wood displaces a volume of water whose weight is greater than the weight of the wood. So the density of wood is less than that of water. Oil floats because it is less dense than water, but mercury sinks to the bottom because its density is thirteen times greater than water.

A ship floats because a large volume of air is contained within its hull, giving it an overall density less than water. However, if it is badly holed by a rock or a torpedo, water floods in which increases its density and it may sink.

Things can also float in air; for example, airships and balloons. This is because they are filled with helium which is less dense than air.

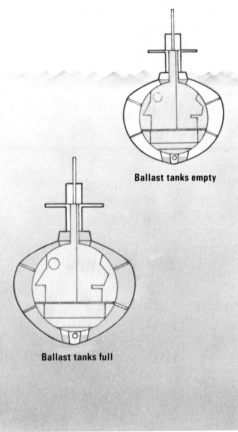

Ballast tanks empty

Ballast tanks full

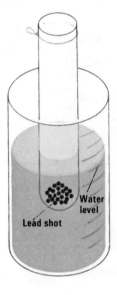

Water level

Lead shot

Left
When a submarine is cruising at the surface its ballast tanks are full of air which keeps it afloat. In order to dive, water is pumped into the tanks to increase the overall density of the ship. The tanks are filled until the submarine reaches a state of neutral buoyancy, when it neither rises nor sinks, but stays at the required depth.

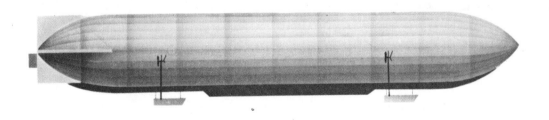

Left
An airship is filled with helium which has a lower density than air. The upthrust by the air on the airship is more than its weight, so it floats.

Development of different types of engine and the resulting forms of transport

Types of engine or power	Ships	Road transport	Rail transport	Air transport
early forms of power — natural and animal	sailing ships; horse-drawn barges on canals	horse-drawn vehicles	horse-drawn trucks	hot air balloons
first efficient steam engine (Watt) 1765, after Newcomen 1712	first successful paddle steam-ship 1783; first propeller steamship 1830	first vehicle driven by steam engine (Cugnot) 1770; more practical horseless carriages 1820	first practical steam train 1812. (Stevenson 1814); first railway (England) opened 1825	
4-stroke petrol engine 1876 (Otto), after Lenoir's internal combustion engine 1860	motor boats	first car 1860 (Lenoir); first petrol driven car 1885 (Daimler; Benz)		first powered flight 1903 (Wright Brothers); first helicopter 1907
Diesel engine 1892	first practical submarines; now in other boats	buses, lorries, taxis, etc.	Diesel trains and Diesel-electric trains	
electrical power		first electric cars 1891. Abandoned, apart from some delivery vans, but being redeveloped (fuel cells)	first electric trains 1879; electrification of railway lines (England from 1950)	
jet engine 1937 (Whittle)	used in a boat (Campbell, 1967) to break water speed record	used in a car (Breedlove 1965) to break the (then) world land speed record	future rail transport	first flight 1937; first supersonic flight 1947
nuclear power; controlled nuclear fission 1942	first nuclear submarine 1952 (Nautilus); used in aircraft carriers, oil tankers, icebreakers, etc.			future space craft

Units and their conversions
TIME
1 year = $365\frac{1}{4}$ days   1 day = 24 hours
1 hour = 60 minutes = 3600 seconds
MASS
1 kilogram (kg) = 1000 grams = 2·2 pounds
1 pound = 16 ounces = 0·45 kg
1 ounce = 28·3 grams
1 ton = 2240 lb = 1016 kg
DISTANCE
1 kilometre (km) = 1000 metres = $\frac{5}{8}$ mile
1 mile = 1760 yds = $\frac{8}{5}$ km
1 metre = 100 centimetres (cm) = 1000 millimetres (mm) = 39·4 inches
1 inch = 2·5 cm   1 cm = $\frac{2}{5}$ inch
1 light year = 9·5 million million km = 5·9 million million miles

Density of some common substances

Substance	Weight compared with weight of an equal volume of water	Substance	Weight compared with weight of an equal volume of water
bamboo	0·4	gold (22 carat)	17·5
brass	8·5	(9 carat)	11·3
butter	0·9	ice	0·92
cast iron	7·0	oak	0·7
cork	0·25	polythene	0·9
diamond	3·5	stainless steel	7·8
glass	about 2·5	wrought iron	7·8

Light, Sight and Sound

Contents

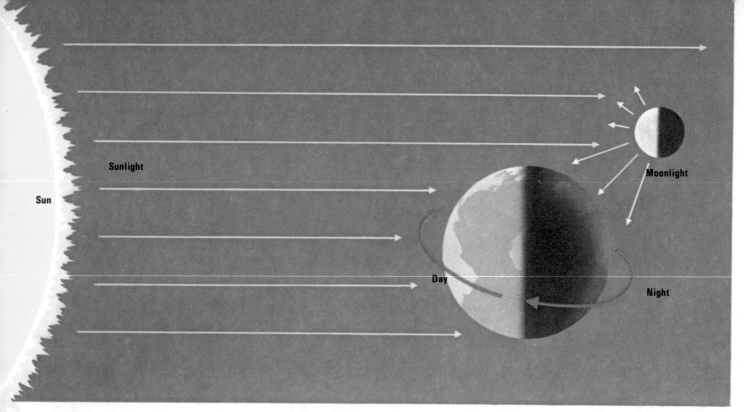

Sunlight

Sun

Moonlight

Day

Night

Light and darkness

Light is a form of energy to which our eyes are sensitive; it enables us to see things. The sun and stars, electric lights, candles, fires, and many other things emit light. These sources of light are very hot. All things are made up of atoms. If a substance is strongly heated, its atoms emit light.

The light given out by the source travels a different distance depending on how bright the source is. A burning match can only be seen up to a few metres away. But we know that light from the sun travels nearly 150 million kilometres.

Darkness is when there is no light. In a room with no windows or openings to the sunlight and with no other form of light, everything seems black or dark; you cannot see anything.

When it is daytime where you live it is night-time or dark on the other side of the earth. The earth rotates on its axis once every 24 hours as it journeys around the sun. On the part of the earth facing the sun it is always light; this is called day. Night comes as this part of the earth rotates away from the sun's light.

Above
The moon does not produce its own light but acts as a giant mirror, reflecting light from the sun to the earth. The moon moves around the earth once a month. As it revolves, we see varying amounts of its surface lit up by the sun at different times each month.

Below right
The electric light bulb contains a coil of thin tungsten wire, called the filament. When an electric current passes through the wire it is heated and emits white light. The brightness of the light depends on the size of the coil.
Sodium lights contain a sealed bulb of sodium vapour. Energy is transferred to the sodium atoms by means of an electric current. This makes the atoms emit yellow light. This colour is good for street lighting. Other gases, such as neon, give off different coloured lights. These lights are used in advertizing displays at night.

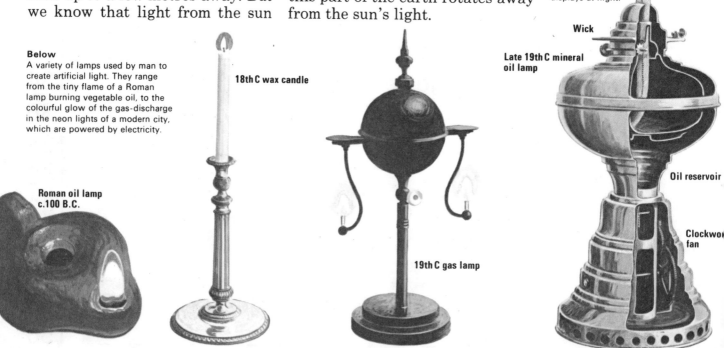

Wick

Late 19th C mineral oil lamp

18th C wax candle

Below
A variety of lamps used by man to create artificial light. They range from the tiny flame of a Roman lamp burning vegetable oil, to the colourful glow of the gas-discharge in the neon lights of a modern city, which are powered by electricity.

Roman oil lamp c.100 B.C.

Oil reservoir

19th C gas lamp

Clockwo
fan

Nature produces a lot of our light. The main natural sources are the sun, the stars, and the moon; lightning flashes are also a source of light. The sun is our nearest star. It is a huge ball of spinning gases that flare and spurt flames out into space.

Apart from the sun, other stars can be seen on a clear night. Like the sun, they are balls of blazing hot gases giving off heat and light. However, since they are very much further away than the sun, they are only seen as tiny pinpoints of light twinkling in the sky.

The full moon, on a clear night, can provide enough light for us to see quite well. The moon is not a star and therefore makes no light of its own; it only reflects the light of the sun onto the earth. So, although the moon is called a natural light source, the actual source of moonlight is the sun.

A light source made by man is called an artificial source. At first man used some form of flame and, later, gas, to produce light. Today, electric light bulbs and fluorescent lights are most commonly used. Artificial light is essential to man's civilized way of life.

There are two main types of artificial light sources. In one, solid or liquid material is heated. An electric light filament, heated by electricity, glows very brightly, producing a whitish light. The

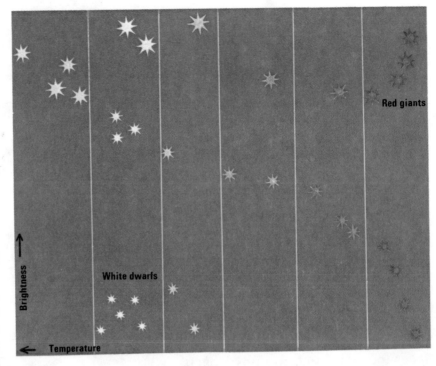

Red giants

White dwarfs

Brightness

Temperature

filament is a coil of thin metal, usually tungsten. The metal magnesium can burn in air, producing an almost blinding white light. The colour of the light emitted by the material depends on its temperature. The hottest materials glow bluish-white. As their temperature is dropped, the glow becomes more yellow, than red, and finally disappears. It is still very hot however.

The other type of artificial source produces light by the heating and resulting glow of the atoms and molecules of a gas. This occurs in some street lights such as sodium vapour and mercury vapour lamps.

Above
The colour of light emitted by stars depends on their temperature. Blue stars and white stars are extremely hot. Yellow and orange stars are cooler—the sun emits yellow light. Red stars are the coolest. The brightness of the star does not depend on temperature. Some red stars, called *red giants*, are much brighter than the white stars known as *white dwarfs*.

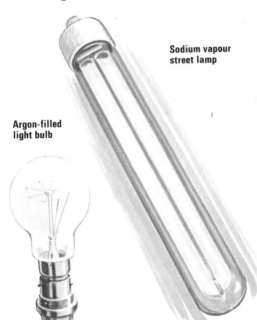

Argon-filled light bulb

Sodium vapour street lamp

Sunlight

The sun, our nearest star, is about 150 million kilometres from the earth. It is a tremendously hot glowing ball of gases held together by gravity. The temperature of its surface is 6000°C; at its centre however, the temperature is about 14 000 000°C. The sun is the main source of the earth's heat and light. This energy is produced by complicated reactions occurring in the centre of the sun. These reactions are called *thermonuclear reactions* (see page 200). They change hydrogen into helium, producing an enormous amount of heat.

During this process the sun loses four million tons of hydrogen per second; it is believed that nuclear reactions will continue for hundreds of millions of years. When the supply of hydrogen is used up, however, the sun will begin to cool down. At present the sun produces so much heat energy that if it were surrounded by ice one kilometre thick it would melt it in about 90 minutes.

The heat in the centre moves out to the surface of the sun. The surface is so hot that it glows bright yellow emitting a tremendous quantity of light. This light and heat energy which is given off by the sun travels through space in all directions.

Left
Without the sun's light plants will not grow. If a log that has lain on grass for a time is moved, the grass lying directly under the log will be pale green or almost white. This is because the grass under the log has not received the necessary light energy to produce chlorophyll or carry on normal growth.

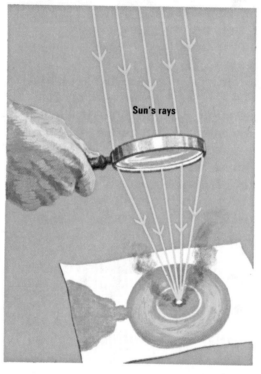

Sun's rays

Left
The heat from the sun can be used to start a fire. The sun's rays passing through the magnifying glass are focused at a point where the strong heat can cause paper, thin twigs, etc. to burn.

Below
A greenhouse is used to provide a warm atmosphere for growing plants. Infrared radiation from the sun can pass through glass and heat up the air inside by transferring some energy to the air molecules. This results in less radiation emerging from the greenhouse than entering. The air therefore stays warmer than the outside air. Some greenhouses have internal heating.

Heat energy is called *infrared radiation*. It cannot be seen, only sensed: anything absorbing these rays becomes warmer. Another form of energy from the sun is *ultraviolet radiation*. Unlike light and infrared rays, very little ultraviolet is able to reach the earth's surface. The fraction that does has a good effect on our health. Some chemical reactions in fact can only take place in the presence of ultraviolet radiation. The heat and light received from the sun is essential to life. Infrared rays keep the earth and atmosphere at a temperature at which we can live. Light rays enable us to see and are essential for plant growth. Without the sun's energy we should live in extreme cold and almost total darkness. We would not survive for long because plants and other forms of life upon which we feed would die without warmth and sunlight.

The process in plants, trees, and grass of absorbing the energy of sunlight is called *photosynthesis*. The green colour of these living things is due to the presence of a dye called *chlorophyll*. This substance absorbs and converts sunlight into chemical energy. Plants and trees use this energy to remove carbon dioxide from the air. Carbon, from the carbon dioxide in the atmosphere, is turned into organic plant material. In this process of photosynthesis the plant gives off

the oxygen which is so essential to both human and animal life.

There is enough heat, light, air, and water on most of the earth's surface for man to survive quite easily. The same conditions do not exist on the other planets in the solar system. None have an atmosphere containing oxygen or any detectable water. The planets nearer to the sun than the earth are extremely hot; those further away are much colder. It is therefore impossible for life as we know it to survive there.

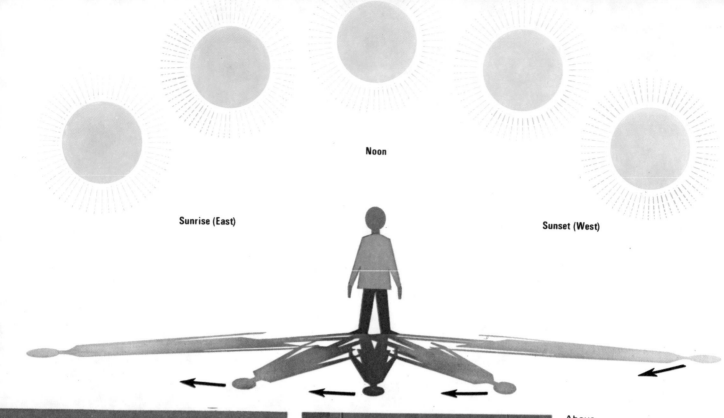

Noon

Sunrise (East)

Sunset (West)

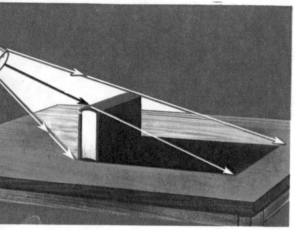

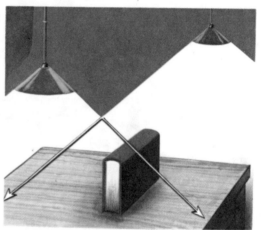

Above
On a sunny day shadows have different lengths and are cast at different angles as the time changes. When the sun is near the horizon, in the early morning or evening, a long shadow is formed by the sun's rays. Its direction depending on whether the sun is rising or setting. When the sun is overhead at midday it casts a short shadow.

Left
A narrow beam of light from a small light source forms a single dark sharp shadow. The length of the shadow depends on the angle of the light beam. With more than one light, producing a wide beam, several indistinct shadows are formed.

Shadows

When light falls on a substance such as glass or water it can pass right through it. These substances are *transparent* to light and we are able to see through them. Other materials, like wood or metal, cannot transmit light (allow light to pass). These materials are called *opaque*.

When light falls on an opaque object, shadows are formed on the opposite side of it where the light cannot get to. They are produced as a result of the simple but important fact that light rays travel in straight lines. Light cannot bend around corners.

Since light travels in straight lines the shadows formed usually have fairly sharp edges. The sharp-

Below
Making a sundial. Fix a piece of paper in a dry sunny position where it can be left. Glue to it a cotton reel with a pencil in it. The shadow of the pencil will move as the day progresses. Every hour mark where the shadow falls and write down the time against it. Now, on a sunny day you can look at the pencil shadow and tell the time from the chart of the sundial.

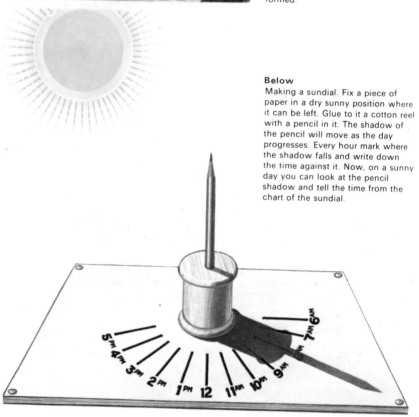

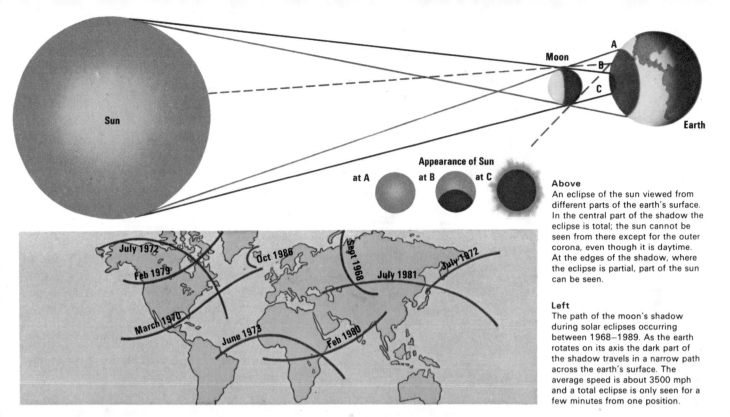

Sun

Moon

A
B
C

Earth

Appearance of Sun

at A — at B — at C

July 1972
Feb 1979
Oct 1986
Sept 1968
July 1981
July 1972
March 1970
June 1973
Feb 1980

Above

An eclipse of the sun viewed from different parts of the earth's surface. In the central part of the shadow the eclipse is total; the sun cannot be seen from there except for the outer corona, even though it is daytime. At the edges of the shadow, where the eclipse is partial, part of the sun can be seen.

Left

The path of the moon's shadow during solar eclipses occurring between 1968–1989. As the earth rotates on its axis the dark part of the shadow travels in a narrow path across the earth's surface. The average speed is about 3500 mph and a total eclipse is only seen for a few minutes from one position.

ness of the edge depends on the position of the light source. A small bright electric light bulb casts a sharp dark shadow behind an object because the light beam is coming from one direction. If there are a number of electric bulbs, the light comes from several directions and the shadows are very indistinct.

The length of a shadow depends on the angle at which light falls on an object. On a sunny day shadows have different lengths at different times of the day because of the changing position of the sun. The sun rises to its highest position at midday then begins to set. In doing so the direction of the sun's rays also changes; shadows are formed in different directions as the day progresses. This changing direction of shadows is used in the *sundial* for telling the time.

Normally, the earth, moon, and sun do not lie in a straight line at any time during the moon's orbit around the earth. But when the moon does pass directly between the earth and the sun (at new moon) it casts a huge shadow on part of the earth's surface. This is called a *solar eclipse*. At the centre of the shadow no light falls on the earth and the eclipse is *total*. At the edges of the shadow some light can reach earth and the eclipse is

A PINHOLE CAMERA

Tin foil

Light rays

Tracing paper

Pin hole

Light-tight box

Above

A pin-hole camera. The image is produced by rays of light from each point on the source passing through the pin hole and falling onto the tracing paper. Together these points of light make up the image.

partial. During an eclipse it grows cold, for we do not receive any heat from the sun.

A *lunar eclipse* can occur at full moon, when the earth, lying directly between the sun and moon casts its shadow on the moon. The moon becomes invisible at places where the eclipse is total or partly hidden where it is a partial eclipse.

You can prove to yourself that light travels in straight lines. Cut a hole out of one side of a box which has a tightly-fitting lid. Cover the hole with tin foil and pierce the centre of the foil with a pin. Remove the other side of the box and replace it with a stout piece of tracing paper. Point the tinfoil end of this pin-hole camera towards a candle some distance away and you will see an upside-down image of the candle on the tracing paper.

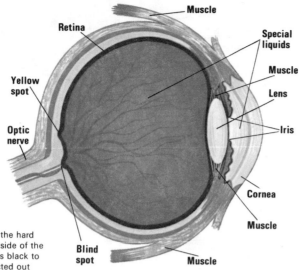

Muscle
Retina
Special liquids
Yellow spot
Muscle
Lens
Optic nerve
Iris
Cornea
Muscle
Blind spot
Muscle

Right
The eye. The sclerotic is the hard white coating on the outside of the eyeball. The inside wall is black to prevent light being reflected out again or causing false impressions by reflection inside the eye. The yellow spot is most sensitive to light detail. A small part of the retina, called the blind spot, is not sensitive to light at all.

Below
A home ciné projector and a segment of a ciné film. When we watch a film the eye sees the slight changes in detail in each picture as a continuous change, which it interprets as movement. The square holes on the edges of the film guide it through the projector.

The eye

Each of your eyes is shaped like a ball, most of which is safely shielded inside your head. At the front of the eye is a transparent outer layer called the *cornea*. The coloured part of the eye is called the *iris*, the middle of which appears black. This is actually a hole, called the *pupil*, that automatically grows bigger or smaller to let in more or less light.

From the pupil the light passes through a lens which can alter its shape to focus images from near or far onto the *retina*. The retina is the backwall on the inside of the eye. It contains millions of light-sensitive cells called *rods* and *cones* (see page 116). These cells convert the light into electrical messages which are carried to the brain by the *optic nerve*.

Every image that is focused on the retina is upside-down. The brain automatically inverts the image to the right way up in our minds. Each eye sees a slightly different view of an object. Be-

cause of this we see a rounded or *three-dimensional* view of things. If we had one eye in the centre of our faces objects would seem much flatter – much as they do in a photograph. A camera uses one lens to produce an image so that the photo only looks *two-dimensional*.

With two eyes we are able to judge the relative position of objects accurately. Close one eye and hold your finger upright so that it is in line with a tall thin object such as a ruler, some distance away. Open that eye and close the other one still holding your finger in the same position. You will find the ruler is no longer in line with your finger.

A ciné film consists of a long series of pictures each slightly different from the last and separated from each other by a short space. When you are watching a film in the cinema your eyes remember the image of the picture just seen until the next one is shown. They cannot form a separate image of each picture (or *frame*) because the film is running through the projector too quickly. The normal speed at which films are shown is 24 frames per second. Because of the changing positions of the object in successive frames we get an impression of movement.

Our brains give us a picture of the outside world by means of the image formed on the retina of the eye. Sometimes the brain is misled and interprets the information wrongly. We then see an *optical illusion*. Straight lines can be made to appear curved, two lines of the same length seem to be of different lengths. The eye is being misled by whatever else is surrounding these lines.

We often have a false impression of movement. If two trains are sitting in a station, each about to move, passengers in one train seeing the carriages of the other train moving often think, incorrectly, that their train is leaving the station. They were expecting to move, and when they see movement assume their train is departing.

Above
The law of perspective. As an object moves into the distance it always appears to grow smaller. In the same way parallel lines, like the edges of a road or a railway line, give the illusion of drawing together as they become further away. These things appear to us in perspective.

Far right
Optical illusion of movement. If you stare at the centre of the picture the lines will appear to move in a most disturbing way. You may even see colours moving out from the centre. Now look quickly at a blank wall and you will continue to see movements of the lines for a few seconds.

Right
Optical illusions. In figs 1 and 2 the two red lines appear to be of different lengths because of the angle of the green lines. They are actually exactly the same length. In figs 3 and 4, the red lines appear curved. In fact they are straight.

Below
This picture can be seen in either of two ways. If you stare at it for long enough you will see first a candlestick then suddenly it will look like two faces. You will not see both candlestick and faces at the same time.

Below right
Which does this look like to you? Is it a duck with a long bill, or a rabbit with its ears back?

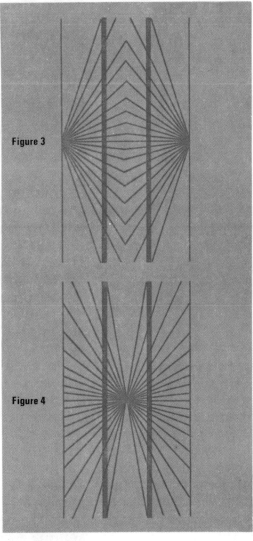

Figure 3

Figure 4

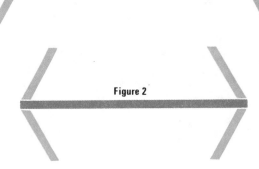

Figure 1

Figure 2

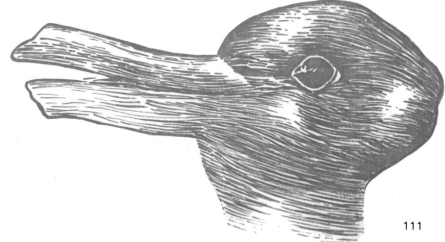

111

Far right
Sir Isaac Newton's famous experiment to split light into its colours, was first performed in 1666 when he was only 23 years old. Newton also performed a similar experiment using two prisms, the second one upside down compared with the first. The first prism split the light into colours; the second prism recombined the colours into white light.

Right
A glass chandelier is an expensive but beautiful light fixture. It is made from hundreds of pieces of glass, which split up the white light emitted from the electric light bulbs.

Right
Glass prisms are used in optical instruments such as binoculars and the periscope. A prism was used by Newton to form his spectrum.

The spectrum

When you look at a glass chandelier which is lit, or at a jewel, such as a diamond, which is cut in a special way, you can see many colours. This happens even though the light shining on the glass or gem appears to be white. This is because properly cut glass, or even a drop of water, can split up white light into many colours. These colours form a rainbow pattern called a *spectrum* of light.

Sir Isaac Newton, was a very great scientist who lived in the seventeenth century. He was the first person to show that light could be split up into different colours. Newton closed all the shutters in his room, to make it dark, then made a small hole in one of them. The sun shone through the hole onto a small piece of glass with triangular sides called a *prism* and then onto a screen. The spectrum on the screen showed coloured bands of red, orange, yellow, green, blue, indigo and violet. Newton realized that the prism had split the white light up into these colours.

Ordinary white light, from the sun or an electric bulb, is in fact made up of thousands of colours, all slightly different from each other. These colours tend to fall into the seven groups of rainbow colours mentioned above.

There are many everyday examples of spectra, such as the rainbow. The bow is formed by the sun shining through thousands of water droplets in a rain storm or in the spray from a waterfall. When different kinds of light are used, different spectra are formed. Look through an odd-shaped lump of glass and see if you can notice the difference between ordinary electric light, fluorescent lighting, and light from a sodium street lamp. You will find that sodium light will not split up at all, for the light is almost pure yellow.

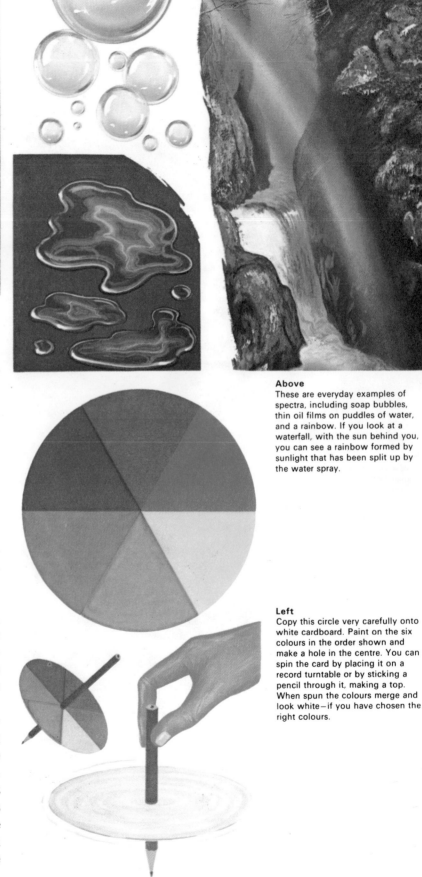

A series of fine lines, close together, can produce a spectrum. You may see colours when you look sideways at a record; similar colours can be seen if you look through your hair or eyelashes into a bright light. Thin films will also split white light into colours; the thin layer of oil on water, which is often seen on puddles after rain, looks multi-coloured, as do soap bubbles.

To test whether white light really is a combination of different coloured lights you can produce it from a mixture of several colours. This is not difficult, but needs care. Copy the picture (right) showing a circle, with the different colours painted in just the right proportions. If you spin this circle all the colours seem to merge until the circle looks greyish white.

When the circle is moving quickly, the human eye cannot see each colour separately, but only the result of mixing them all together. Whenever you look at white light you are really seeing all the colours of the rainbow. However, your eye cannot distinguish between them unless they pass through some material that separates them.

Above
These are everyday examples of spectra, including soap bubbles, thin oil films on puddles of water, and a rainbow. If you look at a waterfall, with the sun behind you, you can see a rainbow formed by sunlight that has been split up by the water spray.

Left
Copy this circle very carefully onto white cardboard. Paint on the six colours in the order shown and make a hole in the centre. You can spin the card by placing it on a record turntable or by sticking a pencil through it, making a top. When spun the colours merge and look white—if you have chosen the right colours.

Primary colours

Sunlight, or light from an electric light bulb, is called white light. White light is actually a mixture of many different colours. We are unable to see these colours as the eye cannot split up white light. However, light can be split up into its component colours by water droplets or bits of glass; the rainbow shows the groups of colours – red, orange, yellow, green, blue, and violet of which light is made. These same colours can be mixed together, in the right proportions, to produce white light.

It is not necessary for all these six colours to be used in forming white light. Only three colours are needed. These colours are called *primary colours*. Red, green, and blue light are one set of primary colours. In the right proportions they can be mixed to give white light. If these proportions are changed, light of a different colour is obtained. *Any* colour can be obtained from certain proportions of these three coloured lights. The primary colours for mixing paints are not the same as those for mixing lights: a different process is involved (see page 119).

You have possibly seen lights mixed in the theatre. Two coloured spotlights can produce a third quite differently coloured circle of light at the point where the beams cross on the stage. You could try similar experiments at home using three torches producing different colours. For the best results, the experiment should be done in a dark room; also the beam of light from the torches should be quite narrow. To obtain the different coloured beams coloured cellophane, fastened over the torch with an elastic band, is useful. Sweet wrappings are ideal for this, but you may have to try several shades of each colour in order to get a good result.

Mixing two of the three primary colours can give interesting results. Red and blue light mixed give a

Right
You can practice mixing coloured lights in a darkened room, using coloured paper and torches. Let the beams cross on a piece of white paper.

Right
The colours you would see on the paper if green, red, and blue light are mixed in the right proportions. Where all three meet the result is white; when only two primary colours cross, a colour is formed which is *complementary* to the third primary colour.

Right
Results you can get by mixing cyan, magenta, and yellow light. When all three lights cross, red, green, and blue light is present in equal proportions, so white light is made. When two, such as yellow and magenta cross, there are enough colours to make white light; but as an extra amount of red is present, the light appears red.

colour called *magenta* (pinkish-purple); blue and green produce *cyan* (greenish-blue); most surprisingly, red and green light mixed together produce *yellow* light.

Any two colours that produce white light when they are mixed are said to be *complementary* colours. Yellow light (a mixture of red and green light) is the complementary colour to blue light. Together they give white light. In the same way magenta is the complementary colour to green and cyan is complementary to red.

A mixture of the correct proportions of red, green, and blue light gives white light. When yellow, magenta, and cyan lights are mixed they can also give white light. Thus these three colours can be considered as a set of three primary colours. Yellow and magenta together produce red light, yellow and cyan produce green light, and magenta and cyan form blue light. If you find paper or cellophane of these three colours with which to cover torches, you can prove this for yourself.

White light can therefore be thought of as being made up of three primary colours. Light of a colour other than white is produced by mixing the right amounts of primary colours.

These facts are the basis of several processes, including *colour vision* and also *colour television* (see page 116). In television systems the reproduction of the correct colour is extremely important.

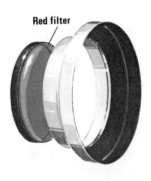

Red filter

(see page 116)

Above
Colour filters, used in photography, consist of a circular sheet of dyed transparent material called gelatin held in a special metal or plastic ring. Coloured glass can also be used. They are usually fitted to the camera in front of the lens.

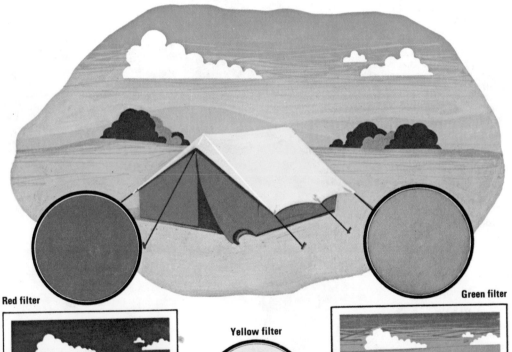

Red filter

Green filter

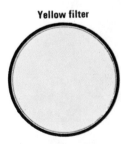

Yellow filter

Left
Colour filters are used to modify the colour of light before it falls onto the film. A yellow filter allows green and red light to pass through, but stops blue light. A red (or green) filter passes red (or green) light. Objects of colours which have not been transmitted appear darker than normal as less light has fallen on the film.

Colour vision

Man has five senses: sight, sound, touch, taste, and smell. The most strongly developed sense is sight. Man lives in a world of colour, of light and darkness. This is not always so with other living things that have often developed other senses, such as hearing or smell, to a much greater degree than ours.

The human eye is a complicated organ. When light falls onto the pupil, it is focused by the eye lens so that light falls on the retina at the back of the eye.

There are two types of cell in the retina that are sensitive to light. They are called *rods* and *cones*. The rods work at night or in dark areas, when there is not much light. They cannot distinguish between different colours. This means we have only black and white vision when it is dark. Bright colours are only seen by the eye as different shades of light or dark grey.

The cones are responsible for our colour vision. It was Helmholtz who first suggested that there are three sets of cones, one set sensitive to red light, one to blue light, and the other set to green light. Any colour can be formed by a suitable combination of red, green, and blue light (see page 114). When light falls on the retina one or more of the sets of cones are sensitized, depending on the colour. Yellow light will produce an equal response in the red and green cones but none in the blue cones. The response of the cones is converted into an electrical signal which is carried by the optic nerve to the brain. Thus the brain is told the colour of the light.

Colour television works in a way that is fairly similar to the process involved in colour vision. When a scene is televised the light is split up into the three colours, red, green, and blue, of which it is composed. Each colour is converted into a separate electrical signal, the strength of which depends on

Right
Hermann von Helmholtz was born in 1821. He studied medicine and physics and made great contributions to both fields, especially in the workings of the eye and the ear, and in electricity and magnetism. He was also a mathematician. He died in 1894.

Helmholtz

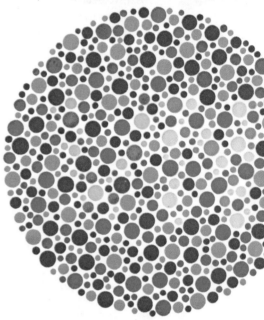

Right
Colour blindness occurs when one or more of the three sets of cones in the eye are not working properly. The person has difficulty in distinguishing between colours; sometimes he finds it impossible. With red-green blindness he would see only the letter N in the diagram. The V would merge into the background.

Below
Man can see all the colours of the rainbow. Other living things cannot see this whole range of colours; some animals possibly have no colour vision and only see in black and white. The honeybee is almost blind to red but it can see ultraviolet very well. It can follow ultraviolet guide lines on the petals of some flowers which lead it to the nectar at the base of the petals. Man is totally blind to ultraviolet light.

The evening primrose as we see it

The evening primrose as the bee sees it, with ultraviolet guidelines on it

the amount of *intensity* of the coloured light.

These three signals are transmitted from the broadcasting station and are received by television sets in the home. The signals are used to produce three electron beams, carrying the red, green, and blue signals. These beams scan the television screen in a way that is similar to the scanning of a black and white television screen by a single electron beam (see page 245).

The screen is coated with over a million phosphor dots, arranged in threes. Each member of the trio emits either red, green, or blue light when electrons fall on it. The three electrical signals are thus converted to red, green, and blue light depending on the strength of the signal.

The tiny phosphor trio is seen as a single pinpoint of light the colour of which depends on the proportions of red, green, and blue light emitted. As the television scene changes, the strength of each electron beam alters and the resulting colours change accordingly.

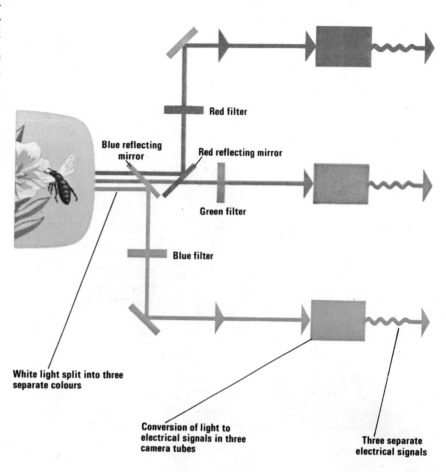

Red filter

Blue reflecting mirror

Red reflecting mirror

Green filter

Blue filter

White light split into three separate colours

Conversion of light to electrical signals in three camera tubes

Three separate electrical signals

Shadow mask: plate onto which electron beams are focused then made to diverge through holes

Part of glass television screen covered with trios of phosphor dots

Above
In colour television, light is split into the correct proportions of red, green, and blue light, by using special mirrors and filters. The mirrors reflect their own colour and transmit the others. The filters only transmit light of their own colour. Each colour, fed into a separate camera tube, is then converted into an electrical signal.

Electron beams carrying the red, green and blue signals

Direction of scan of electron beams

Left
A colour television screen is covered in phosphor dots arranged in trios. The electron beam carrying the red signal is made to fall on one member of the trio which will then emit red light. The 'blue' electron beam must fall on the phosphor that emits blue light, similarly for the green signal. These three lights are seen as a single pinpoint of coloured light.

Coloured objects

Mixing coloured lights gives results which are quite different from those obtained by mixing paints. Mixing blue and yellow lights gives white light. A mixture of blue and yellow paint gives green. Two different processes of colour formation are involved.

The colour of objects depends on what colours of light they can *reflect*. When exposed to light, materials *absorb* some of the colours and *reflect* the rest. Light from the sun or an electric light bulb is a mixture of red, orange, yellow, green, blue, and violet. However it can also be considered as a mixture of the three colours red, green, and blue (see page 114). These three are a set of *primary colours*.

If white light falls on an object and it absorbs green and blue, but reflects red light, then it is a *red object*. All coloured objects absorb every colour of light except the one which is reflected: this is the colour which your eye sees.

This is, of course, true for colours other than red, green and blue. Yellow light can be made by mixing

Above
Coloured objects absorb certain colours from light and reflect the rest. The eye sees the reflected light only, which is therefore the colour that the object appears to be.

Right
When light falls on the surface of a blackboard every colour in the light is absorbed; none are reflected. The white chalk marks however reflect every colour. The combination of these colours makes the reflected light appear white.

Above
The picture drawn in red and green appears normal when viewed in white light. In red light both the white paper and the red marks on it reflect red light; the red marks will therefore merge into the background and disappear. As there is no green light to reflect, the green marks appear black.

Right
A colour negative is in complementary colours to the finished photo. The guardsman's jacket is peacock blue (blue and green mixed). He is standing on purple (blue and red mixed) grass; the sky is yellow (red and green mixed). His hat and trousers are white. The final photograph is seen on the right.

green and red light together; a yellow object absorbs only the blue part of white light; it reflects both the red and the green.

A black object looks dark because it absorbs *all* the light falling on it, and reflects no colour at all; white things absorb *no* coloured light; they reflect every colour falling on them. When they are illuminated by white light, they reflect white light. If the light shining on an object is not white, the colour of the object will change. You may have noticed this when you look at people at night, under yellow sodium street lighting. In white light, blue materials absorb red and green. In yellow sodium light they become black, because sodium light contains no blue light to be reflected.

Mixing paint is not like mixing light. For painting, the primary colours are red, blue, and yellow. When these three colours are mixed in the right amounts blackish-brown paint is produced. Other mixtures are used to produce different colours. You cannot, however, make white paint by mixing other colours.

Mixing lights (additive)

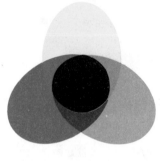

Mixing paints (subtractive)

Above
The different colours obtained when coloured lights (*top*) and coloured paints (*bottom*) are mixed.

When cloth is dyed, or a coloured magazine picture is printed, the coloured ink or dye is put on in successive layers of primary colours, so that the mixing is just right to get the necessary colour tones in the pattern or picture.

Colour film consists of three layers of emulsion (see page 214). The image of a red object will be recorded on one layer sensitive only to red light, a green object on a layer sensitive only to green light, and a blue object on the third blue-sensitive layer. A yellow object appears on both red- and green-sensitive layers. The colours on the negative, however, are *complementary* to the actual colours. The red object appears blue-green, the green object red-blue, and the blue object yellow. In the same way yellow objects will appear blue, purple objects green, and so on. Black objects are white and vice versa. A complementary colour, such as yellow, mixed with its primary colour, blue, produces white light. In the final photo, produced by another complicated process, complementary colours are reconverted to their primary colours.

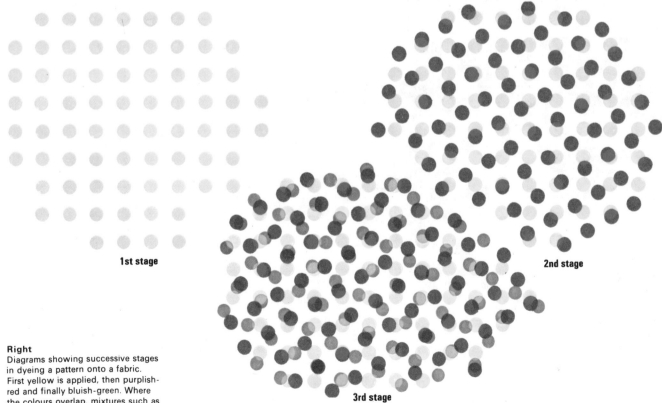

1st stage

2nd stage

3rd stage

Right
Diagrams showing successive stages in dyeing a pattern onto a fabric. First yellow is applied, then purplish-red and finally bluish-green. Where the colours overlap, mixtures such as red or green are made.

119

Right
First law of reflection. The angle of
incidence at which light from the
candle hits the mirror, is equal to the
angle of reflection. If the light arrives
at right angles to the mirror, it will be
reflected in the same direction; the
angles of incidence and reflection
are both equal to zero.

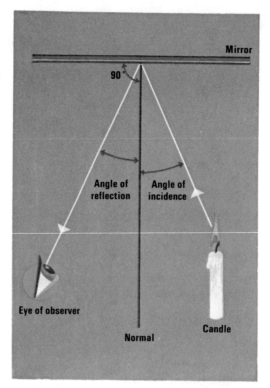

Mirror

90°

Angle of
reflection

Angle of
incidence

Eye of observer

Normal

Candle

Far right
You can see yourself as you look to
other people by looking in two
mirrors of a dressing table, set at
right angles to each other. Two
images are formed.
By making the angle between the
mirrors small, several images of an
object can be seen.

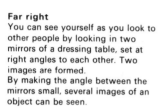

Below
Mirror-writing is laterally inverted.
Look at the image of some writing
in a second mirror. The writing will
be inverted a second time and will
be turned back to normal.

Reflection of light

When light is bounced off a surface,
it is said to be *reflected*. When you
look in a mirror you see a picture of
yourself – your reflection. The picture of an object seen in a mirror is
called its *image*. An image is only
seen if the mirror is flat. Rough or
uneven surfaces can only form a
distorted image.

In addition to being flat, a good
reflecting surface must also be
shiny. A piece of flat rubber does

not form a reflected image. Rubber
is an example of a *matt* or non-shiny
surface.

Metal is a good reflector of light,
but it is difficult to make it perfectly flat. Nevertheless, very early
mirrors were made of pure metal or
bronze; these must have given distorted images and were easily
dented. It was a long time before
better mirrors were produced.

A modern mirror is made of a
small sheet of glass which can be
made perfectly flat. The light is
reflected off a thin layer of shiny
metal, such as silver or aluminium,
on the back of the glass. To prevent
the metal from being scratched it is
protected by a coating of paint.

The laws of reflection can be used
to find out where the image of an
object, in front of a mirror, will be
formed. The first law states that the
angle at which the light from an
object hits a mirror (called the
angle of incidence) is equal to the
angle at which light leaves the
mirror (called the *angle of reflection*). These angles are measured
from a line at right angles to the
mirror called the *normal*. The
second law is that the incident ray,
the normal, and the reflected ray
lie in the same plane. This means

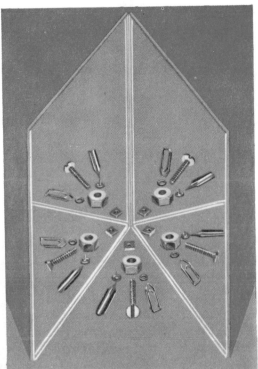

Left
Make a pattern of small objects on a piece of paper. Stand two mirrors, two edges touching, on the paper, with the pattern lying between the mirrors. Looking down into the mirrors you will see the pattern repeated several times. The smaller the angle between the mirrors, the more images are seen.

Below
To make a kaleidoscope, first tape the back of the long edges of two mirrors together and roll a piece of cardboard round them. Tape a piece of clear polythene over one end, lay several bits of paper, coloured side down, on it and cover them loosely with a second piece of polythene. Cover the other end with a piece of paper making a small viewing hole in it. Hold the kaleidoscope towards the light when you are looking through it. Shake it to make the pattern change.

that they can all be drawn on a flat piece of cardboard.

The laws of reflection can be checked by using a small flat mirror. Hold an object, such as a pencil, to one side of the mirror and move your head until you see the image of the pencil. It is only seen when light from the pencil makes an angle with the mirror equal to the angle at which your eye is looking at the mirror.

The shapes of an object and its image, formed by a flat mirror, are the same. The image is no bigger, smaller, fatter, or thinner than the object. It is, however, *laterally inverted*. This means that the left-hand side of the object appears on the right-hand side of the image and vice versa. A reflection of your left hand in a mirror looks like your right hand because your two hands are mirror images of each other. As a result, no one sees themselves as they really are when they look in a mirror.

Plane mirrors are used in many optical instruments. In the *microscope* it directs light onto the object. In the *sextant*, an instrument used by navigators, a plane mirror is used to determine the exact angle of the sun above the horizon.

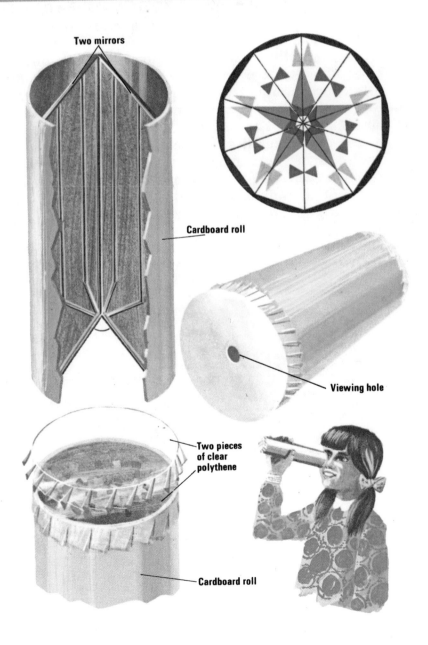

Two mirrors

Cardboard roll

Viewing hole

Two pieces of clear polythene

Cardboard roll

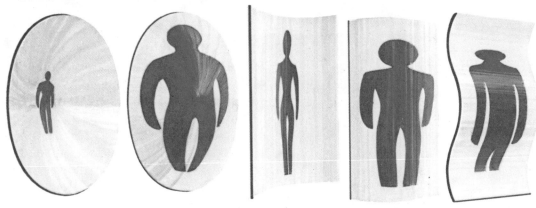

Left
Hall of mirrors. When convex and concave mirrors are combined on one piece of glass, very funny effects can be seen. These distorting mirrors are sometimes part of a fun-fair, and make people look as though they have odd faces, and arms and legs of the wrong length.

Curved mirrors

Curved mirrors are made in a similar way to flat mirrors except that the pieces of glass are curved as though they were part of giant spheres or bubbles. A *concave* mirror curves inwards, (into a 'cave' shape); *convex* mirrors bulge outwards. The laws of reflection are the same for curved mirrors as for plane or flat mirrors.

A beam of *parallel* light consists of light rays travelling in the same direction. If rays of parallel light fall on a concave mirror they are reflected so that they converge to a fixed point, called the *focus* of the mirror. The focus lies on the *principal axis* of the mirror. The distance between the focus and the centre of the mirror is called the *focal length*. Convex mirrors do not bring light to a focus; instead, the reflected rays are spread out (diverge) as though

they came from a point *behind* the mirror. This point is called. a *virtual* focus.

A curved mirror can change the size of an object positioned in front of it. The effect depends on whether the object lies between the focus and the mirror or beyond the focus. The position of the image is found by drawing *ray diagrams*.

Shaving mirrors are concave mirrors with a focal length of about one metre. If a person stands very close to this mirror (between the focus and the mirror) rays of light from the person's face produce an image in the mirror which appears to be of a much larger face. This is a *magnified* image. However if the mirror is pointed at an electric light bulb a long way off, the mirror concentrates the light from it; a very small bright image of the bulb can be seen on a piece of paper held at the focus about one metre away from the mirror. This image is upside down (*inverted*). Coloured

Left
Hall of mirrors. When convex and concave mirrors are combined on one piece of glass, very funny effects can be seen. These distorting mirrors are sometimes part of a fun-fair, and make people look as though they have odd faces, and arms and legs of the wrong length.

Right
Convex mirrors spread out the light from a distant object, so it *appears* to have come from a focus behind the mirror.

Right
A ray diagram showing how an object lying between the focus and a concave mirror is magnified by the mirror. Any ray parallel to the principal axis must pass through the focus. The image is formed where two rays cross.

Right
If the object is a long way from the focus of a concave mirror, a small, inverted (upside-down image) can be seen on a piece of paper held near the mirror.

Right
Convex mirrors collect light from a very wide area round the mirror, producing a small upright image. As the image appears to be formed behind the mirror, it is called a *virtual* image.

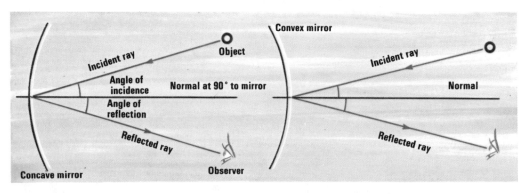

Left
All curved mirrors obey the same laws of reflection as plane mirrors. That is, the angle of incidence is equal to the angle of reflection.

Left
If a concave mirror is held facing the sun, the parallel rays of sunlight are focused, forming a bright spot. On a hot day, the focused light can set paper alight.

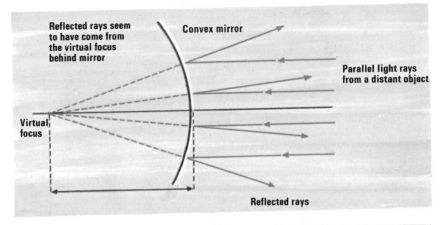

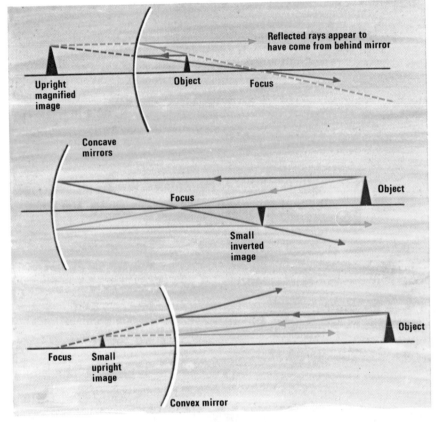

images of brightly lit scenes out of doors can be shone onto a piece of paper in the same way. The *camera obscura* works like this.

Convex mirrors behave differently. They can collect light from objects which are widely spread round the mirror, and reflect this light in a narrow beam. Because of this, convex mirrors can be used as driving mirrors, as the driver can see a large area of the road behind him in a small mirror.

Very large *concave* mirrors are used to collect light from distant objects in one spot. This is the way the big astronomical telescopes work. For the best results the mirror is shaped not like part of a sphere, but more like the inside of an eggshell. This *parabolic* shape can bring light to a perfect focus. Concave mirrors are also used in car headlamps. A parallel beam of light is made by putting the bulb at the focus of the mirror.

Convex mirrors are used where the observer needs to see a large area in the mirror. Apart from driving mirrors, other examples are in buses, where the conductor needs to see a whole deck of the bus from upstairs or downstairs; and a supermarket where the manager needs to see all the shopping area at one glance, to detect shoplifters.

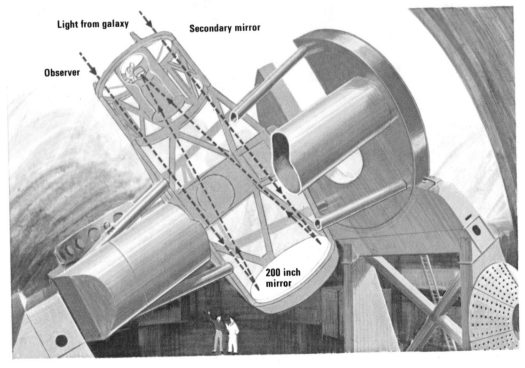

Left
An astronomical telescope, using a parabolic mirror, collects light from the stars at a small accurate focus. This image can then be photographed.

Left
The calm surface of a lake will produce a perfect reflection of the surrounding buildings and trees. When the wind ruffles the surface, the light is reflected in all directions and the sharp image disappears.

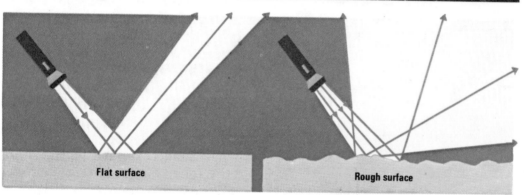

Flat surface   **Rough surface**

Left
If a torch beam is pointed towards a shiny flat surface, the reflected beam remains fairly narrow. If the surface is not flat, the light is reflected in all directions; however, the laws of reflection are still obeyed.

Reflecting surfaces

A silvered mirror is not the only surface that can reflect light. If you can swim, you may have looked upwards at the surface of the water when you were diving. The surface looks very bright from underneath because the sky is above it, but it is also shiny, like a mirror; it is therefore possible to see reflections of things in the water.

You can also see reflections if you look from air onto water. The sharpness of the image depends on how calm the water is. At the seaside, although the water is constantly moving you can see the blurred shadow of a seagull or an aircraft as it flies over.

Many materials can be made smooth enough to reflect light well, but the most common are metals, glass, and liquids, like water. Nearly everyone has noticed their own reflection in a car or train window, and of course the image is much better if it is dark outside, so that no confusing light is passed through the glass. Reflections in

Left
You can see your reflection in a car or train window. It looks quite clear if it is dark outside.

Below
Pepper's ghost. This theatrical effect can be used to produce a ghost-like image which seems to materialize in the centre of the stage. In fact, it is only a reflection on a sheet of glass across the stage, of a person or object standing in the wings against a black background. In this case the ghost is a lighted candle. Shine a torch on it, and from the front the candle will appear to be standing inside the bottle of water – still burning. Switch off the torch and the candle disappears.

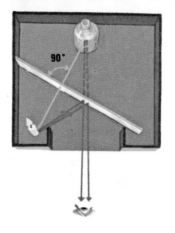

90°

shop windows often prevent the objects on show being clearly seen. Some shops and showrooms therefore have specially curved glass in their windows. Sunlight or street lighting is then reflected in such a way that it does not confuse the observers' view of the display.

Every substance reflects some light, but unless it is smooth the reflections are scattered in all directions. Rooms are bright in the daytime even if the sun does not shine into them; this is because the sky and everything else reflects light in all directions. When the sun is covered in cloud, sunlight enters the cloud and is reflected or scattered off the particles of water vapour at odd angles. Some of this light enters buildings through windows and open doors. In a room, the ceiling and walls reflect light too. This means that no hard shadows can be formed and the light is much softer than it is on bright sunny days.

When light enters a transparent medium such as glass or water, most of it passes straight through but some of it can be reflected at the second surface. If the angle of incidence of the ray at this surface is greater than a *critical angle* no light will pass straight through; it will *all* be reflected. This is called *total internal reflection*.

A prism is a piece of glass with triangular ends. If the angle at which the light ray hits a prism is greater than the critical angle, total internal reflection occurs, and the prism can function as a mirror. Prisms are used as reflectors in binoculars, and in submarine periscopes. With a periscope, objects can be seen that are not in a direct line of sight.

You can make a model periscope at home by using mirrors instead of prisms. Two mirrors must be arranged immediately above each other at 45° to the vertical. With this you can look over the heads of a crowd, or see round a corner.

Some optical illusions involve reflections, such as Pepper's Ghost, a popular theatrical effect.

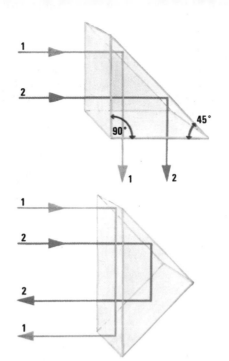

Left
Total internal reflection in a prism. Depending on the shape of the prism and the position of the incident beam, the reflected beam can be turned through 90° (as in the periscope), turned through 180°, returning in the same direction, or simply turned upside down.

Below
To make a model periscope, cut a hole at each end of a large, long cardboard tube, on opposite sides of it, then cover the ends of the tube. Wedge two small flat mirrors into each end, vertically above each other, and adjust their angle until you can see the image of some object above you, reflected from the upper mirror into the lower one. Fix the mirrors in place with tape.

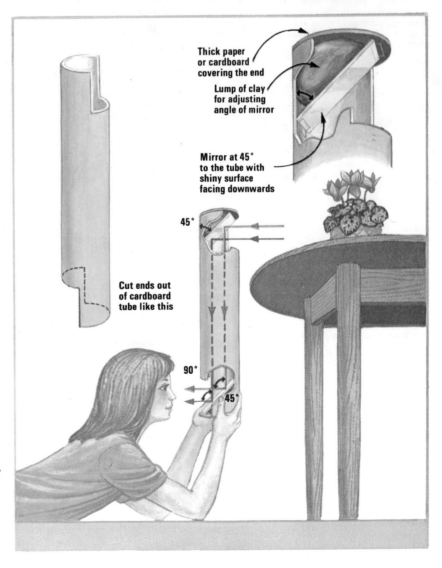

Thick paper or cardboard covering the end

Lump of clay for adjusting angle of mirror

Mirror at 45° to the tube with shiny surface facing downwards

Cut ends out of cardboard tube like this

Refraction of light

Put a pencil in a jam jar of water and look at it carefully. From some angles the pencil will look bent. If you have a pencil torch which produces a narrow beam of light, try shining it into the jar. In a darkened room you can see that the light bends when it passes from air into water. This bending of light, which occurs in both these experiments, is called *refraction*.

Above
A narrow beam of light is bent upwards slightly as it passes from air into water. When it emerges from the water into air again it is bent downwards. It is then travelling at the same angle as it was before it entered the water.

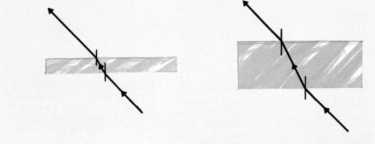

Right
A swirling effect is seen as hot sugar solution (containing coffee) is poured into a jam jar of water. Light travels more slowly in the denser sugar solution than in water and the resulting bending of the light rays produces the swirls.

Light travels at different speeds in different transparent materials; because of this, when light passes from one material to another its direction changes slightly. Refraction causes the shimmering effect just above the ground on a hot day. Light travels through the hot air rising from the ground faster than it travels through the cooler air above, and so a heat haze is produced. You can produce the same effect at home by shining a powerful torch beam at a plain wall just above a candle flame; dancing patterns and shadows appear on the wall behind the candle.

If you dissolve some sugar, about one teaspoonful, in a very small amount of hot water, and then pour this solution into water in a jam jar, you can see a swirling effect as the denser solution sinks to the bottom; this is because light travels slower through the sugar solution than through pure water.

Above
As a ray of light goes from a less dense medium (air) to a more dense medium (glass), it is bent towards the normal. Passing from a more dense to a less dense medium, the light ray is bent away from the normal. The ray of light coming out of the glass is parallel to the ray going in, but it is displaced sideways. The amount it is displaced depends on the thickness of the glass.

Right
A coin in a glass of water will appear much nearer to the surface than it really is, due to refraction of the light ray from the coin to your eye. The eye sees the image as if the ray has travelled straight to it. Real depth divided by apparent depth gives the refractive index of water (1·5).

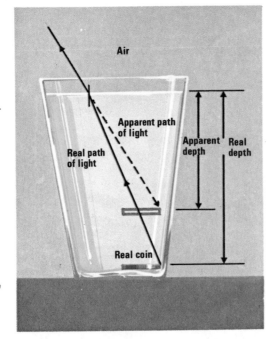

Air

Apparent path of light

Apparent depth

Real depth

Real path of light

Real coin

Refraction is caused by light travelling at different speeds in different materials. If light travels from a less dense to a more dense material (say from air to glass), it is bent or refracted towards the normal. Light passing from glass to air would be refracted away from the normal. (The *normal* is an imaginary line perpendicular to the refracting surface). The light always bends by a definite amount. This amount depends on the *angle of incidence*, the angle at which the light strikes the surface of the material, and on the material itself.

The *refractive index* of the material tells us how slowly light

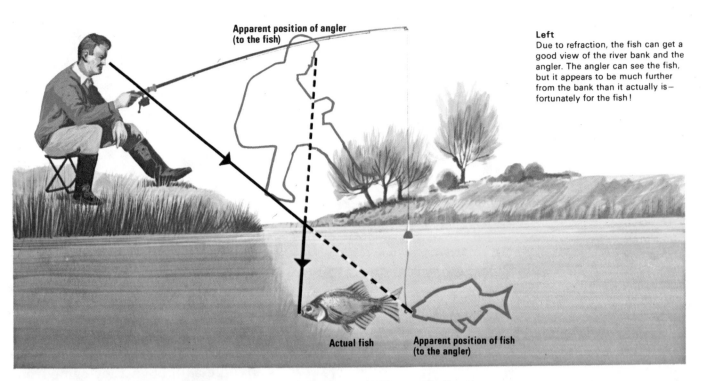

Apparent position of angler
(to the fish)

Actual fish

Apparent position of fish
(to the angler)

Left
Due to refraction, the fish can get a good view of the river bank and the angler. The angler can see the fish, but it appears to be much further from the bank than it actually is—fortunately for the fish!

will travel through the material and hence how much it will be bent. The refractive index equals the speed of light in air divided by the speed of light in the material. For glass it equals 1·5, for water it is 1·3. The denser the material, the higher the refractive index.

Drop a coin into a jam jar of water and look into it from above. Put a chalk mark on the jar where you think the coin is. You will probably find that the coin is much lower down than you had expected. This too is a result of refraction. Swimming pools and rivers may look very shallow when you look in, but are really much deeper.

Prisms or water can split light into the colours of the spectrum (see page 112). This is because the different colours in white light are refracted by the glass or water by different amounts. Violet light is refracted most, and red light least, when white light passes from air into water or glass.

In a rainbow, the sunlight is refracted when it goes into the droplets of water. It is reflected inside them and refracted again as it passes out. The colour seen by an observer will depend on the angle at which he looks at each droplet.

Below
When sunlight falls on a raindrop, the light splits into colours, since the violet end of the spectrum is refracted more than the red end. The colours are reflected inside the drop, and then refracted once more when they emerge.

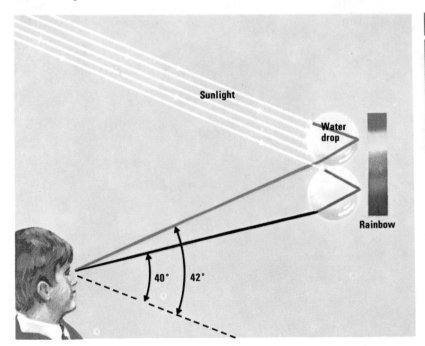

Sunlight

Water drop

Rainbow

40°   42°

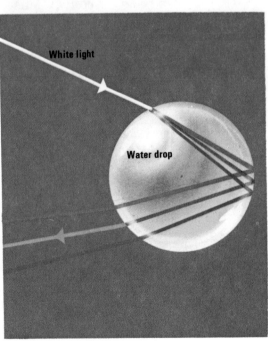

White light

Water drop

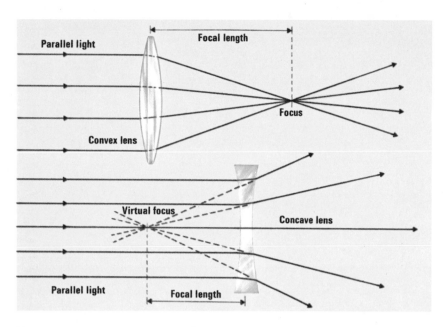

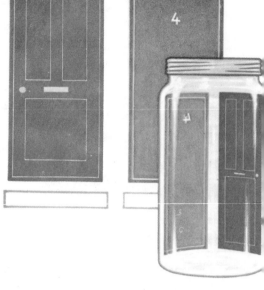

Lenses

A lens is a piece of glass or other transparent solid, cut so that it has at least one surface shaped like part of a large sphere.

Lenses are used to *diverge* light (spread it out), or *converge* light (bring it closer together). They do this by the process of *refraction.*

When light passes from air into glass it is bent towards the normal (perpendicular to the glass surface). When the light emerges it is bent away from the normal.

The actual path of the light rays (whether they converge or diverge) depends on the shape of the lens. The two main kinds of lenses are *convex* lenses, which bulge out on each side, and *concave* lenses which cave in towards the centre.

Convex lenses make parallel light rays falling on them converge to a single point called the *focus*

of the lens. Concave lenses make parallel light rays spread out or diverge as though they came from a *virtual* focus. In each case the distance between the focus and the centre of the lens is called the *focal length* of the lens.

A convex lens makes a good magnifying glass. If an object is placed between the lens and its focus, and you look at it from the other side of the lens, it will appear larger, and further from the lens that it really is. If the object is beyond the focus, you will not see an image at all, but you should be able to form a real inverted (upside down) image by holding a piece of paper on the opposite side of the lens to the object, especially if the object is as bright as a light bulb. For a concave lens, no matter where the object is, the image is always on the same side of the lens as the object, and is smaller than the object.

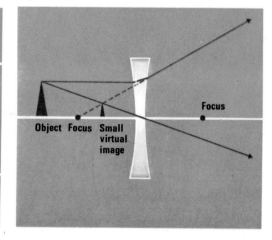

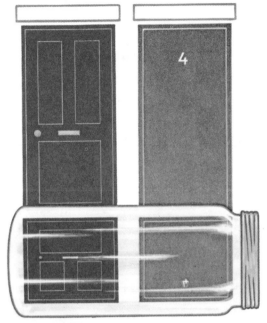

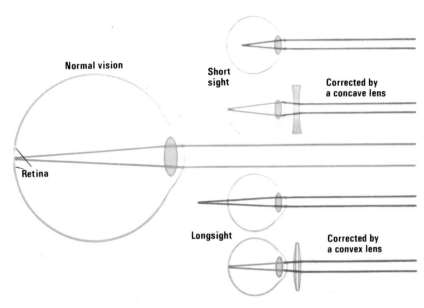

Normal vision

Retina

Short sight

Corrected by a concave lens

Longsight

Corrected by a convex lens

To find the position of the image formed by a lens, *ray diagrams* are drawn. These are similar to the diagrams drawn for curved mirrors and their images. A ray of light parallel to the axis of a thin lens must pass through the focus. If the ray goes through the centre of the lens, it does not change direction.

The human eye contains a convex lens which focuses light onto the *retina* at the back of the eye. Some people's eye-lenses focus the light before it reaches the retina – these are short-sighted people; others focus light beyond the retina because they are long-sighted. Spectacles contain specially made lenses, to bring light to a focus on the retina where it forms a sharp image.

Lenses are used in many optical instruments such as cameras, microscopes, projectors, binoculars, and telescopes. For the biggest telescopes curved mirrors are used, as very large lenses are difficult to make and they also suffer from colour distortion.

All lenses bend light by refraction. The colours, of which white light is composed, are refracted (bent) by different amounts in glass. The light emerging from a lens is therefore slightly coloured. This is always a problem with instruments using lenses. It is possible to reduce this coloration by sticking together two lenses, of different shapes and types of glass. This lens combination is called an *achromat* and is widely used.

Above left
A closed jar full of water makes a simple convex lens. Light from the sun or a torch bulb can be brought to a focus by this lens. If you look at objects through the water they will seem distorted. Their shapes depend on whether the jar is held upright or on its side.

Above
A normal eye-lens focuses light on the retina. If a person is short sighted, light is focused in front of the retina. Concave lenses in spectacles are used to diverge light so that the eye lens can focus it on the retina. If a person is long sighted, light is focused beyond the retina. Convex lenses in spectacles help the eye to focus the light on the retina.

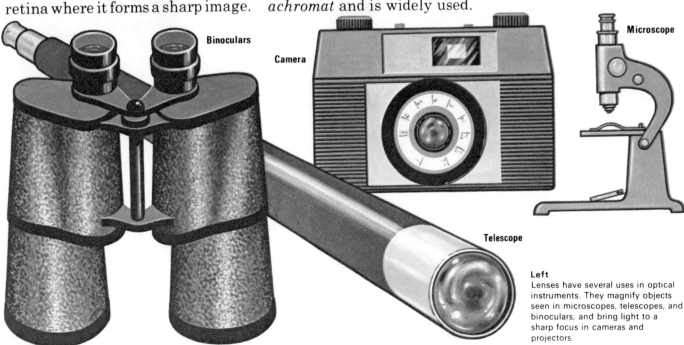

Binoculars

Camera

Microscope

Telescope

Left
Lenses have several uses in optical instruments. They magnify objects seen in microscopes, telescopes, and binoculars, and bring light to a sharp focus in cameras and projectors.

Above
A plane mirror produces a laterally inverted image; that is, the right hand side of the image appears opposite the left hand side of the object, and vice versa. Mirrors have been used for centuries, both for practical purposes and for decoration.

Right
Some historical optical instruments. A model of the first microscope devised by Leeuwenhoek.
Centre A copy of the microscope like the one devised by Hooke before he published his book on microscopy in 1665. *Right* A model of a lamp and condenser system designed by Hooke.

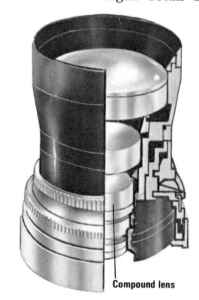

Leeuwenhoek's microscope

Hooke's microscope

Optical instruments

In order to see a small object clearly, we bring it closer to the eye, which gives a wider angle of view of the object and increases its apparent size. With the unaided eye, however, the object can be brought no nearer than about 25 cm from the eye (for somebody with normal vision). Closer than that, the object looks blurred.

To increase the size of a tiny or distant object, without straining the eye, a microscope or telescope must be used. These are optical instruments which use lenses or mirrors to help us see small objects more clearly.

The mirror is the oldest optical instrument. Mirrors have been used for over 2000 years. A mirror changes the direction of a beam of light by *reflecting* the light from a shiny metal surface.

The lens is the main device used in optical instruments. It changes the direction of a light beam by

Right
A single-lens reflex camera. The one lens system is used both for viewing and focusing. The photographer views the subject through the view-finder which is linked optically to the lens system by a pentaprism and a mirror. The mirror is hinged so that when the shutter is opened to expose the film, the mirror lifts up.

Far right
A compound lens. The parts of the lens are set in a precision-made mounting which will rotate but will not let in the light.

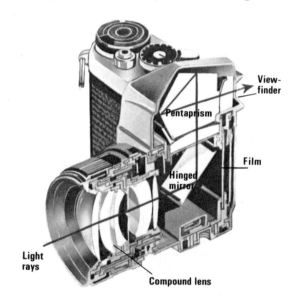

View-finder

Pentaprism

Film

Hinged mirror

Light rays

Compound lens

Compound lens

Right
A simple refracting telescope with a converging objective lens and a diverging convex lens for the eyepiece.

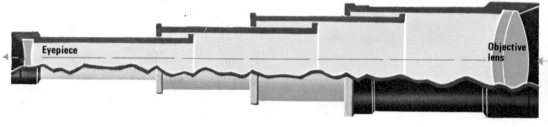

Eyepiece

Objective lens

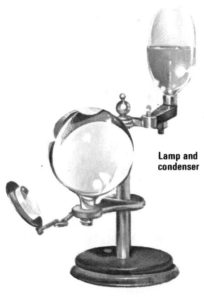

Lamp and condenser

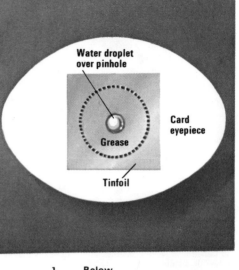

Water droplet over pinhole

Card eyepiece

Grease

Tinfoil

Right
The water-droplet microscope. Place the monocle in your eye. Illuminate a small object, such as a hair, with a strong light and hold the microscope close to it. Adjust this distance until you see a clear and enlarged image.

Below
Prisms are used in some optical instruments, such as the periscope. In this, the prisms act as mirrors. They reflect the light through 90° by means of total internal reflection. There is also a system of lenses in a nautical periscope, to magnify and focus the image.

bending or *refracting* the rays as they pass through it. When lenses are in certain positions they can produce a larger or magnified image of the object. The *magnification* of an optical instrument is equal to the image size divided by the object size. A magnifying glass, consisting of a single convex lens, forms an image several times larger than the object.

The magnification of an instrument can be greatly increased by using more than one lens. Both the simple telescope (page 132) and the microscope (page 216) use two convex lenses separated by a set distance, enabling them to form a greatly enlarged image of the object. Other lenses are used in the instrument to improve the quality of the image.

It is not possible to go on increasing the magnification of an instrument simply by improving its optical system. This is because there is a limit to the magnification set by the laws of physics. To view an object under a microscope it must be illuminated by a beam of light. The magnification limit is determined by the *wavelength* of the light (see page 138). Since the wavelength is a fixed quantity, the maximum magnification of a light microscope or telescope is also fixed.

The camera is a different type of optical instrument. It produces a permanent image of an object or scene by focusing light from the object onto a photographic film. One or more lenses are used for

this and the lens system can be extremely complicated.

Some optical instruments contain an important substance called Polaroid. Light waves normally contain vibrations in all directions perpendicular to their direction of travel. It is said to be unpolarized. Polarized light contains vibrations in only one direction. Polaroid transmits polarized light. Polarization cuts down glare from scattered or reflected light. Polaroid produces this effect. It is used for sun glasses, filters for cameras, and many other optical instruments.

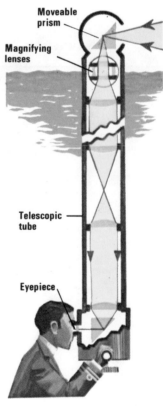

Moveable prism

Magnifying lenses

Telescopic tube

Eyepiece

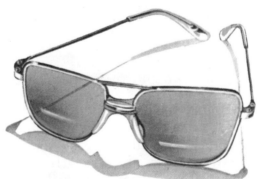

Left
Polaroid sunglasses cut down glare from scattered or reflected light. The lenses are made from polaroid, a substance that transmits light waves which have vibrations in only one direction. Unpolarized light waves normally contain vibrations in all directions.

Refracting telescopes

Telescopes are optical instruments used for observing distant objects. It is believed that the first telescope was made by Hans Lippershey in Holland, in 1608. He was a spectacle maker, and whilst examining a pair of lenses, one behind the other, he accidentally discovered that objects appeared closer. By 1610, an Italian named Galileo, had made a much improved telescope, called the Galilean telescope. It had a magnification of 33 times. From then on many improvements by other scientists and astronomers gradually followed.

Telescopes that use lenses instead of mirrors are called *refracting telescopes* because the light is bent by refraction through the glass.

GALILEAN TELESCOPE

Distant object

Erect virtual image at infinity

Convex objective

Convex eyepiece

Convex objective

Concave eyepiece

Distant object

Focus

Inverted virtual image at infinity

ASTRONOMICAL TELESCOPE

Galileo used his telescope for making astronomical observations. He was able to discover the moons of the planet Jupiter. He also observed that there are hills and valleys on the moon. Galileo's telescope used a convex lens at the front. This is the *object lens* or *objective*. The other lens is called the *eye lens* or *eyepiece*. This was a concave lens in Galileo's telescope. With this lens arrangement the image and object are the same way up.

Later telescopes used two convex lenses. The object lens brings the light to a focus between the two lenses. Another convex lens, the eyepiece, magnifies this image

to produce a larger image seen by the eye.

The image formed by this type of telescope is upside down (*inverted*). This does not really matter in astronomy and these telescopes were used for many investigations of planets and stars.

Refracting telescopes are often called astronomical telescopes. The largest one in existence is the Yerkes telescope in Wisconsin, U.S.A. It is over 18 metres long and the objective lens has a diameter of 40 inches (1 metre).

The early refracting telescopes had the disadvantage that the images formed had coloured fringes around them. This is because a lens focuses light of different colours at slightly different positions, breaking up the different colours that make up white light into coloured fringes. This is called *chromatic aberration*. It is possible to make lenses that do not have this defect. They are used in all modern refracting telescopes. Reflecting telescopes do not suffer from chromatic aberration.

Astronomical telescopes with their two convex lenses are unsuitable for land viewing because they give an inverted image. If a third convex lens is placed in the tube of the telescope the final image is upright. It can then be used for land viewing and is known as a *terrestrial telescope*.

Galileo's telescope, although used for astronomical work, was also a terrestrial telescope because it gave an upright image.

Lippershey, who invented the telescope, is also said to have invented the first binocular telescope in 1608. Unfortunately this idea of using an instrument with both eyes caused little interest.

In 1823 the binocular telescope was re-invented by another Dutchman called J. Voigtlaender. Opera glasses and inexpensive field glasses consist of two telescopes, of the Galilean type. Their magnification is only small. Binoculars use convex lenses for both object lenses and eyepieces.

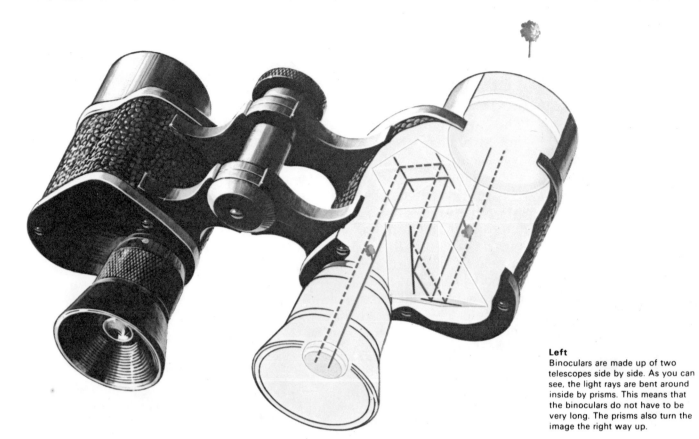

Left
Binoculars are made up of two telescopes side by side. As you can see, the light rays are bent around inside by prisms. This means that the binoculars do not have to be very long. The prisms also turn the image the right way up.

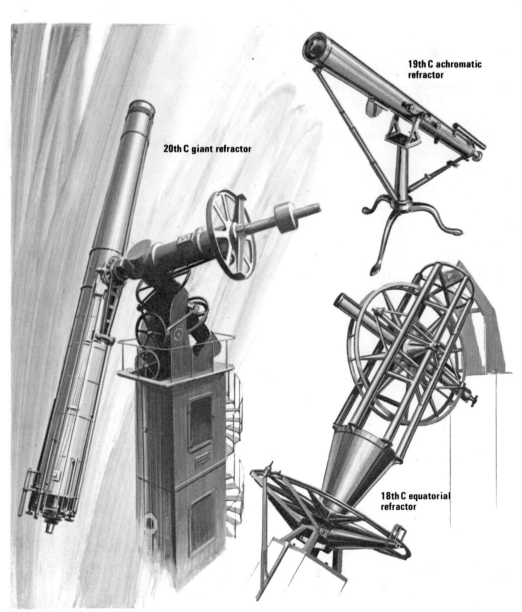

19th C achromatic refractor

20th C giant refractor

18th C equatorial refractor

Left
An eighteenth century equatorial refractor with a 4·2 inch objective, made for the Shuckburgh observatory. A nineteenth century achromatic refractor with a 3·25 inch objective composed of two lenses.
A giant refractor of the twentieth century with a 26 inch object lens. This telescope is at the Naval Observatory in Washington U.S.A.

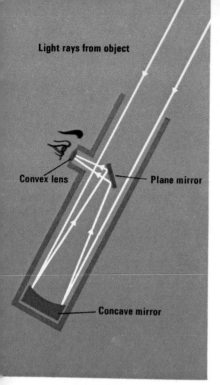

Light rays from object

Convex lens — Plane mirror

Concave mirror

Above
In Newton's telescope a large concave mirror is used. This has a parabolic shape (see page 123). It brings parallel beams of light to a point. A small plane mirror is used to reflect the light out of the telescope through an eyepiece. Usually photographs are taken with an attached camera.

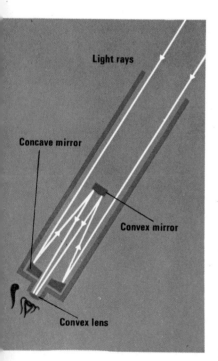

Light rays

Concave mirror

Convex mirror

Convex lens

Above
A later instrument is the *Cassegrainian telescope*. The light is first collected with the large concave mirror. It is then reflected back through a hole by a small convex mirror.

Reflecting telescopes

The early refracting telescopes did not give clear, sharp images. This was because it was difficult to make good lenses. In 1668, Sir Isaac Newton invented a *reflecting telescope*. This telescope had no object lens at all. The light came down an open tube to fall onto a curved mirror at the bottom. The mirror reflected the light back up the tube onto a second flat mirror placed at an angle. This directed the rays to the side of the tube onto the magnifying convex lens of the eyepiece. Newton's telescope produced clearer images free of the colour fringes from which refracting telescopes suffered.

The world's largest telescopes are of the reflecting type because mirrors are free from colour fringes, they can give very sharp images and are much easier to make than large lenses.

Most of the objects studied by astronomers are extremely distant and faint. They can be seen only in telescopes which collect a lot of light. Large modern reflecting telescopes have enormous light-gathering power and reveal fine detail. Very large numbers of very faint, very distant stars can be seen.

Cameras are often fitted to these telescopes and with long exposures they can gather a tremendous amount of extra information about stars and galaxies. No telescope yet built is able to show a star as anything more than a dot of light. Telescopes, however, can still tell us much about the stars. They can show the different star colours. Double and quadruple stars (groups of two or four stars close together) can be seen.

Galaxies (or star systems) have thousands of millions of stars in them and outside our own galaxy there are over 1000 million other separate galaxies. Only three can be seen with the naked eye.

Many galaxies have been photographed using telescopes. Astronomers can only learn a limited amount about the stars with visual telescopes. Other instruments have been developed which can tell us much more about the make-up of the stars. The most important of these instruments is the spectroscope (see page 137).

A large reflecting telescope is found in nearly every major observatory. Throughout the world there are over 300 observatories and 64 radio observatories, and many others that are run privately.

The largest reflecting telescope in the world is at the Mount Palomar Observatory, California, U.S.A. There, the favourable climate and atmosphere enable the telescope to be used, on average,

Left
One of the largest telescopes is on Mount Palomar in California. It is housed in this observatory. The dome weighs 1000 tons. It has a shutter through which the telescope points at the sky. The dome can be revolved so that the telescope can point in different directions

300 days every year. The concave mirror is made of glass, coated with a thin layer of aluminium to give it high reflecting power. It is 200 inches in diameter and the telescope can be used in Newtonian or Cassegrainian form. There are also other smaller telescopes at the Mount Palomar Observatory.

Above
Tycho Brahe (1546–1601) was a Danish astronomer. He set up magnificently equipped observatories at Uraniborg and Stjerneborg near Copenhagen. His most famous work was his accurate observations of the planets, which provided information used by Kepler when he worked out the laws of motion of the planets.

Above right
This is the Hale telescope inside the dome at Mount Palomar. The concave mirror is 200 inches in diameter. It is mounted on the bottom end of the steel framework tube. The astronomer sits in a small cage at the top end to make his observations. The horseshoe shape and the tubes joined to it are a framework to support the telescope. They enable it to be rotated in any direction.

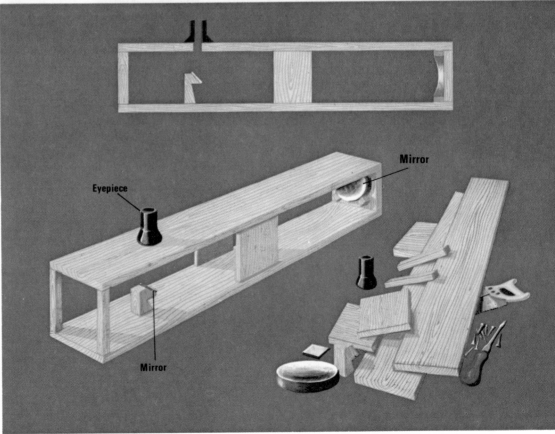

Mirror

Eyepiece

Mirror

Right
You can build a simple Newtonian reflector in a rigid wooden case. You will need a plano-concave mirror, a paraboloid mirror and an eyepiece.

Scattering and absorption of light

When sunlight reaches the earth's atmosphere it hits the minute particles (molecules) of air and the dust suspended in the air and is *scattered* or deflected in many directions.

The scattering of light can explain the colour of the sky. White light is a mixture of colours all having different wavelengths. Not all wavelengths are scattered by the same amount, however. Blue and violet light is deflected more than the other colours. During the day the sky is blue because more blue light is deflected towards the earth. In the morning and evening the sun is low in the sky and light from the sun has to travel through more atmosphere to reach us. If we look towards the sun the light reaching our eyes has lost blue and violet wavelengths. These colours have been deflected away by small particles of dust in the atmosphere. Red and orange light have longer wavelengths so are not deflected away and therefore the sun appears reddish at sunrise and sunset.

When light falls on a substance, some of it is reflected, some transmitted, and the rest is *absorbed* by the material. The amounts depend on the type of substance. An opaque material, such as wood or metal, transmits no light and can only reflect some if it has a shiny surface. Most of it is absorbed. A transparent substance, such as water or glass, transmits most of it. Light, or any other form of energy such as heat or ultraviolet, is absorbed by the atoms and molecules making up the material that it strikes.

Molecules are made up of groups of two or more atoms. Atoms are able to absorb light usually of only one colour. Light is made up of thousands of different colours; the six colours of the rainbow are groups of colours of about the same shade. Each of these numerous colours has its own *wavelength* and *frequency* (see page 138).

When white light falls on a material the atoms absorb some of the different colours that make up white light. The remaining colours are reflected or transmitted. The reflected colours, seen by the eye, give the colour of the object.

When an atom absorbs light, or ultraviolet, its energy increases. It becomes *excited*. An excited atom is

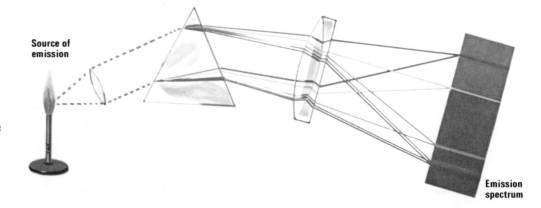

Source of emission

Emission spectrum

unstable–it must get rid of this extra energy. It does so by re-emitting light or ultraviolet radiation of the same wavelength. Some atoms absorb light of one wavelength and re-emit it at a longer wavelength, immediately. These atoms are *fluorescing*; the substance is *fluorescent*. If there is a brief delay between absorption and emission the substance is said to be

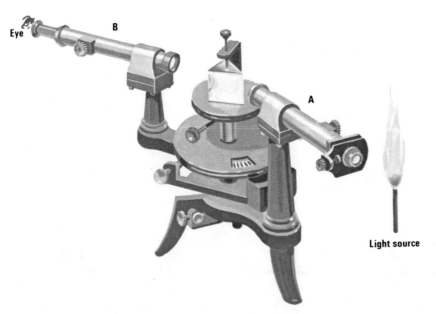

Eye · B · A · Light source

phosphorescent–it is a *phosphor*. Phosphors are used on TV screens.

The study of the absorption and emission by atoms is called *spectroscopy*. Spectroscopy is used in scientific research, medicine, industry, and astronomy. It provides a method of analysing and identifying materials, yielding valuable information on the structure of atoms and molecules.

A *spectrograph* is used to study emission and absorption. This instrument splits up light, by means

of a prism, into its different colours or wavelengths. The light then falls onto a photographic plate and an *emission spectrum*, or *absorption spectrum* is recorded.

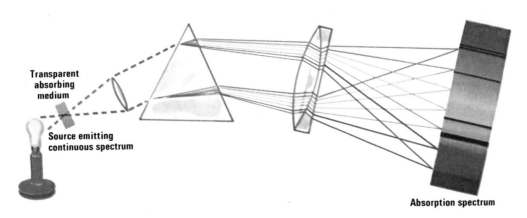

Transparent absorbing medium · Source emitting continuous spectrum · Absorption spectrum

137

Fresnel

Young

Above
The wave theory of light, proposed by the Dutch scientist Christiaan Huygens, 1629–95, was studied by both Augustin Fresnel, 1788–1827, of France and Thomas Young, 1773–1829, of England. Young proved the theory in 1801.

Planck

Above
Max Planck, 1858–1947, a German physicist. Many processes, including absorption and emission of light could not be explained by wave theory. In 1900, Planck suggested that electromagnetic radiation could also be thought of as a stream of small bundles of energy, called *quanta*. Each quantum, travelling at the speed of light, has an energy proportional to the frequency of the radiation. A light quantum is called a *photon*.

Right
If you throw a stone into a calm pond, a series of ripples will be set up moving outwards in circles from where the stone hit the water. These ripples are waves of energy travelling through the water. The distance between successive crests is the wavelength of the wave.

Waves

Light enables us to see; it makes plants grow. Light is in fact a form of energy. A light beam can travel through empty space; the energy must therefore be carried by the beam itself. The passage of this energy does not rely on the surrounding air or on the material through which it passes.

We can tell from the sharp edges of shadows that rays of light travel through air along a straight path. They cannot bend round corners.

It is therefore useful to think of light rays themselves as straight lines. This can explain reflection and refraction. In 1680, Huygens suggested that light rays were in fact *waves*, but it wasn't for over a century that his theory was shown to be true.

Light certainly travels in one direction but the ray itself is moving up and down in continuous crests and troughs. This wave has a similar shape to ripples on a pond. As it moves through space, there is always the same distance between two neighbouring crests or troughs. This distance is called the *wavelength*. It is an extremely tiny distance measured in minute fractions of a metre. The height of a crest or the depth of a trough is called the *amplitude*. The greater

the amplitude of the wave, the greater its energy. As the energy decreases, the amplitude grows less and less.

After the wave has gone through one crest and one trough–after it has travelled one wavelength– the wave has completed one *cycle* of its motion and is ready to repeat itself. The number of cycles in one second is called the *frequency* of the wave, and it never changes for that wave.

Waves move at tremendous speed. The speed is always the same in one particular medium such as air, but decreases when waves enter denser material, such as glass or water. This change in speed causes refraction of the light beam producing an increase in wavelength. The speed of a light wave in any medium equals its wavelength multiplied by its frequency. The greatest speed of light is in a vacuum, such as outer space. The speed in air is very close to this value. The maximum speed is equal to 300 000 km per second. *No object moving in a vacuum can travel faster than this speed.*

Each light wave has its own wavelength and each of these wavelengths corresponds to a slightly different colour. Red light has almost twice the wavelength of violet light. Yellow, green and blue light have wavelengths between these values.

Light is not the only form of energy transmitted by waves. Radio waves, infrared and ultraviolet radiation, X-rays, and gamma rays also travel as wave motions. All these waves move at the speed of light. However, the wavelengths (and hence frequencies) are very different. It is the different wavelengths that give each type of radiation its special properties. They are all examples of *electromagnetic radiation*, and they all travel as electromagnetic waves.

The chart showing the different electromagnetic radiations in order of increasing wavelength (or decreasing frequency) is called the *electromagnetic spectrum*.

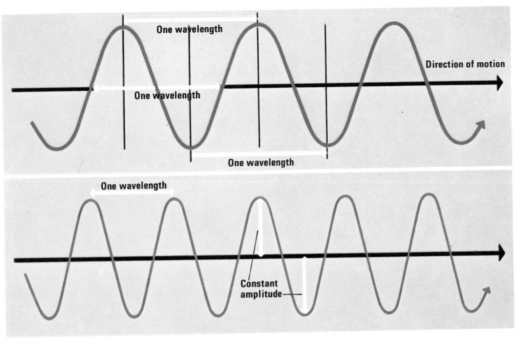

Left
The wavelength of red light is almost twice that of blue light. The frequency is the number of complete wave cycles in one second. The frequency of red light is almost half that of blue light.

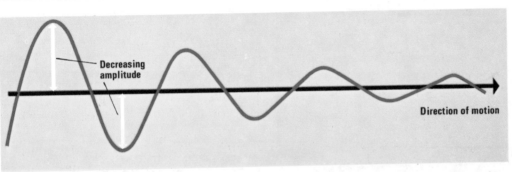

Left
The amplitude, or maximum height of a crest or trough, only remains the same if the wave is not transferring its energy to another medium. If it is losing energy rapidly, the amplitude also decreases, but at a much slower rate. The square of the amplitude (amplitude times amplitude) gives a measure of the energy.

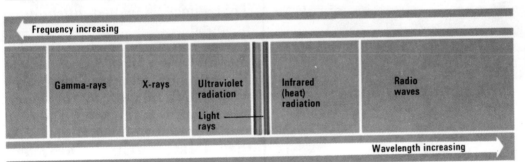

Left
The electromagnetic spectrum. Radio waves have much longer wavelengths than light waves which in turn have greater wavelengths than X-rays and gamma rays. The visible part of the spectrum is very narrow compared with other parts.

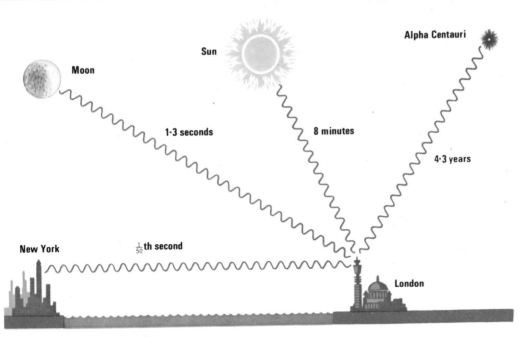

Left
The speed of light. It takes the time shown for an electromagnetic wave to travel between London and the places shown in the diagram.

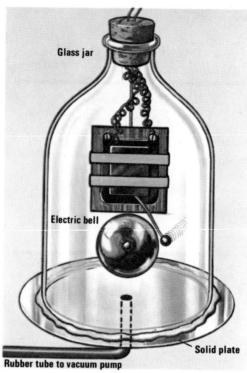

Glass jar

Electric bell

Solid plate

Rubber tube to vacuum pump

Above
The elastic band will make a twanging sound if pulled then let go. This is caused by the elastic hitting against the air molecules as it vibrates rapidly back and forth.

Right
If an electric bell is put inside a jar and all the air is pumped out, no sound will be heard. The hammer can be seen to vibrate rapidly making the bell ring, but because there is no air the sound will not travel.

Hammer   Anvil

Semicircular canals

Acoustic nerve

Cochlea

Eardrum

Outer ear

Stirrup

Above
The ear has three parts. The outer middle, and inner ear. In the middle ear the movements of the ear drum affect three tiny bones. These are named from their shapes, the hammer, anvil, and stirrup. They carry sound to the cochlea in the inner ear.

Right
A drum is a percussion instrument. It consists of a piece of skin, parchment, plastic, or nylon stretched tightly over a wooden or metal frame. The bass drum is the largest orchestral and military drum. The diameter is much greater than the depth. Usually it is played with a felt-headed stick.

Bass drum

Toy drum

Sound

Sound is always made by some kind of movement, for example, hitting your hand against a table or plucking a guitar string. There are many different kinds of sounds; they can be pleasant or unpleasant. Music has rhythm and is usually pleasant to hear. You might like pop music, but your mother may think it is noisy. Noise is any sound that is unpleasant to a person. It is not usually as rhythmic as music.

When something vibrates it produces a sound. Vibrations are movements to and fro. The energy or strength of the vibrations is passed on to the tiny particles (molecules) in the surrounding air and makes them move. The stronger the vibrations the louder the sounds. To make the molecules move requires energy. The further a sound travels the more molecules are moved. The energy of the vibration is therefore slowly used up and the sound becomes quieter. This effect is called *attenuation* of sound.

The vibrations moving through the air are called *sound waves*. You cannot see them, but they would look similar to the movement of corn in the wind. The corn stalks are blown over slightly. As they vibrate to and fro, wave movements are seen to travel across the field although each corn stalk moves only a short distance.

Sound waves move the molecules of air against each other. Each minute particle bumps its neighbour, which in turn bumps its neighbour. The molecules therefore crowd together and then move back again. This crowding together causes a slight increase in *pressure*. As the molecules move apart the pressure drops. A sound wave therefore produces a change in pressure as it travels through the air. If there were no air, as in outer-space, sound would not travel. No sounds would be transmitted so nothing could be heard.

In fact it is only when the sound

wave falls on the ear that a sound is heard. The flap of the outer ear is a funnel to collect the sound waves, which pass along a short tube to the ear drum. The sound waves make the drum vibrate, causing tiny bones in contact with it to vibrate. These carry the sound to the inner ear. Here the vibrations are converted, by a shell-shaped organ called the *cochlea,* into electrical messages. These are carried by nerves to the brain.

There are many ways of producing a musical note. *Percussion instruments* are played by striking a surface in a particular manner. In a bell, the surface, which is usually metal, is struck by a heavy clapper. The oldest bell in the world, found near Babylon, is over 3000 years old. The largest is the *Tsar Kolokol* (King of Bells) in the Kremlin, Moscow. Cast in 1734 it weighs 220 tons and stands on the ground where it fell whilst being hung. The earliest English bell, 1296, is at Claughton, Lancashire. The largest is Great Paul, weighing 17 tons and hanging in St. Paul's Cathedral, London. Big Ben (London) and Great Tom (Oxford) are two other famous English bells. The most famous bell in the U.S. is the Liberty Bell (Philadelphia).

Above
Alarm clocks can be mechanical (wind up) or electrical. This one has bells on top, but usually they are inside. The hammer between the bells starts to vibrate against the bells at the set time.

Left
Different types of bell. When the lever on a bicycle bell is pressed a metal propeller revolves inside the bell, hitting the sides and making them ring. A hand bell is rung by swinging it so that the hammer inside hits the metal. In an electric bell an electric current makes the hammer vibrate. Two famous bells are the oldest bell in the world, which is over 3000 years old and the Liberty Bell, rung on the signing of the Declaration of Independence, 1776, in America.

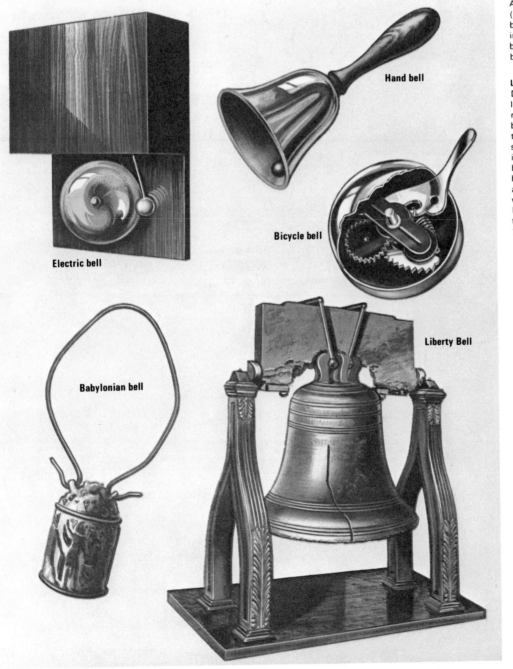

Electric bell

Hand bell

Bicycle bell

Babylonian bell

Liberty Bell

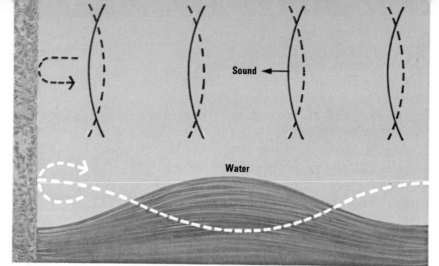

Above
The sound wave of an echo bounces back by reflection, much like water waves bouncing from a wall.

Right
As a bat flies about, it is constantly producing high-pitched sounds. When these sounds hit an insect, they echo back to the bat's ears. This makes the bat produce more frequent sounds, resulting in more echoes. Following the path of the echoes, the bat traps its insect prey.

Echoes and acoustics

An echo occurs when sound waves hit a barrier like a cliff, hill, or high wall. The waves bounce off and the sound is heard again. This is called reflected sound. The time between the sound and its echo is the time taken by the sound wave to hit the barrier and return to the listener. The sound wave loses energy as it travels so the echo is fainter than the original sound.

Whales, porpoises, bats, and some other living creatures can navigate and also locate their prey by using echoes. They emit a stream of sounds in all directions. The path of returning echoes shows where obstacles or prey are.

Echoes are useful to fishermen for detecting shoals of fish and to geologists for finding minerals beneath the earth's surface.

Acoustics is the study of sound as it travels through space. It is especially concerned with the

Right
A cutaway view of an oil deposit in the earth. An underground explosion directs sounds downwards. Oil reflects a certain pattern of echoes, which are recorded by a sensitive instrument called a *seismograph*. The geologist can therefore locate the oil and find the best place to sink a well.

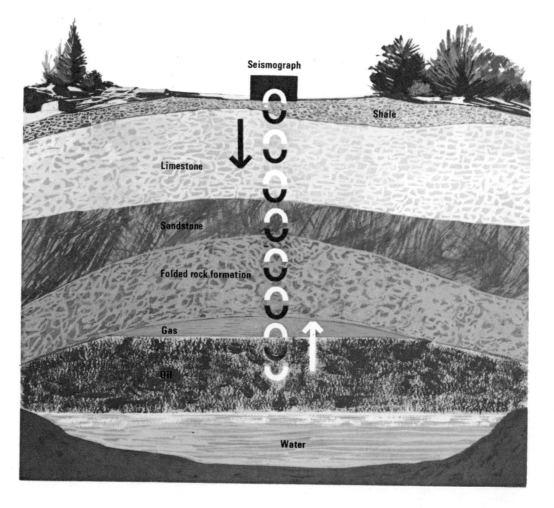

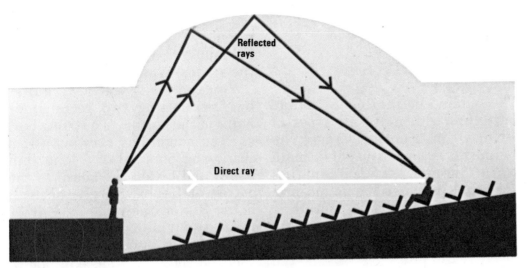

Left
Acoustics of a domed hall. The clearest speech is heard when there is a time lag of 1/20th of a second between the reflected rays and the direct rays SO. The reflected rays then travel 20 metres more than the direct rays. For music, the time lag should be 1/15th of a second, with a path difference of 27 metres.

transmission of sound in cinemas, concert halls, classrooms, any place in fact where sounds must be clearly heard by an audience. In a large room with wide hard un-broken walls, the sound echoes off the walls. The audience hears a jumble of noises making it impossible for even the slowest, clearest speaker to be understood. This is called *reverberation*. It can be reduced by padding the walls, hanging curtains, and using padded seats. These absorb some of the sound and the echoes become less loud. There are fewer echoes in a full hall because people also absorb the sound.

The shape of a hall is specially designed so that, if possible, every sound can be heard clearly by everyone there. Some of the sound is heard directly; the rest is reflected off the walls and ceiling. The distances travelled by these two sets of waves are carefully estimated to minimize the echo.

Sound must travel through a medium, such as air. The molecules of the medium carry the vibrations from the source of sound to the listener's ears. Liquids and solids transmit sound even better than air.

Sound waves travel at a speed that depends on the medium. They travel faster in a denser medium such as water or glass, than in air. The speed of sound in air can be measured by placing an explosive charge 1km from some measuring instruments and then exploding it. The flash of light is recorded by one instrument; a few seconds later a second instrument records the noise of the explosion. Sound does not travel nearly as fast as light. The time between the flash and the noise, found to be three seconds, is the time taken for sound to travel 1km through air.

In a thunderstorm, lightning will always be seen before the accompanying clap of thunder. This is because light travels so much faster than sound. Count the number of seconds between the lightning flash and the first sound of thunder and divide the answer by three. This gives the distance, in kilometres, of the flash.

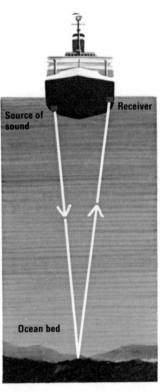

Above
The ocean depth can be found by measuring the time between sending out a sound signal and receiving the echo reflected from the ocean bed. Half this time, multiplied by the speed of sound in sea water, gives the depth. Many readings can be taken in a short time and a whole coastline plotted.

Left
The Whispering Gallery of St. Pauls. If someone whispers up against the wall in one part of the gallery, the sound is reflected around the wall and can be heard on the other side of the gallery.

143

Stringed instruments

The violin, guitar, cello, banjo, harp, and zither are all types of stringed instruments. These instruments are made up of two main parts: the strings, and another part that enriches the sound produced when the strings vibrate.

The strings can be made to vibrate in various ways. Guitar strings are plucked – this is the oldest and most common method; piano strings are struck; a bow is drawn across violin strings; air is blown onto the strings of a special but rare kind of harp.

The strings are stretched across some form of hollow container, usually made of wood. The vibrations of the strings set the air inside the container vibrating. The strings and the air are then in *resonance*; the resulting sounds are louder and richer than those of the strings alone.

You can make your own guitar by first cutting two rectangular holes in the bottom of a strong box, such as a cigar box. Saw out a 5 cm section at one end of a long thin board and fasten the board to the bottom of the box with glue or small bolts. Fasten the lid shut. Buy or make two violin pegs and fasten them tightly into drilled holes at the free end of the piece of board. Cut a triangular piece of wood for a *bridge*, to support the strings.

The vibrations of the strings are passed to the body of the instrument through the bridge. Run two guitar strings from a screw at the end of the box, over the bridge to the pegs. Wind the strings tight. Now you can start to play.

The *pitch* of a note is how high or low it sounds. Pitch depends on the

Above
The guitar, traditionally the instrument of Italy and Spain has six strings, which are plucked or strummed. Different notes can be played by pressing a finger on any one of the strings at certain positions down the neck. The positions are indicated by metal ridges, called *frets*.

Below
Making your own guitar. Bolt the neck to the cigar box as described. Stretch the guitar strings between the screw and the two violin pegs. Buy strings of different thickness. Although they are the same length, when they are plucked the thin one will produce a higher note than the thick one.

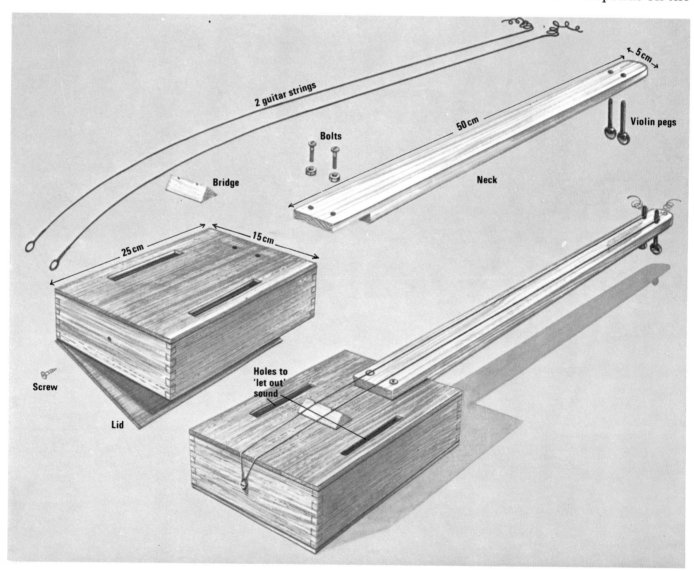

number of vibrations made by a string each second. The more vibrations per second of a string, the higher the pitch.

Tighten one of the guitar strings more than the other. When the strings are plucked two notes of a different pitch will be heard. Tightening the string is one way of increasing the pitch. Pluck the tight string and notice the pitch. Place a finger firmly in the middle of the string, pluck it, and again notice the pitch. As the plucked string gets shorter, the pitch gets higher.

The ancient Greeks found that if a tightly stretched string produces a note of a certain pitch, then a string half as long produces a note with a pitch exactly 8 notes higher on the scale. This note is an *octave* higher than the first.

If you pluck very hard on your guitar strings they will make louder notes than if you pluck gently. You may be able to sing a note in the same pitch as a train whistle but you cannot sing as loudly. The loudness of a sound depends on the amount of energy that goes into making the sound. So, by plucking hard on the guitar strings you put in more energy and thereby obtain louder notes.

Above
The inside of a musical box. The drum is rotated by clockwork motor. As it rotates, metal prongs on its surface hit thin metal strips making them vibrate. Each strip produces a different note. As the prongs hit them in a definite order, a tune is played.

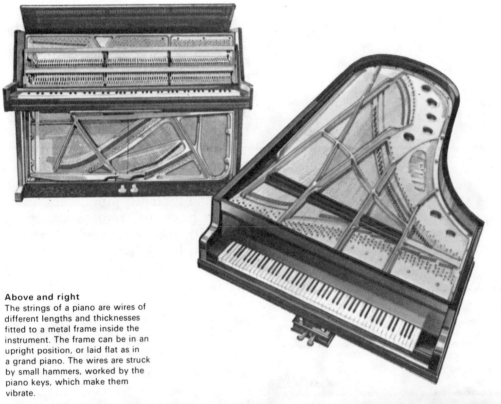

Above and right
The strings of a piano are wires of different lengths and thicknesses fitted to a metal frame inside the instrument. The frame can be in an upright position, or laid flat as in a grand piano. The wires are struck by small hammers, worked by the piano keys, which make them vibrate.

Above
The harp consists of an upright triangular frame. It has 46 strings of different lengths, that are played by plucking.

Left
A chamber orchestra. The two people in front are playing violins. The larger instrument is a cello. This is a four-stringed instrument which is bowed like the violin. The fourth member of this string quartet is playing the viola.

Right

A pipe contains a sharp edge against
which the air is blown. The edge
causes air to move to either side of
it. Sound waves are created in the
air outside the pipe and in the air
colum itself inside the pipe. These
waves produce the musical note.

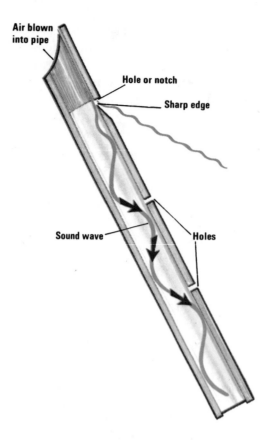

Air blown
into pipe

Hole or notch

Sharp edge

Sound wave

Holes

Pipes

Wind instruments that come under
the heading of pipes are the trombone, trumpet, bugle, tuba, flute, pic-
colo, clarinet and saxophone. When
you blow into one, the column of air
inside vibrates, producing a note.

Air can be made to vibrate as it
is blown into the pipe by making it
move past a sharp edge. This edge
causes eddies or waves in the air
column. If you could see them, they
would look like the waves on a flag
flapping in the wind.

The frequency (number of vibrations each second) of the vibrations
depends on the length of the air
column inside the pipe.

The shorter the air column, the
higher the frequency, or pitch, of
the note produced. By opening or
closing holes at different places on
the tube, the length of the vibrating
air column is altered which changes
the pitch.

Pipes are called *open pipes* if
both ends are open and *closed pipes*
if one end is closed off. An open
pipe and a closed pipe of the same
length have different tones. In an
open pipe the frequency, and therefore the pitch, is twice that of a
closed pipe of the same size. This is
because the waves have a different
shape in the two pipes. At an open
end the molecules of air have their
largest vibrations; at a closed end
they do not vibrate at all.

The waves inside the pipes can
have different wavelengths—as
long as there is a *node* (no vibrations) at a closed end and an
antinode (greatest number of vibrations) at an open end. As the
wavelength gets shorter, the frequency or pitch of the note gets
higher. This means that when you
blow down a pipe, the note produced is coloured by the presence
of other fainter notes of higher
pitch. These are called *overtones*.
The overtones give an instrument
its characteristic sound.

A simple pipe can be made from
bamboo and soft wood. Cut a notch
in the pipe. Carve a short cylinder

Below
A diagram of a wave. Where the
lines cross, the molecules are at
rest; this is called a *node* (N).
Where the lines are widest apart
the molecules are vibrating most
and have their greatest energy; this
is called an *antinode* (A). The
wavelength of a wave is the
distance between alternate nodes or
between alternate antinodes.

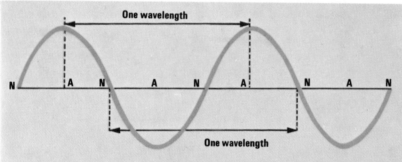

One wavelength

One wavelength

N A N A N A N A N A N

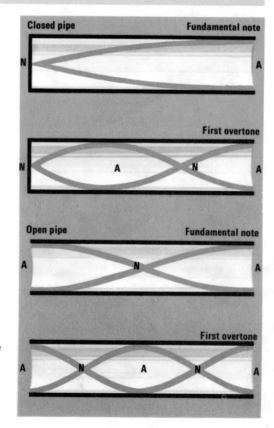

Closed pipe — Fundamental note

N — A

First overtone

N — A — N — A

Open pipe — Fundamental note

A — N — A

First overtone

A — N — A — N — A

Right
Waves in open and closed pipes. The
fundamental note has the longest
wavelength and thus the lowest
pitch or frequency. The frequency of
the overtones are all whole number
multiples of the frequency of the
fundamental.

of wood, shave off one side to make it flat, then push it into the pipe in front of the notch to make a mouthpiece. It should fit tightly. Carve another long cylinder of soft wood which will fit loosely into the open end of the pipe. Glue this cylinder to a pencil.

Blow into the mouthpiece of the pipe near the notch and you will hear a whistle. The air is hitting the edge of the notch and causing the column of air in the pipe to vibrate. By pushing the cylinder on the pencil in and out of the pipe while you blow, you can produce different notes.

The organ is the largest of all musical instruments, covers the widest frequency range, and has the greatest variety of tone. Air is blown into the many pipes, either by hand bellows or now mainly by motor-driven fans. The long, wide organ pipes make low-pitched sounds and the short narrow pipes make high-pitched sounds.

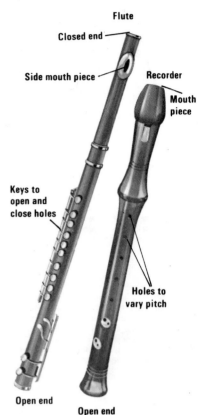

Flute
Closed end
Side mouth piece
Recorder
Mouth piece
Keys to open and close holes
Holes to vary pitch
Open end
Open end

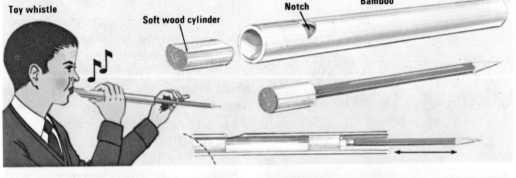

Toy whistle
Soft wood cylinder
Notch
Bamboo

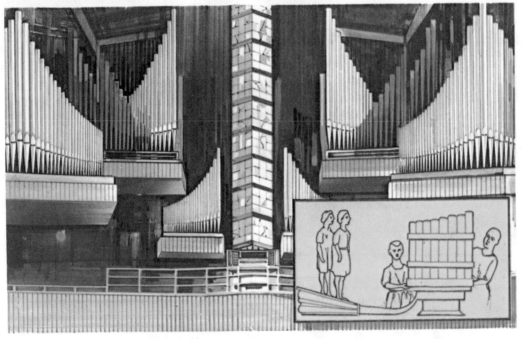

Above
The recorder, first made in the sixteenth century can be up to four metres long. It is played by blowing down the mouthpiece; different notes are produced by opening and closing holes down its length.
The flute is a side-blown wind instrument, closed at one end. The holes are opened or closed mainly by keys operated by the fingers. It produces a very pure clear note.

Above left
A toy pipe made from a piece of bamboo. By sliding the loose cylinder up and down the pipe you can alter the pitch because you are varying the length of the column of air inside the pipe.

Left
The organ. One picture shows an Ancient Roman organ, dating back to the fourth century. The other picture shows a modern organ, built in 1959, at Valparaiso University, USA.

Left
Bottle organ. Fill eight bottles of the same type with different amounts of water. Blow across each bottle in turn. The more water in the bottle the higher the note it produces. With the right amount of water in each bottle you can play a musical scale. You can use a vacuum cleaner hose to blow air across their tops.

147

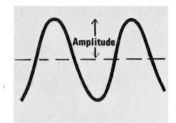

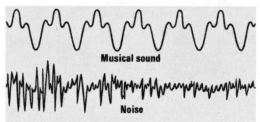

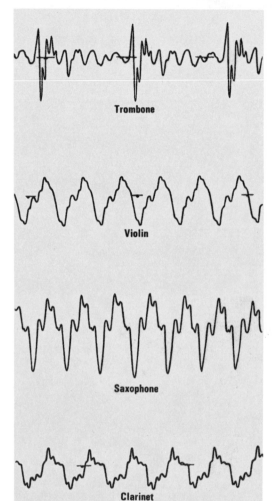

	Doh	Ray	Me	Fah	Soh	Lah	Te	Doh'
Number	1	2	3	4	5	6	7	8
Name	C	D	E	F	G	A	B	C'
Frequency	262	294	330	349	392	440	494	523

Musical sounds and scales

Any sound that we consider pleasant to hear is said to be musical. Music is the sound made by an orchestra, a musical instrument, a singer or a choir.

The ancient Greeks were the first people to study music scientifically. They put together a series of musical sounds in ascending (higher) and descending (lower) pitch to make a *scale*.

Musical instruments can be put into four main sections: strings, percussion, wind, and electronic instruments. The different designs and shapes of the instruments and the different materials from which they are made causes them to have different sounds. The thickness and quality of the wood from which one violin is made will cause it to make different sounds to a similar looking violin made from thinner or poorer quality wood.

Two other important factors are an instrument's size and the musician's skill.

In good music, only the desired vibrations are heard. If the vibration has the right pitch and amplitude (loudness), a musician should be able to recognise which note is being played, for example the note 'A' of the musical scale.

Each musical note has a definite pitch or frequency that is the same for every instrument. It is called the *fundamental frequency*. The note A on a piano has the same fundamental frequency as that note played on a guitar or a flute. It is produced by 440 vibrations of the string or air column in one second.

No musical instrument produces a perfectly pure note of one frequency. Instead it is coloured by a number of fainter *overtones*, produced at the same time as the fundamental frequency (see page 146). These overtones can have two, three, four, five, six times the frequency of the fundamental. Different instruments produce different amounts of some or all of these overtones. This is why they produce such different sounds. Each instrument therefore has a definite and recognizable *quality*.

Musical scales are made up of groups of twelve notes, called *semitones*. The notes are arranged on a scale or 'ladder' which rises from low to high pitch. Each group of notes is called an *octave*. Each note in an octave has a frequency that is 1·0595 times higher than the frequency of the note immediately below it. If you multiply 1·0595 by itself 12 times

you get the answer 2. This means that a note one octave above another one has twice its frequency. The frequency of upper C is 523·2 vibrations per second, twice that of middle C (261·6).

Lord Rayleigh was one of Britain's greatest scientists. He worked out a new method for measuring the strength and loudness (amplitude) of sound vibrations. He wrote the *Theory of Sound* which describes the movement of sound-producing objects, and how they cause the surrounding air to vibrate.

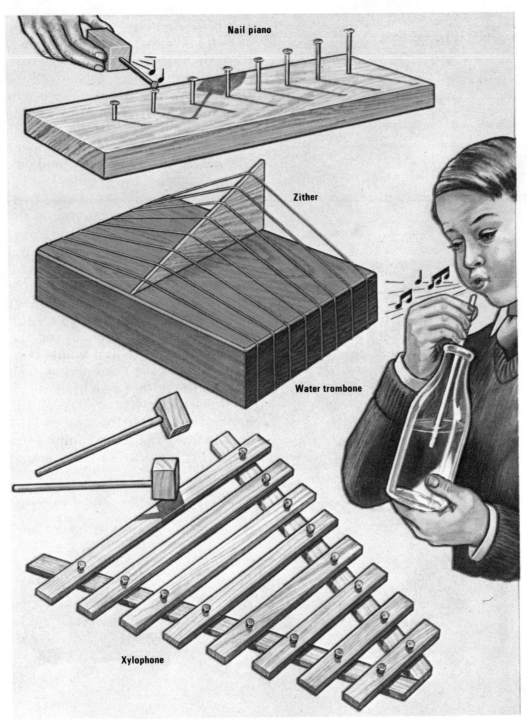

Nail piano

Zither

Water trombone

Xylophone

Left
You can make up an orchestra of home made musical instruments. Here are several made out of ordinary materials. The nail piano and the xylophone both work in a similar way. Each nail or piece of wood is a different length so produces a different sound. The shorter it is, the higher the note. The zither is made of elastic bands. In this case, the longer the band, the higher the note because it has been stretched more. The bottle trombone will need some practice. To produce a note blow across the top of the tube when the other end is dipped in water. To get a higher note, shorten the tube by dipping it further into the water. For a lower note, raise it higher out of the water.

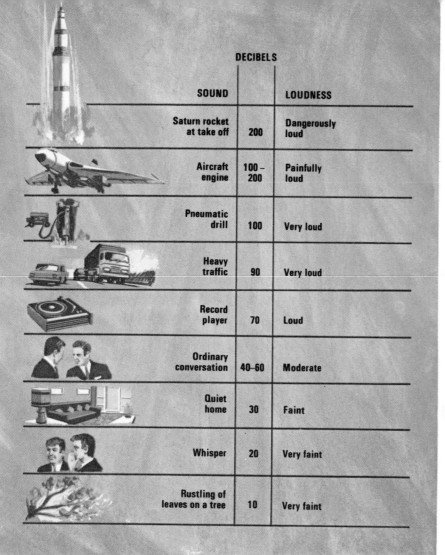

SOUND	DECIBELS	LOUDNESS
Saturn rocket at take off	200	Dangerously loud
Aircraft engine	100 – 200	Painfully loud
Pneumatic drill	100	Very loud
Heavy traffic	90	Very loud
Record player	70	Loud
Ordinary conversation	40–60	Moderate
Quiet home	30	Faint
Whisper	20	Very faint
Rustling of leaves on a tree	10	Very faint

Noise

Any sound that a person finds unpleasant can be called noise. A noise to one person, however, might be thought a nice sound by somebody else. In scientific terms noise is sound made by an irregular pattern of waves.

There are many things which could make our world unpleasantly, even dangerously, noisy. These include jet aircraft taking off, road drills, and heavy traffic. Too great a noise can damage the ears. Laws have been made to forbid the making of noise above a certain level.

You may have noticed that a car horn or fire engine siren seems to have a higher pitch as the vehicle rushes towards you, than when it is moving away from you. This is most noticeable as the vehicle reaches you, for at that moment the pitch of the horn suddenly drops to a much lower note.

Sound waves move outward from the horn. The waves moving in the same direction as the vehicle travel towards you at the speed of sound plus the speed of the vehicle. As a result, if the car is coming towards you, more than the normal number of sound waves reach you each second, so the frequency of the waves is higher than it would be if the vehicle were not moving. The pitch of the note is also higher.

When the car has passed you the sound waves reach you at the normal speed of sound minus the speed of the car. Fewer sound

Above
A scale of noises. The loudness of a noise is found by measuring the energy of a sound wave. Loudness is usually measured in decibels. A sound of zero decibels is just too faint for the human ear to hear. Lorries are not allowed to make a noise above 90 decibels. Sounds above 140 decibels are dangerous to the unprotected ear.

Right
The sound waves of a musical note and a noise. Fig. *a* shows the waveform of a piano note. The waves have a regular pattern and the note makes a pleasing sound. Fig. *b* shows the waves made when a piano pedal is pressed down. There is no regular pattern and the sound, being unpleasant, is called a noise.

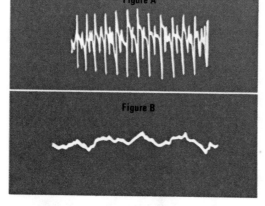

Figure A

Figure B

Right
The Doppler effect. As the fire engine rushes away from you, ringing its siren, fewer sound waves reach you than when it approached you. The pitch of the siren's note drops suddenly as it passes you.

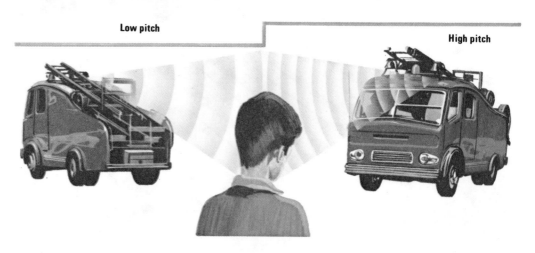

Low pitch

High pitch

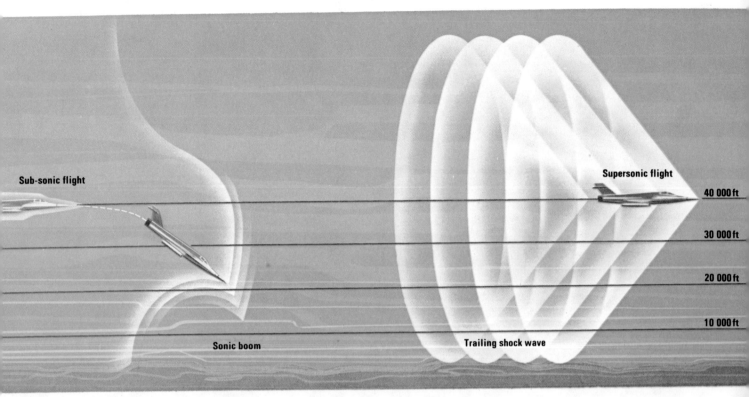

Sub-sonic flight

Supersonic flight

40 000 ft

30 000 ft

20 000 ft

10 000 ft

Sonic boom

Trailing shock wave

waves reach you per second, which means that the frequency is lower than when the vehicle is stationary. The pitch of the note is lower. As the vehicle passes you, the pitch suddenly drops.

This seeming change in pitch of a moving sound is called the *Doppler effect*. It is named after Christian Johann Doppler who worked out the reason for it in 1842. The Doppler effect also occurs with light waves.

If a source of light, such as a star, is moving towards or away from an observer, the normal frequency of the light waves is increased or decreased. This effect is very useful in astronomy for calculating the velocities of stars.

One very recent noise is the sonic boom produced by supersonic aircraft. As an aircraft flies, it pushes air in front of it in waves; these are like the waves you see moving forward and outward from the bow of a moving ship. As the aircraft flies faster it pushes the waves of air against each other until there is a wall or barrier of compressed air in front of it.

At about 1200 km per hour (750 mph) an aircraft reaches the speed of sound. At this moment the powerful air pressure wave at the nose of the aircraft is disturbed and turns into a sound wave. A noise like a tremendous clap of thunder is heard directly below the aircraft; this is called the *sonic boom*.

Above
Sonic boom. Flying below the speed of sound, the aircraft compresses the air in front of it. At 1200 km per hour, the speed of sound, the nose pressure waves become sound waves. This produces a shock wave in the air that causes the sonic boom.

Left
Supersonic aircraft. There are many aircraft that can fly faster than the speed of sound. Most of these are military aircraft. The world's fastest jet aircraft is the Lockheed SR-71. This American plane has reached a speed of 3520 km per hour (2200 mph). Concorde has been developed jointly in Britain and France and will be used to carry passengers. It will fly at more than twice the speed of sound, travelling over 7000 km non-stop.

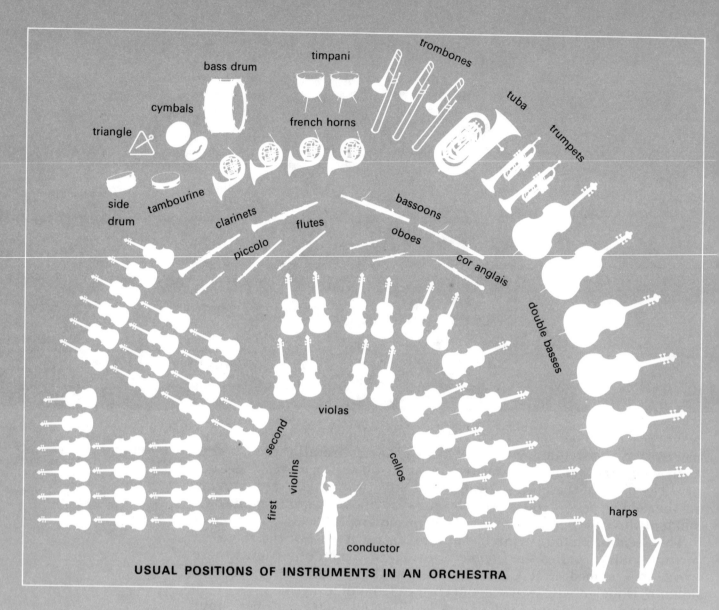

USUAL POSITIONS OF INSTRUMENTS IN AN ORCHESTRA

Invention of optical instruments

Instrument	type	date	inventor	country
microscope	optical	1590	Janssen	Holland
	electron	1939	Zworykin	USA
telescope	refracting	1608 1610	Lippershey Galileo (first practical model)	Holland Italy
	reflecting	1661 1668	Gregory Newton (first practical model)	Scotland England
	radio	1952	built at Jodrell Bank	England
camera		1826	Nièpce, used to take first photograph	France

Electrons at Work

Contents

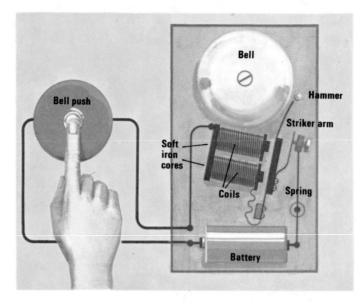

Electrical appliances

Energy can exist in many forms. The most convenient form is electrical energy because it is easily moved from one place to another. Therefore many devices which we use in our homes depend on electrical energy. Usually the devices convert electrical energy into some other form of energy. For example, a light bulb converts it into *light*. An electric fire turns it into *heat* (and a small amount of light when the element glows red). In an electric bell the energy is transformed into *sound*. In these three cases electrical energy is changed into other forms using wires.

Electricity can also be made to pass through a gas when the gas is at a very low pressure. This makes the gas glow as it does in the brightly coloured lights used in neon signs, advertising displays and in sodium street lighting.

When an electric current passes through some liquids, new substances are sometimes formed or liberated from the liquid. This is a *chemical* effect and is used in industry to produce materials such as aluminium and copper. The process is called *electrolysis*.

The telephone is one of the most important appliances used in homes and offices. It too relies on the use of electricity. In 1876 Professor Alexander Bell sent his assistant the first telephone message ever transmitted, 'Mr. Watson, please come here; I want you.' Though the instrument used by Bell has been greatly improved the

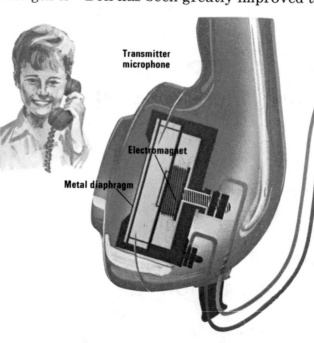

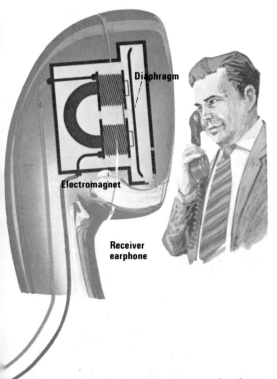

Diaphragm

Electromagnet

Receiver earphone

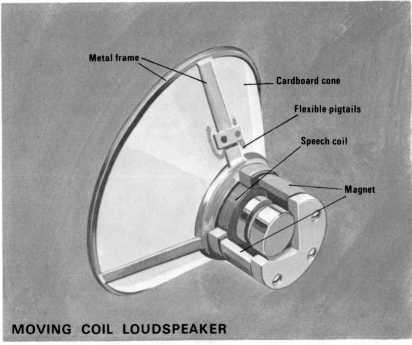

Metal frame

Cardboard cone

Flexible pigtails

Speech coil

Magnet

MOVING COIL LOUDSPEAKER

Above
In the loudspeaker the electromagnet makes a cardboard cone vibrate in sympathy with the current passing through it. The vibrating cone creates sound waves.

principle of the modern telephone remains the same. In a simple telephone the conversion of sounds into electric currents relies on an electromagnet. This consists of a piece of soft iron with a coil of wire wound round it. This electromagnet is placed just behind a thin disc of metal called a diaphragm. The diaphragm in the microphone vibrates in the sound waves and as it vibrates it causes a change in the strength of the magnetism of the electromagnet. This in turn causes an electric current to flow through wires joining the microphone to the receiver. The current changes rapidly at a speed that depends on

how quickly the sounds change; the strength of the current depends on the strength of the sound. In the receiver there is another electromagnet and a diaphragm. The varying current causes this diaphragm to vibrate in the same way as the first so that it reproduces the sounds sent from the microphone.

The *loudspeaker* is a similar device to this simple earphone receiver, but instead of using a vibrating diaphragm the loudspeaker uses a cardboard cone. The electromagnet makes the cone vibrate and this moves a much greater quantity of air. This means that more energy can be changed from the electrical form into sound. Loudspeakers therefore do not have to be held close to the ear.

ELECTRIC QUIZ BOARD

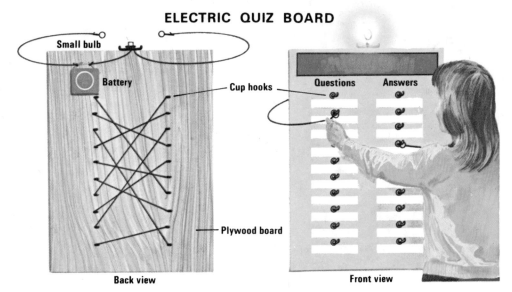

Small bulb

Battery

Cup hooks

Questions   Answers

Plywood board

Back view

Front view

Left
Make a quiz board with a light that flashes to show the right answer. Attach a battery and a small bulb to a board. Wire them together and make two long leads with metal clips on the ends. Test that the bulb will light by touching the clips together.
Screw two lines of metal hooks through the board. Paste down your questions against one line, and the answers, jumbled up, against the second line.
Connect each question to its correct answer by a wire on the back of the board, fastened to the ends of the hooks.
Ask a friend to clip one lead to a question and clip the other lead to what they think is the answer. If they are right, the bulb will light because the connecting wire on the back of the board completes the circuit.

Ampère

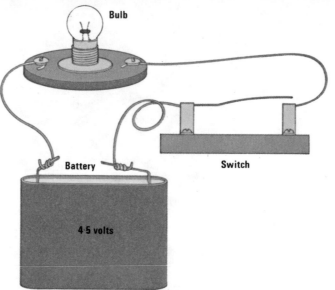
Bulb

Battery

4·5 volts

Switch

Left
A simple circuit consisting of a torch bulb, a battery, three pieces of wire and a switch. When the springy metal strip of the switch is pressed down the electrons flow round the circuit and the light bulb lights up.

André Marie Ampère (1775–1836) was a French scientist and mathematician. After hearing of Oersted's discovery he performed many experiments in electromagnetism. He showed that two wires carrying currents exert a force on each other because of the magnetic fields produced. The unit of electric current, the *ampere* or *amp*, is named after him.

Right
A simple switch made from two drawing pins and a bent paper clip.

Below
The atomic nucleus consists of tiny particles called protons and neutrons. The proton is positively charged and the electron is negatively charged. The charges are equal but opposite and balance each other out. In the hydrogen atom the nucleus consists of one proton and there is only one electron. This atom, like any other atom, has therefore no charge. Neutrons are not charged. They occur in all nuclei except hydrogen.

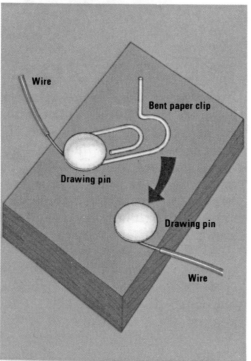
Wire

Bent paper clip

Drawing pin

Drawing pin

Wire

Electric current

If you connect a torch bulb to a battery through a switch you have a simple electric circuit. When the switch is open there is no flow of electricity. When you complete the circuit, electricity flows through the wires from the battery to the bulb. What exactly is it that flows through the wire when the switch is closed? What makes an electric current? The answer is that an electric current consists of a flow of *electrons* and it is this flow of electrons that the switch interrupts.

An electron is a tiny negatively charged particle. It is very tiny indeed. To make the torch bulb

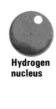
Hydrogen nucleus

Carbon nucleus

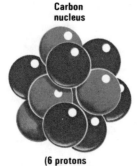

(6 protons 6 neutrons)

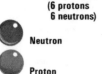
Neutron

Proton

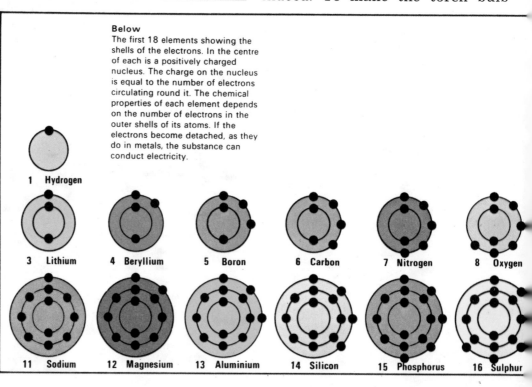
Below
The first 18 elements showing the shells of the electrons. In the centre of each is a positively charged nucleus. The charge on the nucleus is equal to the number of electrons circulating round it. The chemical properties of each element depends on the number of electrons in the outer shells of its atoms. If the electrons become detached, as they do in metals, the substance can conduct electricity.

1 Hydrogen

3 Lithium   4 Beryllium   5 Boron   6 Carbon   7 Nitrogen   8 Oxygen

11 Sodium   12 Magnesium   13 Aluminium   14 Silicon   15 Phosphorus   16 Sulphur

stay alight for one second takes a flow of about one million million million electrons. These electrons occur in atoms (see page 84). Lord Rutherford discovered that the atoms of the different elements all have different numbers of electrons. He also found that atoms consist of a central *nucleus*. The electrons move round the nucleus, at different distances from it, in groups called *shells*. The simplest atom is hydrogen consisting of one electron circling round the nucleus. The diagram shows 18 different elements, all with different numbers of electrons moving round the nucleus.

Groups of eight electrons are very stable in atoms. When atoms combine with each other to form molecules, the tendency is for the combining atoms to end up with an outer shell of eight electrons. However, some atoms, those with one, two, or sometimes three electrons in their outer shells, combine with each other in a different way. These outer electrons detach themselves from the nucleus and wander at random around the atoms. Elements which can combine in this way are called *metals*; they conduct electricity because these detached electrons are free to move.

The function of the battery in the simple circuit described is to push the free electrons in the metal wire so that they all move in the same direction. When a current flows through a wire, it consists of these detached outer electrons all flowing in the same direction. When the switch is turned off and the battery is disconnected the electrons cease to have this push and they return to random motion.

When the torch switch is pushed down, the electrons flow through the wire and pass through the very thin wire in the bulb. This wire is called a *filament*. The wire is so thin that the collisions between electrons and atoms are much more frequent. This increases the temperature of the wire and makes the atoms emit light (see page 105), first red light and then, when it gets hotter, white light.

Electrons not only flow through wires, they also flow through nerves in the body. For example, when you see something, an electrical impulse travels from your eye to your brain. These impulses consist of a flow of electrons passing down the optic nerve from the retina of the eye to the optic centre of the brain. Muscles, too, are controlled by a flow of electric pulses from the brain passing down nerves to the muscles.

Thomson

Above
Sir Joseph John Thomson (1856–1940), the Cambridge scientist who discovered the electron in 1897. This enabled us to understand electric current.

Rutherford

Above
Lord Rutherford (1871–1937), a New Zealander who came to work at Cambridge under J. J. Thomson. He discovered the structure of the atom.

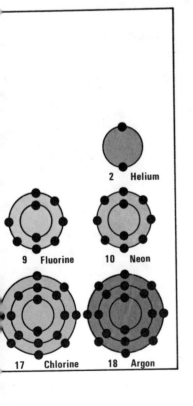

2 Helium

9 Fluorine   10 Neon

17 Chlorine   18 Argon

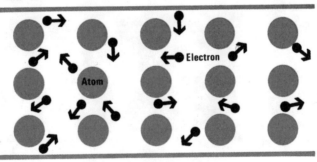

Electron

Atom

Electrons moving at random – no current

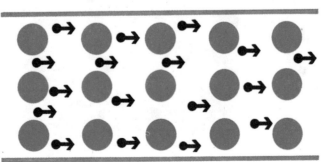

Electrons moving in same direction – current flows

Left
In a metal wire the outer electrons move at random about the atoms. When a current flows these electrons all move in the same direction.

157

Conductors and insulators

In metals, like copper, the atoms combine with each other to form crystals in which the outer atomic electrons are free to move about. When these free electrons move in one direction an electric current flows (see page 157). In non-metals, like sulphur, the electrons are bound to the atomic nuclei and no current can flow. These substances are called *insulators*. Most compounds are insulators and some, like rubber, are particularly good insulators. Wires are usually covered with rubber or plastics to make them safe to handle. In fact we use conductors to carry electricity to where it is needed and we use insulators to prevent it from leaking into a place in which we do not want it.

One of the main uses of insulators is to protect our bodies from electric current. This is because our bodies can conduct electricity, especially when they are wet. If, by mistake, you touch live mains wires you will get a very nasty shock. If your hands are wet the shock can kill you. Never touch electrical appliances when you have wet hands—if there is a fault in the insulation it can be very dangerous. Never take electrical appliances into the bathroom and never touch light switches or plugs when your hands are wet.

The thickness of the insulator needed to protect a wire depends not on the current flowing through it but on the voltage driving the electrons through the wire. If the voltage is high, for example in the wires leading to the plugs of a petrol engine, the insulation has to be thick. The voltage in this case is several thousand volts. On the other hand, the insulation used on wires connected to a torch battery can be very thin as the voltage is only about $1\frac{1}{2}$ volts.

Apart from conductors and insulators, there is a third class of substances called *semiconductors*.

Metal lightning conductor

Left
The lightning conductor provides a harmless path for the lightning discharge to reach earth. It travels down the metal lightning conductor instead of down the side of the building which might catch fire.

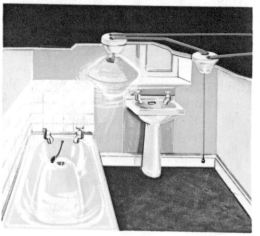

Left
In bathrooms, and sometimes in kitchens, ceiling switches are used. They consist of a switch, operated by a piece of string, attached to the ceiling. With these switches there is no danger of electrocution even when the light is switched on or off with wet hands. The current-carrying wires are embedded in the ceiling.

Below
Mains cables may be made of copper, which is a very good conductor, or aluminium, which is cheaper. The cables are usually insulated with the plastic PVC. Those that come from the power station carry a high voltage and have to have special insulation for carrying the current.

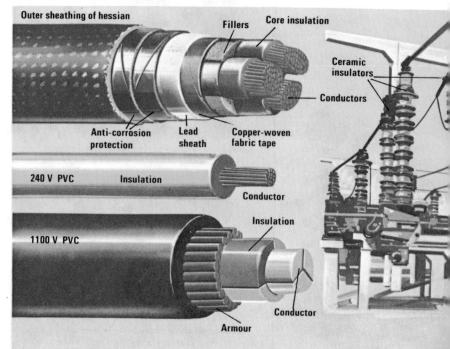

Outer sheathing of hessian

Fillers

Core insulation

Ceramic insulators

Conductors

Anti-corrosion protection

Lead sheath

Copper-woven fabric tape

240 V PVC   Insulation

Conductor

1100 V PVC

Insulation

Conductor

Armour

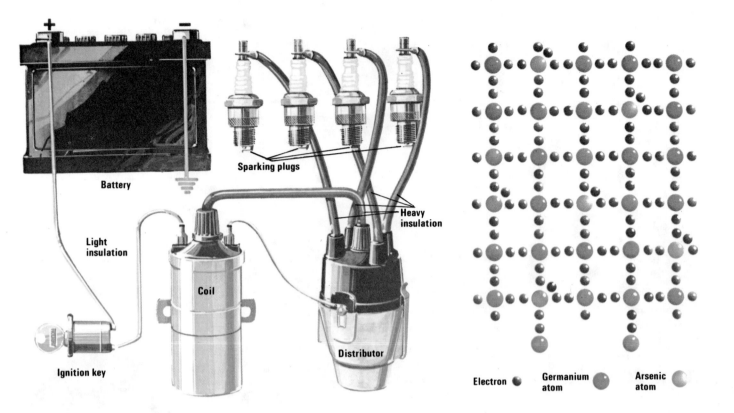

Battery

Sparking plugs

Light insulation

Heavy insulation

Coil

Distributor

Ignition key

Electron ●   Germanium atom   Arsenic atom

In the atom of these substances, some of the electrons can, under certain conditions, break free from their shells round the nuclei. Examples of semiconductors are silicon, germanium, and selenium. One way to make them conduct electricity is to heat them, but a more effective way is to add certain impurities.

If arsenic is added to germanium, free electrons occur in the crystal. This is because the germanium atom has four electrons in its outer shell and arsenic has five outer electrons. When atoms combine they tend to make up groups of eight electrons, so in this case there is one electron over. This electron can be used as a conduction electron; when a voltage is applied the electron moves away from its atom and flows like the electrons in a metal. This type of conduction is called *n*-type. If another element called indium is added to the germanium there is a different type of conduction. Indium has only three outer electrons and therefore when it combines with germanium there is a missing electron. This missing electron or *hole*, as it is called, can also act as a conductor. This is called *p*-type (positive) conduction. Various types of semiconducting material are used in making transistors (see page 239).

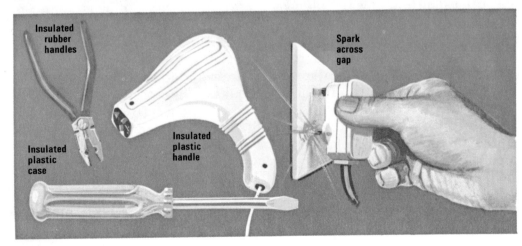

Insulated rubber handles

Insulated plastic case

Insulated plastic handle

Spark across gap

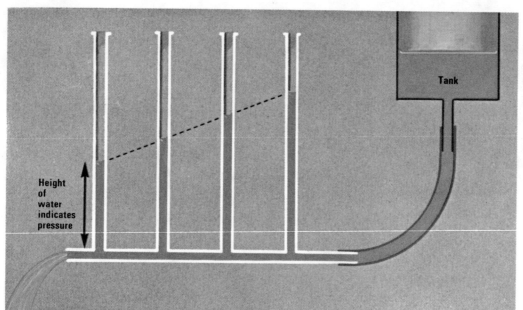

Height of water indicates pressure

Tank

Left
The flow of electricity through a wire is similar in some respects to the flow of water through a tube. Water flows from a tank through a horizontal tube. Because of friction between the water and the walls of the tube, the pressure along the tube is reduced. You can see this if you have vertical tubes sticking out of the tube. The height of the water in the tube shows the pressure in the tube. In the same way, the voltage falls along a wire, due to the resistance. The current is like the quantity of water flowing, the potential difference is like the pressure.

Voltage and resistance

In some ways an electric current resembles the flow of water in a tube. In both cases power is necessary to maintain the flow–the weight of the water or a pump in the case of a tube, and a battery or mains supply in the case of an electric current.

Of course electrons do not flow as a fluid down the wire as in the tube of water, but there are some similarities. Imagine a steady flow of water passing through a narrow horizontal tube. If vertical tubes are fixed to the horizontal tube they can act as pressure gauges, the height of water in the vertical tubes indicating pressure. If you were to carry out this experiment you would see the pressure in the tube fall between the inlet end and the outlet. The flow of water always depends on the *difference of pressure* between the two ends of the tube. In the case of the electric current this difference of electrical pressure, which forces the electric current through a wire, is called the *potential difference* (p.d.). Again the current or flow of electricity depends, like the flow of water, on the potential difference between the ends of the wire. This relation was first discovered by Georg Ohm and is known as *Ohm's law*. This

states that the current increases and decreases in porportion to potential difference.

The size of the potential difference is measured in *volts*, a unit named after the Italian scientist called Volta. The pressure falls along the tube of water because of the friction between the water and the sides of the tube. Similarly with an electric current, consisting of a flow of electrons, there is *resistance* to the electron flow. This is caused by the electrons bumping into atoms or into each other. In fact the resistance of a wire or conductor is equal to the potential difference divided by the current in amperes. This is another way of putting Ohm's law and the unit of resistance is called the *ohm*.

Ohm's law is used in calculating the resistance of the fuses in our homes. A fuse is used to protect an electrical appliance if the insulation breaks down and the current flows where it should not be flowing. If, for example, you knock over a table lamp that is switched on and the glass bulb breaks, it is possible for the two wires attached to the ends of the filament to touch each other. This is called a *short circuit* and there will now be a very high current flowing through the flex, as the current is no longer limited by the high resistance of the thin filament wire. If this were allowed to con-

Ohm

Above
George Simon Ohm (1789–1854). A German scientist who discovered that the current is proportional to potential difference (Ohm's law). The unit of resistance, the ohm, is called after him.

Volta

Above
Count Alessandro Volta (1745–1827). The Italian scientist who first worked out the idea of electric currents. He also made the first battery. The unit of potential difference, the volt, is named after him.

tinue for any length of time it could start a fire in the house because the flex would become very hot.

In order to avoid this danger, nearly every device now has a fuse in the plug. This consists of a piece of thin wire which melts and breaks the circuit if the current is greater than it should be for safety. The high resistance of the fuse restricts the amount of current that can be drawn. It is important to use fuses of the correct resistance for each electrical appliance.

Below and left
Some fuses are built into cartridges, some are bare wire. In older houses the fuses are all together in a fuse box, in modern houses, each plug has its own fuse.

Cartridge fuse

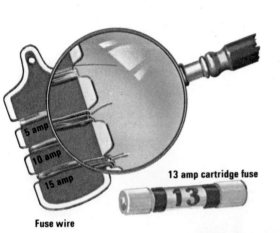

5 amp
10 amp
15 amp

Fuse wire

13 amp cartridge fuse

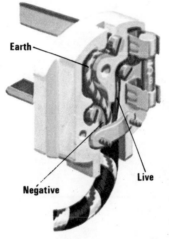

Earth

Negative

Live

13 amp plug with cartridge fuse

Wired fuse

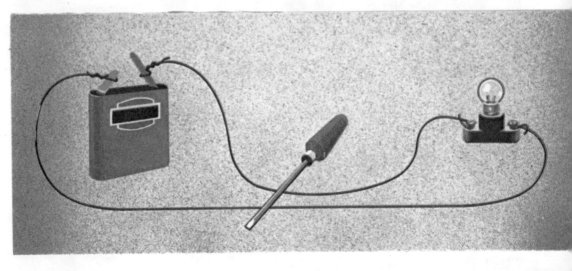

Right
A simple demonstration of a short circuit. Wire up a small bulb to a battery with bare wire. Place a metal conductor, such as a screwdriver, across both wires and see the bulb go out. The screwdriver has caused a short circuit. The current flows through it rather than through the bulb as the thick screwdriver has a lower resistance than the thin bulb filament.

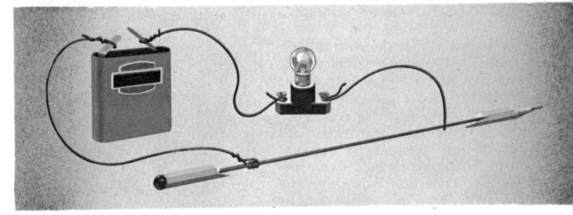

Right
A variable resistor is called a rheostat. You can make one from a piece of pencil lead. Attach wires to each end so that one wire can slide along the lead. As you increase the length of lead in the circuit you increase the resistance and the bulb will grow dimmer.

Right
The domestic iron is heated by an element consisting of a conducting wire wound onto an insulating sheet. It contains an adjustable control which cuts off the current when the iron reaches a certain temperature. This consists of a strip of two metals (*bimetallic strip*) which bends when it is heated owing to the different rate of expansion of the two metals. The bending causes the contact points to open which stops the current flowing so that the element cools down.

Below
An electric hair drier. When you switch it on, the heating coils behind the nozzle start to glow. At the same time an electric motor starts the fan rotating. This sucks a stream of air in through the side vent and out through the nozzle. The air stream is heated as it passes over the coils.
Do not cover up the air vent when the drier is on, because without the air stream, the coils grow hotter and hotter, and would melt the case.

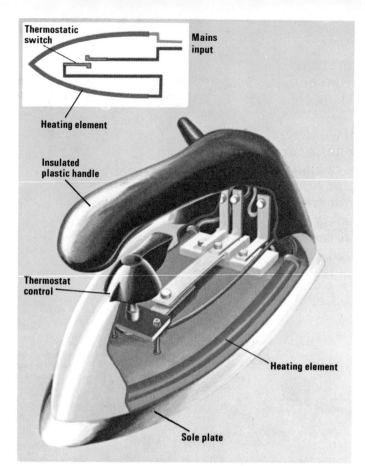

Thermostatic switch
Mains input
Heating element
Insulated plastic handle
Thermostat control
Heating element
Sole plate

Right
Thermocouple. Two wires of different metal are connected together to form a loop. A sensitive ammeter, which measures current, is connected to one wire. One of the junctions is heated by a candle, the other is cooled in ice. The greatest current is shown on the ammeter when the temperature difference is biggest. Take away either the flame or the ice and the current is reduced.

Right
A thermocouple can be used to measure the strength of the sun's rays. It consists of two glass hemispheres. The top one is facing the sun, the bottom one faces the ground. Each glass hemisphere supports a blackened disc. Between the two blackened discs a series of thermocouples are arranged so that one set of junctions is heated by the rays direct from the sun, whereas the bottom junctions are heated by the reflected rays. The difference in temperature between the two sets of junctions creates a current which can be recorded. The record shows the variations in the strength of the sun during the day.

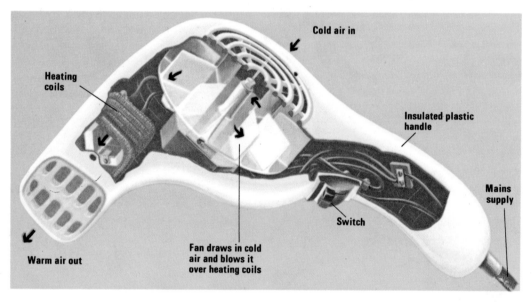

Cold air in
Heating coils
Insulated plastic handle
Mains supply
Switch
Fan draws in cold air and blows it over heating coils
Warm air out

Right
The reverse of the thermocouple effect occurs when a current is passed through wires of two different semiconductors. One junction is then cooled and the other warmed.

Heating coils

Electric current has to overcome resistance as it flows through a wire. Every conductor, however good, has a resistance, although some have only a very small resistance. Electricity produces heat as it forces its way through a resistor. The greater the resistance the greater the heat produced. Sometimes the conductor becomes warm and sometimes red hot, as in an electric fire. Sometimes the conductor becomes white hot as in

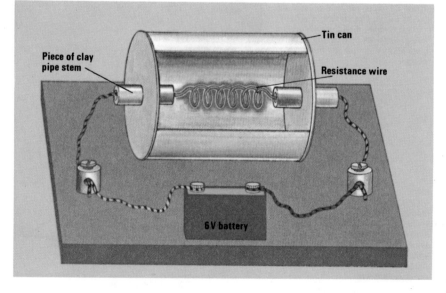

Tin can
Piece of clay pipe stem
Resistance wire
6 V battery

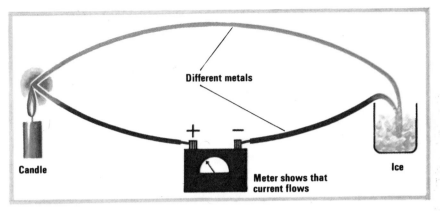

Candle · Different metals · Meter shows that current flows · Ice

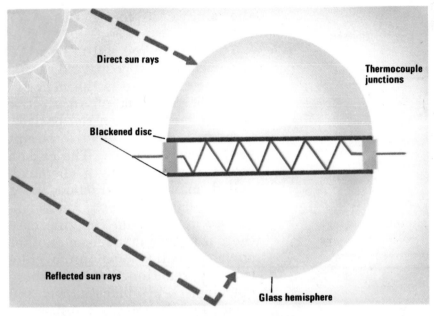

Direct sun rays · Thermocouple junctions · Blackened disc · Reflected sun rays · Glass hemisphere

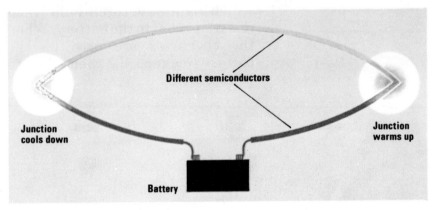

Junction cools down · Different semiconductors · Junction warms up · Battery

Left
A small home-made electric heater. The reflector is a soup can, cutaway. The insulators are pieces of the stem of a clay pipe and the element is made from resistance wire that has been wound onto a knitting needle. The device needs a 6 volt battery to operate it.

which is sometimes called an *element*, becomes red hot.

To make a small electric fire you need a tin can about 10 cm in diameter and 13 cm high with half of the side cut out, a broken stem of a clay pipe and about 30 cm of No 24 SWG *nichrome* wire.

Knock a small hole in each end of the tin and insert a piece of clay pipe in each hole to act as an *insulator* for the wire. Wind the *nichrome* resistance wire on a knitting needle, withdraw the needle, and put the ends of the wire through the holes of the two bits of clay pipe. Connect these ends to two terminals on a wooden base. Finally, nail the tin can to the base. Connect the terminals to a 6 volt battery and the element will glow red. The heat from the element will be reflected from the inside of the tin.

Electric heating elements are a way of converting electric energy into heat. To reverse the process – to create electric energy from heat – a *thermocouple* can be used. A thermocouple consists of two wires of different metals joined at two places so that they form an electrical loop. If the two junctions are at different temperatures a small current will flow through the wire. This current depends on the difference in temperature between the junctions; the higher the temperature difference the higher the current. If the ends of a copper wire are joined to the ends of an iron wire and one junction is placed in a glass of ice and the other in a candle flame, a current is registered on a sensitive ammeter. The current is too low to light a torch bulb, but it is very useful for measuring temperature.

This effect also works in reverse. If a current is passed through the loop containing the two metal junctions, one junction will be cooled and the other will be warmed. The effect is too weak with metals to be of much value but it can be made stronger by using two different types of semiconductor.

the case of an electric light bulb. Thick copper wires have a very small resistance, and thin wires made of special mixtures of metals have large resistances. These mixtures, or *alloys*, are used to make *heating coils*. Heating coils are used in electric fires, irons, toasters, kettles and immersion heaters to heat bath water.

In an electric iron the coil becomes hot but not red hot, otherwise the iron might burn the clothes. In an electric fire and an electric toaster the heating coil,

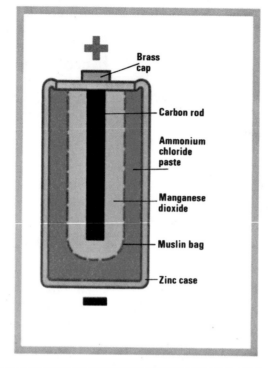

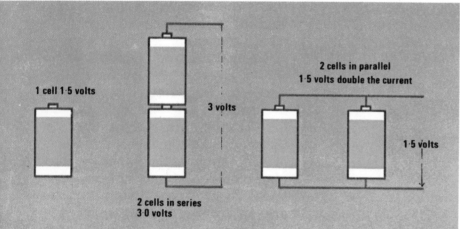

Dry batteries

If you undo a torch you will find
inside one or more *dry batteries*,
sometimes called cells. If you take
a battery to pieces you will find
that it is made of a zinc metal case.
In the centre of one end of the case
there is a brass cap which forms
one terminal. Under this cap there
is a rod of carbon. The bottom of
the zinc case forms the other
terminal.

The carbon rod with the brass
cap is called the positive terminal
and the zinc case is the negative
terminal. We talk of an electric
current flowing from the positive
terminal round an electric circuit
to the negative plate. The carbon
rod is surrounded by a chemical,
called manganese dioxide, in a
muslin bag. Between the manganese dioxide and the zinc case
there is a paste made from another
chemical called ammonium chloride. A reaction between these
chemicals takes place slowly and
produces the potential difference
which lights the torch bulb when
it is connected to the battery. When
the chemicals are used up the
battery weakens and then it has to
be replaced.

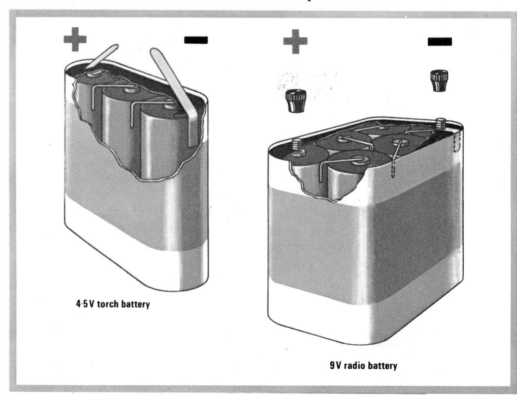

4·5 V torch battery

9 V radio battery

This sort of battery is called a *primary* cell. The normal dry battery has a fixed potential difference or voltage of about 1·5 volts. A small torch needs only one battery, and does not shine very far; a larger torch has two batteries one on top of the other. This increases the voltage to about 3 volts and the torch gives a stronger light.

Some dry batteries which have a much higher voltage, 10 or 20 volts, are in fact a number of single dry batteries joined together.

There are two ways of joining batteries together. If they are connected end to end so that the brass positive terminal of one touches the negative case of the other, the voltages add together. This is called connecting the batteries *in series*. If both brass terminals are connected together and both cases are connected together the batteries are connected *in parallel*. In this case the potential difference is only 1·5V, but the total current available is doubled.

Batteries are used to provide the power for a number of domestic appliances. For example, portable radios using transistors use only one or two batteries in series. On the other hand some portable tape recorders have the batteries driving the motor connected in parallel.

Some devices are very small and therefore require only tiny batteries; toy cars, electric razors, and deaf aids are some examples. These devices only take a small amount of power and they can therefore use very small batteries. Sometimes a different type of cell is used in these small devices. This is called a mercury cell and some types of mercury cell can be recharged. Electric toothbrushes often contain this type of cell. The toothbrush itself fits onto a vibrator unit containing the batteries. When not in use the vibrator unit fits into a charging unit.

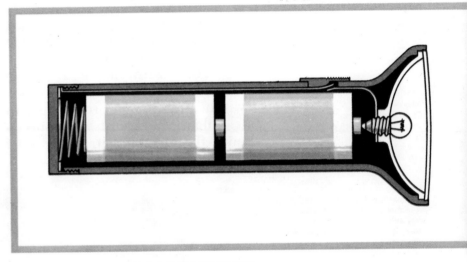

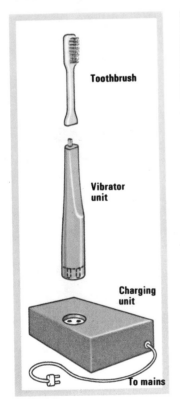

Toothbrush

Vibrator unit

Charging unit

To mains

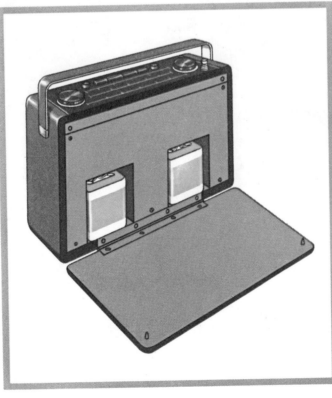

165

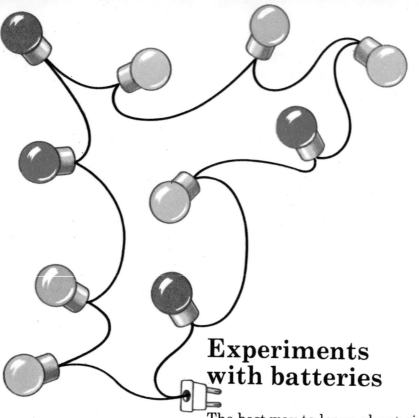

Experiments with batteries

The best way to learn about circuit electricity is to build some simple circuits with batteries.

To start with, make a simple circuit with a 4·5 volt battery, a switch, and a 4·5 volt torch bulb in its holder. A circuit is simply a route for electric current like a motor racing circuit.

Make a simple switch from a piece of wood with two brass drawing pins stuck in it. Straighten out a paper clip and attach it to one of the drawing pins. To make contact simply press the paper clip down onto the other drawing pin.

Now connect into the simple circuit an extra bulb, so that the current passes first through one bulb and then through the other. These bulbs are *in series*. Press the switch and notice how bright the bulbs are; they will not be as bright as when only one bulb is used. This is because when the two bulbs are having to share the 4·5 volts between them, they do not each receive the full voltage for which they are designed.

Now replace the bulbs in their holders by two bulbs which have a lower voltage than the last bulbs. Using a 4·5 volt battery, this time try two 2·5 volt bulbs in this series circuit instead of 4·5 volt bulbs. Notice that the bulbs are brighter this time. They are each receiving about the correct voltage. Now try the two first bulbs connected in a

Above
Christmas tree lights. There are ten coloured bulbs each of 24 volts connected in series to the mains. If one bulb fails the circuit is broken and all the lights go out.

Right
To make a model set of traffic lights, wire three torch bulbs to a three-way switch made out of four drawing pins and a paperclip. Wire the three bulbs together and connect them to a 4·5 volt battery. Connect the other side of the battery to the paper clip switch. Paint the bulbs red, amber and green. These bulbs are connected in parallel so that they can be switched on separately.

Far right
To make a model street lighting system, build a row of wooden lamp posts. Fix a bulb on each post. Wire the bulbs in parallel so that if one bulb fails, the rest will still stay lit. Connect them to a battery via a paper clip switch.

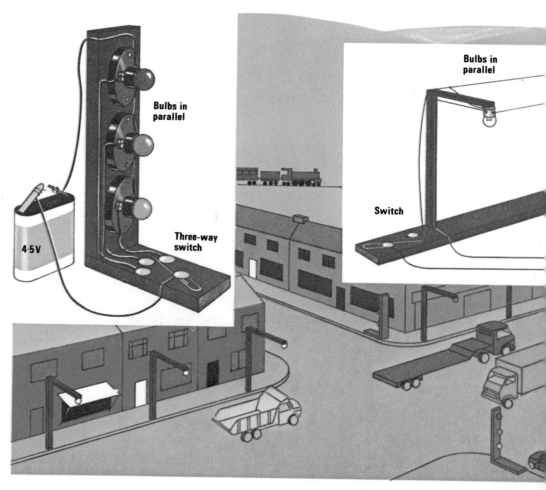

Bulbs in parallel

4·5V

Three-way switch

Bulbs in parallel

Switch

parallel circuit. Notice that both bulbs are bright this time even though the same battery is being used. In this kind of circuit the battery is doing twice as much work and it will not last long. Both bulbs are receiving the full 4·5 volts from the battery and therefore they are working correctly. The small lights used on Christmas trees are connected in a series circuit. The total voltage of all the bulbs is the same as the voltage of the mains which supplies the electricity to light them. This is usually 240 volts. Therefore if each bulb is 24 volts there will be 10 bulbs in this series

If a room needs more than one bulb, they are connected in parallel. In this way two bulbs can be switched on at the same time and they will both be as bright as all the other lights in the house.

You can put your circuits to the test by making some useful models and toys out of them. Use a simple electromagnet to make parts move. You can equip a doll's house or a model village with lighting and a train set with signals.

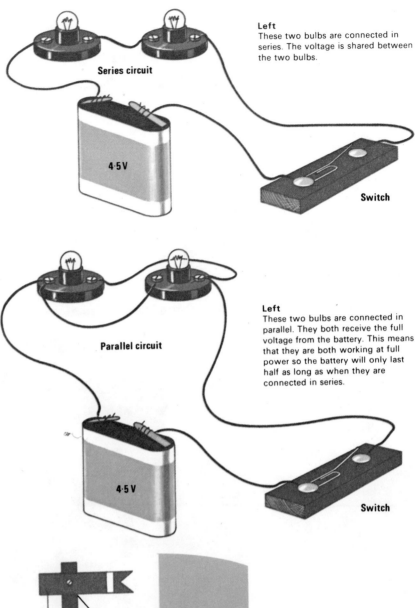

Series circuit

4·5 V

Switch

Left
These two bulbs are connected in series. The voltage is shared between the two bulbs.

Parallel circuit

4·5 V

Switch

Left
These two bulbs are connected in parallel. They both receive the full voltage from the battery. This means that they are both working at full power so the battery will only last half as long as when they are connected in series.

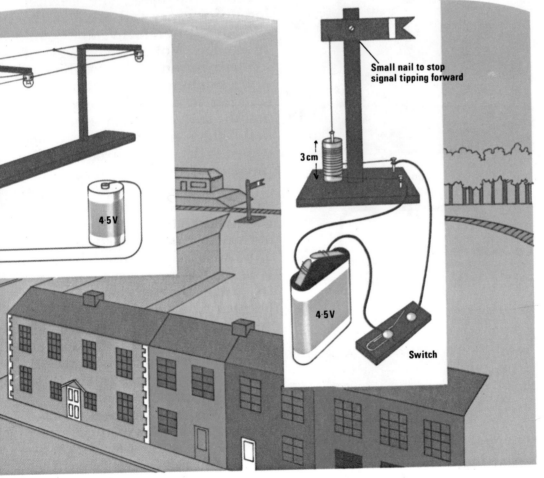

4·5 V

Small nail to stop signal tipping forward

3 cm

4·5 V

Switch

Left
To make a model railway signal take some insulated copper wire (s.w.g. No. 36 is best) and wind it round a piece of thin tube, such as a piece of the barrel of a ball-point pen. Wind the wire round about 1000 times. Make the winding about 3 cm long. This is the first part of the *electromagnet* which will work the signal. Make the signal on a wooden base and fix the signal arm so that it can move up and down easily. Glue the winding to the base close to the upright piece. Tie a piece of thread to the back of the arm of the signal and attach a nail to the other end of the thread. Arrange the length of the thread so that the nail goes in and out of the electromagnet as the signal arm goes up and down. Now connect the ends of the winding wire to two nails on the wooden base. Connect the two nails to a switch and a 4·5 volt battery. The model is now ready to operate — when you close the switch the signal will rise. The electromagnet pulls the nail downwards when the current flows, and this lifts the signal.

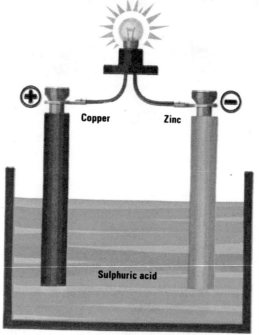

Copper   Zinc

Sulphuric acid

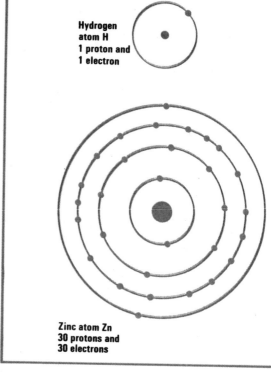

Hydrogen atom H
1 proton and
1 electron

Zinc atom Zn
30 protons and
30 electrons

Far right
This shows how positive ions are formed from atoms. The hydrogen atom (H) has 1 proton and 1 electron so it has no charge. If an electron is taken away a single proton remains. This is a hydrogen ion (H^+). It has a positive charge. The zinc atom (Zn) has thirty protons and thirty electrons. If it loses one electron it has one more proton than electrons and therefore has a positive charge. Thus it has become a zinc ion (Zn^+).

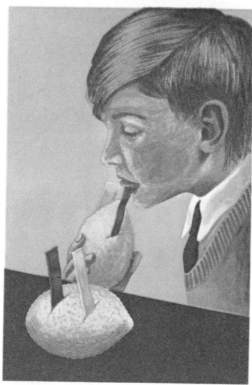

Right
You can make a simple electric cell from a lemon and two metal strips, one of zinc and one of copper. Roll the lemon about to make it juicy inside. Stick the two metal strips into it, making sure they are not touching inside. Touch the two ends with your tongue and you will feel the tingling sensation of the current that the cell is generating.

Battery

Anode   Cathode

Copper

Copper sulphate solution

Right
In a voltaic cell a chemical reaction causes an electric current. In the same way if an electric current is passed through an electrolyte it can cause a chemical reaction. This is called *electrolysis*. Here a current is passing through a solution of copper sulphate. The cathode becomes coated with a thin layer of copper. This is an example of electroplating. At the anode, oxygen gas is given off.

Cells and electrolysis

The dry cells used in electric torches are examples of primary cells. In these cells electricity is made by chemical changes. The earliest form of primary cell is called the *voltaic cell* after its inventor Count Alessandro Volta. It consisted of a copper rod and a zinc rod dipping into a sulphuric acid solution. This solution is called the *electrolyte* and the rods are called the *electrodes*. If the copper electrode is connected to the zinc electrode outside the electrolyte then a current flows.

To understand how this happens we must think of the structures of the atoms and molecules. An atom of zinc contains a nucleus made up of protons and neutrons. The protons have a positive charge and this makes the nucleus positive. A number of electrons are moving around the nucleus and these all have negative charges. There is the same number of electrons as protons and this makes the total charge of the atoms neutral.

If an atom of zinc loses an electron there are now more protons than electrons and the atom is no longer neutral. It has a positive

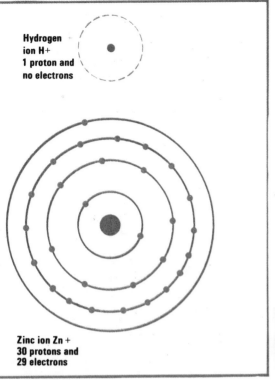

Hydrogen
ion H+
1 proton and
no electrons

Zinc ion Zn +
30 protons and
29 electrons

charge. These charged atoms are called *ions*.

If an atom gains an extra electron there are more electrons than protons and the atom has a negative charge. It has become a negative ion. It is these ions that produce electricity in batteries.

Now think of the zinc and copper rods in the sulphuric acid solution. The zinc rod consists of many zinc atoms. Some of these change into positive zinc ions and go into the solution. The electrons are left behind on the zinc rod and a negative charge builds up on this rod. At the copper rod a different process takes place. In the solution the sulphuric acid gives positive hydrogen ions. These combine with electrons from the copper rod and turn back into hydrogen atoms. This causes bubbles of hydrogen gas to form on the rod. It also causes the copper rod to build up a positive charge because it is losing electrons. Thus the zinc rod contains more electrons than protons and the copper rod has less electrons than protons. If they are connected by a wire outside the solution, the electrons in the zinc move through the wire to the copper. In other words there is a flow of electric current.

In the cell the zinc rod dissolves in the sulphuric acid to give zinc ions. Sulphuric acid is a compound and is sometimes called hydrogen sulphate. It has lost its hydrogen as hydrogen gas. The electricity has been produced by a chemical reaction in which zinc and hydrogen sulphate have changed to zinc sulphate and hydrogen. The copper has not been changed by the production of electricity but it is necessary to have a copper rod to give electrons to the hydrogen ions. In the voltaic cell the copper is the positive electrode and the zinc is the negative electrode.

Above
Electrolysis is used for coating metal objects and parts with a thin layer of a different metal. Here are some objects that have been coated in this way. The part to be coated is hung in a bath of electrolyte and made the cathode of a cell. The anode is made of a piece of the metal to be deposited. When an electric current is passed, the object is covered with a layer of this metal. This is called *electroplating*. Usually objects are electroplated with expensive metals, such as gold, silver, copper, and chromium. Car bumpers, for instance, are made of steel and covered with chromium to make them shiny. It would be too expensive to make the whole bumper out of chromium.

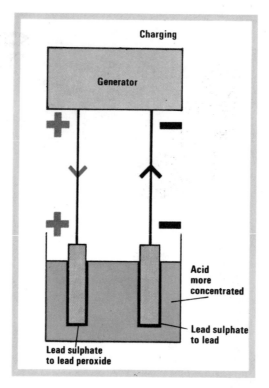

Charging

Generator

Acid more concentrated

Lead sulphate to lead

Lead sulphate to lead peroxide

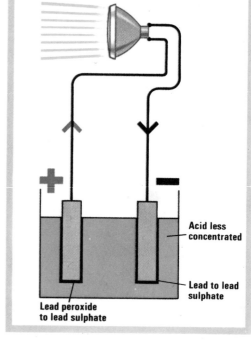

Discharging

Acid less concentrated

Lead to lead sulphate

Lead peroxide to lead sulphate

The car battery

In a normal dry battery the chemicals which produce the electric current are used up and the whole battery has to be thrown away when it no longer works. Cells of this kind are called *primary cells*. They are expensive and also cannot be used to produce large currents. So a cell has been developed which can store electrical energy when this is passed into it. The electricity can then be drawn from the cell in the form of an electric current. Such a cell is called a *secondary* cell or, sometimes, an *accumulator*, as is the car battery.

In an accumulator two lead plates are used as electrodes in a solution of sulphuric acid. By passing a current through the lead plates chemical changes take place in the electrodes, the sulphuric acid solution gets stronger and the cell becomes capable of driving an electric current. We call this *charging* a battery.

When the charging current is stopped, the battery can then be connected to a circuit, like a light bulb. Current will then flow for a time from the anode to the cathode. The chemical change which took place during charging is now reversed as electricity is drawn from the accumulator. However the materials in the accumulator are not used up, merely changed. Therefore the whole process can begin again. When the accumulator is providing an electric current it is said to be *discharging*.

The accumulator does not make electricity in the way that the dry battery does. It only stores it, and electricity has to be put in before any can be taken out. The same amount of electricity can be obtained from a cell as was put into it.

In a normal petrol driven car the battery is used to produce the electric spark which starts the engine. It also supplies current for the car headlights and indicators, the heater fan, windscreen wipers, and horn. The battery is

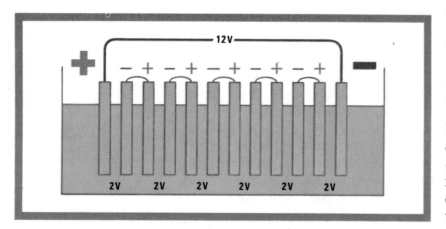

12V

2V 2V 2V 2V 2V 2V

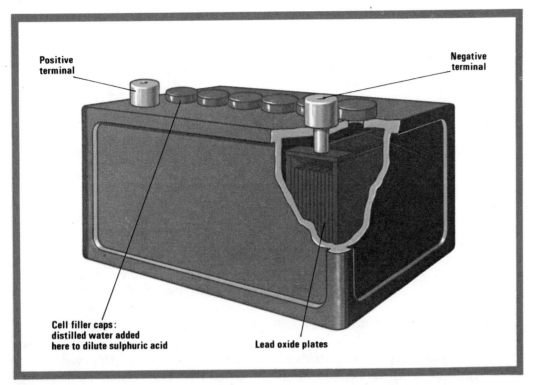

Positive terminal

Negative terminal

Cell filler caps: distilled water added here to dilute sulphuric acid

Lead oxide plates

Left
A cutaway diagram of a car battery, or accumulator. It shows the set of lead plates immersed in the electrolyte solution, which is dilute sulphuric acid. At each end of the battery there is a large connection point, or terminal, where the heavy duty leads are attached.

charged up by a dynamo which is turned by the car engine, or by a battery charger.

Today we are greatly concerned about the pollution of the air we breathe caused by the large number of cars, and especially lorries on the road. The gases that come out of their exhausts are poisonous.

One well known vehicle does not poison our air. This is the milk float which is driven by electricity. It has an electric motor instead of a petrol or diesel engine. The power comes from large accumulators which are charged with electricity every night. Because no fuel is burnt there are no poisonous exhausts to pollute the atmosphere. Several car manufacturers have been trying to develop battery driven cars for use in towns. The problem is to make accumulators that can hold large amounts of electricity and are not too heavy. Better and better accumulators are now being made for use in electric cars.

Left
Different types of vehicle powered by an electric motor.

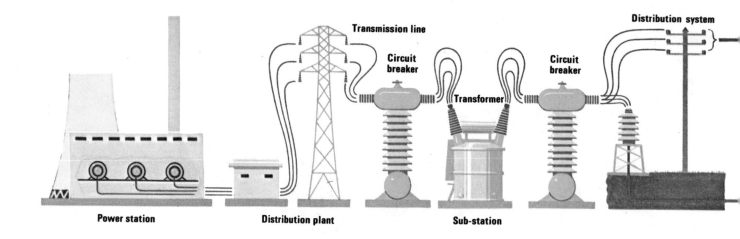

Power station   Distribution plant   Sub-station

Mains supply electricity

Primary cells (dry batteries) are expensive and have to be thrown away when used up. Accumulators, or secondary cells, are also expensive and need electricity to recharge them. In our homes we use a large number of electrical appliances apart from lighting. Such things as cookers, washing machines, mixers, drills, fires, television, and many more are operated by electricity. To run all these appliances from batteries would not only be very expensive, but each house would need an extra room in which to put all the bulky batteries.

An alternative source of electricity is provided by the mains supply, generated in power stations (see page 182) and transmitted by wires to homes, offices, and factories. There is a network of these wires running throughout the country and this is called the *grid*. The British grid consists of 235 power stations and has 13 000 km (8000 miles) of wires. The voltage carried by these wires is very

high – sometimes as high as 400 000 volts. The wires are mostly carried on pylons that are a familiar sight in the countryside. From the high-voltage wires carried by pylons, the current is fed to sub-stations in which the voltage is reduced by transformers (see page 180). This reduced voltage is transmitted to the users, usually by underground cables, but sometimes by overhead wires.

In most countries the mains supply is *alternating current* (a.c. for short). This means that the voltage varies up and down and is not steady as it is in *direct current* (d.c.). Alternating current is used because its voltage can be changed by a transformer – direct current cannot be changed in this way.

When the electricity enters a home or factory it has to be metered because we have to pay for the electricity we use. The more you

Far right
Electricity meters consist of a special kind of electric motor which drives a counting device. This shows the number of units (kilowatt-hours) used. It is most important that the aluminium motor disc does not rotate after the current has ceased. A braking magnet is used to stop the disc.

Right
The mains electricity supplied to homes is alternating current. This means that the voltage rises from zero to a maximum value of about 340 volts; it then declines to zero again. This is called half a cycle. The remaining half cycle is a negative voltage – the minimum voltage being – 340 volts. The average of each half cycle is 240 volts. The number of times this cycle is repeated in one second is called the frequency. In Britain this is 50 hertz (1 hertz is a frequency of 1 cycle per second); in the USA it is 60 hertz.

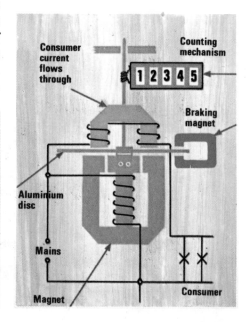

Left
All these devices used in homes rely on mains electricity. The supply is usually 240 volts in Britain (117 volts in the USA) and nearly always alternating current.

Below left
These devices are used in offices. In the electric typewriter a key has only to be lightly touched. This saves the typist a great deal of effort and enables her to type much more quickly. The electronic desk calculator uses transistors and is very quick and silent. It is replacing the old adding machines and mechanical calculators.

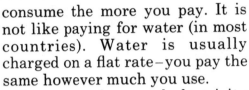

consume the more you pay. It is not like paying for water (in most countries). Water is usually charged on a flat rate—you pay the same however much you use.

To measure how much electricity you have used a meter is installed. This consists of a special type of motor connected to a counting device. This has a little dial that shows the number of units you have used. At regular intervals throughout the year a man from the electricity company comes to read the meter and then a bill is sent to the consumer. The bill is worked out on the number of kilowatt-hours used. If you have a 2 kilowatt heater and you keep it on for one hour you will be charged for 2 kilowatt-hours. For a 3 kilowatt heater burning for 2 hours the consumption would be 6 kilowatt-hours.

The price of electricity, in most countries, depends on the time at which it is used. It is usually cheaper at night than in the day. So some heaters, called *storage heaters*, are heated by electricity during the night and give out their heat during the day.

Left
Many industrial machines work on mains electricity. Heavy machines require special installations.

173

Magnetism

About 500 B.C. the ancient Greeks discovered that a certain type of black stone had the power of attracting pieces of iron. This mineral was an ore of iron and is called *magnetite*. Anything that has this property of attracting iron is called a *magnet* and the property itself is *magnetism*.

Magnetite is a compound of iron and oxygen. The common magnets that you see are made of iron or steel. A magnet can have any shape but is usually in the form of a *bar* magnet or a *horseshoe magnet*.

If you have a magnet you can experiment with iron filings. These are very small pieces of iron or steel. Touch the iron filings with the magnet and you will notice that they tend to stick onto the ends of the magnet. The magnet is stronger in these regions. These are called the *poles* of the magnet.

Tie a piece of thread around the middle of a bar magnet and hang it up so that the magnet is balanced horizontally. You will notice that the magnet always comes to rest with its ends pointing in the same direction. In fact one

Below
This is a piece of magnetite. It is sometimes also called lodestone.

Below
The bar magnet and the horseshoe magnet are the two commonest forms of magnet.

Left
The iron filings tend to stick to the ends of the magnet where the magnetism is strongest. These regions are called the poles. If a bar magnet is cut in two you do not get single poles. Instead, two separate magnets are produced.

Below
Try suspending a magnet like this. It always points north and south. If you already know the direction of north you can find which is the north pole of the magnet and which is the south pole.

Right
A chain of pins can be hung from a pole of a magnet. Each pin is made into a magnet as shown here. Notice that the north pole of the bar magnet induces a south pole on the end of the pin.

end of the magnet always points in the direction of the north pole of the earth and the other points in the direction of the south pole.

This effect is used in the compass (see page 176). The end pointing towards the north magnetic pole is called the north-seeking pole of the magnet–or *north pole*. The other is called the *south pole*.

If you play with a magnet you will also notice that not all materials can be attracted to it. You can pick up pins and nails with it but it will not attract wood, plastic, or paper. It will also not affect many other metals, such as copper, aluminium, and gold. Materials that are attracted to a magnet are called *magnetic materials*. Other materials are said to be *nonmagnetic*.

There are very few magnetic materials. The most common one is iron. Two other metals, nickel and cobalt, are also magnetic. Alloys of these three metals are magnetic too. Steel is an alloy of iron and carbon, with small amounts of other metals. It is strongly magnetic.

If you have two bar magnets find out which is the north and which is the south pole of each and mark them. Now try putting the two magnets together. You will find that the north pole of one attracts the south pole of another. The north pole of one magnet pushes away the north pole of another and two south poles also *repel* each other.

If you hang a pin from one pole of a magnet you will find that a second pin can be hung from the first pin and a chain of pins can be built up. Each of the pins is changed into a magnet and they are said to be *magnetized*. You may find that the pins are still slightly magnetized when they are removed from the magnet. A better way of magnetizing a piece of steel is to stroke it with a magnet. Make the strokes one on top of the other, always starting at the same end, and lifting the magnet well clear between strokes.

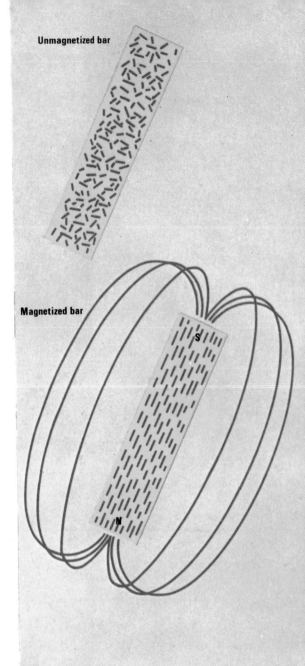

Unmagnetized bar

Magnetized bar

Right
In magnetic materials like iron the atoms themselves are little magnets. Usually they are all pointing in different directions so the metal is not a magnet. In a magnet the atom magnets all point in the same direction. If it is brought close to the unmagnetized metal it causes the atom magnets to line up and thus makes the metal into a magnet. When magnets are heated, they lose their magnetic properties because the heat disarranges the atoms. A magnet can also be demagnetized by hammering it or dropping it.

Below
Stroking a piece of iron with a magnet is one way of making it into another magnet. Always start at the same end.

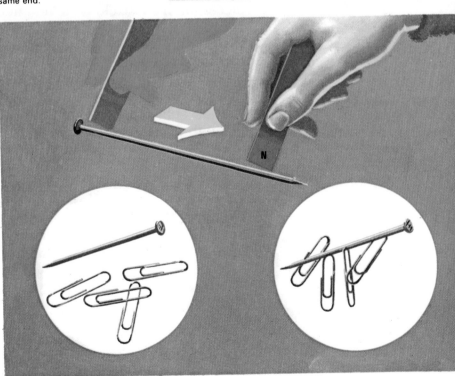

Right
A piece of iron can be moved about by a strong magnet under a piece of cardboard. This is because the effect of the magnet passes through the card.

Far right
This is how iron filings are used to show the field of magnets. There are lines of force running between the poles of the magnet.

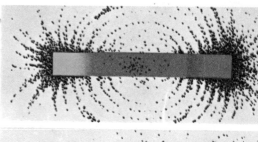

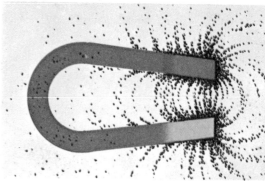

Above
Magnetism also passes through liquids. You can use a magnet to control a model boat in a shallow tray of water.

Magnetic fields

The Greeks used to think that pieces of iron stick to a magnet because it has small hooks on its surface. It is easy to show that this cannot be true. If you push a magnet close to a pin the pin will jump to the magnet. You can also attract objects by magnetism through a piece of paper.

Two things do not have to be touching one another to be attracted by magnetism. How do they affect one another? How does the pin know that the magnet is close to it? Obviously there must be some influence of the magnet passing through space. One way in which scientists have tried to explain this influence is by thinking of magnetic fields. The magnet affects the region around it and can influence other magnets or magnetic materials in this region.

This region is called a field of force – or a *magnetic* field.

It is possible to show a magnetic field by laying a piece of paper over a magnet and sprinkling iron filings onto it. The paper is then tapped and the filings arrange themselves into a pattern. The iron filings cluster together in the regions in which the magnet has most effect, that is, in the places where the field is strongest. You can see that there are more filings close to the poles of the magnet. They also tend to arrange themselves in lines running between the poles of the magnet. These are called lines of force and are imaginary lines running from the north pole of the magnet to its south pole. They show the direction in which the magnet acts when anything is put into its field. The influence of a magnet falls off as one gets further away from it. We say that its field gets weaker.

The earliest use of magnets was in compasses, for showing direction. This use depends on the fact that the earth has a magnetic field. It acts like a large bar magnet. Think of the earth spinning on an imaginary axis. One end is the North Pole and the other the South Pole. These are called the geographical poles of the earth. The earth acts like a large bar magnet lying almost along this axis. Any magnet suspended in the

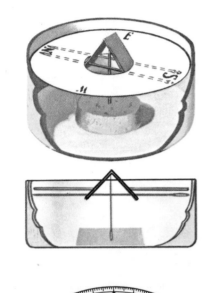

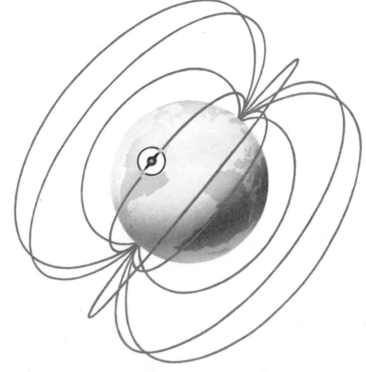

field will line up with the lines of force. The needle of a compass is a small magnet and always points north and south. The end of the magnet pointing north is called its north seeking pole, or north pole. The other is its south pole.

In fact a compass needle does not point to the true North Pole. It points to the *magnetic* North Pole which is several hundred miles from the true North Pole.

Navigators always have to make a correction for this *variation* of the compass. This is complicated by the fact that the positions of the magnetic poles vary slightly from year to year. In some places the needle of the compass does not read true because of magnetic material such as iron ore in the earth, or a large piece of steel nearby. A compass can be shielded from stray magnetic fields by a piece of soft iron.

Above
The earth acts as a large magnet and this is why a compass needle can be used to show north and south. The needle is a small magnet balanced on a pivot and it always comes to rest along the lines of force. In fact, the earth's magnetic field is not symmetrical, as shown, because it is distorted by the influence of the sun's magnetism.

Above: top left
You can easily make a small compass. First magnetize two large sewing needles by stroking them with a magnet (see page 175). Then stick them side by side on a round piece of cardboard. Make sure that you place them so that their north poles are both in the same direction. This card can be pivoted on another needle as shown. Before marking the points of the compass on the card you have to find out which end of the needle points to the north.

Above left
Compasses were used for finding direction by the Chinese over 2000 years ago. This is the compass card of a mariner's compass. The compasses used on ships are mounted on pivots so that they always stay horizontal no matter how the ship pitches and rolls.

Left
This is the *aurora borealis* or northern lights. It is seen at night in Arctic regions and is caused by charged particles from the sun trapped by the earth's magnetic field. In the Antarctic the *aurora australis* is seen.

177

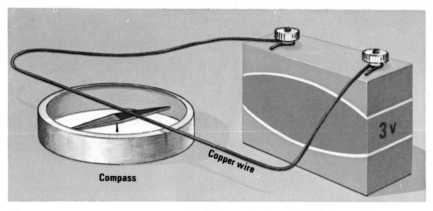

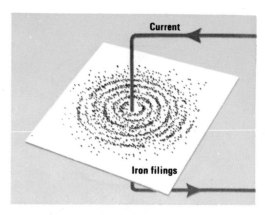

Iron filings

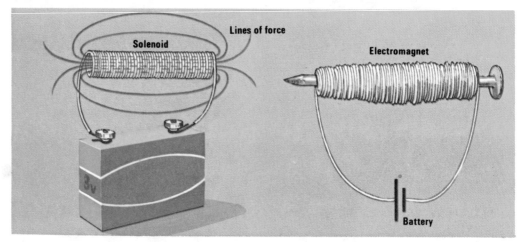

Lines of force

Solenoid

Electromagnet

3v

Battery

Oersted

Above
Hans Christian Oersted (1777–1851) was a Danish scientist. He believed that there was a connection between magnetism and electricity and discovered the magnetic effect of an electric current in 1820.

Above
A model of the apparatus used by Hans Oersted to demonstrate the magnetic effect of an electric current on a compass needle.

Electromagnetism

In 1820 a Danish scientist, Hans Christian Oersted, made a very important discovery. He noticed that a magnet was affected by an electric current flowing in a wire.

You can easily demonstrate this yourself. Take a 3 volt battery, a length of copper wire, and a small pocket compass. Connect one end of the wire to one terminal of the battery and lay the wire over the compass. Now touch the free end of the wire to the other terminal of the battery. The compass needle will change direction. When you remove the end of the wire it swings back to its original position. Do not keep the battery connected for too long or it will soon go flat.

This experiment shows that a flowing electric current produces a magnetic field. The shape of this field is not the same as that of an ordinary bar or horseshoe magnet but it has the same properties. In fact a current in a wire can be made to act just like an ordinary magnet.

If you wind a coil of wire round a

pencil you have a *solenoid*. Pass a current through it and put each end in turn near a compass needle. You will see that one end of the solenoid attracts the north pole of the needle and the other repels it. The solenoid has a north and south pole just as a bar magnet has.

Find out what happens when you change the direction of the current by connecting the battery the other way round. Magnetism produced by an electric current is called *electromagnetism*.

The electromagnetism of a solenoid is increased if it is wound around a piece of magnetic material, the *core*. If you wind turns of wire around a large steel nail and connect it to a battery you produce a strong magnetic field. A magnet of this kind is called an *electromagnet*.

If you switch off the current (by disconnecting the wire) you will probably find that the nail still acts as a magnet. It has been magnetized by the effect of the current. Magnets of this kind are called *permanent magnets*.

If, instead of steel, you had used

Left
If iron filings are used they can show the field of a single wire. This experiment requires a high current and you could not do it with a small battery.

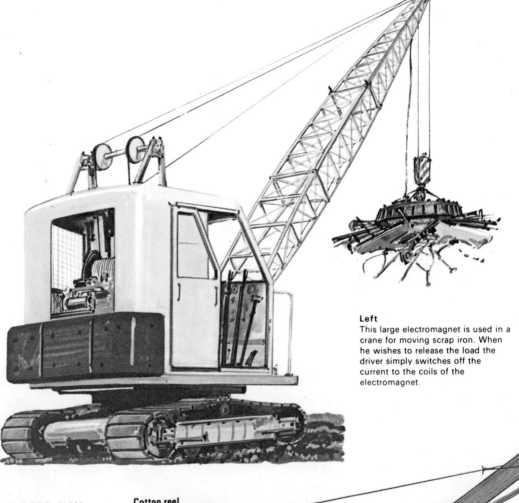

Left
A coil of wire like this is called a *solenoid*. It acts as a magnet. You can make a good electromagnet by wrapping a coil around an iron core. Note that the more turns of wire you use the stronger the magnet. The wire used has to be covered with an insulator.

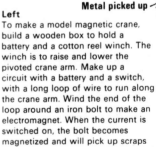

Left
This large electromagnet is used in a crane for moving scrap iron. When he wishes to release the load the driver simply switches off the current to the coils of the electromagnet.

a piece of soft iron as a core you would find that the magnetism disappeared when the current was switched off. It is not easy to do this experiment as soft iron is difficult to find. You may be able to make a piece by heating an iron nail to red heat and letting it cool slowly. The soft iron does not keep its magnetism like steel. It is a temporary magnet.

Electromagnets have many uses: they are used in electric bells, loudspeakers, electric motors and generators.

Because we know that an electric current can also create a magnetic field we can also realize where the magnetism of permanent magnets comes from. In a piece of magnetic material the atoms themselves all act as little magnets (see page 175). An electric current in a wire is just a flow of electrons along it–so a magnetic field is formed by movement of electrons. We also know that atoms contain moving electrons. Thus we can see that the magnetism of a permanent magnet is caused by the motion of electrons in its atoms.

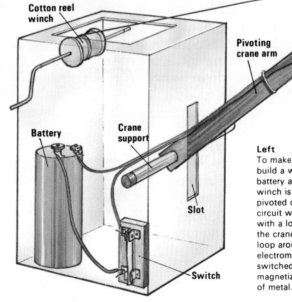

Cotton reel winch

Pivoting crane arm

Electromagnet

Battery

Crane support

Metal picked up

Slot

Switch

Left
To make a model magnetic crane, build a wooden box to hold a battery and a cotton reel winch. The winch is to raise and lower the pivoted crane arm. Make up a circuit with a battery and a switch, with a long loop of wire to run along the crane arm. Wind the end of the loop around an iron bolt to make an electromagnet. When the current is switched on, the bolt becomes magnetized and will pick up scraps of metal.

Left
A large electromagnet can be used to remove steel splinters from the workman's eye.

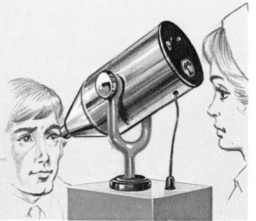

179

Electromagnetic induction

After Oersted had shown that an electric current could produce a magnetic field, scientists began to wonder whether they could use a magnetic field to produce an electric current. There were many attempts to do this. All were unsuccessful until in the 1830s Michael Faraday began a series of experiments with magnets and coils.

To detect an electric current some kind of instrument has to be used. The earliest form of current detector was the *galvanometer*. This was simply a compass surrounded by a flat vertical coil of many turns of wire. A current flowing through the coil produces a magnetic field which affects the compass needle.

One of the experiments performed by Faraday was to take a large wire coil (solenoid) and connect it to a galvanometer. When a bar magnet was placed near the coil of wire the galvanometer was not affected. No electric current is produced by the magnet. However when the magnet was pushed into the solenoid the galvanometer needle moved slightly and then went back to its original position. When the magnet was pulled out of the solenoid the needle 'kicked' in the opposite direction. Faraday realized that an electric current was being produced when the magnet was moving. The direction of the electric current depended on the direction in which the magnet was moved. This behaviour is called *electromagnetic induction*: the moving magnet has *induced* an electric current in the solenoid.

This discovery was of immense importance. Up till then electric currents had been produced by electric cells. Now a method existed for converting mechanical energy into electrical energy.

For example, if the magnet was continually pushed and pulled in and out of the solenoid an electric current first flowed one way and then the other. This produced an alternating current. A mechanical engine was used to move the magnet making a simple generator.

The current is induced in the solenoid when the magnet is moved because the magnetic field is changing. The same effect is obtained if a wire is moved through a field as the conductor cuts the lines of force.

Faraday also did experiments on the opposite effect. If a wire is placed in a magnetic field and a current passed through it the wire moves. There is a force on it due to the effect of the current and the field. Thus we see that if a wire is moved through a magnetic field, a current flows in it. This principle is used in generating electricity (see page 182). If a wire carrying a current is placed in a magnetic field, the wire is made to move. This principle is used in electric motors (see page 184).

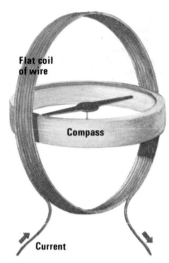

Above
In a simple galvanometer a current passing through the flat coil produces a magnetic field. This deflects the compass needle and so the current is detected.

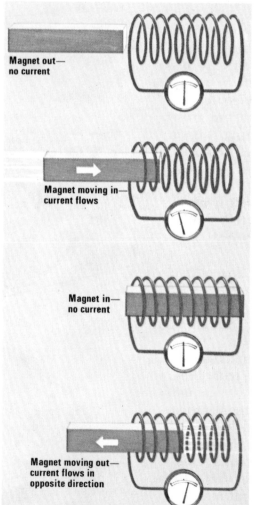

Left
When the magnet moves into the coil the galvanometer needle moves one way. When it is pulled out of the coil the needle moves in the opposite direction. The current only flows when the magnet is moving.

Maxwell

Above
James Clerk Maxwell (1831–1879) was a brilliant Scottish physicist and mathematician. He produced a mathematical theory of electromagnetic fields and showed that light was electromagnetic waves.

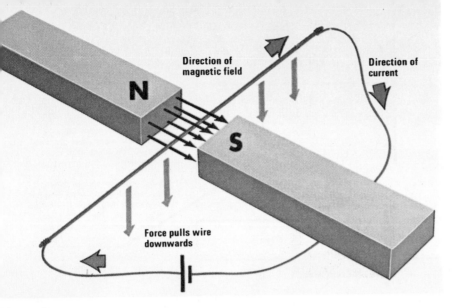

Direction of magnetic field

N

S

Direction of current

Force pulls wire downwards

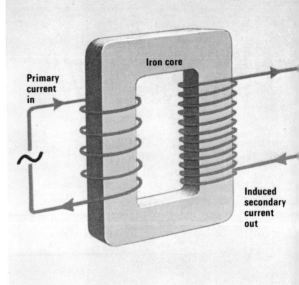

Primary current in

Iron core

Induced secondary current out

Above left
Electromagnetic induction occurs when a conductor moves through a magnetic field. The opposite effect is used in electric motors. A current is passed through the wire and it experiences a force and moves.

Above
Transformers also work by electromagnetic induction. They are used to change an alternating current of one voltage to an alternating current of another voltage. The current to be transformed is passed through the first coil. As the current increases and decreases it produces a magnetic field which also increases and decreases. This changing magnetic field induces a current in the second coil which has a different number of turns. The difference in the number of turns causes a difference in the voltage.

Left
This is a large transformer used in a power station. The two coils of wire are wound onto the same iron core, one over the other. There are more turns of wire on the first coil than on the second. Because of this the voltage in the second coil is less than in the first. Transformers like this are called *step-down* transformers because they reduce the voltage. Step-up transformers are also used.

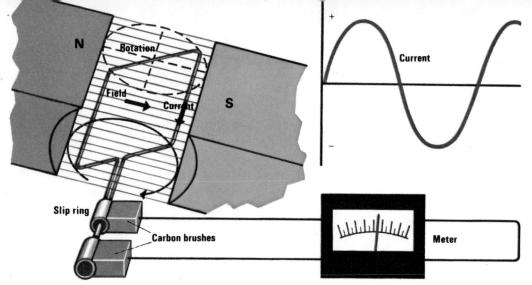

Electric generators

There are two principle ways of making electricity. The first is to generate it in a cell by chemical reactions. The second is to produce it by the electromagnetic effect using a rotating machine. Rotating machines are called *generators* (the small ones are sometimes called *dynamos*).

The principle of the generator was discovered by Michael Faraday. He showed that if a conducting wire is moved across a magnetic field an electric current is generated in the wire.

The most convenient way to arrange this conducting wire is to rotate a coil of it between the poles of a permanent magnet. This is exactly what Faraday did in 1831, and it is no exaggeration to say that the whole of our present way of life is based on his discovery.

Without electricity modern society would come to a standstill—no heating or lighting, and no movement from the millions of electric motors that we use for

trains, lifts, factory machines and the hundreds of other electrical appliances we use every day.

Faraday's first generator was a small laboratory-bench model that he rotated by hand. In the modern power station the machines are rotated by mechanical means. In a coal, oil, or nuclear power station the generators are rotated by steam turbines (see page 234). The turbines are connected directly to the generators and the set is called a *turbogenerator*.

In a hydroelectric station the rotation of the generator is produced by a water turbine. These power stations are situated on

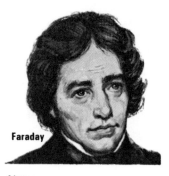

Above
Michael Faraday (1791–1867) was a great British scientist. He made many discoveries in electricity and magnetism and studied electrolysis.

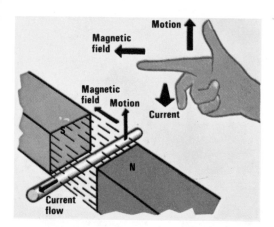

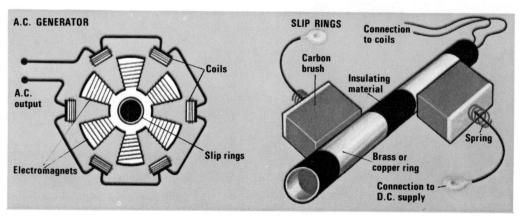

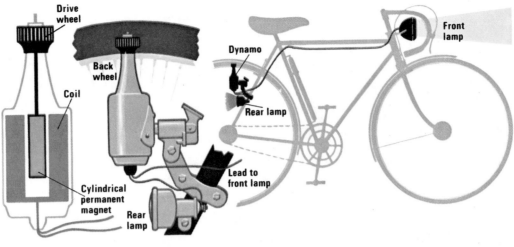

Right

In a bicycle dynamo the motion is obtained from the bicycle wheel. The drive wheel of the dynamo rubs against the tyre and is thus made to rotate. The drive wheel is connected to a cylindrical permanent magnet that rotates inside a coil. Only one wire is needed to the rear light and front light because the dynamo is earthed to the frame which provides the other connection. In some bicycles the dynamo is built into the hub of the wheel.

Drive wheel

Back wheel

Coil

Dynamo

Front lamp

Rear lamp

Cylindrical permanent magnet

Lead to front lamp

Rear lamp

rivers at points at which there is a fall of level, usually at a natural waterfall. A dam is built to restrict the waterfall and the water is lead through a large pipe to the lower level where it rotates a water turbine. In all cases the turbine-generator set is a means of converting mechanical energy into electrical energy.

Fleming devised a rule, Fleming's Right Hand Rule, to work out in which direction the current flows in a conductor when it is moved through a magnetic field. (*See caption* on page 182).

Gauss

If the conductor is in the shape of a coil, the current is obviously going to change direction as the coil rotates. So the current produced by this type of machine is going to vary from nothing, to a maximum in one direction, falling again to nothing when the coil is vertical. The current then reverses direction and builds up to a maximum in the opposite direction, finally returning again to zero. This series of events is called an *alternating current*. The number of times this cycle changes in one second is called the *frequency*. Alternating currents are produced in all our power stations because the voltage can easily be changed by a transformer (see page 181).

In small machines such as a bicycle dynamo the magnetic field is produced by a permanent magnet. But in the large machines the electromagnet is rotated inside the coil of wire instead of the other way round. The effect is exactly the same, the electricity is generated in the stationary coil (*stator*) by the changing magnetic field produced by the rotating magnet (*rotor*).

Above

The generator room of a modern power station. The huge steam pipes feed the steam turbine which drives the generator in the foreground.

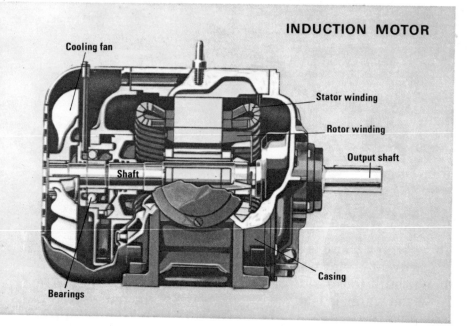

INDUCTION MOTOR

Cooling fan

Stator winding

Rotor winding

Output shaft

Shaft

Casing

Bearings

Above
An electric induction motor. The rotor and the stator have identical windings.
The two windings behave rather like a transformer.
The magnetic field induced in the rotor causes it, and the attached drive shaft, to rotate.

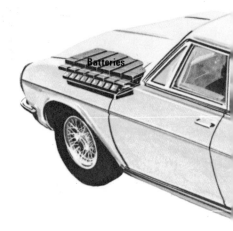

Batteries

Above
The electric car is still experimental but the electric motors now available are perfectly adequate. The problem is to produce batteries that hold enough electricity and do not weigh too much.

Electric motors

Electric motors depend on the same principle as the generator invented by Michael Faraday. In the generator, a current is produced in a conductor by moving it through a magnetic field. In the motor, current is passed through a conductor placed in a magnetic field and this produces a force on the conductor which tends to make it move. Again, as in the generator, the most convenient arrangement is to make the conductor into a coil of wire and place it between the poles of a magnet.

You can easily make a very simple motor from a large cork, a length of fine wire, a knitting needle, some stout pins, and two small bar magnets. As you will see, current has to be supplied to the coil through a device called a *commutator*. The commutator used in the model is a very simple one, but those used in large motors work on the same principle. The commutator reverses the direction of the electric current after the coil has made half a rotation. If there were no commutator, the coil would come to rest after half a turn, with the coil horizontal. The change in direction of the current makes it rotate through another half rotation, and so on.

On a large motor there is not one coil but a series of coils, each being displaced by a small angle from the previous one. The com-

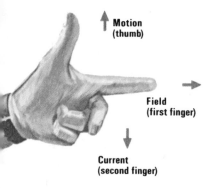

Motion (thumb)

Field (first finger)

Current (second finger)

Above
Fleming's left hand rule gives the direction of motion for motors. The first finger gives the direction of the magnetic field, the second finger indicates the direction of the current, and the thumb then gives the direction of motion.

Right
A vacuum cleaner uses an electric motor to suck up dust. The motor drives a fan which sucks in the air through the dust bag. The motors are usually a.c. synchronous motors as no change of speed is needed.

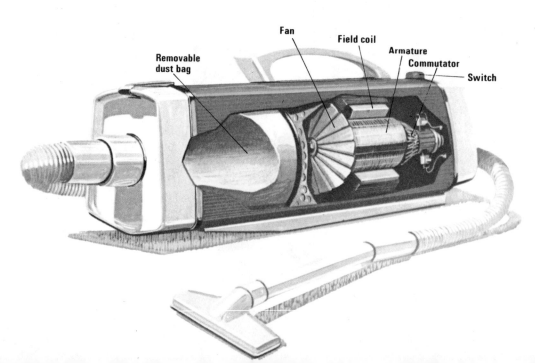

Fan

Field coil

Armature

Commutator

Switch

Removable dust bag

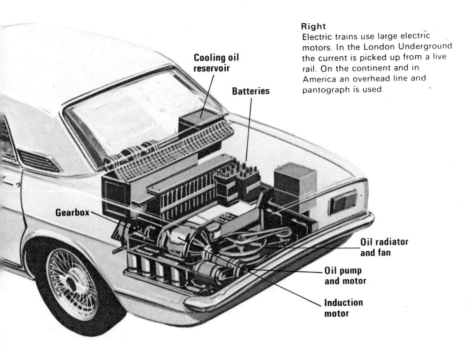

Cooling oil reservoir
Batteries
Gearbox
Oil radiator and fan
Oil pump and motor
Induction motor

Right
Electric trains use large electric motors. In the London Underground the current is picked up from a live rail. On the continent and in America an overhead line and pantograph is used.

Live wire
Pantograph
Live rail

mutator, too, has many segments, one for each separate coil. The current is fed to each segment of the commutator by the carbon brushes as it rotates between them.

Electric motors have a wide variety of uses, from tiny fraction-of-a-kilowatt motors that drive electric shavers, to enormous motors that drive trains and industrial machinery. Some motors are designed to run on alternating current, some on direct current (d.c.), and some can be used on either (universal motors). The d.c. motors used in electric trains are the same type as the model described, except that the permanent magnet is replaced by an electromagnet.

Synchronous a.c. motors run at a constant speed that depends on the frequency of the supply; they are therefore not used when it is necessary to vary the speed to any great extent.

The a.c. induction motor, which is widely used in industry, has rotatory windings (the rotor) very similar to the stationary winding (the stator). The two windings then behave rather like a transformer. Some of these motors will not start themselves and therefore need a separate starter motor.

Electric motors are a very convenient and clean means of obtaining mechanical energy. The electric car would reduce the pol-

lution in our cities enormously. It would produce no exhaust fumes and would be very much more silent than cars driven by internal combustion engines.

One of the advantages of electric motors is that they produce rotary motion directly. In a petrol engine the back and forward motion of the piston has to be converted into rotary motion.

Some electric motors, called *linear motors,* do not produce rotation. They are a type of induction motor in which the stator and rotor are both straight and parallel. This type of motor may one day be used to provide economic intercity transport by monorail. One winding would be on the vehicle the other winding would be on the single track used.

Below
To make a simple electric motor, first take a large cork and wind onto it, lengthways, 25 turns of No. 26 SWG insulated copper wire. Hold this winding in place by two or three rubber bands. Make connections to the two ends of the wire using two stout pins which must be left protruding from the cork by about 2cm. Now pass a knitting needle through the centre of the cork and support the whole device on two crossed nails at each end as shown. The magnetic field is produced by two bar magnets supported on matchboxes. A 6 volt battery is connected by two wires to two bent paper clips held in position by drawing pins. The pins from the cork must just touch the paper clips. The motor is not self-starting and to start it the cork must be rotated.

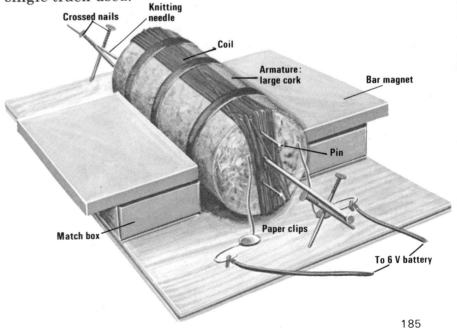

Crossed nails
Knitting needle
Coil
Armature: large cork
Bar magnet
Pin
Match box
Paper clips
To 6 V battery

185

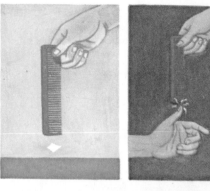

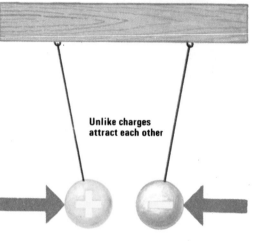

Unlike charges attract each other

Like charges repel each other

Coulomb

Electrostatics

Some 600 years before the birth of Christ a Greek philosopher, called Thales, discovered that a type of stone called (in Greek) *elektron* had the ability of attracting small pieces of fluff or feather, after being rubbed with fur. We call this stone, which is a fossil resin, amber. This discovery laid the basis for the whole science of electricity. The British scientist, William Gilbert (1544–1603), first suggested that the word *electricity* (from the Greek elektron) should be used to describe this force.

If you comb your hair with a plastic comb you will find that the comb has the ability of attracting small pieces of paper. This is an exact replica of Thales' experiment. If you comb your hair in a dark room and then hold the comb close to your thumb you will see a small spark. This is because the energy stored in the charge is making the air atoms between the comb and your thumb emit light. This is what happens in a lightning discharge.

What creates this force of attraction and where does the energy of the spark come from? Until the end of the nineteenth century no one knew the answer. Now we know part of the answer, but not all. We know that matter is made up of atoms and that atoms are made up of three kinds of particles: electrons, protons, and neutrons.

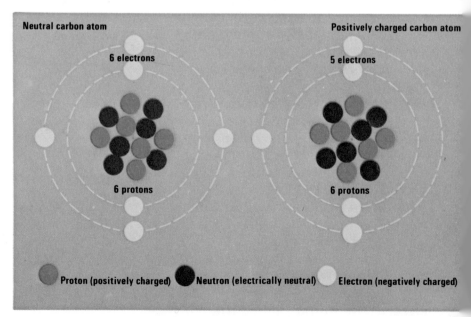

Neutral carbon atom

6 electrons

6 protons

Positively charged carbon atom

5 electrons

6 protons

Proton (positively charged)   Neutron (electrically neutral)   Electron (negatively charged)

Right
To show repulsion between like charges take a strip of newspaper about 5 cm wide and 30 cm long, lay it on a table, and stroke it about 20 times with a piece of woollen material. Now hang the strip over a plastic ruler and you will see the ends repelling each other.

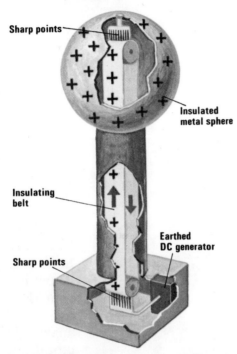

Sharp points

Insulated metal sphere

Insulating belt

Earthed DC generator

Sharp points

Right
To produce a high electric charge for use in science laboratories a Van de Graaff generator is used. The air molecules are broken up at the lower points, positive charge being conveyed to the moving belt. This charge is then conveyed to the insulated metal sphere by the upper set of points.

Right
An experiment to show the behaviour of an electrostatic charge. Hang a small ball of pith, balsa wood or cork on a fine thread. Rub a stick of sealing wax on your sleeve to charge it up. Bring it close up to the pith ball. The ball will be attracted to it. Let them touch so that some of the electrostatic charge is transferred from the sealing wax to the ball.
Take the wax away and then bring it close again. This time the ball will swing away because both the ball and the wax have the same type of charge and like charges repel each other.

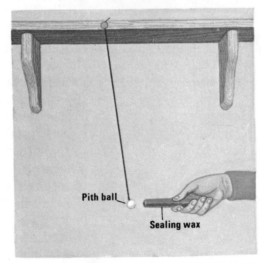

Pith ball

Sealing wax

Left
In a carbon atom the nucleus consists of 6 protons and 6 neutrons; 6 electrons circulate round the nucleus, so the atom is electrically neutral. When a comb containing carbon atoms is run through hair some of these electrons remain on the hair. If one electron from each carbon atom is lost to the hair the remaining carbon atom will be positively charged and will be attracted to the electrons in the atoms of the paper.

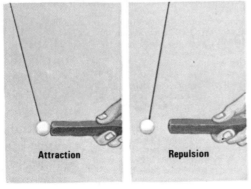

Attraction

Repulsion

The central nucleus of an atom consists of protons and neutrons. Protons have a property called positive electric charge, neutrons have no electric charge, and electrons have a negative electric charge. The electrons circle round the central nucleus, each atom containing the same number of electrons round the nucleus as there are protons within it. As the charge on the electron is exactly equal, but opposite in sense, to the charge on the proton, an atom is electrically neutral.

When you pull your comb through your hair some of the electrons from the outside atoms of your comb are left behind on your hair. This means that the protons in these atoms do not have sufficient electrons to balance them. The result is that the comb is positively charged. The protons in the comb are then able to attract the electrons in the atoms of the paper. This creates the force between comb and paper.

This explanation is based on two facts. The first is that particles of matter can be charged electrically in two different ways; we call one positive, the other negative. The other fact is that unlike charges exert an attractive force on each other. (As we shall see later, like charges exert a repulsive force on each other).

We can measure attraction and repulsion of electric charges, we know all about electricity in atoms, but we still do not know exactly what an electric charge is or what the difference is between negative and positive charge.

Atmospheric electricity

If the electricity in a charged body is rapidly discharged through a conductor held close to it, but not touching it, a spark will jump between the two. In 1708, a British scientist called William Wall was the first to suggest that a lightning flash in the sky was a similar process on a grand scale.

Fifty years later an American inventor, Benjamin Franklin, carried out an experiment to try to prove that a lightning discharge was, in fact, caused by electricity. In a thunderstorm he flew a kite to which he attached a metal wire. The wire was connected to a silk thread, the other end of which was held by Franklin. A metal key was attached to the thread just above Franklin's head. Franklin flew the kite into a thundercloud and then held a finger close to the key. A spark jumped across the gap. Each time Franklin flew the kite into the thundercloud he made the key spark. This proved that thunderclouds were charged with electricity and that some of the charge was being conducted down the silken thread to the key. The build-up of charge on the key then caused a spark to jump the gap to his finger.

It was a brilliant experiment but a very foolhardy one. The next person to try it was killed by the discharge. Franklin was very lucky to escape with his life. However, the risk he took turned out to have been well worth it. Having shown that lightning is caused by an electric discharge, Franklin went on to invent a way of protecting tall buildings from being struck by lightning. The invention was a simple logical step from the kite experiment. He attached a metal rod to the highest point of a building and connected the rod by a wire to the earth. Thus if lightning struck the building the charge was led safely down the wire to earth.

Damage by lightning has been

Above
Benjamin Franklin's experiment with a kite. He could have electrocuted himself by allowing the thundercloud to discharge through the cord of his kite. A later experimenter was killed because the charge in the cloud built up to such an extent that the current passing through him to earth was large enough to be fatal. A current of only 15 thousandths of an ampere is sufficient to kill a man.

Left
In rain clouds there is a separation of charge resulting from the breaking down of air molecules. Many theories have been suggested to account for this but none are definitely accepted. The cold (−10 to −40°C) upper part of the cloud contains the positively charged particles. The middle region at about 0°C contains the negative particles. The rain areas at the base of the cloud are sometimes positively charged. When lightning flashes from the negative part of one cloud to the positive part of another cloud it is called cloud-to-cloud lightning. When it flashes to earth it is called cloud-to-earth lightning.

greatly reduced by the use of lightning conductors. Even so, throughout the world, on average some twenty people a day are killed by lightning.

Lightning can pass from one cloud to another or from a cloud to the ground. In both types a single flash usually consists of between five and ten closely spaced strokes following the same channel. The interval between the strokes is only a few hundredths of a second and to a human eye they appear as one flash. The current carried by each discharge heats the air causing it to expand. The repeated expansions and contractions caused by the five to ten strokes generate massive sound waves. This is the thunder. As light travels more quickly than sound there is a delay between seeing the flash and hearing the thunder. For every second's delay between seeing the flash and hearing the sound the thunder has travelled 330 metres as the speed of sound is 330 m per second.

Below
St. Elmo's fire is a bluish glow sometimes seen on the wings of aircraft during an electrical storm. Storm clouds carry a heavy electrical charge at their bases. The static charge acquired by pointed objects on aircraft discharges into the oppositely charged cloud with a visible light. It used to occur on the masts of wooden ships and is named after St. Elmo, the patron saint of Mediterranean sailors.

Lightning conductor

Above
The metal lightning conductor at the top of the church tower conducts the electricity of the discharge down the metal conductor safely to earth. The lightning conductor was invented by Benjamin Franklin.

Right
Electrical transmission lines are sometimes struck by lightning, as they have sharp points sticking up from the ground. When lightning strikes a pylon, large voltages build up across the insulators. This can cause them to break down with a serious flashover. This may mean that the line has to be taken out of service.

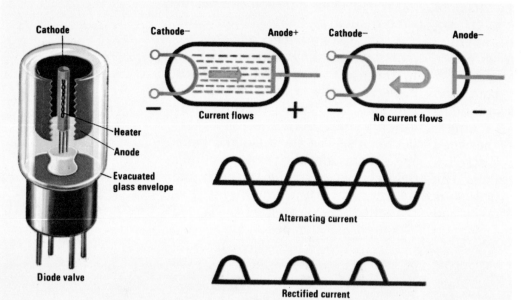

Cathode · Heater · Anode · Evacuated glass envelope

Diode valve

Cathode− · Anode+ · Current flows · +

Cathode− · Anode− · No current flows · −

Alternating current

Rectified current

Left
The diode. An alternating voltage makes the anode positive and then negative in one cycle. As current will only flow when the anode is positive, the negative half of the cycle is lost. Alternating current is thus changed to direct current. The diode therefore acts as a rectifier.

Right
Diagram of an X-ray tube. The cathode is specially shaped so that a narrow beam of electrons is directed onto the tungsten disc in the anode. This produces a fairly narrow beam of X-rays which leaves the tube through a thin metal plate. The energy of the X-rays depends on the difference in voltage between anode and cathode.

X-rays and valves

The electrons in a metal can move about freely. If they are given enough energy they can escape from the metal completely. This energy can be supplied by heating the metal. If the metal is heated strongly enough a stream of electrons is produced.

Electrons have a negative charge. A negative charge is always attracted towards a positive charge, but never towards another negative charge. This fact is used in a device called the *valve* used in electrical circuits.

The *diode* valve contains two electrodes–a *cathode* and an *anode* –inside a glass container from which the air has been removed. When the cathode is heated, electrons are emitted. These are attracted towards the positively charged anode. A current therefore flows through the valve, but only in one direction–towards the positive anode. If the anode became negatively charged, no current would flow.

The *triode* valve has an anode, a cathode, and a third electrode called the *grid*. The flow of electrons from cathode to anode is affected by the charge on the grid. As the grid becomes more positive a greater number of electrons flow through it. The voltage on the grid therefore controls and can also increase (*amplify*) the current flowing from cathode to anode.

Transistors (see page 238) can perform the same jobs as valves. They have replaced valves in many circuits because they are much smaller, last longer, and require no heat to produce the flow of electrons.

The production of a stream of electrons by heating a metal is still used in many instruments including the *electron microscope* (see page 217) and the *X-ray tube*. X-rays are similar to light, since they also move as waves (see page 138), but the wavelength is very much smaller. Unlike light waves, they are invisible. The energy of X-rays is very high. They can travel a great distance inside an object and sometimes pass straight through it.

X-rays are produced in an X-ray tube when a narrow stream of electrons emitted from a heated cathode is strongly attracted towards the anode. The anode is at a very high voltage. This means that the electrons are moving very fast towards the anode and therefore have a large amount of energy. The anode contains a small disc of heavy metal such as tungsten. When the electrons strike the tungsten atoms, they give up their energy to electrons in the inner electron shells of the atom. To get

Below
Wilhelm Konrad Roentgen, 1845–1923, a German physicist. He discovered X-rays in 1895 and studied many of their properties. The discovery of X-rays started a new era in physics and medicine.

Roentgen

Fleming

Above
Sir John Ambrose Fleming, 1849–1945, an English physicist. He invented the diode valve in 1904 and also made a great contribution towards the development of the electric light.

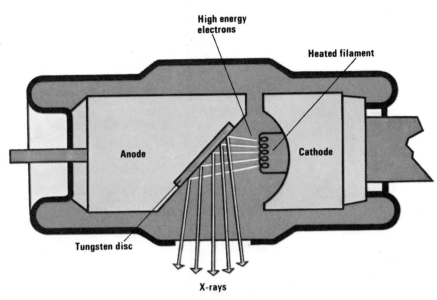

High energy electrons

Heated filament

Anode

Cathode

Tungsten disc

X-rays

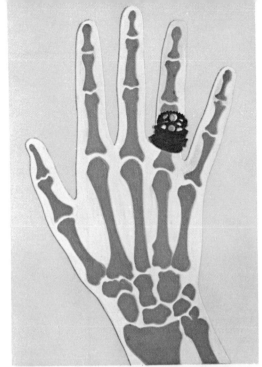

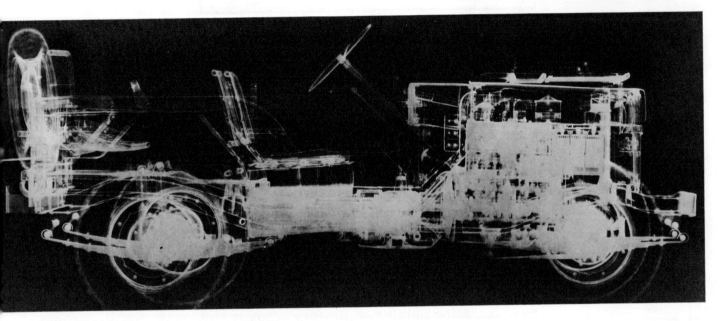

rid of this excess energy, the atoms emit X-rays.

X-rays have various uses in medicine. X-rays, like light, can produce an image on photographic film. If a person stands between a low-energy source of X-rays and a film, a photo of the bone structure is obtained. Broken or badly formed bones can be seen. Much higher-energy X-rays are used to treat cancer, since X-rays are a form of ionizing radiation (see page 195). X-rays are also used in scientific research to find out how atoms and molecules are arranged in crystals and how they are grouped together in some of the giant chemical compounds found in the body, such as DNA and cytochrome c. This

type of research is called X-ray crystallography.

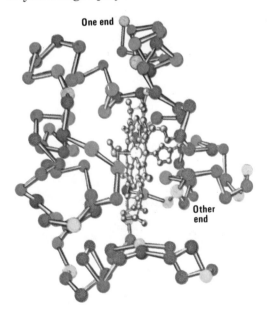

One end

Other end

Above top
An X-ray photograph of a hand with a ring. Dentists take X-ray photos to check that your teeth are growing correctly and to see if you need any fillings. Only bones and teeth show up on the negative of the film. The film is blackened by X-rays which are able to pass straight through skin and air. Bones and teeth absorb most of the X-rays and therefore appear whitish.

Above
An X-ray photograph of a jeep. Engineers use photographs of this type to detect faults in assembly or to show up some types of defect in the metal.

Left
The chemical structure of cytochrome C. This is a giant molecule present in the cells of the body. Its complicated structure was unravelled by the use of X-rays. Each coloured ball represents a different group of atoms. Knowing its structure helps scientists to learn about how it works.

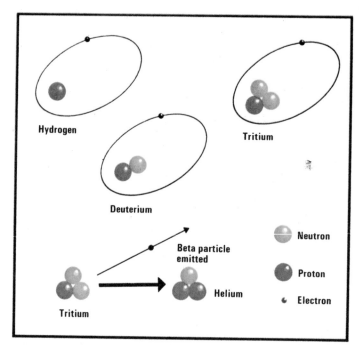

Hydrogen

Tritium

Deuterium

Beta particle emitted

Tritium

Helium

Neutron

Proton

Electron

Becquerel

Radioactivity

An atom consists of a number of electrons moving around a central nucleus. The nucleus contains tiny particles called *protons* and *neutrons*. The nuclei of any particular element, such as carbon, always have the same number of protons, equal to the number of orbiting electrons. The positive charge of the protons is thus balanced by the negative charge of the electrons. However, the number of neutrons in the nucleus of an element can vary. Atoms in which the nuclei have the same number of protons but a different neutron number are *isotopes* of that element. Every element has several isotopes.

The nuclei of many isotopes always remain unchanged–they are *stable* isotopes. Other nuclei are unstable. At any moment they can emit energy, in the form of radiation, in order to reduce this instability. These are nuclei of *radioactive* isotopes, called *radioisotopes* for short. Radioactivity was first reported in 1896 by Becquerel. He found that some form of energy was being emitted by uranium salts. It was found that this emission came from the nucleus, and did not involve the orbiting electrons.

A radioisotope can lose energy in various ways, but the two most important processes are the emission of an *alpha particle* and the emission of a *beta particle*. An alpha particle consists of two protons and two neutrons; it is actually the nucleus of a helium atom. After its nucleus has emitted an alpha particle, a radioisotope is changed into the isotope of another element having two less protons. The weight of the nucleus is reduced by losing the alpha particle.

A beta particle is an electron. There are no electrons in a nucleus, however, so where does it come from? It results from the sudden change or *disintegration* of a neutron into a proton and an electron (plus another particle called a *neutrino*). This disintegration only

Marie Curie

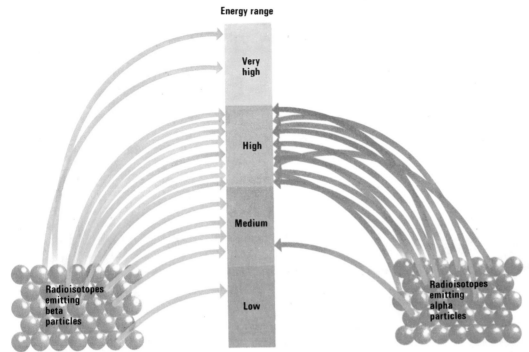

Very high

High

Medium

Low

Radioisotopes emitting beta particles

Radioisotopes emitting alpha particles

Left
The energy of particles emitted by different radioisotopes can vary widely.
If an alpha and beta particle have the same energy, the beta particle will be stopped by a thin sheet of perspex, whilst the alpha particle would not pass through a sheet of paper. A gamma emission would require thick steel, concrete, or lead to stop it.

Below
The radioactive series of uranium, starting with the disintegration of a radioisotope of uranium containing a total of 238 protons and neutrons (92 protons) and ending in the production of a stable isotope of lead. Half-lives are shown for some of the disintegrations.

occurs in nuclei of radioisotopes, never in the nuclei of stable isotopes.

After the emission of a beta particle, the radioisotope is therefore transformed into an isotope of another element having one more proton than the original. The weights of these two isotopes are about equal, since the neutron and proton have approximately the same weight.

A radioisotope often changes or decays into an isotope that is also radioactive. In turn, the second isotope may decay into a third radioisotope, and so on. This process will continue until a stable isotope is formed. The radioisotopes involved form a *radioactive series*. Four such series are known, one of them being the *uranium series*.

The time taken for half of the nuclei of a radioisotope to disintegrate is called its *half-life*. The values of the half-life for different radioisotopes vary from a minute fraction of a second to many million million years. In radioactive material the number of nuclei of the radioisotope present grows less and less as more of them decay.

The *activity* of a radioactive material is measured by the number of disintegrations in a second. It therefore decreases with time, the rate depending on the half-life of the radioisotope.

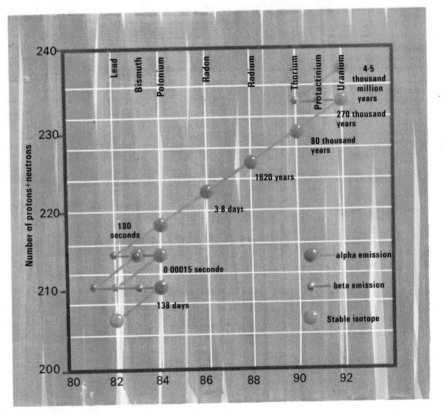

Lead Bismuth Polonium Radon Radium Thorium Protactinium Uranium

4·5 thousand million years
270 thousand years
80 thousand years
1620 years
3·8 days
180 seconds
0·00015 seconds
138 days

alpha emission
beta emission
Stable isotope

Number of protons+neutrons

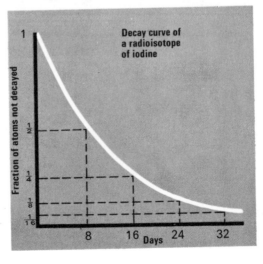

Decay curve of a radioisotope of iodine

Fraction of atoms not decayed

Days

Left
The decay curve of a radioisotope of iodine, having a half-life of eight days. After 16 days only a quarter of the original number of nuclei remain. This fraction is reduced to an eighth after 24 days and to a sixteenth after 32 days.

Radioisotopes

Several radioisotopes occur naturally in the rocks on the earth's surface. One out of every 100 000 atoms of potassium is radioactive. Many rocks, including granite, contain potassium compounds. The radioisotope of potassium decays into a stable isotope of argon, the half-life being over one thousand million years. By measuring the amounts of these two isotopes present in a particular rock it is possible to calculate the time at which the potassium isotope first started to decay. This is the time at which the rock was formed. By finding the age of rocks it is possible to estimate the age of the earth. This method, called *radioactive dating*, gives the age of the earth as being between three and four thousand million years.

Radiocarbon dating can be used to find the age of objects several thousand years old. These objects must be made from organic material, that was once living, such as wood. All plants obtain carbon from the carbon dioxide in the atmosphere. This carbon contains a very small but constant proportion of a radioisotope (half-life 5730 years). The absorption of carbon from the atmosphere stops when the material dies. The radioisotope of carbon however, continues to decay. By determining the amounts of stable carbon and the radioisotope present in the object, the time of death of the sample material can be found.

Radioisotopes occurring naturally on earth all have extremely long half-lives. Radioisotopes with short half-lives probably disappeared from the earth, by disintegration, thousands or millions of years ago.

As these isotopes are very useful in medicine, industry, and scientific research, man must produce his own supply. They are called *artificial radioisotopes*. Most are formed by bombarding elements with low-energy neutrons.

Below
Radioisotopes are very useful to both archaeologists and geologists. Here, the sodium-24 radioisotope is being used as a source of X-rays to radiograph one of the fallen stones at Stonehenge, so that the structure of the stone can be investigated.

Right
A picture (scan) of the amounts of a radioisotope present in different areas of the liver. The colours dark blue, green, through to red represent increasing amounts. The greatest quantity of radioisotope should collect in the centre of the liver. The dark blue area near the centre of the scan indicates the presence of a cancer tumour.

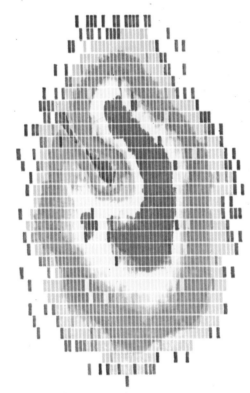

Below
Radioisotopes can be used to control the thickness of a piece of metal being produced as a long thin sheet. The amount of radiation reaching the counter will change if the thickness of the sheet changes. An electrical signal is then sent to correct the spacing of the rollers.

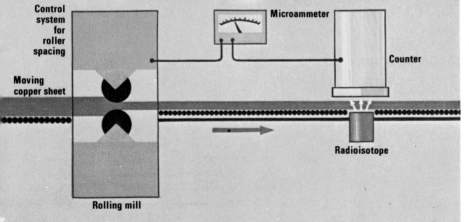

Control system for roller spacing

Microammeter

Moving copper sheet

Counter

Radioisotope

Rolling mill

194

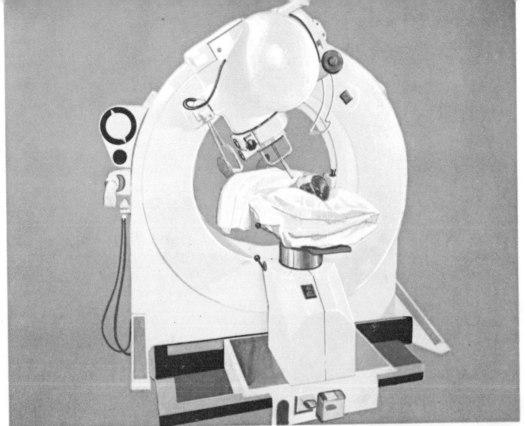

A radioisotope has the same chemical properties as the stable isotopes of the same element. If a radioisotope is introduced into the human body, by injection say, it will follow the same path as a stable isotope of the same element. Certain elements, such as iodine, collect in one particular part or organ of the body. If the organ is not working properly, too much or too little collects there. The amount of radiation emitted by a radioisotope can be measured very accurately. It is therefore possible to detect how much radiation is given off by a radioisotope in the body and to find out if there is any disease, such as cancer, in the area involved.

The streams of alpha or beta particles emitted by a radioisotope are types of *ionizing radiation*. X-rays and ultraviolet radiation are other examples. These rays and particles have enough energy to remove the outer electrons from the atoms or molecules of the material through which they pass. This ionizing action is used in medicine to treat cancer.

Many molecules in the body have very complicated structures which can be damaged by ionizing radiation. This would prevent the molecules from controlling processes going on in the cells, and the cells would eventually die. Cancer cells are dangerously overactive and ionizing radiation can be used to kill them. Ionizing radiation is therefore useful to man but it is a dangerous tool and great care has to be taken with it.

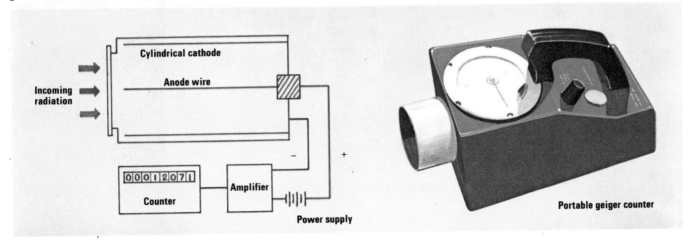

Incoming radiation

Cylindrical cathode

Anode wire

− +

Counter

Amplifier

Power supply

Portable geiger counter

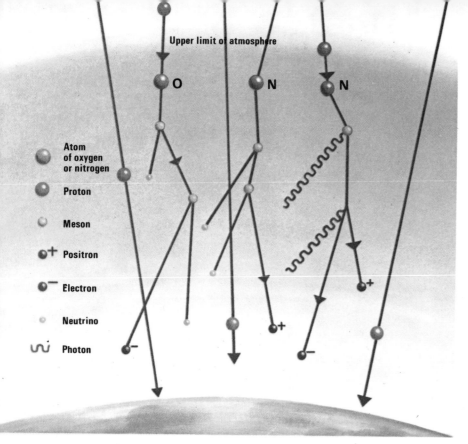

Upper limit of atmosphere

O   N   N

Atom of oxygen or nitrogen

Proton

Meson

Positron

Electron

Neutrino

Photon

Above
Cosmic rays from outer space. This high-energy radiation consists mainly of protons and some alpha particles. These particles collide with molecules in the air and produce other elementary particles. At sea level about one particle per square centimetre arrives every minute. The source of cosmic rays is uncertain; they possibly come from exploding stars (supernovas).

Elementary particles

Matter consists of groups of atoms. In the early nineteenth century John Dalton thought that atoms could not be divided into anything smaller. This is now known to be incorrect. Atoms are composed of a central nucleus around which move electrons. The nucleus contains protons and neutrons. Electrons, protons, and neutrons are *elementary particles*. This means that they cannot be divided into smaller particles. They are the basic units of matter.

Although these particles cannot be subdivided, some can change or *decay* into other elementary particles. They are therefore *unstable;* and only last for a certain time.

When the neutron is outside the nucleus it is unstable. It lasts about 12 minutes then changes into a proton, an electron, and another elementary particle called the *neutrino*. These three particles are all stable and do not decay into other particles. The neutrino is a strange particle. It has *no* mass and no charge. It is a tiny bundle of energy. It is therefore extremely difficult to detect, and was only discovered in 1956.

The photon is an elementary particle. Like the neutrino, it is stable and has no mass or charge; it is also a bundle of energy. Radio waves, light, and X-rays can all be thought of as a stream of photons (see page 138). These types of radiation only differ in the amounts of the energies of the photons.

There are a large number of elementary particles apart from those already mentioned. They are all unstable, some of them decaying in minute fractions of a second. Elementary particles can react together to produce other particles, but reactions can only occur if certain laws are obeyed. The total charge of the particles reacting together (or decaying) must equal the total charge of the particles formed. When a neutron decays, its zero charge is balanced by the positive charge of the proton and the equal but negative charge of the electron. This is called *conservation of charge*. Many other

Right
A model of the cloud chamber used by Wilson to show the tracks of elementary particles in a gas saturated with water vapour.

Far right
A bubble chamber photograph. A bubble chamber contains liquid hydrogen. When charged particles enter the machine, tiny bubbles form along their tracks, which can therefore be photographed. When they collide with protons in the hydrogen nucleus other elementary particles are produced forming additional tracks. The shape of the track helps to identify the particle.

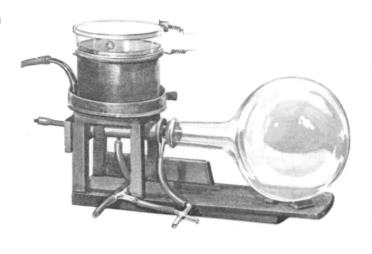

Lawrence

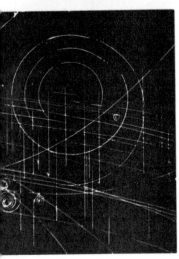

properties, apart from charge, must also be conserved.

The properties and reactions of elementary particles are studied by *nuclear* physicists. Several particles have been discovered in *cosmic rays*. Cosmic rays come from outer space and consist mainly of very high energy protons; alpha particles and nuclei of slightly heavier atoms are also present.

When cosmic rays enter the earth's atmosphere they collide with the oxygen and nitrogen molecules of the air. These collisions produce elementary particles such as electrons, neutrinos, protons, and *mesons*. There are a number of different types of meson, some of which are charged and all much lighter than the proton.

Scientists are now able to produce a beam of high-energy protons. Machines, called *particle accelerators*, are used for this purpose. The first accelerators were built in the 1930s. Since then, extremely complicated machines have been designed to produce beams of protons, and also of electrons, having energies many thousands of times greater than those of the original accelerators. These beams are made to collide with atoms, especially hydrogen, and the resulting reactions are studied. From these studies information is gained about the basic structure of matter and the parts played by the different elementary particles.

CHARGES ON SUB-ATOMIC PARTICLES

Electron	charge: $-e$	
Quark	charge: $-\frac{2}{3} \times$ electron charge $= \frac{2}{3}e$	
Quark	charge: $\frac{1}{3} \times$ electron charge $= -\frac{1}{3}e$	
Quark	charge: $\frac{1}{3} \times$ electron charge $= -\frac{1}{3}e$	
Neutron	charge: $+\frac{2}{3}e - \frac{1}{3}e - \frac{1}{3}e = 0$	
Proton	charge: $+\frac{2}{3}e + \frac{2}{3}e - \frac{1}{3}e = e$	

Nuclear fission

Above
A chain reaction in uranium−235. One neutron causes a nucleus to split. The split nucleus breaks into two large fragments and either two or three fresh neutrons. These neutrons each collide with further nuclei causing more fissions.

Neutron

Fission products

Uranium−235

Mushroom cloud

Right
Fissile uranium−235 and plutonium −239 can be stored safely if the quantity is small (less than a few kilograms). This is because so many neutrons escape from the surface of the material that the chain reaction cannot continue. This smallest quantity capable of maintaining a chain reaction is called the *critical mass*. Above the critical mass enough neutrons are kept inside the material to keep the chain reaction going. In an atom bomb two masses smaller than the critical mass are brought together to make one lump above the critical mass.

1 critical mass

2 subcritical masses

When the nucleus of an atom breaks up, the pieces into which it breaks fly apart with great speed. The kinetic energy (energy of motion) of these fragments is equivalent to heat and this heat can be put to useful work in power stations. It can also be used for destructive purposes in the atom bomb.

To make this energy available it is necessary to start a *chain reaction* in a radioactive material. A chain reaction occurs when the fragments from one atomic nucleus collide with another nucleus causing it to split, the fragments from this nucleus then causing other nuclei to split, and so on. The *fission* (or splitting) of a large radioactive nucleus, like uranium, is caused by bombarding it with atomic particles. A *neutron* is a particularly suitable atomic particle as it has no charge and is therefore not repelled by the nucleus. When a neutron strikes the nucleus of certain isotopes of uranium, the uranium nucleus splits into two approximately equal large fragments and either two or three neutrons. These neutrons then fly off and cause two or three more uranium nuclei to break up. This is how the chain reaction starts.

In the atom bomb all the energy of this *nuclear reaction* is released in a fraction of a second, in the form of a tremendous, devastating explosion. To make this happen the fuel must consist of pure uranium-235 or plutonium-239. Both of these isotopes are *fissile*, that is, they split up when struck by a neutron.

In a nuclear reactor arrangements have to be made to slow down the devastating explosion that takes place in a bomb. This is done by using a mixture of the fissile isotope of uranium and the more plentiful, but much more stable iosotope, uranium-238.

Natural uranium, as it comes from the ground, contains only 7 fissile uranium-235 atoms in every 1000. This makes it one of the most

Above
Enrico Fermi (1901–1954), the Italian physicist. Working in America in 1942 he built what was then called an atomic pile in the squash court of Chicago University. It was the forerunner of both the atom bomb and nuclear reactors.

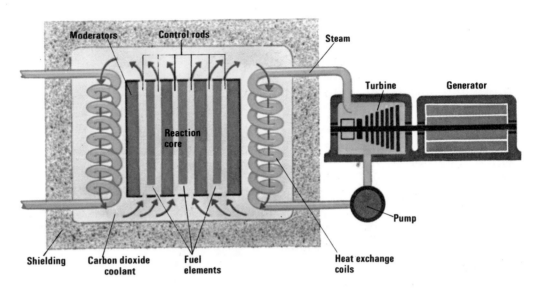

Above
A thermal reactor. The core consists of fuel elements and moderator. The rate of reaction is controlled by control rods made of a substance (such as cadmium or boron) that absorbs neutrons. The control rods are raised and lowered into the core. The coolant extracts the heat from the core and raises steam in a separate circuit. The steam drives a turbogenerator.

valuable and sought after minerals on earth.

It is not possible to build up a chain reaction in this material. In order to start a chain reaction it is necessary to increase the percentage of uranium-235 atoms in natural uranium–or to add plutonium to it. This is called *enriching* the natural fuel.

There are various types of reactor. Fast reactors, such as the Los Alamos, Clementine which uses pure plutonium-239, are called *fast* because the fission process involves the interaction of fast neutrons with the nuclei, whereas in *thermal reactors* a different principle is used. In these reactors the fuel is mixed with a substance called a *moderator*. This is a neutral substance consisting of light atoms (such as carbon or water) with which the neutrons emitted during fission collide. These collisions slow down the neutrons. Fast neutrons are often absorbed when they collide with the stable uranium-238 isotopes but slow neutrons are not. The introduction of the moderator produces more of the slow neutrons so that more are available to cause fission of the uranium-235 isotopes. This process generates a large amount of heat.

The heat produced in the core of a nuclear reactor (which contains the uranium fuel and the moderator) is used to heat up a liquid called the *coolant*. The coolant then becomes very hot and is able to make water boil. The steam produced is then used, as in coal or oil-fired power-stations, to rotate a turbine which drives a generator. Many countries today have nuclear power stations to supply their growing populations and industries. The reactors of the future will be fast breeder reactors.

Left
Nuclear energy can also be used for transport. The NS *Savannah* was the first nuclear ship. Launched in 1959 but now retired, she could remain at sea three and a half years without refuelling. One kilogram of uranium contains the equivalent energy of 2000 tons of coal. This is a tremendous advantage for ships and submarines.

Nuclear fusion

The fission of heavy nuclei is one way to obtain nuclear energy. Another way is the fusion (or joining together) of light nuclei. Deuterium is an isotope of hydrogen, sometimes called heavy hydrogen. When two atoms of deuterium come together to form helium an enormous amount of energy is released. In fact, when 1 kg of deuterium is converted to helium the energy released is six times greater than the energy released by the fission of 1 kg of uranium.

These *thermonuclear reactions,* as they are called, will only take place if the deuterium atoms collide with each other with great energy. This means that they must be moving very rapidly which, in turn, means that they must be at a very high temperature – over ten million °C. Temperatures as high as this do not normally occur on earth, although they do occur in the interior of stars. In fact, the energy of the sun and other stars is derived from thermonuclear reactions.

In the interior of the sun (see page 106), hydrogen is being converted into deuterium, and deuterium into helium. This happens because the gravitational attraction in the centre of the sun forces all the hydrogen atoms (protons) close together, creating a high pressure and a high temperature. When a neutron collides with a proton a deuterium nucleus is formed. When two deuterium nuclei collide, a series of reactions occurs leading to the formation of helium. The effect of all these reactions is that the total mass of deuterium is greater than the total mass of helium formed. This difference in mass, called the *mass defect,* is converted into energy in accordance with Einstein's Law.

It is extremely rare for the high temperatures required for thermonuclear reactions to occur on earth. The atom (fission) bomb is one source of such temperatures,

Einstein

Left
Albert Einstein (1879–1955), the great German physicist who settled in America. His theory of relativity showed that mass and energy are different forms of each other. In thermonuclear reactions some of the mass of the deuterium atoms is converted into energy. This is the source of the energy of the sun and also the H-bomb.

Hydrogen and Deuterium reactions

Neutron   Proton

Left
Thermonuclear reactions occur between deuterium nuclei. A deuterium nucleus consists of one neutron and one proton. In the first reaction two deuterium nuclei fuse to produce a helium–3 nucleus (two protons and one neutron) and one spare neutron. In the second reaction, which also can occur, the hydrogen isotope called tritium (one proton and two neutrons) is formed. In the last two reactions tritium and helium–3 react with deuterium to form helium–4.

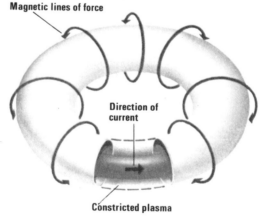

Magnetic lines of force

Direction of current

Constricted plasma

Left
The central problem of thermonuclear reactions is to contain them in a vessel. One solution relies on magnetic fields to keep the reaction away from the walls of the tube. At the high temperature of a thermonuclear reaction the atoms lose their electrons becoming a collection of electrons and positively charged nuclei. In this state a gas is called a *plasma.* In a toroidal (ring-shaped) reaction vessel the plasma is created by passing an enormous current through the gas. This current itself produces a strong magnetic field which constricts the plasma to the centre of the tube keeping it away from the walls.

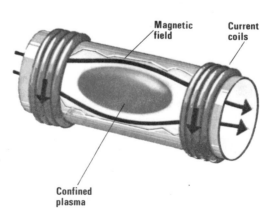

Magnetic field   Current coils

Confined plasma

Left
Some experimental reaction vessels are straight and the plasma is stopped from touching the ends by magnetic mirrors (strong magnetic fields round the end of the tube). In some experiments the plasma is created by a laser beam.

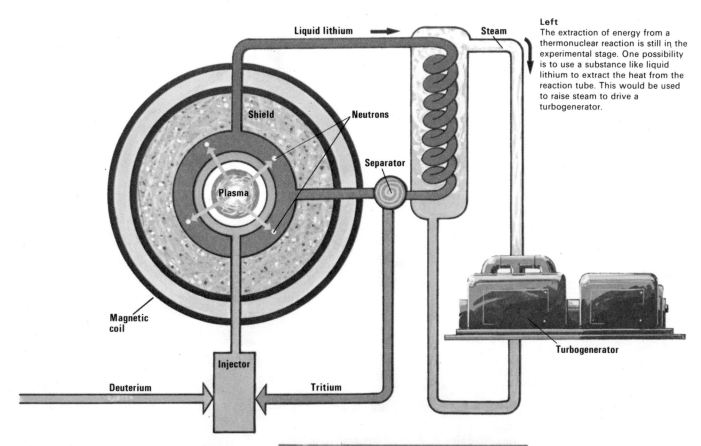

Left
The extraction of energy from a thermonuclear reaction is still in the experimental stage. One possibility is to use a substance like liquid lithium to extract the heat from the reaction tube. This would be used to raise steam to drive a turbogenerator.

Liquid lithium

Steam

Shield

Neutrons

Separator

Plasma

Magnetic coil

Turbogenerator

Injector

Deuterium

Tritium

and this is the basis of the *hydrogen bomb*.

If it were possible to make a fusion reactor this would have very great advantages over the fission type of reactor. Hydrogen is much easier and cheaper to obtain than uranium. Two out of every three atoms of water are hydrogen and 15 out of every 100 000 hydrogen atoms are deuterium atoms. Sea water would therefore provide plenty of fuel.

At the other end of the process, too, there is another great advantage. A fission reaction produces dangerous radioactive waste products that have to be disposed of, usually in the sea. A fusion reactor does not produce any dangerous wastes.

Unfortunately, although many laboratories are trying to make fusion reactors, none has so far succeeded. There are three main problems. The first is to create a high enough temperature, called the *ignition temperature*, to start the reaction. The second is to construct a vessel to contain a reaction taking place at several million degrees. All known materials vaporize instantly at

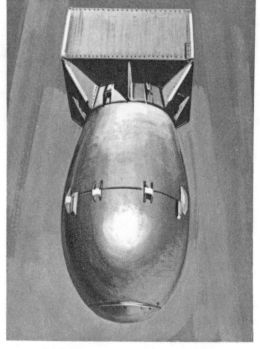

Left
A nuclear bomb. This atom bomb was called Fat Man and weighed about 4500 kg.

these temperatures. Finally, a way has to be found of extracting the energy from the reaction. The ignition temperature has been reached in several devices but only for a tiny fraction of a second. The problem now is to extend this time.

The problem of *containment* (containing the reaction is a vessel) is partly solved by using magnetic fields as vessel walls.

History of Communications and Entertainment

Device	Type	Date	Inventor	Country	Event
telegraph	single wire	1835	Morse	USA	first transatlantic signals transmitted
	under-water cable	1866	Field	USA	
telephone		1876	Bell	USA	first successful telephone message
gramophone	cylindrical record	1877	Edison	USA	first successful machine
	flat record	1887	Berliner	USA	
cinema	silent film	1895	Lumier Brothers	France	first public demonstration
	plus sound	1923	de Forest	USA	first public demonstration
radio		1896	Marconi	Italy	first successful communication by radio waves
		1906	Fessenden	USA	first public demonstration
tape recorder		1899	Poulsen	Denmark	
television	black and white	1926	Baird	Britain	first public demonstration
	colour	1954	—	USA	first successful public demonstration

Electrical components and their uses in electrical circuits

Component	Symbol		Use in circuit
battery			acts as a source of voltage, supplying current to the circuit
resistor		fixed value variable value	increases the resistance to the flow of both alternating current (a.c.) and direct current (d.c.)
capacitor		fixed value variable value	stores electricity; a.c. can flow through it if frequency of the current is high enough; d.c. cannot pass
inductor (coil)			opposes changes in current, smoothing out ripples, allowing d.c. to pass; a.c. can flow through it if frequency of current is low enough
transformer			used to increase or decrease the voltage in a circuit
diode		valve semiconductor	used to change a.c. to d.c. (rectification); can supply large currents at high voltages
triode			used to control the flow of current, to increase (amplify) the voltage and to produce electrical oscillations
transistor		p.n.p. n.p.n.	performs same functions as triode, but can work at lower voltages, and is smaller, cheaper and more reliable
aerial			for transmitting and receiving radio waves
earth			any point in the circuit at zero voltage

Discoveries and Inventions

Contents

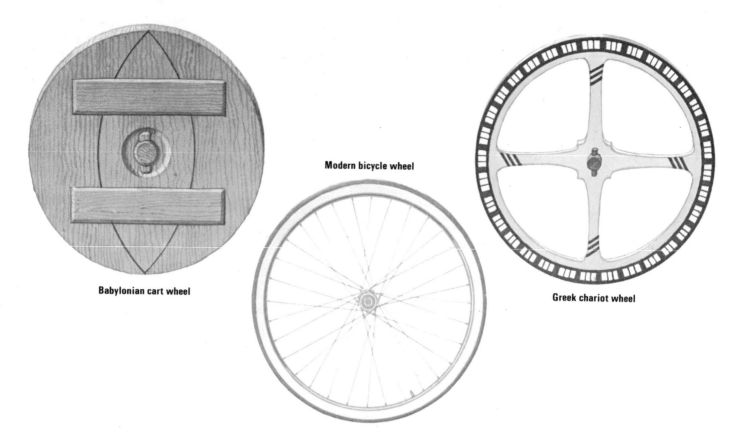

Modern bicycle wheel

Babylonian cart wheel

Greek chariot wheel

Above
Some examples of wheels:
(left) a very old cart wheel from
Mesopotamia; (right) a Greek
chariot wheel with spokes; (centre)
a wheel from a modern bicycle.

The wheel

Imagine living in a lonely place with no trains, buses, cars, or bicycles. You would have to walk everywhere. This is what life was like in primitive times. Gradually, many thousands of years ago, men started to live in groups near rivers. They built huts to live in and began to grow crops in the land around their settlements. Men had learnt to be farmers. At first animals were used to carry men and their goods. With the invention of the wheel civilization took a tremendous leap forward. You can get an idea of the use of wheels by putting a heavy book on a table and pushing it along. Then take some round pencils and rest the book on them. It is now much easier to move the book by making the pencils roll

Below
It is much easier to push a book
along on rollers. This is because
the surfaces in contact roll over
one another rather than sliding
and this involves less friction.

underneath it. We say that there is less *friction* when things roll, than when they slide. The large stones at Stonehenge were probably moved on tree trunk rollers.

Nobody knows who first had the idea of using wheels. In Asia, about 4000 B.C., men had carts with wheels that were solid circles of wood. Two wheels on either side of the cart were joined by a pole which we now call the *axle*. The axle was joined to the cart. These carts were first pushed by men. Later they were pulled by horses.

By 1750 B.C., the Ancient Egyptians were using spokes on their wheels. The spokes came out of the *hub* at the centre of the wheel. They were attached to an outer rim which moved over the ground. The wheels, made of wood, were much lighter than the older, solid wheels. Vehicles could therefore move

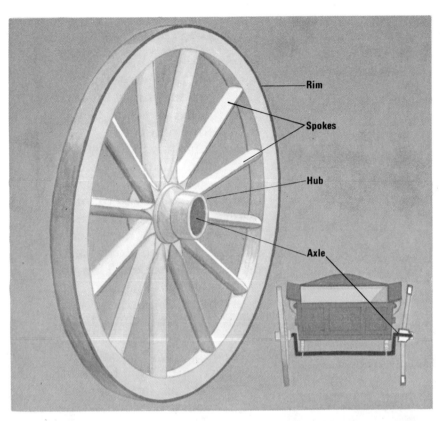

Rim

Spokes

Hub

Axle

much faster. Egyptian chariots had spoked wheels and were greatly feared by opposing armies because of the speed at which they could move. Instead of wood, the Romans used iron to make their spoked wheels; they therefore lasted much longer but were very heavy.

When a wheel is turning it moves on the axle, which goes through a hole in its centre. The point where the axle goes through the wheel is called the *bearing*. When the wheel moves, the axle is fixed and the hub of the wheel rubs against the axle. This friction makes it more difficult for the wheel to go round and the parts quickly wear out. It also makes the hub and axle very hot when the wheel turns quickly.

To make it easier for the hub to slide on the axle it is coated with grease or oil. Early man probably used animal fats for this.

Ballbearings were first used in the nineteenth century. They are used in many modern wheels. A number of steel balls are held between the inside of the hub and the axle. Instead of sliding on the axle the hub rolls around it, just as the book moves along the rollers. Because the balls roll instead of sliding, the wheel turns more easily.

Ball bearings

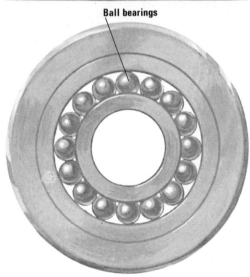

Above
When rubber was invented it was a better material than iron for making tyres. The tyres on this penny-farthing are made of solid rubber.

Above left
The first wheels were made of wood. In the sixteenth century the first tyre was made. This was a band of iron in the shape of a hoop, which was made to fit tightly around the wheel. These wheels were lighter than solid iron wheels and lasted almost as long. Wheels were also made with a saucer shape. They were held on the cart as shown in the diagram. This made them stronger. They were called *dished wheels*.

Left
An aeroplane tyre. This is an example of a pneumatic tyre (first invented in 1845). Pneumatic means filled with air. The air is pumped into the tyre through an opening with a special stopper called a valve. The air inside makes the wheel more bouncy than one with a solid tyre. Most vehicles have pneumatic tyres nowadays. The pattern cut into the rubber is called the tread. It prevents the aeroplane skidding when it takes off or lands.

Left
Ballbearings make the wheel move more easily on the axle.

Printing

Before the invention of printing, books had to be written by hand. It took months, often years, for a man (called a *scribe*) to make a single copy of a book.

Printing in its most simple form was invented in China over 2000 years ago. Parts of a flat wooden block were cut away to form raised letters or designs. The raised surface was covered in ink and a sheet of paper pressed down onto it to print on the paper. This was still very slow and expensive.

In the 15th century a German printer, Johann Gutenberg, made it possible to print books faster and cheaper. Instead of carving an entire page out of one block of wood, he carved each letter separately on small blocks of wood of the same height. These pieces (called *characters*) could be placed in any order to form words and sentences. When the printing was completed, the pieces of type could be used again to make new words. Instead of pressing a piece of paper against the inked type by hand, a mechanical press was used to force the paper against the type. Even with this improvement, it was still slow.

William Caxton was one of the first English printers. After learning the art of printing in Europe in 1471, he returned to London and set up his own press in Westminster. Early books were mainly on law and religion, but Caxton also

Above
Separate pieces of type being selected by hand to form words. They are placed in a special tray called a *composing stick*.

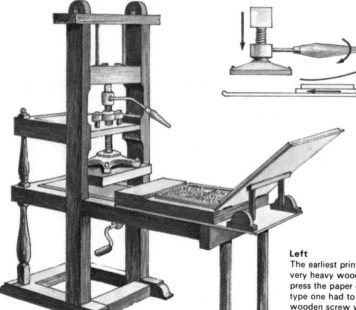

Left
The ancient Chinese method of printing from wood or stone blocks. The modern hobby of lino cutting is done in a similar way, using lino blocks.

Left
The earliest printing presses were very heavy wooden machines. To press the paper down onto the inked type one had to tighten a big wooden screw which forced down a heavy wooden plate onto the paper.

Left
William Caxton, 1422–1491, one of the first English printers. His first book in English was printed in 1475. He translated many books from foreign languages before printing them. He printed a total of nearly 100 different books. One of the earliest of these was about the game of chess.

Right
The Linotype setting machine, invented in America in the late 19th century by Ottmar Mergenthaler, a German printer. It was one of the most important inventions in printing since Gutenberg invented movable type over 400 years earlier. With this machine the printer is able to work much faster because most of the operations are performed automatically.

WEB OFFSET LITHO MACHINE

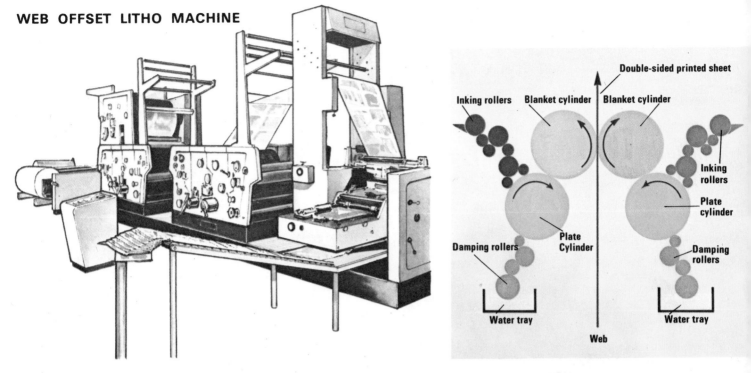

Double-sided printed sheet
Inking rollers
Blanket cylinder
Blanket cylinder
Inking rollers
Plate cylinder
Plate Cylinder
Damping rollers
Damping rollers
Water tray
Water tray
Web

printed books on other subjects. In the five hundred years since Gutenberg first used separate pieces of type, many improvements have been made in both the speed and quality of printing.

Except in special cases, type is no longer set by hand. Large modern setting machines, with keyboards like a typewriter are used to produce lines of type or film automatically. From these, *printing plates* are made, either by moulding or photographically.

The plates are used on the giant modern printing presses that are run by electricity. These are capable of printing thousands of books or newspapers every hour.

There are three main methods of printing: *letterpress*, *photolithography* and *gravure*. Letterpress uses plates with a raised moulded surface. Photolithography uses plates with a flat surface. These are produced photographically. Gravure printing uses plates with an engraved surface, produced by chemical etching.

The two main types of printing machine used are the *sheet-fed* and the *web-fed*. In sheet-fed machines, single sheets of paper are automatically fed into the machine and printed individually. In a web-fed machine, a continuous roll of paper is fed through the machine. Both types of machine can print up to four colours on either one or both sides of the paper at once. The paper goes through a different set of plates for each colour. Some machines can also cut up the sheets and fold them into pages.

Above
A Web Offset machine. This can print on both sides at once of a continuous web of paper fed from a roll. The plate cylinder is damped and then inked by rollers. The impression is transferred, or offset, onto a blanket cylinder which prints it onto the paper.

-FED ROTARY PRESS

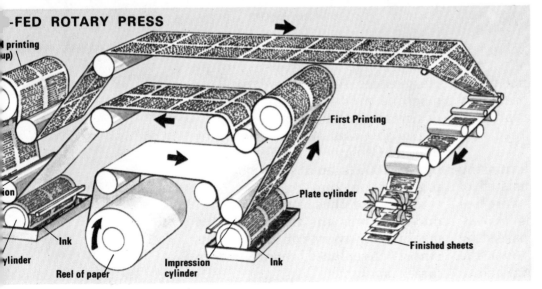

printing
up)

First Printing

ion

Plate cylinder

Ink

Finished sheets

ylinder

Reel of paper

Impression cylinder

Ink

Left
A modern web-fed Rotary Press. This uses a continuous roll of paper to print on instead of separate sheets. Newspapers and books are often printed on such a press because of its great speed. These presses cut and fold the pages automatically.

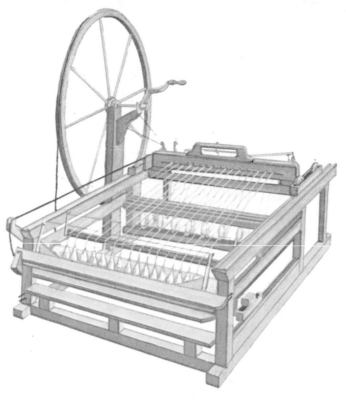

Crompton

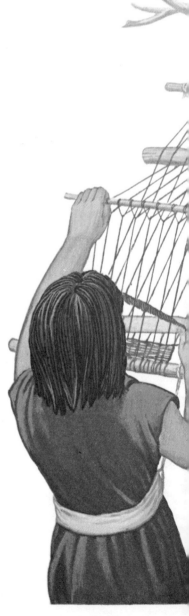

Cloth

Spinning and weaving are two of man's oldest industries. There are many types of woven material, such as matting, fencing, or wicker for baskets; the most important one, however, is cloth. Before cloth can be woven, thread must be spun from animal hair, parts of plants, or some other substance. Cotton, wool, and flax were certainly used in 2500 B.C. In fact, the earliest piece of cloth dates back to about 4500 B.C.

In Europe, spinning was done by hand up to the fourteenth century. The spinner would draw out a piece of fluff from a mass of raw wool, or cotton. He would twist it, overlapping the ends of several bits, to form a long thin thread. This was wound onto a stick called the *spindle*. The process became faster when the spindle was rotated by using the foot treadle of a *spinning wheel*. This produced thread of a more even thickness.

Thread is woven into cloth using a *loom*. Early looms consisted of two wooden bars. Threads were tied between the bars. A long thread, wound on a *shuttle* was passed by hand under one thread, over the next one, then under again, and so

on. On the way back, the shuttle was passed over a thread which it had previously gone under, and vice versa. The threads are therefore interlaced at right angles to each other. The shuttle thread forms the *weft* of the material; the fixed threads form the *warp*.

Weaving became much faster when alternate threads could be lifted all at once. The shuttle could then be thrown back and forth through the space between the two lots of threads. Gradually looms became more complicated and fancy patterns could be easily woven.

In 1733, John Kay invented the *flying shuttle*. The weaver pulled cords causing the shuttle to move rapidly across the loom. Now, thread could no longer be spun quickly enough for the weavers. This problem was solved in 1767 by Hargreaves' *Spinning Jenny*. This machine produced many spindles of thread at the same time.

The *spinning mule,* invented by Samuel Crompton in 1779, enabled up to 1000 spindles to be spun together on one machine. Any thickness of thread could be produced. It was the main spinning machine for over a century but has since been replaced by more modern faster machines.

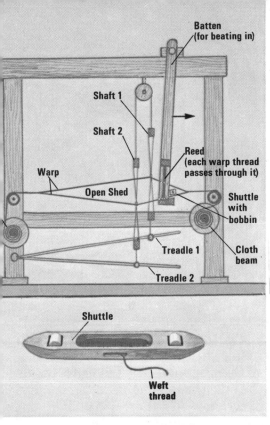

Batten (for beating in)

One of the two sets of two shuttles on either side of the loom: 4 different coloured warp threads can be used

The dobby: controls which shafts should be lifted for the shedding process

Shaft 1

Shaft 2

4 shafts

Reed (each warp thread passes through it)

Warp

Open Shed

Shuttle with bobbin

Treadle 1

Treadle 2

Cloth beam

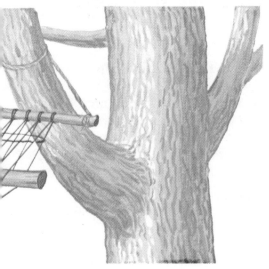

Shuttle

Weft thread

To produce cloth quickly, and of a high quality, the principal steps in weaving should be done by mechanical means. There are four main processes: arranging the warp threads so that they remain tight and equally spaced (*warping*); raising those warp threads under which the shuttle must pass (*shedding*); passing the shuttle through the resulting space, or shed (*picking*); making each weft thread horizontal and equally spaced (*beating in*).

Kay's flying shuttle was one step towards automation. Gradually power-driven looms replaced hand-looms. The first one was built by Cartwright in 1785. There have been many developments since.

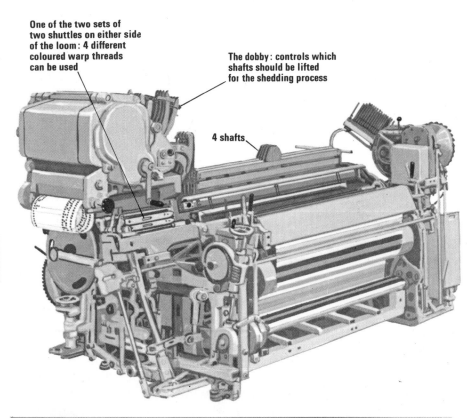

A SIMPLE LOOM

Warp thread. Pass through a loop in middle of twisted string. Tie firmly at both ends

2 pieces of twisted string (make 40 for each frame)

Frame of twisted wire (make 2)

Glue or nail together pieces of wood to make frame

25 cm

50 cm

8 cm

Alternate threads lifted by string loops on one frame

Left
Building a simple loom. (a) Make the wooden and wire frames as shown. *Two* wire frames are necessary. (b) Pass the red threads through the central string loops on the first wire frame. The blue threads are passed through the loops on the second wire frame. They should lie between the red threads. The threads should be tied fairly tightly to the ends of the loom. (c) Wind a very long piece of green thread on a piece of cardboard. Lift the first wire frame and the shuttle can pass beneath the red threads. Then lift the second frame and it passes under the blue threads. Use a long knitting needle to push the green threads close together.

View of loom from above

2 frames for lifting alternate warp threads

Alternate threads lifted by string loops on other frame

Shuttle

Weft thread

Only a few warp threads are shown. There should be about 40 threaded through each frame. (About 80 warp threads altogether)

Use wire frame (not shown) to lift one set of warp threads

Pattern of weaving (shown loosely) Push weft threads together

Pass shuttle across between the two sets of warp threads

Right

Cotton is a cool strong fibre which has many uses. It can be treated with chemicals, making it stain-resistant.

Wool is the most useful natural fibre. It can be woven into both thick and thin material.

Linen is very tough and lasts a long time.

Far right

Silk is the most luxurious and costly material. It has a unique sheen and can be dyed many beautiful colours. Silkworms are mainly reared in Eastern countries like Thailand and China. There is a silkworm farm in Britain but the silk is not of such good quality as that from Asiatic countries.

Cotton

Wool

Linen

Below

You can make several natural dyes from vegetable matter.

Take some blackcurrants, for example, soak them in water overnight and then boil them for an hour. Strain off the juice and soak a clean piece of white cloth in it. Simmer the cloth in the juice until it is dyed to a deep colour. The colour will be lighter when the cloth dries.

Be careful not to get any of this dye on your own clothes, and wear rubber gloves to protect your hands. This type of dye will wash out, or run, if the cloth gets wet.

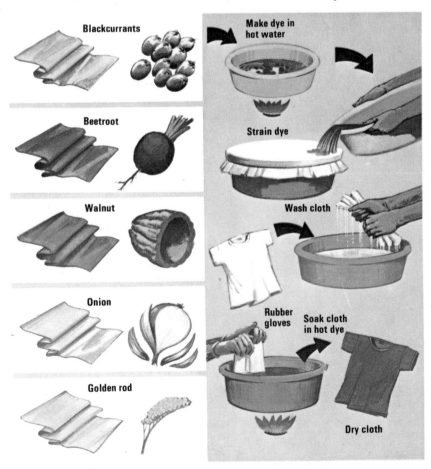

Blackcurrants

Beetroot

Walnut

Onion

Golden rod

Make dye in hot water

Strain dye

Wash cloth

Rubber gloves

Soak cloth in hot dye

Dry cloth

Clothing materials

Today all clothing materials are made from threads (*fibres*) which are woven into cloth. Before 1891 all fibres came from plants and animals. *Cotton* comes from the fluffy seed pods of cotton plants which grow in hot countries such as Egypt. *Linen* is made from the stalks of a plant called *flax*. Flax grows well in cool moist places, such as Ireland. The hair clipped from a sheep or goat is made into *wool*. *Silk* is made by a kind of caterpillar called a silkworm. It spins the silk to make a cocoon inside which it changes into a moth. If the cocoons are put into water the silk thread can be loosened and unwound. All these materials can be spun, woven, and dyed.

Today, besides all these fibres, we have others called man-made or artificial fibres. *Rayon* is made from wood. This is beaten up with water into a pulp. The wood pulp is then mixed with two chemicals called *caustic soda* and *carbon disulphide*. These dissolve the wood pulp and a thick liquid is formed called *viscose*. The liquid is then forced through a small nozzle into a bath of acid. The acid causes the viscose to set into a solid thread which can be wound onto a spool.

Besides rayon there are many other man-made fibres. Materials like Terylene, Acrilan, and nylon are made from chemicals in oil or coal. The chemicals are mixed together and heated, forming new substances which can be made into threads. Nylon was first made in 1932 by an American chemist, W. H. Carothers.

Natural fibres and rayon can easily be dyed. They will absorb water like blotting paper. The coloured dyes are mixed with water and the materials dipped into them. Either the thread or the woven cloth is dipped into the dye. Often the plain material is laid flat and a coloured design is printed on it. Man-made materials like nylon cannot easily be dyed. Their surface is slippery, rather like plastic. They

Silk

Man-made fibres

Left
These fabrics look like the natural materials, but all are man-made fibres. They are much easier to wash and keep clean; often they do not need to be ironed. Clothes are often made from a mixture of natural and man-made fibres.

are usually coloured while they are being made into thread.

At first materials were sewn together by hand to make clothes. In 1832 an American, Walter Hunt, built the first sewing machine. Another type of machine was made by Isaac Singer in 1851.

In a sewing machine there are two pieces of thread. One length is on a special bobbin inside the machine. The other is on a cotton reel on top of the machine. This is threaded through a moving arm and then through the eye of the needle. In a sewing machine needle the eye is at the pointed end. The cloth is made to move under the needle, which moves up and down. As the needle goes through the material it carries the thread with it; this is looped around the other thread inside the machine to make the stitch. Under the material are two rows of blunt metal teeth, called the *feed dog*. When the machine is working, the feed dog moves backwards to carry the cloth along. Then it drops down a little and moves forward to its original position, moving the next piece of material backwards.

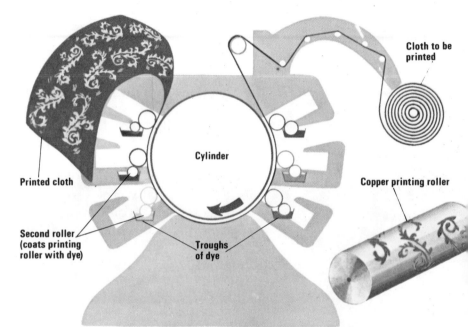

Printed cloth

Cloth to be printed

Cylinder

Copper printing roller

Second roller (coats printing roller with dye)

Troughs of dye

Above
Roller printing, used to print patterns onto cloth. The pattern is cut out of a copper roller and the gaps filled with a coloured dye. This machine has six rollers each with a different pattern and filled with a different coloured dye. As the cloth passes each roller, the separate colours are printed onto it.

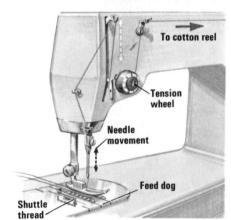

To cotton reel

Tension wheel

Needle movement

Feed dog

Shuttle thread

Left
A sewing machine threaded ready for use.

INTERLOCKED STITCHING

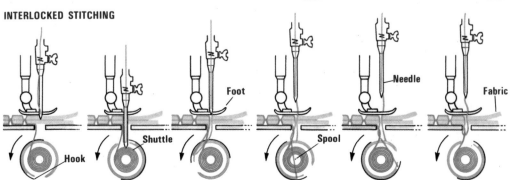

Hook

Shuttle

Foot

Spool

Needle

Fabric

Left
A diagram showing how the top thread and the one inside a sewing machine lock together to form a stitch.

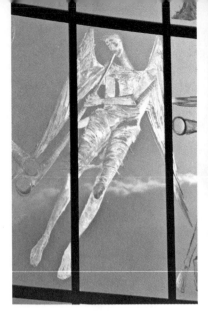

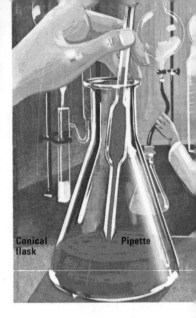

Conical flask   Pipette

Above
Two cathedral windows that show entirely different decorative uses of glass.
(Right) The beautiful stained glass rose window in the Cathedral of Chartres in France, built in the twelfth century. *(Left)* The Flying Angel etched on the Great Glass Screen in Coventry Cathedral, England, finished in 1961.

Glass

Today we are very familiar with materials like nylon, perspex, and bakelite. These are not found naturally, like wood and stone. They are said to be man-made materials. The oldest man-made material is glass, which was first used about 3000 years ago.

Glass is made from a mixture of sand, soda, and limestone. These are ground together and heated to about 1500°C. They form a clear jelly-like substance. When this cools it sets into a hard brittle glass. To produce coloured glass, small amounts of other chemicals can be added. Sand always contains some iron, which, if not removed, gives glass a greenish colour.

Glass is used for making jars, bottles, and other vessels. About 2000 years ago it was found that a piece of hot soft glass on the end of a metal tube could be blown out into a bubble which could then be shaped. Nowadays glass-blowing can be done by machine. Glass is also used in windows. At first only small pieces were made. These were joined together on lead frames. Later windows were made by blowing a piece of glass into a large bubble and flattening it, so that it formed a plate. Windows made like this have a lump in the middle where the bubble was joined to the glassblowing tube.

Today bottles and jars are nearly all made by machine, in moulds. Window glass is made by flattening the soft hot glass between rollers and allowing it to cool slowly. It is then polished. It has also been

Above
Glass has always been prized for its beauty. This wine goblet is decorated with diamond-point engraving. It was made in 1686.

Right
Some everyday uses of glass: sheet of plate glass; light bulb; milk bottle; jam jar; windscreen; thermometer.

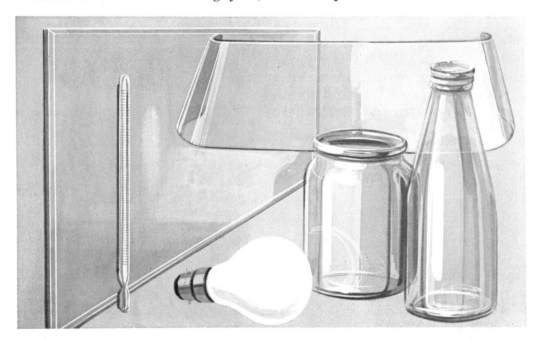

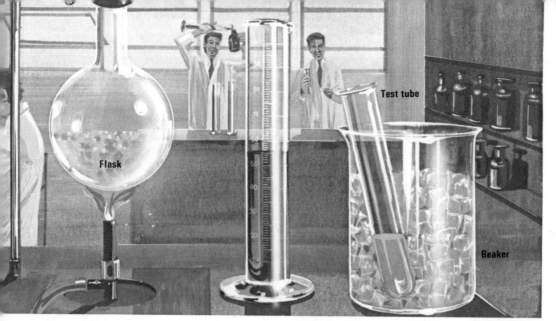

found that different kinds of glass can be made by adding other substances to the sand, soda, and limestone.

The glass in a car windscreen is very strong. When a windscreen cracks it breaks into many small pieces. These do not have sharp edges, so the driver does not get cut. Glass can be made to withstand heat. Ordinary glass would crack if it were heated but *Pyrex* glass does not. Neither does it break as easily when it is dropped. It is therefore used for making cooking dishes. When rockets and spacecraft are sent into space they have to stand extremely high temperatures. They are therefore covered with a coating of a special glass called *Pyrosil*. This is also used to make cooking dishes now.

Glass can be made into very fine threads. This is called *fibreglass*. It can be woven into a cloth which is very hard wearing and does not burn. The cloth is often used for making curtains. The glass fibres can also be mixed with plastic to make a very light strong material. It does not rust like iron or rot like wood. Car bodies and the hulls of boats are often made of fibreglass.

In our modern world there are many substitutes for glass, such as perspex and other plastics. These are lighter than glass and do not break as easily. Many bottles are now made of plastic. But plastics are not as heat-resistant as glass and are affected by chemicals.

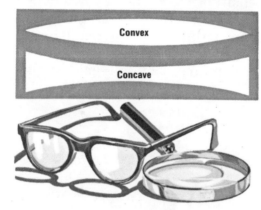

Convex

Concave

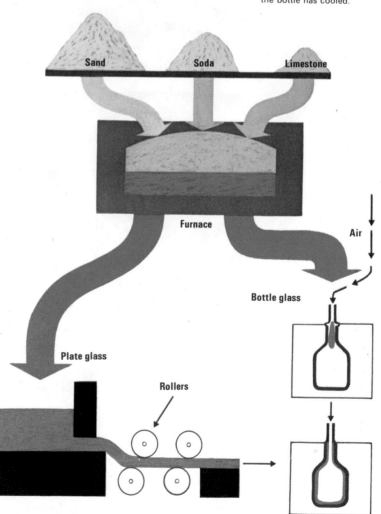

Sand **Soda** **Limestone**

Furnace

Air

Bottle glass

Plate glass

Rollers

Left
Glass is used for making lenses. As light passes through the lens its direction is changed. The amount the light is bent depends on the type of glass used and on its shape. Lenses are used in spectacles and in many instruments such as telescopes, binoculars, microscopes, and cameras. The glass used for making these lenses has to be of very good quality and have no flaws. It is called *optical glass*.

Below
Making plate glass and bottles. The bottles are blown into a mould which can then be opened up when the bottle has cooled.

Photographic film

It has been known for centuries that some chemicals change colour when light falls on them—they are *light-sensitive*. Light makes certain silver compounds turn black (after they are treated with the right chemicals). It is these compounds, and in particular *silver bromide*, that are used in the manufacture of photographic film.

There are many types of film and they all have at least one light-sensitive layer. This layer is called the *emulsion*. In black-and-white film, a thin layer of emulsion is coated onto a plastic or glass base. It contains tiny silver bromide crystals in a jelly-like substance called *gelatin*.

Light, reflected or given out by the subject being photographed, is focused by the camera lens onto the emulsion, when the shutter is opened. The light from different parts of the subject activates the silver bromide crystals by varying amounts; the stronger the light, the greater the reaction. An image of the subject is formed in the emulsion, but until the film is developed it cannot be seen. It is called a *latent image*.

To make this image visible, the film has to be treated with certain chemicals. This is done in a *dark room* to prevent any more light falling on the emulsion. The film

Fox Talbot

Above
Joseph Niépce (1765–1833) produced the first photograph (a very blurred one) in about 1826. He worked for many years with Louis Daguerre (1787–1851) improving his methods of processing film. Daguerre continued after Niépce's death. Fox Talbot (1800–1877) worked on a different process and was producing small negatives in 1835.

Niépce

Daguerre

Right
Film development using a lightproof tank. In total darkness the film is fed into the spiral groove of the reel by turning the top. The reel is then put inside the tank and the chemicals poured in and out: first developer, then water, and then fixer. After washing again in water for about 45 minutes the film is taken out and dried.

Spiral groove

Tank Reel

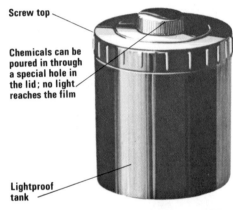

Screw top

Chemicals can be poured in through a special hole in the lid; no light reaches the film

Lightproof tank

Right
An enlarger. This instrument contains a glass convex lens acting as a magnifying glass (see page 216). The negative is placed above this lens and is illuminated by a flash of light from above. An enlarged image of the negative is formed on the photographic paper placed beneath it.

Far right
The negative and final photo of a subject taken with black-and-white film.

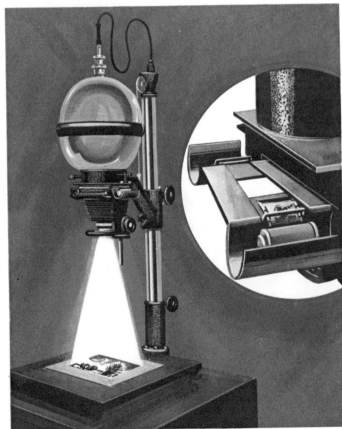

Negative print

Positive print

is placed for a certain length of time, at about 20°C, in a dish or tank containing *developer*. The developer turns the light-activated crystals to grey or black metallic silver. The shade of grey or black depends on how much light fell on a particular area of the film. In this image light and dark are reversed; dark shadows on the original subject appear clear (the film is transparent) while bright spots are black. The individual pictures on the film are therefore called *negatives* of the subject.

After washing the film in water, it is immersed in another chemical called *fixer*. This dissolves away the unactivated silver bromide and also makes the image stay in position. The film is then washed and dried.

To obtain a photograph from this negative, it is placed against a special photographic paper. This paper also contains a layer of light-sensitive crystals. The paper and negative are exposed to a brief flash of light. The dark areas of the negative will let only a little light through onto the paper; the clear parts allow much more light through.

The photographic paper is then developed and fixed in the same way as the film. The final image produced on the paper is white in areas that are dark in the negative, and vice versa. It is therefore identical to the subject that was originally photographed.

Films are now much smaller than they used to be. If the negative is placed in contact with the paper, a rather small photograph, the same size as the negative, is obtained. An *enlarger* is used to produce a larger photograph, or to enlarge one part of a photograph.

A *Polaroid camera* uses a special type of film. This Polaroid film is developed by a process inside the camera. Black-and-white photographs are obtained about 10 seconds after the picture is taken. Colour photographs and X-ray photographs can also be produced in this way.

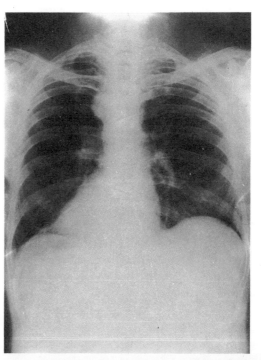

Left
An X-ray photograph of the chest, showing the ribs. Film can be made sensitive to X-rays. For a chest X-ray, a person stands close to the film, between it and the X-ray machine. X-rays are stopped by bones, but pass through skin. The final image shows up the bones, appearing white in areas where X-rays have landed on the film.

Below
An infrared photo, taken from the air, of some defoliated trees (trees without leaves). These appear blue whereas healthy trees are purplish red. Film can be made sensitive to invisible infrared radiation. All warm things give off or reflect different amounts of infrared. The amount determines the colour. Grass and leaves reflect it strongly. It passes through haze in the atmosphere; faraway objects show up easily on these photographs.

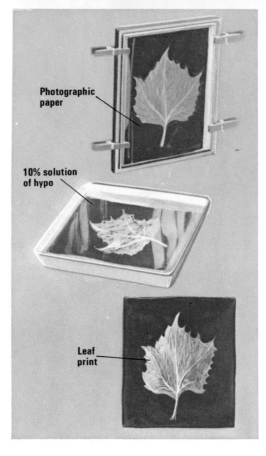

Photographic paper

10% solution of hypo

Leaf print

Left
You can make a type of photograph without using a camera. Get a piece of slow photographic printing paper. Place something flat, like a leaf, on the sensitive side of the paper and press it between a board and sheet of glass. Leave it in the sun until the paper turns dark violet.
Take out the paper and you will have a pale print of the leaf. The thick veins will show up white because they let the least amount of light through. To fix the print, soak it for five minutes in a solution of hypo containing one part silver nitrate to ten parts water. Rinse, dry and press it.

Microscopes

Some objects are so small that they cannot be seen clearly by eye. A microscope is used to form an enlarged picture or *image* of the object. The *magnification* of a microscope is the size of the image divided by that of the object. If the magnification is × 100, the image is 100 times larger than the object.

An optical microscope uses glass lenses to produce the enlarged image. The simplest type is a *magnifying glass*. This is merely a converging or convex lens – a lens which bulges out in the centre. It is held a short distance above the object and moved towards the eye until the image becomes clearly seen (*focused*).

A microscope used in a scientific laboratory is more complicated. It contains a number of different lenses; only two are used in the actual magnification. The tiny object (or *specimen*) is placed on a thin glass plate and strongly lit from below. The convex lens just above the object is called the *objective*. It produces a magnified image in the same way as the simple magnifying glass. This image is formed between the objective and the second convex lens, called the *eyepiece*. The eyepiece magnifies this first image even more. The total magnification of the instrument is the magnification of the objective multiplied by that of the eyepiece. The final image can be over 1000 times the size of the object. Tiny details of objects such as parts of plants, creatures in pond water, or hairs can be seen.

Above
A magnifying glass. It is useful for looking at small objects such as stamps, insects, and small print in books.

Right
A compound microscope with a multiple nosepiece. Three different objective lenses can be interchanged by swinging the nosepiece round. This provides different magnifications. The cutaway objective lens system shown on the right, gives a magnification of × 100. The cutaway Huyghenian eyepiece shown above it is composed of two lenses. Eyepieces usually have a magnification of about × 5 or × 10 The total magnification of a compound microscope is found by multiplying together the magnifications of the eyepiece and the objective.

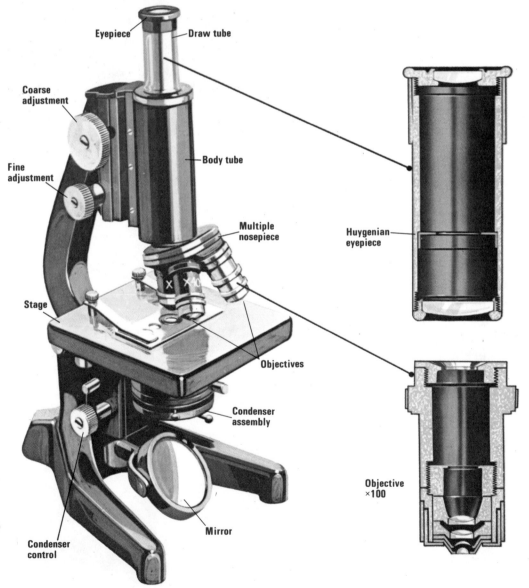

When even greater magnification is needed, an *electron microscope* is used. Instead of using light to illuminate the object, a beam of *electrons* is used. An electron is a minute particle of matter found in the atom (see page 156) and is too small to see. A beam of electrons (also invisible) can be produced by heating a thin coil of wire to a high temperature. Glass lenses cannot change the direction of (converge or diverge) an electron beam. In the electron microscope special magnets are used for this job. These are called *magnetic lenses*. The electron beam passes through the specimen which must be very thin; it can be a slice cut from the object being studied. The electrons bounce off the atoms and molecules making up the thin slice. They are then focused by one of the magnetic lenses to form an image of the object. Although the electron beam cannot be seen, the final image is visible, being formed in the same way as the picture on a television screen. This image can be up to one million times larger than the object!

With this enormous magnification, extremely small things can be studied to find out how they work – or why they don't work. There are therefore many fields of science, such as medicine, chemistry, and physics where the electron microscope is a valuable tool.

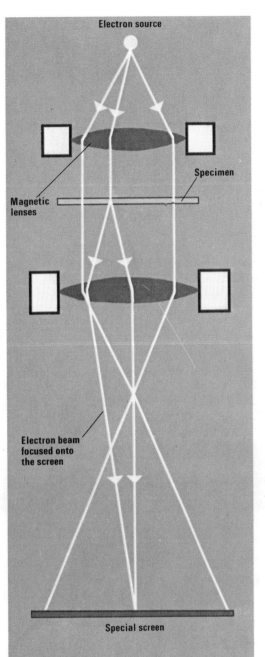

Electron source

Magnetic lenses

Specimen

Electron beam focused onto the screen

Special screen

Left
A diagram of an electron microscope. The image is formed in a similar way to that in the optical microscope, but the magnification is much greater. A tiny part of an animal can be shown in great detail. Images of nerves, blood cells, and viruses, for example, are used to find out how these living things work.

Far left
Seen through a simple microscope, this fly's wing looks ten times its real size.

Left
Red blood cells, magnified 5000 times. Blood contains a large number of red cells, as well as many other substances. The red cells carry oxygen from small blood vessels in the lungs to different parts of the body. The image was produced by a scanning electron microscope, a slightly more complicated form of the ordinary electron microscope. It produces more life-like images.

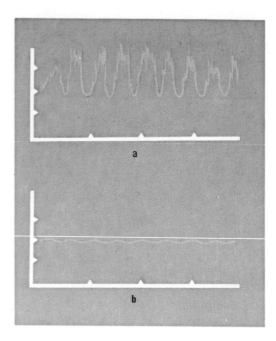

a

b

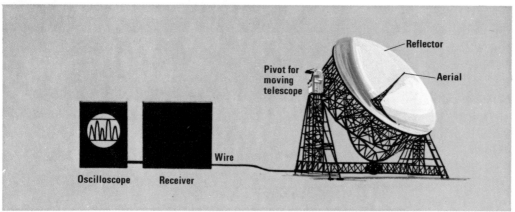

Reflector

Pivot for moving telescope

Aerial

Wire

Oscilloscope   Receiver

Above left
The Jodrell Bank telescope. This is one of the world's largest radio telescopes. It is 250 feet (over 74 metres) in diameter. This telescope can be swung round to the required angle. The sheets of metal of the reflector can also be moved. This enables more accurate collection of the radio waves.

Left
This is a much simplified diagram of a radio telescope. Radio signals are caught on the reflector and picked up by the revolving aerial. The aerial collects them and sends them back to the receiver.

Above
The receiver does not form a picture of the radio sources. It obtains details about the power given out by these sources. This information is recorded as lines. The diagram shows the lines of the sun (a) when it is active, (b) when it is quiet (when very few signals emitted).

Radio astronomy

The sound you hear on radio has been carried through the air by radio waves. These waves travel between broadcasting station and radio receiver which are separated by up to several thousand kilometres. Radio telescopes pick up waves which are travelling through the air from much further away. These radio waves come from stars in different parts of the universe and can travel for millions of years before they reach the earth and are picked up by the telescope.

They were first discovered by accident in 1932 by Karl Jansky. He was using a radio receiver with a movable aerial. When he pointed the aerial towards the Milky Way he received signals from the stars.

Most radio telescopes are built in isolated places where they will not be too disturbed by radio waves from earth. Some radio telescopes, like the famous one at Jodrell Bank near Manchester, England, are made of sheets of metal joined together in a bowl shape. This bowl is called the *reflector*. In the centre of the bowl is the *aerial*. The bowl is fixed to a rotating stand which enables it to move in all directions.

The reflector is made of shiny metal similar to the metal behind an electric fire. They both work in the same way. When the bars of the fire give off heat the metal catches the heat rays and throws or 'reflects' it back. The reflector of a radio telescope receives radio waves travelling through the air and reflects them to the central aerial. The aerial is constructed of wire mesh and it revolves quite separately from the reflector picking up the radio waves reflected on to it. It sends the waves back through wires to the *receiver*. The receiver changes the radio waves

Lovell

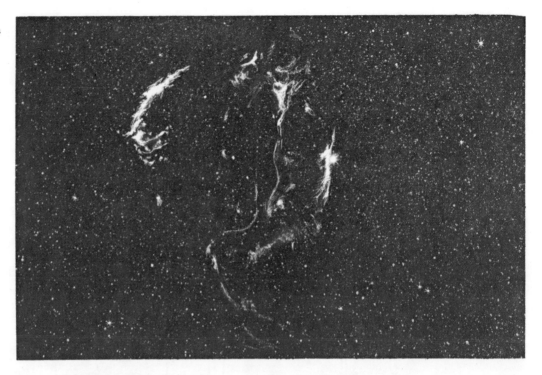

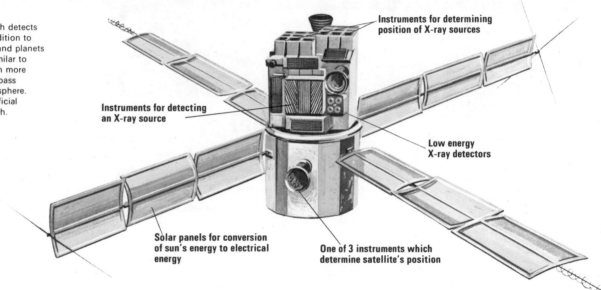

Instruments for determining position of X-ray sources

Instruments for detecting an X-ray source

Low energy X-ray detectors

Solar panels for conversion of sun's energy to electrical energy

One of 3 instruments which determine satellite's position

into a special kind of picture. These pictures are made up of lines as you can see in the diagram.

Radio Astronomy is the study of the patterns of lines made by the radio waves. The astronomer uses many instruments to help him understand the line patterns. From the patterns he can learn many facts, such as how hot a star is or how fast it is moving.

Many stars send out radio waves, including the sun. Many of these signals are very difficult to detect. However, special radio sources exist called *quasars* and *pulsars* which give out strong signals. Pulsars, first discovered in 1967, are tiny stars that rotate extremely rapidly (some in less than one minute) and give out radio waves at very regular intervals. Pulsars are a type of dying star. The remains of the star that exploded in 1054 forming the Crab Nebula is a pulsar. It is about 30 km in diameter and makes one complete rotation in about three hundredths of a second.

Very little is known about quasars. They seem to be star-like objects at enormous distances from us. The radio signals given out by them must be extraordinarily strong since they are easy to detect even after travelling these great distances through space.

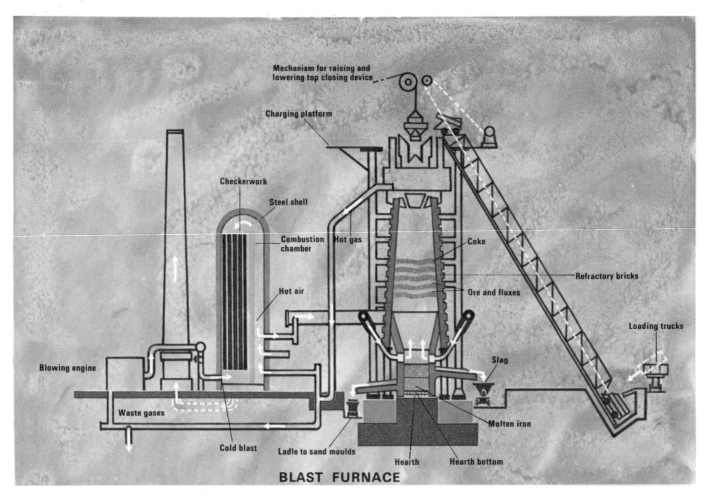

Labels on diagram:

Mechanism for raising and lowering top closing device

Charging platform

Checkerwork

Steel shell

Combustion chamber

Hot gas

Hot air

Coke

Refractory bricks

Ore and fluxes

Loading trucks

Blowing engine

Slag

Waste gases

Molten iron

Cold blast

Ladle to sand moulds

Hearth

Hearth bottom

BLAST FURNACE

Above

Blast furnace. Trucks carry the ore, coke, and fluxes (mostly limestone) to the top of the furnace, which may be 70 metres high. Hot air (about 800°C) is blown into the brick lined furnace causing the coke to burn and produce carbon monoxide. This acts on the ore and raises its temperature to about 1600°C. The molten iron falls to the bottom and is drawn off and run into sand moulds to form pig iron. The slag floats on the iron and is run off at a higher level.

Bessemer

Above

Henry Bessemer, who was born in 1813 and died in 1898, developed his process for making steel from iron because cast-iron cannon balls were too weak to be used in the rifled cannons he had invented.

Iron and steel

Primitive man made his first tools and weapons from bones and stones or from wood. Gradually he discovered that metals–the hard shiny materials he found on meteorites or sometimes in the ashes of a fire–could be made into sharper and tougher tools. The first metal to be obtained in any quantity was copper, but this was too soft except when it was found mixed with tin. This mixture of copper and tin is called *bronze*, and about 3500 B.C. the Egyptians were using bronze tools and weapons. This was the beginning of the *Bronze Age*.

Iron had been known for as long as bronze, but the only source in the Bronze Age was the occasional meteorite. Then somewhere in Asia, about 1500 B.C., men found that by heating certain minerals with wood they could make iron themselves. The Hittites were the first to have an army using iron weapons–they soon defeated the armies who had bronze weapons,

as bronze swords are no match for iron ones.

This was the start of the *Iron Age,* which we are still in today. Iron and steel are still the most important metals of construction. Cars, factory machinery, agricultural machinery, and weapons are all made mostly of iron and steel. Large buildings have a steel framework. **Over 600 000 000 tons of iron** and steel are used throughout the world every year. Think of what your life would be like without iron and steel.

Today we obtain most of our iron from the minerals, or *iron ores,* called *haematite* and *magnetite*. These occur in many places all over the world and are easily mined from the earth. They are converted to iron in a *blast furnace*. In the blast furnace the ore is burnt with coke and limestone to produce liquid iron which is run off into moulds and allowed to set **into slabs. This is called *pig iron* and can be used to make *cast iron*.**

To make 100 tons of iron takes about 190 tons of ore, 100 tons of

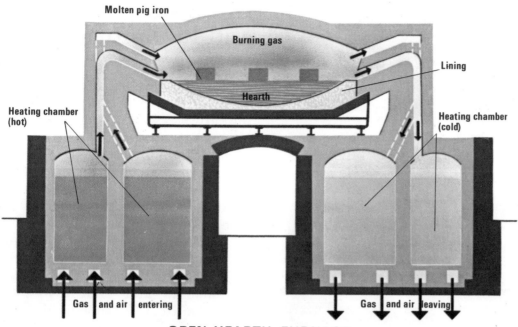

Molten pig iron

Burning gas

Lining

Hearth

Heating chamber (hot)

Heating chamber (cold)

Gas and air entering

Gas and air leaving

OPEN-HEARTH FURNACE

Left
The open-hearth steel-making furnace. Air and gas are heated by being passed over hot brickwork. The gas and air burn over the molten pig iron and the burnt gases are used to heat the brickwork to warm the incoming gas and air. The furnace is lined with special bricks that absorb some of the sulphur and phosphorus in the iron. The steel is tapped off and the slag floating on it can be used as a fertilizer as it contains phosphorus.

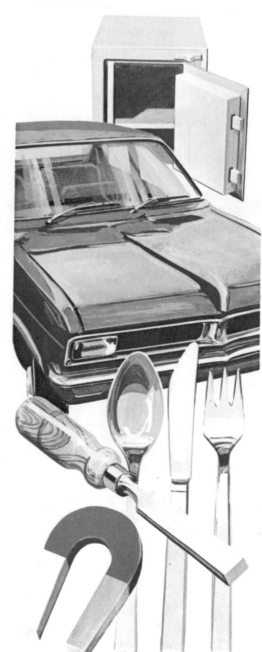

Far left
All these objects are made of plain steel: nail; horse-shoe; wire-wool.

Left
These objects are made of steel alloys. Manganese steels are used for safes, chrome-vanadium steel is used in cars, stainless steel is used for cutlery. Chrome-tungsten steel is used for tools like this chisel. Tungsten, silicon, or cobalt steels are used to make magnets.

Below
A simple experiment to show how quickly iron or steel rusts in damp air.
Put some wire wool in the bottom of a jar and leave it standing upside-down in a saucer of water. In a day or two the wool will turn rusty red. The grey iron has been changed to red iron oxide.
You will also notice that the water has risen up inside the jar to replace the oxygen in the air that has been used up in oxidizing the iron. Keep some steel wool in a dry, screw-top jar for comparison.

coke and 50 tons of limestone. At the same time 50 tons of *slag* are made. This is used to make cement and concrete.

Pig iron is not pure iron; it contains 3–4 per cent of carbon. This makes it rather brittle. The most useful form in which iron is used is *steel*. Steel is iron with most of the carbon removed, leaving only 0·2–1·5 per cent. A cheap way of doing this was discovered by Henry Bessemer in 1856. It consists of sending a blast of air through the molten iron so that most of the carbon forms carbon dioxide with the oxygen in the air. Today the Bessemer process has been replaced by the open-hearth and basic oxygen methods of steel-making.

Steel is much stronger and more versatile than iron. By adding other elements it can be made stronger, or rust-proof, and can stand up to higher temperatures. If 13 per cent of manganese is added to steel it becomes much harder. Nickel and chromium added to steel give the stainless steels which do not rust.

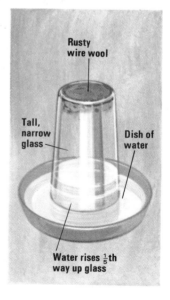

Rusty wire wool

Tall, narrow glass

Dish of water

Water rises $\frac{1}{5}$th way up glass

Engines and locomotion

It is almost impossible to imagine now how difficult it used to be to move about the country. Before the railways were developed in the nineteenth century, land transport depended entirely on the horse. Seas were crossed by sailing ships. The need for the horse and the sail were abolished by the invention of an efficient steam engine by James Watt. Watt was born in 1736, in Greenock, Scotland. At seventeen he learnt to make mathematical instruments and had a job as 'Mathematical Instrument Maker' to Glasgow University. One of the jobs they asked him to do was to repair a model of Newcomen's steam engine. This rather inefficient engine was used to pump water out of mines.

Watt improved on Newcomen's design and then he completely altered it. His new engine used only a third of the fuel that Newcomen's engine required. Watt also made his engine capable of rotary movement, using a crank and gear wheels. By 1782 this engine was working up to 40 machines in a factory. This was the beginning of the *Industrial Revolution* when manpower began to be replaced by machines.

The earliest steam engines were stationary; the first attempt to use them for transport was in 1787 when the American John Fitch built a workable steamship. By

Above
Watt's steam engine. Steam from the boiler enters the cylinder through a valve and pushes the piston down. At the bottom of the stroke another valve opens and steam pushes the piston up. The up-and-down (reciprocating) motion of the piston is converted to rotary motion by a system of cranks and gears.

Above
John Fitch's paddle steamboat. It worked but was not financially successful. Fitch died unknown.

Right
George Stephenson's steam locomotive called the 'Rocket'. It won a competition in 1829 covering 12 miles in 53 minutes.

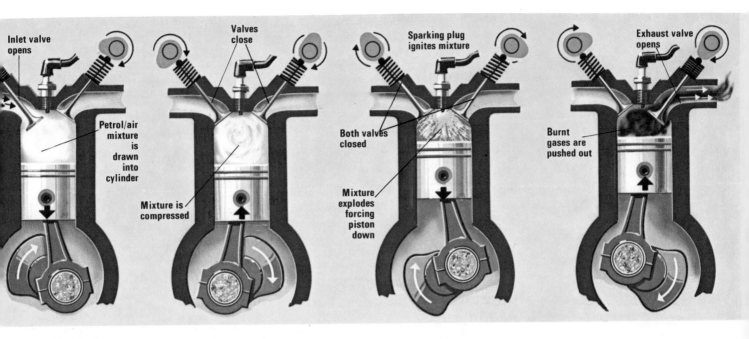

Inlet valve opens

Valves close

Sparking plug ignites mixture

Exhaust valve opens

Petrol/air mixture is drawn into cylinder

Mixture is compressed

Both valves closed

Mixture explodes forcing piston down

Burnt gases are pushed out

1850 propeller driven steamships were regularly crossing the Atlantic. The first successful steam train, built by George Stephenson in 1814, began the era of land travel by railway. For land transport the steam engine had the great disadvantage that it was necessary to carry coal or wood around to make the fire. The search then began for a lighter fuel and an engine in which to burn it. The result was the internal-combustion engine, a gas version of which was made by the Frenchman Etienne Lenoir in 1860. However, the modern engine we use in our cars is based on the first four-stroke engine, built by Nikolaus Otto in 1876. The cycle of strokes on which it works is still called the Otto cycle. Modern cars have engines consisting of 4, 6, or 8 cylinders; the more cylinders the more smoothly the engine runs.

The first practical petrol cars were built in Germany in 1885 by Gottleib Daimler and Carl Benz.

In 1892 the German engineer Rudolf Diesel introduced a modified type of engine using oil as the fuel. This engine does away with the sparking plugs, the explosion taking place when the oil is sprayed into the cylinder which contains highly compressed air. Diesel engines are used for buses, taxis, lorries, and some trains and boats.

Small petrol and Diesel engines are often two-stroke engines. In this type of internal-combustion engine there are no valves, the piston uncovers parts, or holes in the cylinder wall, as it moves up and down. Some motor cycles, cars, and lawnmowers have two-stroke engines. You can recognize them by the 'pop-pop' noise they make at each stroke.

Above
In the Otto cycle, on the first stroke the piston goes down and the inlet valve opens permitting air and petrol vapour to be sucked into the cylinder. On the second stroke the piston rises compressing the mixture. The sparking plug then fires and the mixture explodes, pushing the piston down for the third stroke. On the fourth upward stroke, the exhaust valve opens and the burnt gases are pushed out. The cycle is then repeated over and over again.

Below left
The Diesel locomotive is not as smooth as the electric train but is cheaper to run because an electrified rail or overhead wire is not required.

Below
In the Diesel engine the air is heated before the fuel is let in. The fuel is sprayed in, in fine drops which ignite spontaneously in the hot air.
In the petrol engine the petrol and air mixture is ignited by the sparking plug. Not all the mixture is burned.

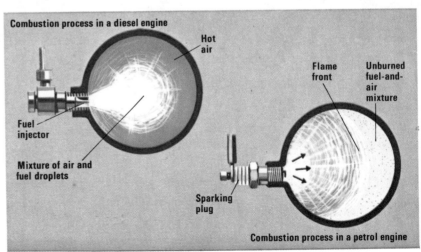

Combustion process in a diesel engine

Hot air

Flame front

Unburned fuel-and-air mixture

Fuel injector

Mixture of air and fuel droplets

Sparking plug

Combustion process in a petrol engine

Motor cars

Below
This was the first successful petrol-driven car. It was invented by Siegfried Marcus in 1874. Though it could be driven under its own power it was heavy and clumsy. It was not a commercial success.

Below, bottom
In 1873, Bollée's L'Obéissante was the first car to have pivoting front wheels, instead of the whole axle moving. This meant that it was more easily steered and manoeuvred. The car was very elaborate. Its steam engine was placed at the back. The wheels were moved by the steam in much the same way as pedals move a bicycle—by turning gear wheels.

Bottom right
The 1911 Ford Model T was the most popular car made at the time. Between 1908–1927, fifteen million were sold.

After Newcomen had invented the steam engine in 1712, attempts were made to harness this device to a cart in place of the horse. It was only with Watt's improved engine that this became possible. The first successful power-driven cart was built in 1769 by Nicholas Cugnot. From then on, all over the world a great variety of extraordinary steam-powered vehicles were produced.

The first practical steam vehicles, called 'horseless carriages', were built in 1820. Good roads, had been built by Telford and Macadam for horse-drawn vehicles. The hard surfaces were ideal for steam carriages.

The early vehicles resembled stage coaches and carried goods and passengers in the same way. They travelled at about 30mph. However, in the 1865 Road Locomotives Act (called the Red Flag Act), the Government restricted their speed to 4mph. This Act slowed down car development in Britain very considerably.

In the nineteenth century, the trend was to develop light vehicles, which were easy to manoeuvre. One problem with a steam engine is that it requires a furnace of some sort to raise steam, and this means carrying large quantities of heavy and bulky coal—like an old-fashioned steam engine. With the development of the oil industry, inflammable liquids such as petrol and paraffin made it possible to do away with external combustion in engines. In their place internal-combustion engines were built, in which the petrol vapour explodes inside the cylinder.

The first successful gas engine was built by Etienne Lenoir in 1860. This inspired a German, N. A.

Marcus petrol car

L'Obéissante

Ford Model 'T'

Right
The Panhard Levassor Saloon Car of 1895, the first to have its engine at the front.

Otto, to build a 'four stroke' internal-combustion engine in 1876.

The world's first practical petrol-driven cars were produced in 1885. In 1889 petrol cars were imported into Britain and the speed limit was raised to 12mph.

At the beginning of the twentieth century more steam engine cars were produced. In 1906 the Stanley brothers in America produced the *Stanley Rocket* capable of travelling at 127mph. However, steam cars disappeared as they were clumsy and expensive to run.

The main development was switched to petrol-driven cars, the important improvements occurring in the period 1907–1930. In 1907, Sir Henry Royce produced his first famous *Silver Ghost*. In this period car bodies became stronger and more streamlined. Front suspension was added and syncromesh gears were invented. Shock absorbers, windscreen wipers, and indicators became standard equipment on every car. Since 1930 major developments include the use of automatic gears and the invention of the Wankel engine.

The first electric cars appeared in 1890, made possible by Gaston Plant's invention of a storage battery. Though popular, they could only go short distances before the battery needed recharging. When petrol cars became self-starting, electric cars went out of favour, though they are still used today for milk floats and other delivery vehicles. Interest in electric cars has revived because they do not cause pollution and it is hoped that new lighter types of batteries or fuel cells can be developed to last a similar time as a full tank of petrol.

Below
The Wankel engine has a rotating piston in place of the two-stroke piston which moves up and down. The principle on which both engines work is similar, but in the Wankel engine the triangular-shaped piston compresses the air and petrol mixture within an elliptical cylinder.

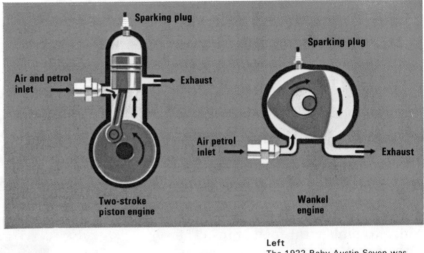

Two-stroke piston engine

Wankel engine

Left
The 1922 Baby Austin Seven was the first mass-produced cheap car. It cost less than £100. It could go as fast as 50mph. It had pneumatic tyres, windscreen wipers, and a rear view mirror; 300 000 models were sold. The 1972 Austin Mini, designed by Sir Alec Issigonis, is the modern counterpart of the Baby Austin.

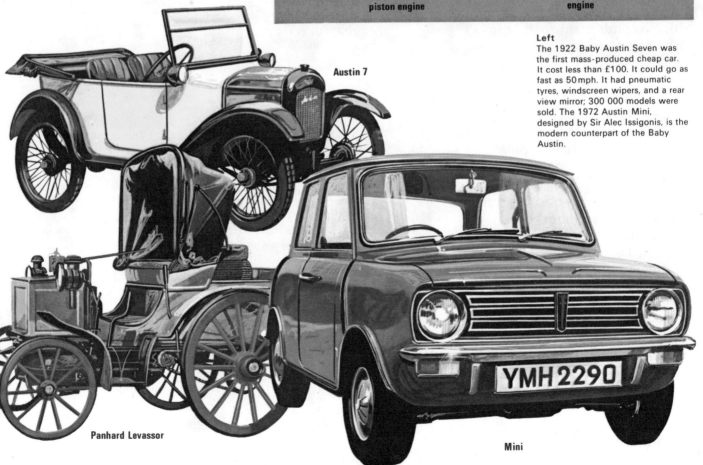

Austin 7

Panhard Levassor

Mini

Submarines

In 1775, David Bushnell built the first practical submarine. It was used during the American Revolution when the Americans tried unsuccessfully to attach a mine to the hull of a British ship. However, they were unable to stay under the water for long enough.

In 1801 Robert Fulton built a submarine called *Nautilus* for the French. Above water it was powered by sail. Under the water it took four men to drive a belt which moved a propeller to drive the boat through the water. It had enough oxygen to enable the crew of four to breathe and keep two candles burning for two hours.

Making the vessel move was the main problem. Steam engines were not suitable and petrol engines were dangerous because of the explosion risk. The invention of the diesel engine solved these problems and by the Second World War submarines were of great importance in the war at sea, being able to stay under water for two or three days. They were used by both sides to sink vital food ships. The submarine is an ideal type of vessel for launching torpedoes.

In the modern submarine, an electric motor is used to drive the propeller. When the vessel is on the surface, the diesel engines drive a generator coupled to the motor. When the submarine is below the surface the motor is driven by batteries which are charged by the generator.

The most recent advance has been in the use of nuclear power. Nuclear submarines have small nuclear reactors (see page 198) which produce heat, which in turn causes water to boil and turn into steam. The steam turns a turbine which drives the submarine's propeller. The great advantage of a nuclear submarine is that it uses only a tiny quantity of atomic fuel (uranium or plutonium) and can remain under the water for several months. An ordinary submarine

Left
A diagram of the inside of the first submarine used in warfare. It was called the *Turtle*. It was built of wood, shaped like a pear and operated by hand using a screw propellor.

Left
A periscope is used in a submarine to look at the sky and the sea when the vessel is under the surface. Prisms are used to reflect the light from above the surface down the tube and then into the observer's eyes.

has to come into port to obtain fresh supplies of oil. It also has to surface frequently to charge its batteries by means of the diesel engine, which requires an air supply to run it.

In 1931 Sir Hubert Wilkins, an Australian, attempted to reach the North Pole by going under the ice in an ordinary submarine. Because he had to surface often for air, his attempt failed.

In 1958 the U.S. Navy attempted the same voyage using the first nuclear submarine, also called *Nautilus*. As she had to sail between the sea floor and the ice ceiling, she had to have special instruments to make sure there was enough clearance.

Echo sounding devices were fitted. *Nautilus* carried three special compasses, since an ordinary compass will not give an accurate reading near the Pole. The second attempt, made in July 1958, succeeded.

Recently, research has been carried out on the effects of living under the sea. The chief problems to be solved are how men will breathe under water and how the human body will adapt to the great pressure of the water.

Off the Californian coast a *sealab* has been constructed on the ocean floor. Three aquanauts live down there for short periods to find out how men can live and work at those depths.

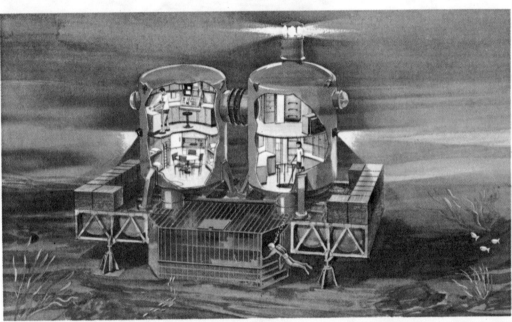

Left
There are four main rooms in the Tektite Sealab: a laboratory, control room, living quarters, a storage area and a wetroom. The wetroom is where the aquanauts enter and leave the Tektite Lab.

Below
This *submersible* was built by Cammell Laird for exploring the sea bed. It is powered by electricity and can move around freely. The electricity is fed through a cable from a ship on the surface. Divers from the submersible can search for oil and minerals and study life on the sea bottom.

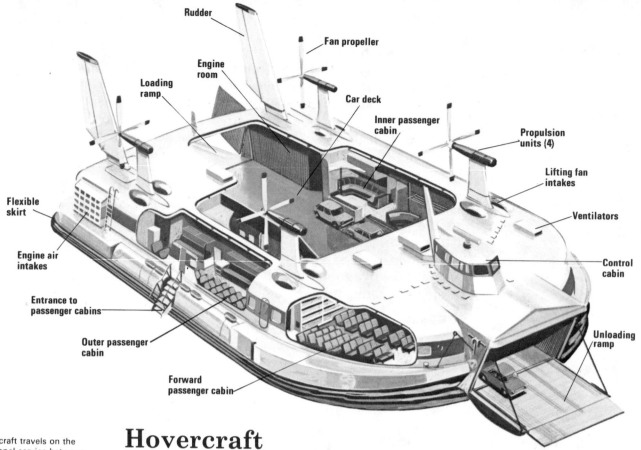

Rudder

Fan propeller

Engine room

Loading ramp

Car deck

Inner passenger cabin

Propulsion units (4)

Lifting fan intakes

Ventilators

Flexible skirt

Engine air intakes

Control cabin

Entrance to passenger cabins

Outer passenger cabin

Forward passenger cabin

Unloading ramp

Hovercraft

In the early 1950s Christopher Cockerell, a British engineer, designed and made the first working hovercraft. A hovercraft is basically a platform floating on a cushion of air. It is pushed along by means of a propeller and steered, like an aeroplane, with a rudder.

The air cushion is produced by a large flat fan which blows air downwards so hard that it lifts the craft off the ground or water. This cushion supports the craft so that there is no contact between it and the surface. There are no wheels and the craft can travel over land or water. At the outer rim of the air cushion, strong jets of moving air are formed which insulate the air cushion. This moving air is contained by a flexible rubber skirt.

The hovering height above the surface depends on the speed of the moving air. However a large platform is needed to provide a big enough air cushion for a reasonable lift. Tests have shown that the best height is one tenth of the platform's diameter, i.e. a platform 5 metres wide should hover half a metre above the ground.

Though a circular platform is the ideal shape for hovercraft, it is not the ideal shape for a travelling vehicle. Hovercraft are therefore usually oval or rectangular. There is now a regular cross-channel hovercraft service from England to the Continent. These large hovercraft can carry 254 passengers and 30 cars. They travel at speeds up to 90 kph and they make the crossing from Dover to Boulogne in 40 minutes. They have 4 propellers which are driven by 4 Rolls-Royce turbo-prop engines.

Hovercraft are used all over the world. These craft are especially useful for travelling along rivers going through jungles, such as

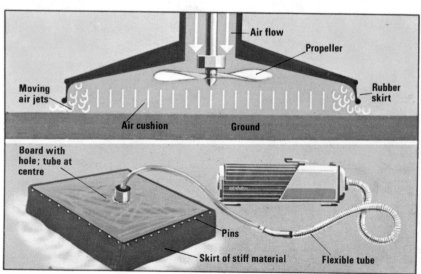

Air flow

Propeller

Rubber skirt

Moving air jets

Air cushion

Ground

Board with hole; tube at centre

Pins

Skirt of stiff material

Flexible tube

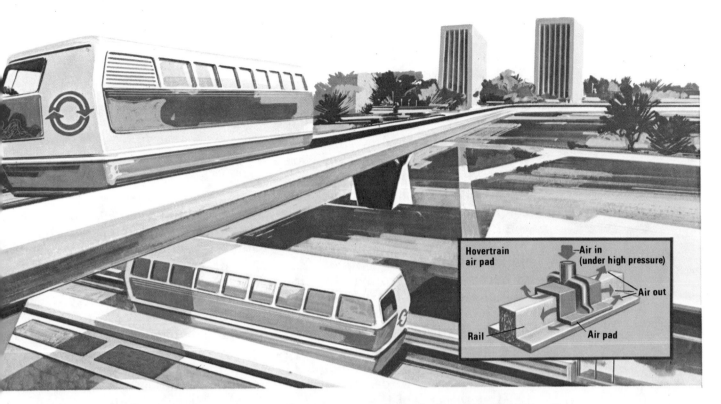

Hovertrain air pad

Air in (under high pressure)

Air out

Rail

Air pad

the Amazon, and across land upon which it would be hard to land an aircraft. Experiments are being carried out in various countries with hovertrains. These could use the present railway tracks but rails and wheels would not be needed. Alternatively, new concrete channels would be built.

The idea of a supporting air cushion is now being applied to everyday equipment. Vacuum cleaners which move over the carpet in this way are now available. Lawnmowers supported on a cushion of air are also widely used. They are particularly useful for mowing banks and slopes.

Hydrofoil boats are similar in that they can 'ski' over the surface of the water. The boat has special foils designed to lift the hull out of the water. To get the boat to take off, speed is greatly increased. The foils work in much the same way as aircraft wings. The foils are laid in pairs underneath the boat and are attached by metal struts to the hull. In the water the boat looks as if it is on stilts. The foils barely touch the surface of the water once the boat is travelling at speed. By getting the hull out of the water in this way, friction between the hull and the water is reduced.

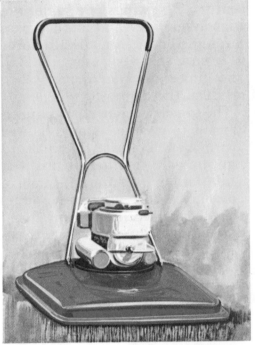

Above
Inter-city transport of the future may be by hovertrains, running in overhead concrete channels. They may be jet propelled and driverless, perhaps travelling at several hundred miles per hour. (*Inset*) A diagram showing the hovertrain pad system.

Left
A small hover-lawn-mower. It is supported on an air cushion and is very useful for rough grass or steep banks.

Below
A hydrofoil in full flight. The struts on either side are attached to the foil, part of which is just under the surface of the water. Hydrofoils are particularly useful on rivers and harbours. They provide services on the River Thames in London, in Sydney Harbour in Australia, and on the Norwegian fiords.

Aircraft

Man has always dreamt of being able to fly. Many machines and devices have been tried for this purpose. The first successful balloons were launched by the Montgolfier brothers in 1782. They were filled with hot air, which being lighter than the cooler surrounding air lifts the balloon off the ground. In 1783 their balloon was used for the first manned flight, although the balloon was tethered to the ground. In 1785 Blanchard and Jeffries crossed the channel in a hydrogen-filled balloon. Hydrogen is lighter than air and provides the required lift.

Gliders, copying the principle of flight used by birds, were also tried at the end of the nineteenth century. The wings of a glider are slightly inclined and as they pass through the air an upward force is created–this is called the *lift*. The glider stays in the air as a result of the lift on its wings.

The great problem with manned flight is to produce enough power to provide the lift and the thrust to give forward motion. Until the invention of the internal-combustion engine this was not possible. The Wright brothers learnt to fly gliders and they used this experience to make aeroplanes powered by petrol engines. Their first successful flight took place on the 17th December 1903. The plane flew for 12 seconds covering 40 metres at a height of about 3 metres. The plane was made of wood and canvas built round the engine (12 horse power).

At first flying was regarded as a dangerous sport. Planes were built for enthusiasts. In the First World War, however, they were used for dropping bombs; after the war it was realized how valuable they were. Planes were soon improved, wood and canvas giving way to metal, particularly aluminium. Instead of being open structures they had enclosed bodies, with seating for a passenger as well as a pilot. In 1919 Alcock and Brown were the first to fly the Atlantic nonstop. In 1934 a DC2 was used to carry passengers from England to Australia. In 1939 Pan American Airways provided the first transatlantic passenger service.

During the Second World War, planes were the most vital part of the fighting force. During these five years, necessity led to great advances in the development of aircraft. The main advances were the use of monoplanes (single wing) in place of biplanes (double wing) and the development of the jet

Below
Orville (1871–1948) and Wilbur (1867–1912) Wright. It was some years after the first flight of these American brothers before their Government became aware of the possibilities of the aeroplane. In France, however, they were acclaimed as heroes. Orville's longest flight lasted 75 minutes, the plane reaching almost 100 metres. This convinced the American Government that it was a successful venture.

Orville Wright

Wilbur Wright

Right
The first historic flight made by the Wright brothers on December 17th, 1903. They made four more flights that day.

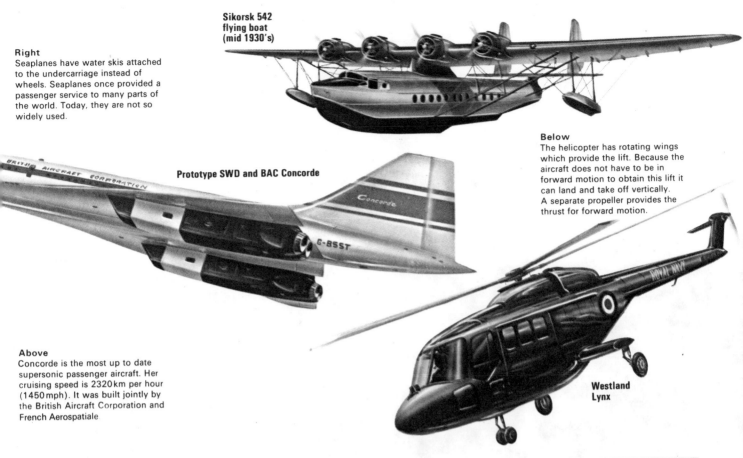

Sikorsk 542 flying boat (mid 1930's)

Right
Seaplanes have water skis attached to the undercarriage instead of wheels. Seaplanes once provided a passenger service to many parts of the world. Today, they are not so widely used.

Prototype SWD and BAC Concorde

Below
The helicopter has rotating wings which provide the lift. Because the aircraft does not have to be in forward motion to obtain this lift it can land and take off vertically. A separate propeller provides the thrust for forward motion.

Westland Lynx

Above
Concorde is the most up to date supersonic passenger aircraft. Her cruising speed is 2320 km per hour (1450 mph). It was built jointly by the British Aircraft Corporation and French Aerospatiale

engine. By the end of the war both sides were using jet fighters.

After the war all these developments were used to provide modern passenger aircraft. For example, the Boeing 707 is a development of B29, the aircraft used to drop the atom bomb on Japan.

In fixed wing aircraft, lift is obtained from stationary wings; a propeller or jet produces the forward thrust. These aircraft need long runways and have high landing speeds. In supersonic flight, aircraft fly faster than the speed of sound–about 760 mph (1200 km per hour) near sea level. The *Concorde* can fly at twice the speed of sound.

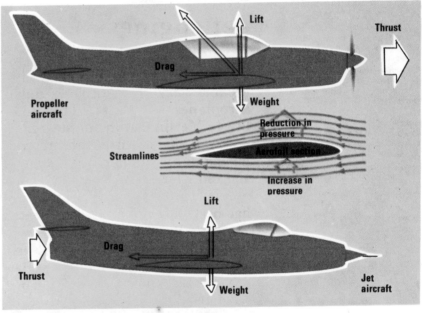

Heat-resistant metals

A —Steel
B —Light Alloy Parts
C —Light Alloy Sheets
D —Titanium

Above
The forces on the wing of propeller and jet aeroplanes. Moving through the air the lift is the force on the inclined wing that supports it. This is counter-balanced by the weight. The friction of the air over the wing surface causes the drag which acts against the thrust. The thrust is produced either by a propeller at the front of the aircraft or by the reaction to the jet at the rear.

Left
A cutaway diagram of an aircraft showing the principal metals used in the frame. It contains some steel and a large amount of light alloys. Titanium is used because it can stand up to great stress and high temperatures.

231

Whittle

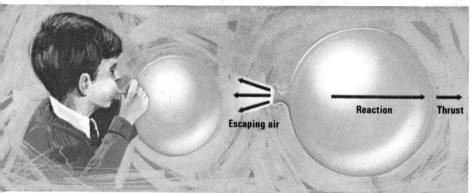

Escaping air   Reaction   Thrust

Above
The principle of reaction propulsion can be illustrated by allowing an inflated balloon to fly across the room with its neck open. The reaction of the jet of air flowing out of the neck, thrusts the balloon forward in the opposite direction to the air jet.

Below
The principle of a jet engine. Air enters at the left end, is compressed by the compressor blades, and then enters the combustion chambers. The fuel burns in the compressed air and passes out of the jet nozzle turning the turbine on the way. The turbine can also turn a propellor as well as the compressor. Engines like these using propellers are called *turboprops*.

Jet engines

During the Second World War it became very important to make aeroplanes fly faster. The Rolls Royce Merlin piston engine which powered the Spitfire fighters was incapable of further development and so the British government decided to develop a jet engine that had been patented in 1930 by Frank Whittle. By the end of the war Britain, America and Germany had several types of jet propelled fighters and since then jet engines have become the main source of power for all large aircraft.

Jet propelled aircraft have no propellers but obtain their thrust from the reaction to a high-speed jet of gas that is produced in the engine when the fuel burns.

If you blow up a rubber balloon and let it go with the neck open it will fly across the room. This illustrates jet propulsion. The air you have blown into the balloon rushes out of the neck and the force of the escaping air reacts backwards on the balloon pushing it forward. In a jet engine, the high-pressure gas is produced by burning a fuel such as paraffin. The air needed for burning the fuel is drawn in from the front of the engine. This burning takes place in a series of combustion chambers arranged around the engine. The hot gas escaping from the combustion chambers is used to rotate a turbine before being allowed to pass out of the jet nozzle at the rear. The turbine consists of a number of blades attached to a shaft. This shaft is connected to another turbine-like device at the front of the engine which compresses the incoming air. As the gases rotate the turbine, the turbine drives the compressor which forces air into the combustion chambers. In this way large quantities of fuel can be burnt. In the *turbofan* type of jet engine some of the air sucked into the front of the engine is not used to burn the fuel but is mixed with the hot exhaust gases at the rear of the engine.

Aeroplanes with a single jet engine, usually military planes,

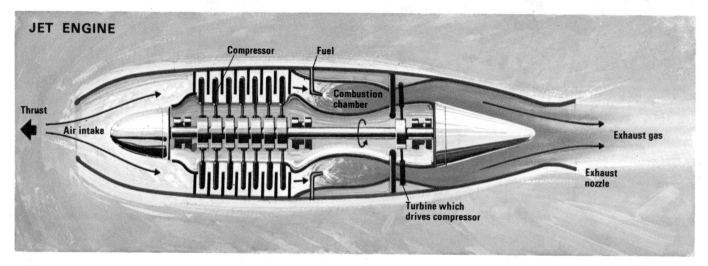

JET ENGINE

Compressor   Fuel

Combustion chamber

Thrust

Air intake

Exhaust gas

Exhaust nozzle

Turbine which drives compressor

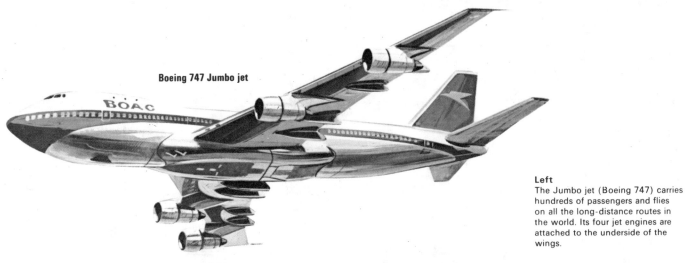

Boeing 747 Jumbo jet

Left
The Jumbo jet (Boeing 747) carries hundreds of passengers and flies on all the long-distance routes in the world. Its four jet engines are attached to the underside of the wings.

are built round the engine, but the larger aircraft have two, three, four, or more engines. These engines are sometimes slung in pods below the wings, attached to the rear of the body, or they form part of the tail.

Without jet engines supersonic flight would not be possible. *Concorde* has specially developed jet engines that enable it to cruise at twice the speed of sound.

The simplest type of jet engine is the *ramjet*. This has no moving parts and consists essentially of a long tube–it is sometimes called a flying drainpipe. The centre of the tube serves as the combustion chamber and the tail as the jet nozzle. As the tube flies through the air, air is forced into the combustion chamber into which the fuel is injected. The burning of the fuel in the air makes hot gases flow out of the jet nozzle at a higher speed than the air flowing in. This produces the thrust to force the ramjet through the air. A ramjet can only work if the machine is already moving rapidly.

JET-PROPELLED BOAT

Below and Left
The jet-propelled boat is powered by the force of a jet of steam escaping when water in the tin boils. The steam boiler is heated by a candle. Jets of steam will make this roundabout rotate. Use wires to suspend the gondolas; balance them carefully round the disc. Decorate it with foil, not paper, and stand it on a metal tray for safety.

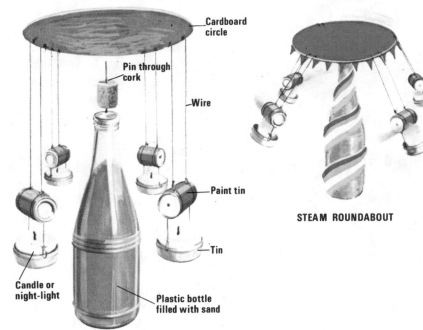

Cardboard circle

Pin through cork

Wire

Paint tin

Tin

Candle or night-light

Plastic bottle filled with sand

STEAM ROUNDABOUT

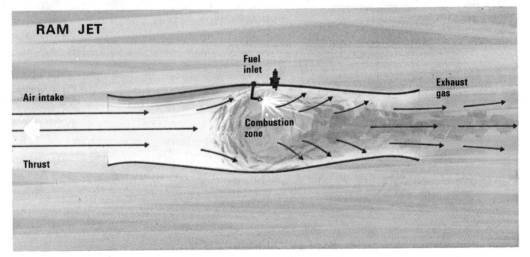

RAM JET

Air intake

Thrust

Fuel inlet

Combustion zone

Exhaust gas

Left
The ramjet, or flying drainpipe, has no moving parts. It only works when the pipe is flying through the air fast enough to produce a high pressure in the centre portion. In this wider centre portion the air is slowed down and the pressure increases. Fuel is added and burnt at high pressure, and hot gases flowing out of the rear nozzle. Rocket assisted ramjets have been used in some guided missiles.

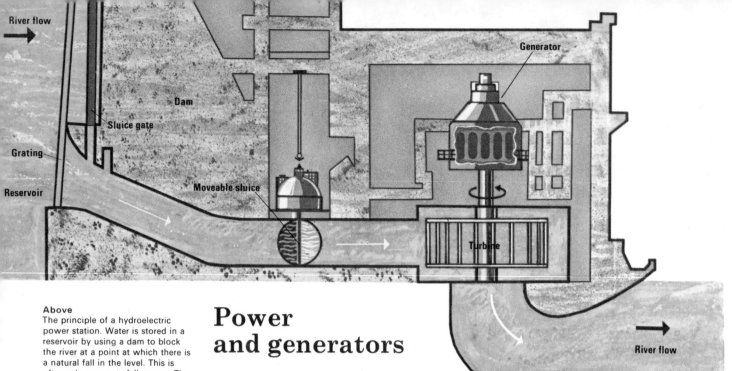

River flow

Dam

Sluice gate

Grating

Reservoir

Moveable sluice

Generator

Turbine

River flow

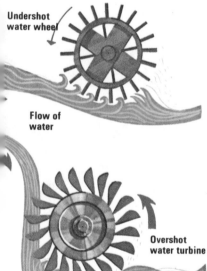

Undershot water wheel

Flow of water

Overshot water turbine

Power and generators

The water-wheel and the windmill were for many thousands of years man's only sources of mechanical power. The water-wheel was a very large wheel placed in a flowing river. The rim was very wide and the spokes were broad and extended beyond the rim so that they formed large flat paddles. As the river water flowed over the wheel, it moved the paddles, thus making the whole wheel turn. The wheel was attached to the side of a mill and the axle was connected to large millstones for grinding corn. As the wheel turned, so did the millstone. The windmill worked in a similar way, using the force of the wind to move the sails to provide a turning force for the axle.

In the nineteenth century the water turbine was developed from

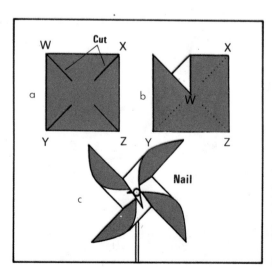

W — Cut — X   X

a   b   W

Y   Z   Y   Z

Nail

c

the simple water-wheel, and was much more efficient. In a turbine, the paddles of the wheel were bucket-shaped. Water, poured from above, filled up these buckets and the weight of this water moved the wheel round. As the paddles reached the lowest position, the buckets emptied themselves. With the discovery of electricity, water turbines were harnessed to generators to produce electricity for light, heat, and power. These are called *hydroelectric generators*. Though hydroelectric power stations cost more to build than coal or oil power stations, they are much cheaper to run as there are no fuel costs. England has little water power, but Wales and Scotland have some. Many countries have built hydroelectric power stations.

The St. Lawrence Seaway project and the power station at Niagara Falls are two important plants in America. The power supply for hydroelectric stations is made continuous by building dams to store large quantities of water.

Hydroelectric power produces only a tiny proportion of the world's electricity. Most of it is produced by burning coal and oil in furnaces to produce steam. This steam is used to drive steam turbines which in turn are coupled to generators.

The simplest type of electric generator or dynamo was invented by Faraday in 1830. It consisted of a copper disc made to rotate between the poles of a magnet. An electric current was produced in the disc as it rotated and cut the lines of force of the magnet. Large modern generators in power stations work on exactly the same principle; the copper disc, however, is replaced by coils of wire and the horseshoe magnet is replaced by an electromagnet. The stationary coils of wire forming the electromagnet are called the *stator* and the rotating coils are called the *rotor*. A bicycle dynamo is a small generator: the turning bicycle wheel rotates a coil of wire between magnetic poles.

So far, two sources of energy for doing work or producing electricity have been mentioned. One is natural wind and water power. The other is coal and oil, formed from plant and animal fossils millions of years ago. There is also a third source of energy available to man. This is *nuclear energy*. Some power stations are now operated by the heat produced when large numbers of uranium atoms are made to split into two parts. This is called nuclear fission. It is the same process as occurred in the atom bomb, but it is very carefully controlled so that it does not occur too quickly and cause an explosion. This heat from the splitting atoms is used, just as in a coal or oil power station, to produce steam and drive a steam turbine.

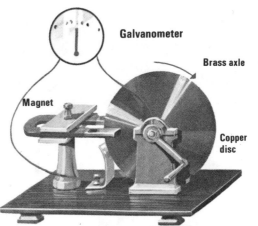

Left
Faraday's dynamo. The rotating copper disc cuts the lines of force of the magnet. This results in a current being produced in the disc. This current is picked up by the wires. The galvanometer is an instrument showing, by the position of the needle on the scale, that a current is flowing.

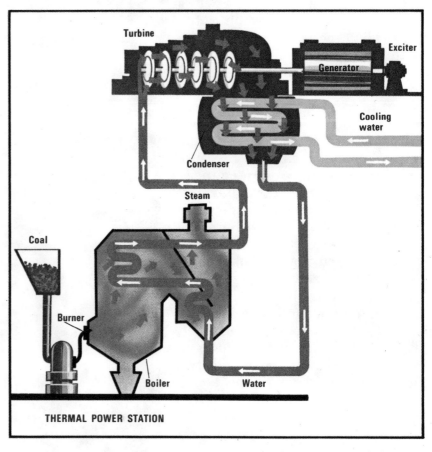

THERMAL POWER STATION

Above
The principle of a thermal power station. Coal or oil are burnt in a boiler to produce steam. The steam drives a turbine which is coupled to a generator.

Left
Solar cells are used in spacecraft to provide energy. Light from the sun is converted directly into electricity by these cells. Solar cells are used in hot countries to provide hot water in houses.

235

Tape recorders

One of the many uses of magnets and electromagnetism is in tape recorders. Magnetic recording of sound was first achieved in 1898 by a Danish inventor, Valdemar Poulsen. He used a reel of steel wire instead of the tape used in modern recorders. The use of tapes was introduced in the 1920s.

In tape recorders a magnet is used to record sounds onto the tape. The tape is a strip of plastic with a coating of a powdered material called iron oxide. This is magnetic. To produce a tape recording the sound is first converted into electrical signals by a microphone (see page 155). In the microphone the varying pressure of air which is the sound is changed into a varying electric current. This is then taken through wires to the *recording head* where the electrical signal is recorded on the magnetic tape that travels past it at a constant rate.

The recording head is a curved piece of iron wound with a coil of wire to make an electromagnet. The iron has a very narrow gap between the ends. As the electric current flows through the coil a magnetic field is produced across the gap between the two poles of the electromagnet. The tape is passed along very close to the gap. The iron oxide on the tape is magnetized by the magnetic field on the recording head. When the current through the coil is large the magnetic field is strong. The tape is then strongly magnetized. When the current is small the tape is weakly magnetized. In this way the changes in the current are recorded on the tape.

When the recording is being played back the tape is moved past a similar head called the *reproducing head*. It is moved at the same speed as was used in the recording. Now the magnetic parts of the tape produce a weak magnetic field in the reproducing head. As the tape goes past, this magnetic

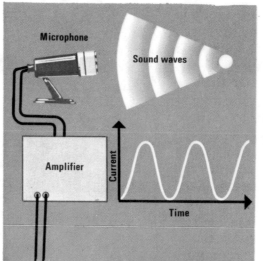

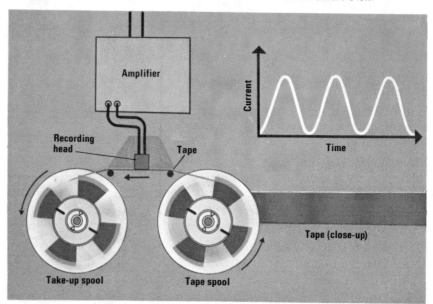

Left
The sound waves are picked up by the microphone. It turns them into an electric current which changes with time. The graph shows how the current first increases, then decreases, increases again, and so on as the sound waves hit the microphone. The small currents produced are put through an amplifier which makes the current stronger.
Below
As the current through the recording head changes the magnetic field changes. When the current is large the field is strong. The field magnetizes the iron oxide on the tape. The red areas in the diagram represent strongly magnetized tape. This happens when the current in the recorder head is high. The brown areas represent weakly or un-magnetized tape. This occurs when the current is low.

Left
This shows the working part inside the recorder head. It is made of iron wound with a coil of wire. The current through the coil produces a magnetic field across the gap. This gap is very small, about ·005 mm. The tape moves along very close to the gap. The reproducing and erasing heads are similar.
Below
When the recording is being played the opposite process is used. The tape is moved past the reproducing head. Small currents are produced. These are amplified and fed to a loudspeaker. This produces the original sound.

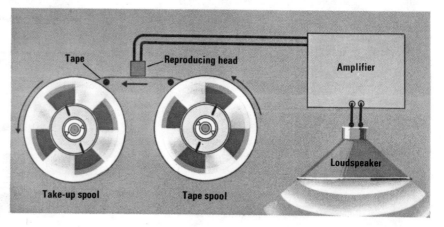

field changes. The magnetic field causes a small current in the coil. This changes as the field changes. It is 'magnified' with an amplifier. The varying electric current produced by the reproducing head is identical to the one produced by the microphone during recording. When it is passed into a loudspeaker the original sound is reproduced.

The advantage of a tape recorder is that the tape can be cleared and used again to record something else. This is done with a third head called an erasing head. The erasing head is similar to the other two heads. It produces a strong magnetic field which increases and decreases very quickly, many times every second. This alternating field demagnetizes the tape so that it can be used again.

The magnetic tape recorder is used to record and play back sounds.

A similar method is used in recording and playing back television pictures for later broadcasts. Both the picture and the sound are turned into electrical signals. These are then recorded onto magnetic tape. This is called *video tape*.

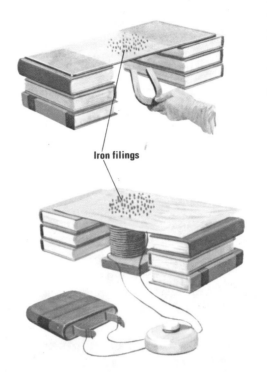

Iron filings

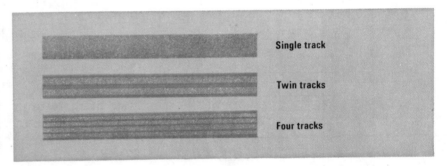

Single track

Twin tracks

Four tracks

Left
Two experiments to show how a magnetic field affects iron filings, just as the electromagnetic recording head of a tape recorder affects the particles of iron oxide on the tape. Put some iron filings on a transparent sheet and move, first a horseshoe magnet, and then a small electromagnet, underneath them. You will see the filings dance and move into a pattern when the magnet comes near them.

Below
Three different types of magnetic tape for recording on one, two or four tracks.

Left
A modern tape recorder, which works by mains electricity. It is also possible to have portable tape-recorders driven by batteries.

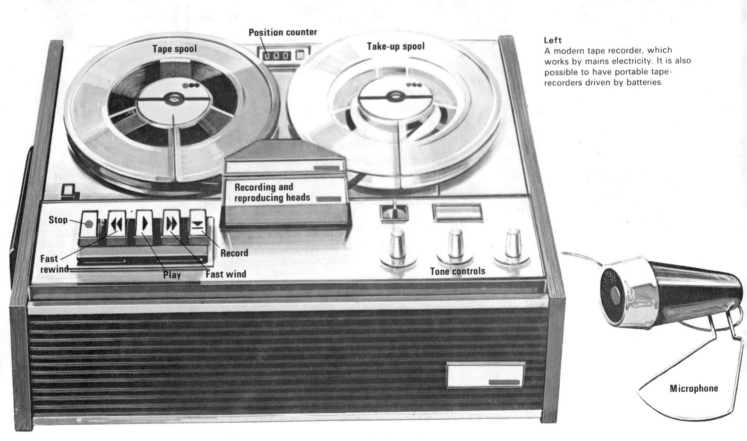

Position counter

Tape spool

Take-up spool

Recording and reproducing heads

Stop

Fast rewind

Play

Fast wind

Record

Tone controls

Microphone

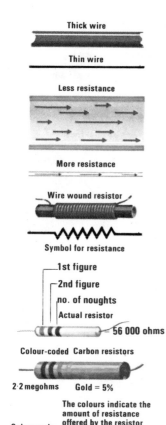

Thick wire

Thin wire

Less resistance

More resistance

Wire wound resistor

Symbol for resistance

1st figure
2nd figure
no. of noughts
Actual resistor

= 56 000 ohms

Colour-coded Carbon resistors

2·2 megohms   Gold = 5%

The colours indicate the
amount of resistance
offered by the resistor

Colour code

Colour		Value
black		0
brown		1
red		2
orange		3
yellow		4
green		5
blue		6
violet		7
grey		8
white		9

Variable resistors

Knob

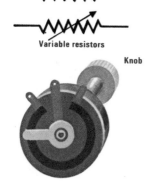

Carbon track

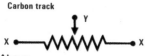

X ——————— X
Y

Above
Wire-wound resistors and the
colour-code. A resistor controls
the amount of current flowing
in a particular circuit.
It can be made of various
materials that slow down the flow
of electrons. When you turn down
the volume control of your radio
you increase the resistance of the
circuit. The signal to the loudspeaker therefore becomes weaker.

Valves and transistors

Electronics is the branch of science concerned with electrical circuits. Circuits are complete pathways for electrons to travel along while they do useful work. This work ranges from lighting a torch bulb to running a huge computer. These pathways are connected to various electrical *components* that each perform different functions; these include *valves*, *transistors*, *resistors*, *capacitors*, and *inductors*.

The diode valve was invented by John Ambrose Fleming in 1904. It consists of a sealed glass tube from which the air has been removed. Two metal elements inside (called *electrodes*) are attached to wires which pass out through the bottom of the tube so that electrical connections can be made to them. One of these electrodes is called the *cathode*. When the cathode is made very hot, by applying an electric current to it, it forces some of the electrons in it to jump out of the metal. This stream of electrons is attracted across a small space inside the tube to the second electrode, called the *anode* (or plate). Such a valve with two electrodes is called a *diode*. Electrons travel only from the cathode to the anode, and this permits alternating current (A.C.) to be changed to direct current (D.C.). The *triode* valve contains a third electrode (the *grid*); other valves have more. The grid controls the flow of electrons through the valve.

During the middle of the twentieth century it was found that an electric current could be made to flow through the crystal structure of a solid material, such as germanium. A large current can be obtained if tiny amounts of a substance, such as arsenic or boron, are added to the germanium crystal.

The arsenic atom has one more electron than the germanium atom in its outer shell (see page 156). These spare electrons can be made to move through the crystal struc-

ture when a proper voltage is applied to wires inserted into the material. This device is called an *n*-type *semiconductor* (*n* standing for negative). In it, the electrons move away from the negative electrode towards the positive electrode. A *p*-type semiconductor (*p* for positive) contains a tiny amount of an impurity such as boron. Boron has one less electron than the germanium atom in its outer shell. This means that electrons can be attracted to the boron atom from the germanium atom.

Gaps are created in the outer shell of the germanium atom. The crystal has electrode terminals attached at each side. By applying a proper voltage to the crystal across the electrodes, these gaps (called *holes*) can be made to move through the crystal from the positive to the negative electrodes. The resulting current is therefore caused by a movement of holes rather than of spare electrons.

A *transistor* consists of a sandwich of an *n*-type, *p*-type, and *n*-

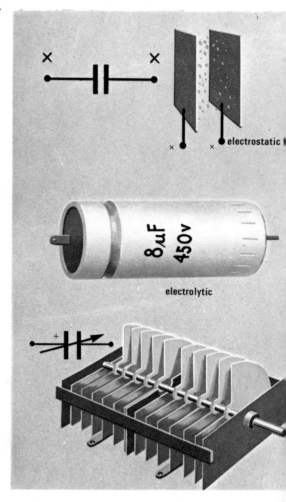

electrostatic

8 µF
450v

electrolytic

type semiconductor (an *n-p-n transistor*). Alternatively, if the order of the semiconductors is changed, a *p-n-p transistor* is formed. A transistor has three basic connections—one to the central semiconductor (the *base*) and two to the semiconductors on each side (the *emitter* and *collector*). These devices perform the same functions as the triode valve which they have replaced in many electrical circuits.

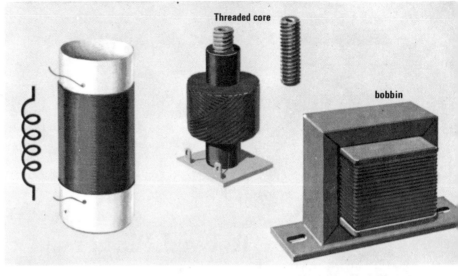

Threaded core

bobbin

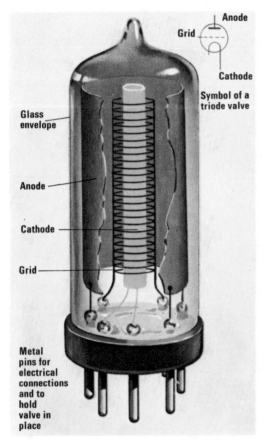

Anode

Grid

Cathode

Symbol of a triode valve

Glass envelope

Anode

Cathode

Grid

Metal pins for electrical connections and to hold valve in place

Above
A coil or inductor consists of wire wrapped round a piece of metal or non-metal. It produces an electromagnetic property called inductance. It has many uses such as smoothing out the ripples of current from a diode valve that has changed alternating current (A.C.) to direct current (D.C.).

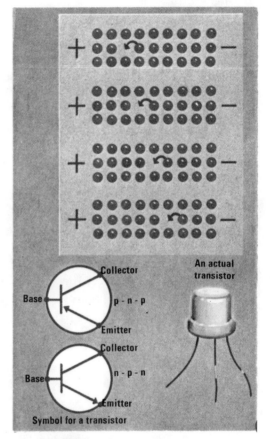

Collector

Base

p - n - p

Emitter

An actual transistor

Collector

Base

n - p - n

Emitter

Symbol for a transistor

Right
Transistors can perform the same functions as valves. They have replaced valves in many circuits because they are small, require no heat to produce a flow of electrons, need much less voltage to run them, last longer, and are more reliable.

Above
The triode valve contains a third electrode (as well as the anode and cathode) called the *grid*. This controls the flow of electrons through the valve. The triode can therefore increase the size of (*amplify*) electrical signals.

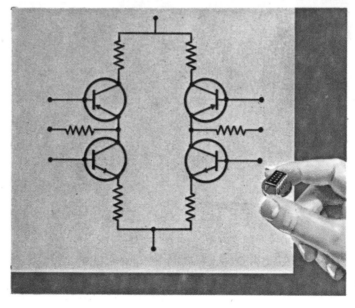

Left
An integrated circuit. Transistors and other electrical components can now be made extremely small. Thousands of components, forming many hundreds of circuits, can be permanently fixed onto a tiny piece of semi-conductor material. This is called an integrated circuit. It is very light, long-lasting, and cheap and is therefore widely used.

Left
A capacitor is used in a circuit to store electrical charge. It consists of two or more metal plates. These plates can be fixed, or one of them can be moved so as to vary the amount of charge stored between them. When you tune into a radio station you move the plates of a variable capacitor.

Edison

Record Players

The first machine to reproduce the human voice was called a *talking machine*. It was invented in 1877 by an American, Thomas Alva Edison. The earliest machines were crude devices and the quality of the sound was very poor. They consisted of a metal drum around which tinfoil was wrapped. The drum had to be turned by hand, as electric motors were not then in common use. These machines, known as *tinfoil phonographs*, both recorded and played back sounds of the human voice. The operator spoke loudly into the *recording tube*, consisting simply of a tube with a diaphragm and stylus (or needle) at one end. While the drum was turned by hand the operator spoke into this recording tube. These sounds made the diaphragm move back and forth (vibrate). The stylus, attached to the diaphragm, recorded these movements by vibrating in the same way against the tinfoil. The resulting marks or impressions made on the tinfoil represented the loudness and pitch of the recorded voice. To reproduce the sound, another stylus was moved along the impressions and the vibrations of the attached diaphragm reproduced the voice in the *hearing tube*.

Further improvements in the talking machine were made during the last few years of the nineteenth century. One was the use of a cardboard cylinder coated with wax in which the sound vibrations were cut into the wax coating by the recording stylus. One version of

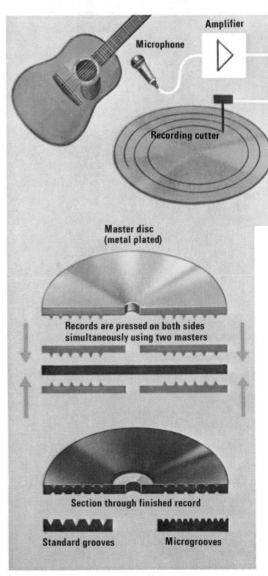

Master disc
(metal plated)

Records are pressed on both sides simultaneously using two masters

Section through finished record

Standard grooves   Microgrooves

Speakers

Record deck

Pickup

Amplifier

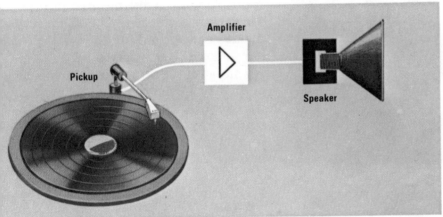

Amplifier

Pickup

Speaker

this device was called a *graphophone*; another was called a *phonograph*. They were first used as dictating machines, but never became very popular. It soon became clear that the talking machine had a more important role in entertainment, by reproducing music.

The first improvement was to operate the machine by a clockwork motor using a spring which could be wound up with a special handle or crank. The next important development was the change of recording surface from a cylinder to a flat circular disc, much the same as we use today. These *recordings* (or *records*) were at first cut or pressed on only one side of the disc.

During the early twentieth century machines were made that could press out thousands of copies of a record from one *master disc*. The master disc is made with ridges instead of grooves. The first mass-produced records were made of shellac in heated presses, the master being stamped against the surface of the soft shellac leaving grooves identical to those cut in the original recording. The play-back needle travels in these grooves and vibrates against the bumps in the grooves thus reproducing the original sound. The play-back needle vibrates in the *pick-up* which converts the vibrations to electric currents. These currents are fed to a valve or transistor amplifier which increases their power so that they can operate a loudspeaker.

By using microgrooves cut in pure hard plastic (vinyl), records today rotate at 33 revolutions per minute instead of the 78 r.p.m. used with shellac records. These improvements combined with lighter pick-up and better electronic circuits and loudspeakers have led to high fidelity (hi-fi) reproduction.

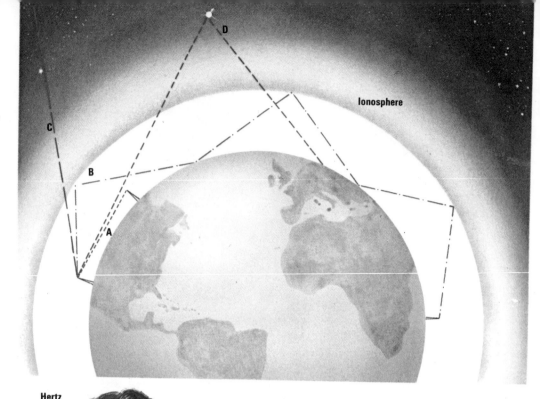

Right
Propagation of Radio Waves.
A. Ground waves following the curvature of the earth for a relatively short distance.
B. Sky waves reflected from the ionosphere, over 80 kilometres high, and sent back to earth. Several bounces are possible and the radio signal may be sent all the way around the world.
C. Sky wave passing straight through the ionized layer. It may continue out into space, getting weaker and weaker, or be reflected back to earth by a special communications satellite.
D. A communications satellite relays radio waves that pass through the ionosphere back to earth.

Right
Heinrich Hertz, a German physicist who was born in 1857 and died in 1894, demonstrated the existence of radio waves in 1886. He found that radio waves behave much the same as light waves. Hertz played an important role in laying the groundwork for the invention of wireless telegraphy.

Far right
The Morse Code and an early type of Morse telegraph system. The transmitter was powered by a battery and the signal was passed on by land lines. At the receiver, the signal was automatically punched out on tape.

Below
Guglielmo Marconi, an Italian electrical engineer who was born in 1874 and died in 1937, invented wireless telegraphy in 1895. He came to England in 1896 and succeeded in transmitting a wireless signal for a distance of nine miles. In 1901 he was able to receive a wireless signal (the letter S in Morse Code) sent across the Atlantic, from Cornwall to Newfoundland. He was awarded the Nobel prize for physics in 1909.

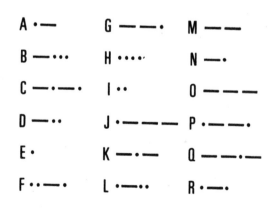

Hertz

Radio

Every hour of every day all over the earth there are millions of radio waves travelling through the air at the speed of light – 300 000 000 metres per second (or 186 000 miles per second). In order to hear them we must have a radio set, which changes the electric signals picked up by the receiving aerial into sounds that we can hear through a loudspeaker. These radio waves can be transmitted on many differ-

A •—	G ——•	M ——
B —•••	H ••••	N —•
C —•—•	I ••	O ———
D —••	J •———	P •——•
E •	K —•—	Q ——•—
F ••—•	L •—••	R •—•

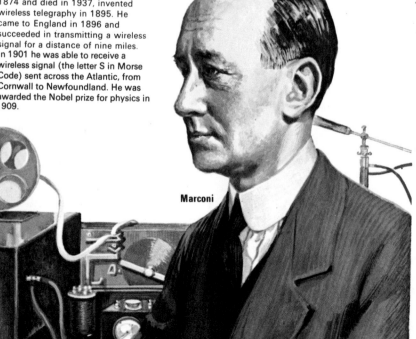

Marconi

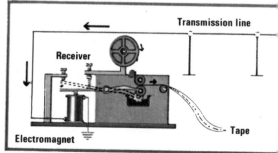

Transmission line

Receiver

Electromagnet

Tape

ent frequencies or wavelengths.

Music and voice were not the first to be transmitted by radio. Before the invention of the *microphone* (which changes sound waves into electrical waves) and the electronic valve (see page 238), radio transmissions were all just a series of dots and dashes representing in Morse Code the letters of the alphabet.

There are two types of radio waves. The *ground wave* can follow the curvature of the earth for a short distance of about 350 km. Ground waves cannot therefore be used for transmitting radio waves between distant countries or even between cities separated by a large distance in the same country. Radio waves can be made to travel much greater distances, however, by being bounced off an electrically-charged layer in the atmosphere. This layer, called the *ionosphere*, is over 80 km above the ground. The reflected radio waves are called *sky waves*.

When short-wave radio waves are transmitted, they are reflected off the ionosphere, and can be received by radio sets many hundreds of kilometres from the transmitting set. These waves can then bounce back to the ionosphere and

be reflected back to earth over and over again in a series of bounces or *skips*. This is how a radio signal from London is able to be heard in Australia, for example, thousands of kilometres away.

Not all sky waves are reflected by the ionosphere. Some high-frequency waves (short wavelengths) pass through the ionosphere into outer space. When short wave radio waves are being transmitted over a great distance they have to be reflected back to earth artificially by a *communications satellite*. When a television programme is broadcast over a great distance, a communications satellite is used to reflect the high-frequency waves.

If the ionosphere reflected every wavelength, it would be impossible to talk by radio to astronauts who have flown beyond it. There would be no field of radioastronomy if the radio waves from distant stars were unable to pass through the earth's atmosphere.

Radio is important not only in giving us information, music, and other forms of entertainment as in broadcasting, but is extremely useful for *two-way* communications between aeroplanes and control towers, and for ship-to-shore links.

Above
The Post Office Tower in Central London is used for mounting radio and TV aerials. A high tower is a good place for aerials as they can transmit ground waves much further than those mounted at ground level.

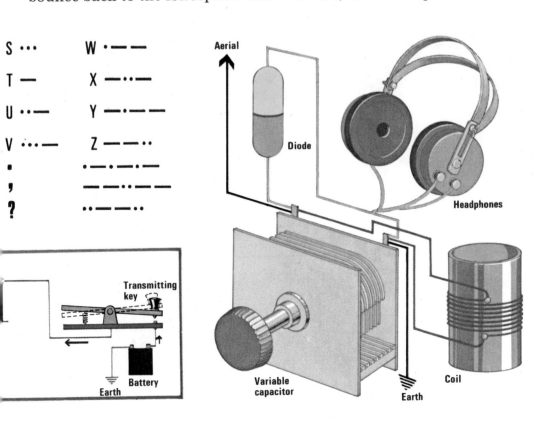

S ···	W ·——		
T —	X —··—		
U ··—	Y —·——		
V ···—	Z ——··		
. ·—·—·—			
, ——··——			
? ··——··			

Aerial

Diode

Headphones

Transmitting key

Battery

Earth

Variable capacitor

Earth

Coil

Left
A simple radio receiver. The signal from the transmitting station is picked up by the receiving aerial and is tuned in by the circuit containing the variable capacitor and coil. The signal then passes through the diode which *detects* or *demodulates* the signal so that it can be heard in the earphones.

Baird

Left
John Logie Baird was born in 1888 and died in 1946. When ill health prevented him from working as an electrical engineer he turned to studying television. He produced the first practical system. His system was used for a short while but then better ways of televising were found. His system used infrared rays.

Below
The picture tube, or cathode-ray tube, consists of an electron gun which produces the electron beam and a number of magnetic coils for focusing the beam and making it scan the screen. The screen is coated with a fluorescent substance that emits light when struck by the electron beam.

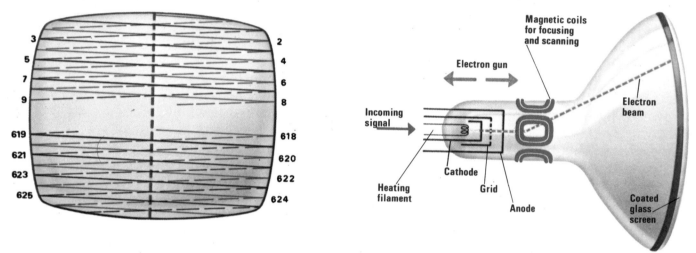

Magnetic coils for focusing and scanning

Electron gun

Incoming signal

Heating filament

Cathode

Grid

Anode

Electron beam

Coated glass screen

3 2
5 4
7 6
9 8
619 618
621 620
623 622
625 624

Above
The electron beam of a black-and-white set scans the screen in a zig-zag. Each frame consists of 625 lines and 30 frames are formed in one second. The lines are at a slight angle because the beam moves steadily down the screen. Each frame is built up by first scanning the odd-numbered lines (shown black) and then the even-numbered lines (red).

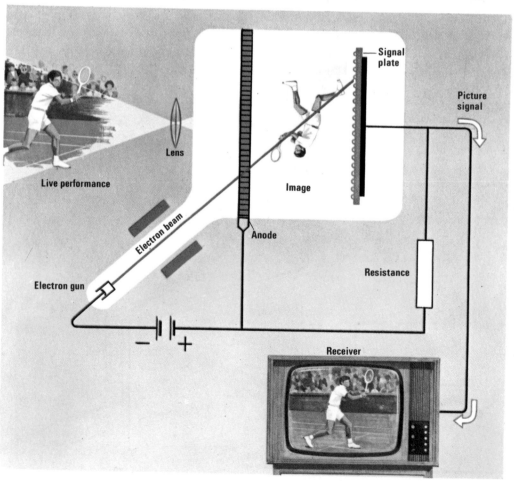

Live performance

Lens

Electron beam

Electron gun

Anode

Image

Signal plate

Picture signal

Resistance

Receiver

244

Television

Television shows still pictures. The pictures appear to move because they are shown one after the other at high speed. To give this impression there must be thirty pictures per second.

Each picture is divided into a number of *lines* (625 on newer sets and 405 on older sets). Each line contains several thousand bits of light or dark. To make a good picture the lines are separated into tiny bits – as many as 200 000 bits altogether. The television camera contains a signal plate covered with photosensitive dots (dots of a chemical that are sensitive to light). Each dot corresponds to one of the 200 000 tiny bits. An electron beam crosses the plate line by line and transmits the signals picked up from the dots. These are amplified and then transmitted. In the television set in your home the signals are received, amplified, and shown on the picture tube (or cathode-ray tube). In the cathode-ray tube, another electron beam is produced. This beam is made to cross the screen 625 times, so making the 625 lines. At the end of each line the beam flies back and starts the next line. These 625 lines are produced in $\frac{1}{30}$ second and each set of 625 lines is called a *frame*. As the beam crosses the back of the picture screen it gets weaker and stronger in accordance with the signals transmitted (that is, in

accordance with the strength of the signals picked up from the photosensitive dots in the camera). The tube contains a special fluorescent screen, coated with chemicals, which glow under the impact of the electron beam. The stronger the beam, the brighter the light. The set also contains a loudspeaker for producing the sound and a synchronizing system for keeping the sound and picture together.

Colour television is more complicated. There are three electron beams each of which carries the signal for one of the colours, red, blue, and green. The screen of the picture tube is coated with $1\frac{1}{4}$ million tiny dots of phosphor, arranged in groups of three. A phosphor is a substance that emits light when an electron beam falls on it; each of the three phosphors used emits only one of the three colours red, blue, and green. So the blue phosphor emits blue light when the electron beam carrying the blue signal falls on it, and so on. These three colours can be combined in different proportions to give all the other colours of the original televised scene.

Television can be either broadcast, as it is for entertainment, or it can be transmitted by wire. This is called *closed-circuit television*. Closed-circuit television is used for a number of purposes. For example, it can be used in hospitals to enable students to see the details of an operation.

Computers

Throughout the ages man has used calculating machines to help him work out his sums. One of the very earliest was the *abacus*. This simple cheap device is still used in many Asian shops and banks to make calculations at great speed. Much more complicated calculating machines have now been built that can perform both simple and highly complex calculations automatically.

John Napier invented a system called *logarithms* which greatly simplify multiplication and division. Each number can be represented by another number called its logarithm. To *multiply* numbers together their logarithms are *added*, to *divide* numbers their logarithms are *subtracted*. The logarithms of numbers can be looked up in tables. To speed up this process, the *slide rule* was invented. It is based on logarithms and is a very useful calculating aid as it is small and portable.

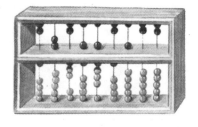

Above
The abacus consists of moveable beads attached to rods. In this one the top row of beads, each bead equals 5 when lowered. In the larger lower group, each bead equals 1 when raised. Skilled abacus operators can produce answers as fast as some machines.

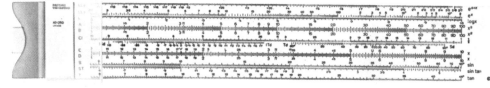

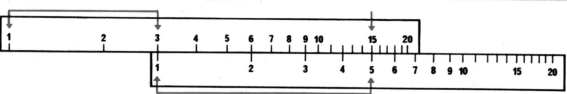

Above right
The top picture shows a slide rule, the bottom one explains the principle of multiplying on a slide rule. Both the scales on the rule have the numbers arranged logarithmically—not equally spaced. These scales are arranged to show the multiplication 3 × 5 = 15. Each number of the lower scale is below a number 3 times as large in the upper scale. A homemade slide rule like this will work very well, but it will not be as accurate as a bought one.

Right
A shop cash register. An assistant presses the key on the keyboard of the till corresponding to the price of the goods bought. When all the items bought have been rung up the total button is pressed and the machine adds up all the prices that have been rung. The total shows in the window.

Right
An electronic calculator. This machine can add, subtract, multiply, and divide. Some devices perform more complicated sums.

Numbers must often be worked out to a high degree of accuracy. Businesses, such as banks, large industries, and scientific laboratories use electrical calculating machines. These devices work extremely fast and some are now being built to run off batteries and are small enough to put in a pocket.

The fastest, most accurate, and most useful calculating machine is the *computer*. Charles Babbage built the first computer in the early nineteenth century. It carried out a long series of calculations and printed out the results. He went on to invent a more modern type of computer but due to lack of interest it was never built.

Modern computers do not rely on levers and cogs like Babbage's machines; they have extremely complex electrical circuits inside them which do the work. At first valves were used in the circuits. Since valves are fairly large and the number of circuits is very great these original machines were enormous and extremely difficult to run properly. The invention of the *transistor* (see page 238) followed by the *integrated circuit* revolutionised the computer industry. Integrated circuits are extremely small, very reliable, long-lasting and cheap. Employing tiny silicon chips, they can form microprocessors in small computers.

A computer can work out calculations and provide answers to complicated problems in minutes, even seconds. A man would take days, or possibly months, to work the same thing out. Before a computer can perform these tasks, it has to be told exactly what to do. Instructions telling the machine how to use the numbers and other information fed into it must be written in a special language by the person using the computer. The instructions and information make up a computer *program*. If the computer gives an incorrect answer it is the program that is wrong, not the machine.

The computer differs from simple electrical calculators in that it has a *memory*. It can store away information and use it some time later. It can therefore be compared with the human brain. It solves problems much faster and with greater accuracy than the brain. It can be made to play games like chess and is able to translate words from one language to another. However it cannot make decisions or think up new ideas but only does what it is programmed to do.

Babbage

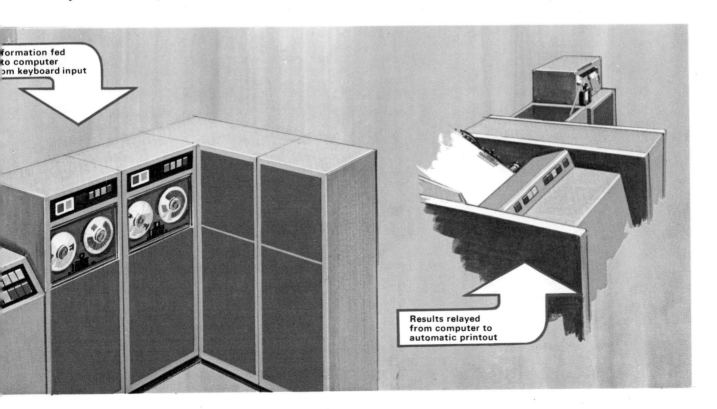

Information fed to computer from keyboard input

Results relayed from computer to automatic printout

Radar

The name *radar* is taken from the initial letters of the phrase *Radio Detecting and Ranging*. Radar is a radio transmitting and receiving system that uses radio waves of very short wavelengths–a few centimetres only. These waves are transmitted from a special type of aerial. The aerial, with its dish-shaped reflector behind, can point in any direction; it receives signals strongest when pointing in the direction of the incoming radio waves. Usually, radar aerials turn automatically and constantly in a complete circle, so they can send and receive signals in any direction.

Unlike ordinary radio waves which can pass through solid objects, the very short waves used by radar tend to bounce off most objects. Radar makes use of this fact to tell how far away an object is, and, in the case of a moving object, in what direction it is travelling and at what speed. This is possible, because when the radio waves sent out by the transmitter hit an object they are reflected back to the radar station in a fraction of a second. During this brief time the transmitter is shut off and the aerial is used to receive the signal and pass it to a special cathode-ray tube resembling a TV picture tube. On this tube, a picture or image is formed of what the radio beam sees.

The returning radio signal is an echo reflected back from whatever solid object it hits. Certain objects, especially those made of metal, reflect back a strong signal. This forms a bright image on the radar screen. Other objects, especially those not made of metal, reflect back weaker signals and form less bright images on the screen. A bigger object reflects back more radio waves, so that with experience an operator can tell if he is seeing a flight of birds or a group of jet planes.

Great technical improvements were made in radar by the British in 1940; they succeeded in developing a special transmitting tube (called a *magnetron*) able to produce very high-powered signals at the extremely short wavelengths needed for radar. This made possible the first *microwave radar* system. At these microwave frequencies smaller aerials could be used, which made radar capable of being used in aircraft.

Radar is used to aid navigation by both aircraft and ships, as well as to tell them if they are about to enter an area of bad weather or collide with another craft or vessel. During the Second World War radar was first used to track enemy aircraft and provide automatic guidance control for anti-aircraft guns. The great advantage of radar over sight is that it works at night and in fog or clouds.

Right
The height above ground and the angle at which the radar aerial is pointed is important in determining the type of objects that can be detected by reflection of the radar beam. A plane may escape being detected by flying very low.

Far right
The cathode-ray tube shows the reflected radar signal (echo) and tells the operator the distance away of an object or storm as well as its speed and direction. The spiral at the top of the screen is a hurricane. The smaller light areas show heavy rainfall.

Far right
One of the important uses of radar is at airports to help aircraft land, especially during bad weather. Two different signals are transmitted from the ground. One signal indicates to the pilot the correct direction of approach for the aircraft; the other shows at what height the plane should be flying. The pilot can therefore tell exactly where he is at every moment during his approach to the runway.

Right
Most radar stations use the same aerial to transmit as to receive. During a very brief instant, between each radar pulse being transmitted, the receiver is turned on to receive the returning signal by means of an automatic switch. This switch changes the aerial connections from the transmitter to the receiver.

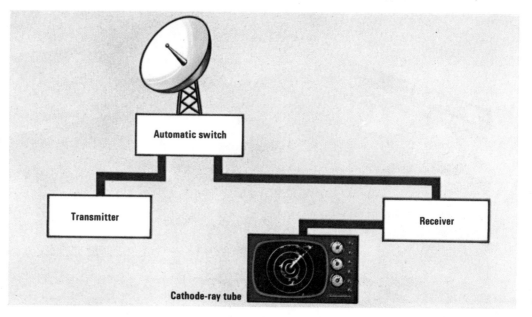

Automatic switch

Transmitter

Receiver

Cathode-ray tube

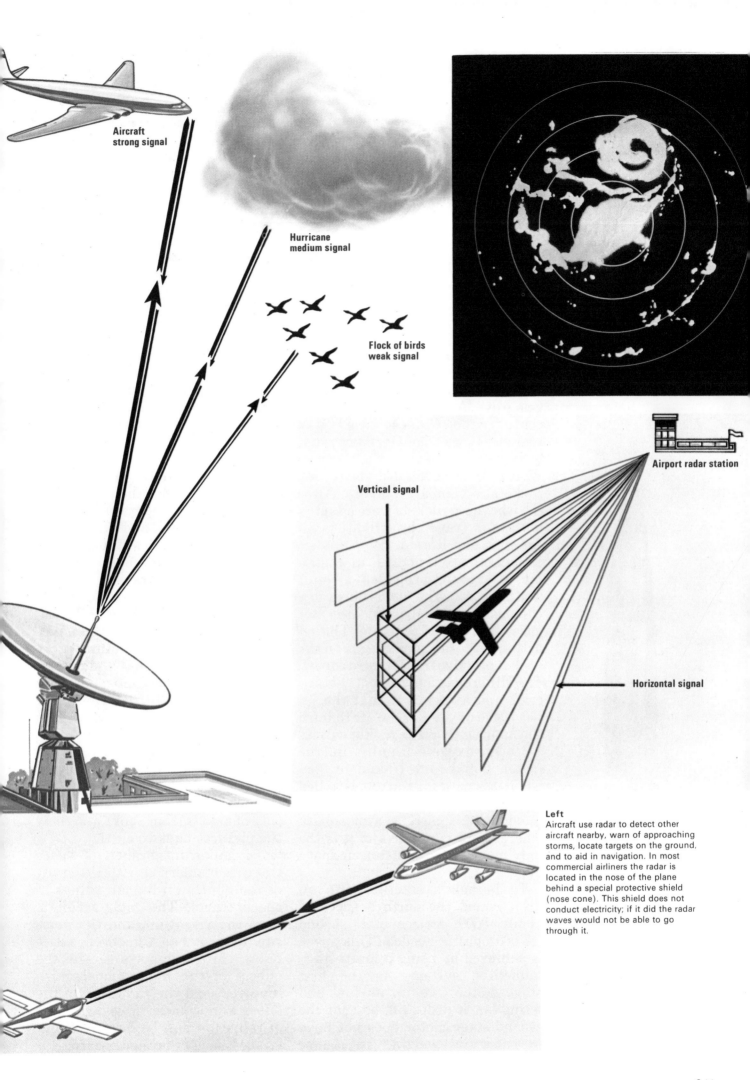

Aircraft
strong signal

Hurricane
medium signal

Flock of birds
weak signal

Airport radar station

Vertical signal

Horizontal signal

Left
Aircraft use radar to detect other
aircraft nearby, warn of approaching
storms, locate targets on the ground,
and to aid in navigation. In most
commercial airliners the radar is
located in the nose of the plane
behind a special protective shield
(nose cone). This shield does not
conduct electricity; if it did the radar
waves would not be able to go
through it.

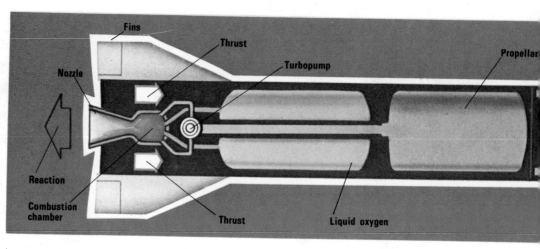

Fins

Thrust

Turbopump

Propellar

Nozzle

Reaction

Combustion chamber

Thrust

Liquid oxygen

Above

Werner Von Braun was born in Germany in 1912. He studied engineering and during the Second World War he perfected the V2 rockets. After the war he worked for the Americans and was responsible for the *Explorer* satellite from Cape Kennedy in January 1958.

Above

The V2 rocket—the first rocket with a liquid propellant. Used to bombard London in the war it is the forerunner of the American space rockets. It was 14·5 metres high and weighed about 13 tons. It carried about 9 tons of propellant (ethyl alcohol and oxygen) and could reach an altitude of 150 000 metres.

Rockets

In the nineteenth century the use of rockets in war was advanced by the studies made by Sir William Congreve. As early as the eleventh century the Chinese used war rockets. It was the Germans who, towards the end of the Second World War, designed huge V2 rockets to bombard London. After the war these rockets were adapted for space travel by scientists in America and Russia.

Rockets are propelled in a similar way to jet-propelled aircraft (see page 232). The fuel is burnt in a combustion chamber and the hot gases flow out of a nozzle. The reaction of the fast moving gas on the rocket produces the forward thrust. The difference between a jet aircraft and a rocket is that the jet needs the oxygen in the air to burn the fuel, whereas the rocket carries its own oxygen–usually in the frozen liquid form (liquid oxygen when it is used for rockets is called *lox*). A rocket therefore can fly outside the earth's atmosphere where there is no air and it is the only means of propulsion in space at present.

To launch a satellite into an orbit round the earth a speed of about 8000 metres per second (18 000 mph) is needed. This speed is achieved by using a multi-stage launching system. As the first stage motor uses up its fuel and burns out it drops off, so that the second stage motor does not have to carry its weight. To escape

from the earth's gravitational pull, the speed of launching must be increased to about 11 200 metres per second (25 000 mph). As the moon's gravitational pull is much less than the earth's, the launching speed from the moon is less; about 2400 metres per second (5300 mph).

Orbiting satellites can be used to find out what space is like just outside the earth's atmosphere. Instruments in the satellites measure the temperature, count the meteorites, and determine other characteristics of space, such as the magnetic field or the strength of cosmic rays.

Satellites are also used to enable television programmes to be broadcast round the world. As the waves carrying television pictures only travel in straight lines and cannot be reflected by the ionosphere (see page 243), satellites have to be used to bounce the rays back to earth.

In *meteorology* (weather forecasting) use can be made of satellites. They carry special instruments for this. They can observe the formation of clouds from above and relay the pictures back to earth.

An important branch of space travel is concerned with the study of the effects on human beings in space travel. The high acceleration, the vibration, and the noise can have a bad effect on astronauts. More important are the effects of the high temperatures involved, and the radiation in the outer atmosphere. Massive doses of radiation can be fatal. Weightlessness is yet another hazard.

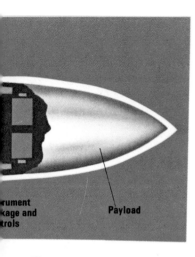

Instrument package and controls

Payload

Above
The principle of the rocket. The rocket carries its own propellant and oxidiser (usually liquid oxygen). The fuel burns in the combustion chamber and flows out through the nozzle. The reaction of exhaust gases on the body of the rocket thrusts it forward.

Far right
The spectacular moment of lift-off of a Mercury-Atlas rocket from its huge gantry.

Right
Saturn V—the rocket used as a launcher for the Apollo spacecraft, which successfully landed men on the moon. It is a three stage rocket, the first stage using paraffin and liquid oxygen, the next two stages using liquid hydrogen as the fuel, also with liquid oxygen. The total height is 110 metres and the total weight 2700 tons. It can carry a payload of 45 tons to the moon.

Far right
Nuclear Rocket. So far rockets used in space exploration have used chemicals for propulsion. The Americans have been developing a nuclear rocket consisting of small nuclear reactors which heat a stream of hydrogen.

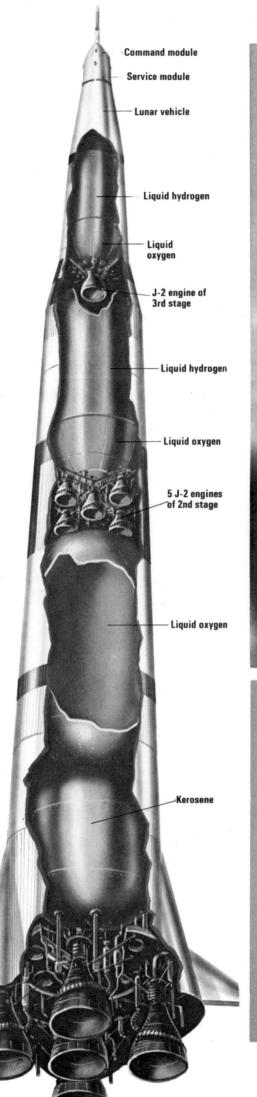

Command module

Service module

Lunar vehicle

Liquid hydrogen

Liquid oxygen

J-2 engine of 3rd stage

Liquid hydrogen

Liquid oxygen

5 J-2 engines of 2nd stage

Liquid oxygen

Kerosene

5 motors type 5-1 of first stage developing 7 500 000 lbs of thrust

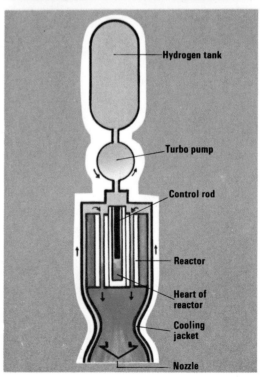

Hydrogen tank

Turbo pump

Control rod

Reactor

Heart of reactor

Cooling jacket

Nozzle

INDEX

Figures in bold type refer to illustrations

ACKNOWLEDGEMENTS

The photographs in this book appear
by courtesy of the following organizations–

Page 17 top left, Associated Press/NASA;
Page 18 top left, NASA/from a
  Woodmansterne transparency;
Page 21 bottom right, Bill Stacey;
  bottom left, Solarfilma, Iceland;
Page 24 top, French Government Tourist
  Office;
Page 42 top centre, British Steel
  Corporation;
Page 124 top left, Department of the
  Environment;
Page 191 centre, Kodak Ltd.;
Page 212 top left, photograph by
  Nicholas Servain, Woodmansterne
  Ltd.; top centre, Hamlyn Group
  Picture Library;
Page 215 top, Kodak Ltd.